ate Due

the **MBA** companion

Palgrave Student Companions are a one-stop reference resource that provide essential information for students about the subject – and the course – they've chosen to study.

Friendly and authoritative, *Palgrave Student Companions* support the student throughout their degree. They encourage the reader to think about study skills alongside the subject matter of their course, offer guidance on module and career choices, and act as an invaluable source book and reference that they can return to time and again.

Palgrave Student Companions – your course ... one source

Published
The MBA Companion
The Politics Companion
The Social Work Companion

Forthcoming
The Cultural Studies Companion
The English Language and Linguistics Companion
The Health Studies Companion
The Literary Studies Companion
The Media Studies Companion
The Nursing Companion
The Psychology Companion
The Theatre, Drama and Performance Companion

Further titles are planned

www.palgravestudentcompanions.com

the MBA companion

paul dainty and moreen anderson

melbourne business school, the university of melbourne, australia

your course ... one source

palgrave
macmillan

First published 2008 by
PALGRAVE MACMILLAN
Houndmills, Basingstoke, Hampshire RG21 6XS and
175 Fifth Avenue, New York, N.Y. 10010
Companies and representatives throughout the world

PALGRAVE MACMILLAN is the global academic imprint of the Palgrave
Macmillan division of St. Martin's Press, LLC and of Palgrave Macmillan
Ltd. Macmillan® is a registered trademark in the United States, United
Kingdom and other countries. Palgrave is a registered trademark in the
European Union and other countries.

ISBN-13: 978–1–4039–9885–9 paperback
ISBN-10: 1–4039–9885–X paperback

This book is printed on paper suitable for recycling and made from fully
managed and sustained forest sources. Logging, pulping and manufacturing
processes are expected to conform to the environmental regulations of the
country of origin.

A catalogue record for this book is available from the British Library.

A catalog record for this book is available from the Library of Congress.

10 9 8 7 6 5 4 3 2 1
17 16 15 14 13 12 11 10 09 08

Printed and bound in China

brief contents

contents

list of figures and tables

figures

tables

acknowledgements

The authors and publishers are grateful to the following for permission to use copyright material:

BusinessWeek Online, for Box 2.1 from 'The First Year', BusinessWeek Online, 24 October 2001.

Team Technology, for Box 4.1, The Myers Briggs Type Indicator™ from Myers Briggs (2006) A Complete Guide and Questionnaires at www.teamtechnology.co.uk.

Penguin Books, London, for Box 4.3 from E. de Bono (2000) Six Thinking Hats, pp. 14–15. Copyright © MICA Management Resources Inc. and McQuaig Group, USA.

Edward de Bono and the McQuaig Group Inc. for Box 4.4.

Nelson Australia Pty Ltd for Box 5.1 from Poole, D. 'Managing Emotional Intelligence', in P. Murray, D. Poole and G. Jones (eds) (2006) Contemporary Issues in Management and Organisational Behaviour (Melbourne: Thomson), p. 347.

The British Psychological Society for Figure 5.1 from 'Occupational sources of stress: a review of the literature relating to coronary heart disease and mental ill health', Journal of Occupational Psychology (1976), **49**: 12.

Elsevier Ltd for Box 5.2 from Holmes, T.H. and Rahe, R.H. (1967–68) 'Social readjustment rating scale', Journal of Psychosomatic Research, **11**(2): 216.

John Wiley & Sons Ltd. for Box 5.5, adapted from Quick, J.C., Nelson, D.L. and Quick, J.D. (1990) Stress and Challenge at the Top: The Paradox of the Successful Executive (New York: John Wiley), p. 190.

Figure 6.1 reprinted with permission of John Wiley & Sons Australia, © 1991, from Bailey, J.E., Schermerhorn, J.R., Hunt, J.G. and Osborn, R.N. (1991) Managing Organisational Behaviour in Australia (Singapore: Jacaranda Wiley), p. 395.

McGraw-Hill Companies for Box 6.2 from Luthans, F. (1995) Organizational Behaviour, 7th edn (New York: McGraw-Hill), p. 426.

Richard Pascale for Figure 9.1, 'The ebbs and flows of business techniques 1950s–1990s', from Pascale, R.T. (1994) Transformation, (London: BBC Enterprises). Simon & Schuster from Pascale, R.T. (1988) Managing on the Edge.

Anupindi, R., Chopra S., Deshmukh, S.D., Van Mieghem, J.A. and Zemel, E. (1999) *Managing Business Process Flows* (Englewood Cliffs, NJ: Prentice Hall) p. 26.

Massachusetts Institute of Technology for Figure 10.2 from Schmenner, R.W. (1986) 'How can service businesses survive and prosper?', *Sloan Management Review*, **27**(3): 25. Copyright 1986. All rights reserved. Distributed by Tribune Media Services.

Henry Mintzberg for Figure 14.1, adapted from Mintzberg, H. (1973) The Nature of Managerial Work (New York: HarperCollins), p. 59.

McGraw-Hill Companies for Figure 14.2 from Luthans, F. *Organizational Behavior*, 7th edn, p. 15. Copyright 1995.

John Storey for Box 14.4 from Simmons, D.E. Shadur, M.A. and Bamber, G.J. 'Optus: New Recruitment and Selection in an Enterprise Culture', in Storey, J. (ed.) (1996) *Blackwell Cases in Human Resource and Change Management* (Oxford: Blackwell), pp. 147–59.

McGraw-Hill Companies for Table 14.1 'Evolution of the 21st Century Manager', from Kreitner, R. and Kinicki, A. (2001) *Organizational Behavior*, 5th edn (New York: McGraw Hill), p. 8. Copyright 2001.

Palgrave Macmillan for Figure 18.2 from White, C. (2004) *Strategic Management* (Houndmills, Basingstoke: Palgrave Macmillan), p. 532.

Every effort has been made to trace copyright holders, but if any have been inadvertently overlooked the publishers would be pleased to make the necessary arrangements at the first opportunity.

contributing authors and principal affiliations

Michael J. Baker, Emeritus Professor of Marketing, University of Strathclyde.

Rob Brown, Professor of Finance, Faculty of Economics and Commerce, University of Melbourne.

Gonzalo Chavez, Professor of Corporate Finance, Instituto de Empresa (Spain).

Mark Crosby, Associate Professor – Economics, Melbourne Business School.

Paul Dainty, Professor of Management Development, Melbourne Business School.

Clare Morris, Professor and Dean of Quality and Standards Development, University of Gloucestershire.

David Trende, Principal Fellow, Accounting, Melbourne Business School.

Kannan Sethuraman, Associate Professor – Operations Management, Melbourne Business School.

Devanath Tirupati, Professor – Operations Management, Indian Institute of Management.

Colin White, Professor of Strategy, Graduate School of Management, La Trobe University.

introduction

The Master of Business Administration degree (MBA) is the most popular business qualification in the world and is fast becoming a prerequisite for management positions.[1] It is offered by business schools and university faculties in many countries and despite regular criticism that the MBA is in decline, it continues to thrive. Linda Anderson of the *Financial Times* points out that 2006 has been buoyant for European business schools with an increase in programmes and robust applications.[2] The same is true of America and also of Asia where interest in the MBA has enjoyed massive growth.

There are several reasons for this, but none more important than the value an MBA can bring to its recipients. As David Wilson, president and CEO of the Graduate Management Admissions Council, notes:

> The MBA continues to demonstrate its strong value proposition. In a knowledge economy, leadership and management demand a complex portfolio of skills and talents. A selective MBA programme gives its graduate those skills.

This is supported by numerous endorsements from educators worldwide. A colleague and professor of marketing strategy, Richard Speed, sums up the benefits as follows:

> MBAs tend to give their graduates choices that their non-MBA peers do not have. They have enhanced skills, increased confidence and a dramatically enhanced network of professional contacts. For the employer, they have a more valuable employee, with a broader range of skills, who has more alternative employment options because they now have more ways to contribute to their employer's business.[3]

Despite the success of the MBA, the many great business schools and scores of outstanding faculties, there are, however, flaws. While an MBA can bring many benefits, it can also result in students failing to capitalize on some of the major opportunities available on the programme. This is because the MBA is usually very intense and demanding. It is also often an expensive experience, both in terms of time and money. Consequently, extracting the full benefits from the degree is critical. This requires a range of skills, attitudes and approaches to learning, which sometimes do not become evident until well into the programme.

The Master of Business Administration degree (MBA) is the most popular business qualification in the world and is fast becoming a prerequisite for management positions.

Many students initially take the degree for the business knowledge it provides. This book helps to improve understanding of some of these most critical areas. But to truly operate at a high level of effectiveness in an increasingly demanding work environment requires a range of capabilities that go beyond business knowledge alone. The book also explores how the degree experience can be better utilized to pursue broader personal developmental goals and indeed even personal transformation. An MBA can literally change your life. But it will only do this, or do this in a way that is personally beneficial, if a proactive approach is taken to learning during the degree.

The book is for both full-time and part-time students who have made the decision to undertake an MBA, or an equivalent postgraduate management degree. The intention is not to replace any MBA subject. Rather, based on research with current and past MBA students, it aims to prepare the reader for what lies ahead both in terms of looking at the skills and requirements of the degree programme, and also in examining ways of maximizing personal and professional development. These issues are explored through two main areas: 'personal capabilities' and 'functional capabilities'.

The first part of the book on personal capabilities is concerned with developing the qualities needed to effectively manage a challenging degree programme or demanding work role. These include the ability to manage oneself and the ability to learn in varied situations and from different approaches, including case studies, presentations and projects. It also includes the ability to analyse and solve problems effectively; to cope emotionally with the stresses and strains of an exacting environment; to communicate and influence others; and to make informed and satisfying career choices. Most importantly, it includes the ability to lead others in a global context, a critical skill for the twenty-first century. The book explores how these capabilities can be developed on an MBA course, both to enable students to successfully complete the degree, but also to enhance their work effectiveness long after graduation.

> We have found tremendous endorsement for this type of postgraduate management degree.

The second part of the book on functional capabilities is concerned with the management subject areas, tools and concepts that are essential to running a business and central to an MBA programme. Management ideas now form the basis of a lucrative 'ideas industry', where management books, consultants and gurus reach worldwide audiences. In this part of the book, we examine how the management discipline has developed and highlight some of the key drivers that have shaped contemporary management ideas. The ensuing chapters review the functional subjects that are often seen as the 'core' subjects of the MBA. These include an understanding of operations management, finance, accounting, marketing, organizational behaviour, quantitative methods, economics and strategy.

Many people have contributed to these two parts. Particularly important are the expert authors who in each of the functional chapters have provided an overview of their subject and identified current trends in their area. These are important and complex subjects and, for many students, uncharted territory. The authors review these areas in a way that demystifies the subject and enables the student to gain some familiarity with the essence of the discipline.

Also important are the many students who provided the research for the first part of the book. In none of our interviews, and indeed in over 25 years of involvement with MBA programmes and hundreds of participants, have we come across a student who felt that the MBA had not been of benefit to them. We have found tremendous endorsement for this type of postgraduate management degree. However, despite this, we have also found a large number of students who felt they could have gained more from their MBA experience. They realized too late that there are many opportunities on an MBA that can be easily missed without a proactive approach to learning. Hopefully this book will go some way to redressing that balance early on and help to make the MBA a life-changing experience.

references

1. Quoted on the European Foundation for Management (EFMD) website, www.mba-courses.com.
2. Anderson, L. 'European business schools report: Confidently facing Bologna', *Financial Times* website, www.ft.com/businesseducation, 4 December 2006.
3. Quoted in Yen, M. 'Moving on up with MBAs', *Human Resources*, 17 October 2006.

studying an MBA 1

1 why take an MBA?

Most readers of this book will be in the process of making a commitment to at least one year (and more likely eighteen months to two years) of full-time study for a business degree that will probably be more demanding than anything you have done in the past. Alternatively, you may have just signed up for an equally, if not more daunting, four years of part-time study while holding down a full-time job. In years to come, you will probably remember your degree period as much for the work/life balance challenges you overcame, as for your course learning.

You will also pay a lot for the experience. If you attend one of the top schools, you will be paying tuition fees of around US$40,000 per annum and for those of you taking the degree full time, an even greater cost in lost earnings while you are out of employment for one or two years.

You will not be alone. Annually, over 200,000 people take the Graduate Management Admission Test (GMAT), the standard international test required for applying to many business schools. But not every school requires the GMAT and the number of MBA graduates is probably double this number worldwide. At least 112,000 people in the USA and 13,000 in the UK will graduate with an MBA through the full-time option. In addition, an increasing number of people take an MBA through part-time study, online or other distance approaches, offered, for example, by the Open University. Add to these those who will graduate with a management qualification, such as a Diploma or Masters of Management, similar to the MBA experience, and you can see that you are part of a worldwide phenomenon.

> today the MBA is the fastest growing post-graduate qualification in the world. Its appeal transcends national borders.'

This is a phenomenon that has grown quickly. In 1956, graduates of business education were virtually non-existent, with only 3,200 MBA degrees awarded in the US. By the end of 2000, there were 341 accredited master's programmes in business in the US, with 900 American universities offering a master's degree in business.[1] While the US has been the main driving force behind this growth, business education has grown around the world. For example, the number of business schools in Britain has risen from 20 in the early 1980s to 120 today. Business education has also spread throughout continental Europe, with many European countries having at least one and sometimes many more highly ranked schools. In addition, there has been a spectacular growth in quality business schools in the Asia Pacific region, particularly in China, Singapore and Australia. As Stuart Crainer and Des Dearlove point out: 'today the MBA is the fastest growing post-graduate qualification in the world. Its appeal transcends national borders.'[2]

Why the appeal? There are many benefits to an MBA. The most obvious one is money and for those attending a top school, the short-term financial benefits seem too good to be true. The average salary in 2006, for graduates completing an MBA in 2003, was US\$166,900 from Stanford, US\$140,200 from INSEAD and US\$135,200 from London Business School.[3] All the top schools in the USA, Europe and Asia have equally impressive figures. As the old saying goes, 'There is gold in them there hills'. For some students, the short-term return is critical, and for everyone taking an MBA, long-term financial returns will be important. However, these have to be seen in perspective.

Although most MBA graduates should expect an improvement in their salaries in the short term, the return over the longer term will depend on many factors, including the business school attended, the reasons for going there, the subsequent job opportunities and, not least of all, their own ability. The vast majority taking an MBA will not graduate from one of the top schools and in the short term are less likely to command the stellar salaries that are achieved by some. The largest annual full-time MBA intake occurs at Kellogg with around 1,200 students and Harvard with around 900. Wharton takes on about 750 students annually, but the rest of the top schools in the US have intakes of between 400 and 500 full-time students a year. Thus, 80% of the 120,000 full-time American MBA students attend schools that are more likely to produce graduates who can expect modest increases in their starting salaries rather than massive immediate returns. The same is true in Europe, where most MBA and postgraduate business students do not take their degrees at the top schools. For example, INSEAD, with an intake of 880 full-time students in 2005, is large by European standards, but IMD has fewer than 100 full-timers each year.[4]

> The largest annual full-time MBA intake occurs at Kellogg with around 1,200 students and Harvard with around 900.

There will be those who see the MBA as their passport to Wall Street (or their country's equivalent), or a job in one of the global consultancy firms. There is nothing wrong with that ambition. However, the overall benefits from an MBA are much greater than a short-term financial fix. Indeed, focus on this too much and you might fail to mine the real gold from a postgraduate business degree.

the benefits of an MBA

Why the stellar growth in business education? The MBA is a long-term personal investment that can yield high returns in many different ways. For some, its value lies in developing an organizational and strategic approach to thinking about business. Jeanne Wilt, assistant dean of admissions and career development at the University of Michigan's business school, argues that an MBA is 'the single best way to get a solid knowledge of the basic business building blocks – accounting, finance, marketing, human resources, and organizational behaviour – and it's the best way to round out your work experience.'[5]

As well as understanding the functional building blocks, developing an ability to analyse problems is central to many business degree programmes. A management qualification provides a systematic way of exploring business issues and provides frameworks that assist in dealing with the complexity of many business dilemmas. Some business schools are increasingly seeing the need to build on this foundation and provide a broader experience. Jackie Wilbur, director of the career development office at MIT's Sloan School, encapsulates this in her comment:

We're already a wonderfully analytical, quantitative school. Now we're trying to put the icing on the cake of the Sloan MBA. We want to make sure we pay equal attention to interpersonal skills and to understanding how the whole aspect of leadership relates to career development. These are the skills that become more important as people advance through their careers.[6]

The notion that the MBA is a long-term qualification – an opportunity for career development and personal enhancement – is an important one. Many MBA students use it effectively in this way, often seeing it as a vehicle to switch career. Functional specialists, in particular, use the qualification to make the vital step into general management. George Bain, former dean of London Business School, says: 'There are a few exceptions, of course. On the whole, though, most people who take an MBA are career changers. They want to have an experience which will change their lives.' Robert Hamada, dean of the Graduate School of Business at Chicago, also emphasizes the career aspect: 'Business school is now seen as a very important career pit stop for ambitious people. This is definitely true in the US and increasingly in other parts of the world including Europe and I would say even more so in Asia.'[7]

An increased salary, better understanding of business, an improved range of skills and a desire to enhance one's career are only of benefit if they also enhance an employer's perception of the business graduate. In many instances they do. For instance, Mark Smith, managing director of Korn/Ferry, the executive search firm, sees the degree as highly desirable:

Most of our clients see the MBA as first and foremost a screening process. People self-select to go to graduate school. They are people who are ambitious, who care about their careers, who are motivated to make the time and investment to get where they want to be.

Robert Hamada says:

In the US and increasingly now in other parts of the world, the MBA is seen as a credential almost like a union card. It is a signal to a potential employer that they are serious about business.[8]

Many companies confirm this view. For instance, Jim Beirne, director of recruiting for the US-based company General Mills, comments:

If you go to the source – it turns out to be a relatively inexpensive method. General Mill's chairman, vice chairman and all its presidents save one were hired off business school campuses. These schools are where we find and nurture our top management.[9]

Adding to this is the networks and alumni contacts that many business schools provide. Some of the bigger schools particularly pride themselves in the networking opportunities their schools have nurtured over many years. For example, Harvard Business School alumni occupy about 20% of the top three executive positions of Fortune 500 companies.[10] Cranfield School of Management, a leading business school in Europe, has 10,000 alumni located in 115 countries worldwide. As Crainer and Dearlove note, alumni networks span the globe like empires.

Consequently, there are many benefits to taking a graduate business degree. The experience is often quite different from an undergraduate programme and the outcomes are also varied. Ultimately, as we argue throughout the book, the MBA and similar educational experiences can be seen as a holistic experience giving the new graduate increased confidence to cope with business problems and enhance personal growth. Jeanne Wilt of the University of Michigan says:

There will always be folk who say you don't need an MBA to get ahead. And they're right. But for many individuals facing their own career development and the knowledge that they need to round out their experience, this will always be a great investment.[11]

what the critics say

With the large amount of money and time invested in business education, it is sometimes easy to turn a blind eye to the criticisms voiced about business qualifications. Jeanne Wilt's comment does, however, highlight the fact that not everyone is convinced of the benefits of an MBA degree. Some question whether this really is a qualification that adds value, often pointing to successful businesspeople like Richard Branson, Bill Gates, Michael Dell, Anita Roddick and Jack Welch – none of whom have MBAs. If they are so good, why is the degree so necessary? In a similar vein, critics also point out that many top-performing firms – Southwest Airlines, Wal-Mart, The Men's Warehouse, ServiceMaster, PSS/World Medical, SAS Institute, AES, Whole Foods Market and Starbucks – do not recruit at the leading business schools and don't emphasize business degree credentials and staffing practices.[12]

> *Often critics fail to point out that there are many roads to achieving business success and business education is just one option.*

One of the unfortunate aspects of this debate is that the views expressed are rarely balanced in their assessment. Often critics fail to point out that there are many roads to achieving business success and business education is just one option. Jack Welch may not have an MBA, but in revitalizing Crotonville, the GE management education centre, he used many highly respected business school professors such as Noel Tichy and Steve Kerr from the University of Michigan. Jeffrey Immelt, Welch's successor, is a Harvard Business School alumnus.

Indeed, there are hundreds of highly successful businesses run by MBA graduates and many highly respected business and government people who have MBAs, including James Wolfensohn, the recently retired president of the World Bank; Phil Knight, president, CEO and founder of Nike; Meg Whitman, president and CEO of eBay; Stan O'Neal, CEO of Merrill Lynch; and Frank Shrontz, the former chairman and CEO of Boeing. Indeed, as this is a young degree, as more people come through the ranks of business and government sectors and the numbers of alumni grow, the criticism in the future may be that it is impossible to get into some organizations without a business qualification. Taking an English literature course doesn't guarantee literary success any more than an MBA guarantees a seat on a corporate board. Indeed, many successful novelists don't have degrees, but this does not prevent thousands taking degrees in literature with the hope of penning a bestseller. In fact, in terms of success in one's chosen career, the MBA would seem to be a much better bet.

However, an MBA alone is not the key to the door of a successful future. What one does with the degree, how one manages oneself on the job, luck and a host of other factors will come into play as with any path through life. Steven Zales, of Spencer Stuart, argues:

Even in the 21st century, an MBA doesn't ensure an easy ticket to the boardroom. The degree certainly gets you ahead in the early years ... After about 10 years into an individual's career, though, there's a shift away from how good an education you've received to how you've been proving yourself on the job. At that point, other factors become much more critical in determining how you move up the organization.[13]

What about the degree's applicability to more immediate business problems? Does an MBA make you better equipped to deal with the business world on a day-to-day basis? In principle, there is little doubt that a postgraduate business qualification will equip the graduate with additional skills. But there have been strong criticisms over the years of the limitations of some business school curricula, and they are worth listening to. Jeffrey Pfeffer and Christina Fong summarize these as:

an overemphasis on analysis at the expense of both integration and developing wisdom as well as leadership and interpersonal skills, or teaching the wrong things in the wrong ways (and perhaps to the wrong people, or at least at the wrong time in their careers).[14]

Some of these criticisms are echoed by others. Crainer and Dearlove complain that business schools

have failed to keep pace with the constituencies they serve. The vast majority continue to take a functional view of what managers do. Teaching remains around functional disciplines or silos that mirror the traditional departments of corporations. But while much of the business school world accepts that this silo approach is outdated, most ... business schools still make little serious attempt at integrating these areas of knowledge into a coherent view of what it means to run a business.[15]

They also believe that 'business schools have spent too much emphasis on teaching students analytical techniques and not enough on managing people'.

Many in the business school community also see an emphasis on analytical skills at the expense of developing other qualities as a shortcoming. Henry Mintzberg believes that 'conventional MBA programmes train the wrong people in the wrong way with the wrong consequences', ignoring the extent to which management is a craft requiring zest and intuition rather than merely an ability to analyse data and invent strategies.[16] In similar vein, Harold Leavitt, the marketing guru based at Stanford, argues:

While we teach the right things on our MBA programmes, we don't teach some critical things we ought to teach ... like leadership, vision, imagination and values, producing critters with lopsided brains, icy hearts and shrunken souls.[17]

responding to the critics: improving the MBA

How have schools responded to these criticisms? The critics tend to be quite pessimistic with responses varying from, not enough, to not at all. But the current situation is much less negative. At General Mills, Beirne, for example, who hires 75 MBAs each year, in response to the criticism that business schools turn out theoreticians divorced from the real world, replies:

There is no question that I would like to see some improvement. The analysis MBAs are taught is outstanding, but it's the practical applications of that analysis, coupled with an ability to lead, that we spend a lot of time on. Can schools teach that? Well, I think they are getting better at it.[18]

Noel Tichy, professor of organizational behaviour at the University of Michigan and director of its global leadership programme, also sees the need for improvement. He comments: 'No one's interested in seeing candidates who are able to use business algorithms. They want them to be better implementers, better communicators, better team players and schools like ours have responded.'[19] For Jeanne Wilt: 'The MBA is all about the ability to learn and practice team skills and to gain the experience of delivering measurable results while working with diverse cultures.'[20]

In an increasingly competitive business school world, many schools like Michigan have had no choice but to respond. This response has come in several different ways. The most notable have been in terms of the way the MBA is delivered and how some MBAs are structured. The major change in delivery has been through the development of the part-time and executive MBA programme, which has seen massive growth. Indeed, some see this as a threat to the mainstream MBA. Beirne comments:

These [EMBAs] are very attractive to us as a business investing in our employees because they don't over expose our high-potential employees to the 300 or 400 recruiting organizations that are out there meeting the full-time day students.[21]

In addition, the internet and online provision has also greatly influenced the delivery of the MBA. Increasingly, schools are using new technology to produce innovative approaches to MBA education. The Instituto de Empresa Business School based in Madrid, for example, has a Global MBA, which integrates online learning with video conferencing and classroom-based activities. These are important and welcome developments. The challenge is to continue to integrate new technology with face-to-face learning experiences. Without peer contact, developing some of the interpersonal capabilities described later in the book becomes difficult. It would be ironic indeed if new technological developments, no matter how sophisticated, directed students away from opportunities to improve in the very areas that MBA programmes have been largely criticized for – the development of interpersonal skills. The balance is important.

> The challenge is to continue to integrate new technology with face-to-face learning experiences.

However, the most notable change in structure has been the move to specialist courses, where the MBA allows a student to specialize in a particular functional area, such as marketing and finance, or an industrial area. As with the part-time and executive MBA, specialist full-time MBA courses have also grown quickly, although in relation to some industrial specialisms, the response seems somewhat overenthusiastic. For instance, SDA Bocconi offers an MBA in fashion and design, Danube University offers an aviation MBA, while Lincoln University offers one in church management. You can even get an MBA in soccer at the University of Liverpool.

What is important about most of these developments is that they predominantly retain the core aspects of the MBA. As Phillip Crotty and Amy Soule note, while the executive MBA is meant to attract older managers with appropriate job experience, the typical curriculum covers the same major course areas as the standard MBA. The same is true of specialist MBAs. For instance, the University of Liverpool's soccer MBA still covers the fundamentals – organizational behaviour, marketing, strategic management and the management context – all compulsory modules.[22]

This emphasis on fundamentals is one of the major attractions of an MBA-style degree. A thorough grounding in the fundamentals of business activity and the development of ways of thinking and learning about business have been the platform for its past success and are critical to its continued success. One cannot graduate with an MBA without having a thorough financial grounding or a good understanding of marketing. To demolish the core aspect of the MBA programme would be to throw the baby out with the bath water and the remarkable consistency among MBA programmes is one of the reasons for its success and its worldwide portability. As Gale Bitter at Stanford says:

At Stanford we pride ourselves in offering a research based framework that managers can apply to any situation. Our programmes don't just try to teach the latest 'flavour of the month' ideas and techniques, they are based on research over many years. What we teach is substantial. It will stand the test of time.[23]

Whether or not you go to Stanford, the principle that you will be getting a set of theories, tools and techniques that have a solid foundation and applicability to a range of business environments is what we believe you should expect.

So what should you have learned on graduating? You should leave your programme with the latest thinking in the major disciplines. You should have a better understanding of what we know, what we don't know, what we can (and what we can't) do in many areas, and you should have a much better ability to sort out ideas without substance from those that may help you in the longer term. In some cases, the principles you learn will not be immediately applicable, but possibly more because you may not yet be in a position to use them. In many areas you should be able to apply your knowledge straight away. If you can't walk into a job and immediately apply the accounting concepts you have studied, or put forward a coherent marketing plan based on what you have learned on your MBA, then you should ask for your money back.

going beyond the fundamentals

However, while you will leave an MBA programme with an understanding of the functional aspects of business, this should not be the whole story. You should not leave an MBA without a range of other abilities, such as a capacity to work in groups, communicate well and influence others. As the criticisms of the MBA discussed earlier have highlighted, the acquisition of these softer skills has, in the past, largely been left to chance. This is less likely to occur now. As Crainer and Dearlove note:

Clearly, the basic functional skills – finance, marketing, operations, HR, and strategy– remain relevant. But it is no longer so easy to justify an entire programme around them. More imaginative and realistic programmes increasingly construct entirely new foundations while covering all the major elements of the functions.[24]

Previous comments indicate that many of the better schools are responding to the need to go beyond the fundamentals. Applying management concepts through project work is more the norm rather than the exception. Many programmes have introduced leadership courses and created additional opportunities for skills development. Some have developed entrepreneurial options and subjects such as managing diversity and improving ethical responsibility are increasingly becoming part of the curriculum. As William Christie, dean of Vanderbilt University's Owen Graduate School of Management, comments: 'If courses in ethics and moral leadership are not already part of the curriculum, they had better be.'[25] Moreover, many schools now provide career assistance, partly driven by the emphasis placed on this by international publications that rank business schools.

But changes in the curriculum are only part of the answer to going beyond the fundamentals. It is rare, although obviously not unheard of, for MBA graduates to say they regret going to business school. It is probably one of the reasons why so many alumni, not just in the USA but elsewhere, are so keen to give back both time and money to the schools they have attended. But while few seem to regret the investment in a business school degree, it is not uncommon for graduates to feel they could have got more out of the degree. For instance, a study by the AACSB, which, along with EQUIS and the Association of MBAs, is one of the main accrediting bodies of MBA courses, found that MBA graduates thought that the ability to communicate effectively with another person was the single most useful skill in their career – but that only 6% of business schools were even moderately effective in teaching that skill.[26]

Clearly, this is an area business schools need to continue to work on. However, rather than seeing responsibility for student development residing solely within the lecture room, tremendous benefits could be gained by broadening the responsibility for learning and placing the individual student more in the spotlight. While the MBA has elements of a 'spoon-feeding' process, students will still get a lot more out of their degree if they see themselves not as passive recipients of sometimes imperfect 'tablets of stone', but as part of a proactive learning process, where they have both choice and responsibility for their own learning and development. Viewed like this, the MBA education process takes on a different light and a new dimension of thinking and new possibilities for development present themselves.

A proactive approach to learning and one that involves personal responsibility and choice on an MBA is not a completely new idea, but it certainly has not been emphasized enough. Pfeffer and Fong argue

that many programmes operate on the basis of some incorrect assumptions about learning, thereby doing things that contribute to poorer learning outcomes ... when students are relieved of any sense of responsibility for their learning and much involvement in the learning process, the evidence is that they learn much less.[27]

You cannot afford to go through an MBA programme being taught a lot, but learning very little. Neither can you afford to place all the responsibility, or blame, on the degree programme for how you come out at the end. If you experience a tremendous learning experience, then that is terrific, but there are many things you can do to enhance your development.

These developmental opportunities on a postgraduate business degree fall into two broad areas. The first of these is the opportunity to develop *functional capability* – or an improved ability in functional skills. These include a better understanding of subjects like strategy, economics, marketing, finance, accounting, operations and organizational behaviour.

The second set of opportunities centre on what can be called *personal capabilities*. These are the skills that are essential for personal effectiveness in a managerial environment. They include improved abilities in analysis, creativity, time management, stress management, communication and teamwork. They also include an ability to manage short- and long-term goals from both a work and a personal perspective.

However, in reality, these two sets of competencies are not independent of each other. Often, both areas have to be used together. In operating in challenging environments, effective professionals will often draw on both a range of functional perspectives and on their interpersonal competencies at the same time. A manager contemplating a merger of two organizations with different cultures will have to take into account many factors, ranging from the strategic and financial imperatives of the merger to the issues of organizational integration, change and leadership.

The problems that face managers today cannot be solved by having a functional understanding alone, although this is clearly an important string to one's bow. Professional businesspeople must also have a range of competencies and use these in an integrated way. Consequently, taking an MBA is about more than expanding your knowledge in any one area. It is about taking opportunities to become a complete and well-rounded businessperson, effective in today's business environment. For many people embarking on an MBA, with gaps in their skills and knowledge, the programme may well be a journey of personal improvement. However, that developmental path is often not laid out clearly on an MBA, or indeed even signposted as a possible objective. Consequently, thought needs to be given early on to the direction that your own journey might take.

conclusion

Postgraduate business education provides many developmental opportunities, but it also has some limitations, as this chapter has highlighted. Capitalizing on the degree's potential requires you to think about not only what you might learn, but also the process of how you learn. You also need to take responsibility for your own development, not just over the next few years, but also in relation to lifelong learning. Consequently, this requires a full understanding of what an MBA programme is meant to do and what you need to extract from it in order to maximize the personal benefits. This book will help with that process. It does not attempt to replace the rich learning available on the degree, but can give you an extra advantage on a degree that already gives you the edge.

references

1. Pfeffer, J. and Fong, C.T. (2002) 'The end of business schools? Less success than meets the eye', *Academy of Management Learning and Education*, **1**(1): 78.
2. Crainer, S. and Dearlove, D. (1999) *Gravy Training* (San Francisco: Jossey-Bass) p. 76.
3. *Financial Times* website, http://rankings.ft.com/rankings/mba/rankings.html, February 2007.
4. Op. cit. Crainer and Dearlove (1999) pp. 84–6.
5. Greco, J. (2001) 'Does that MBA really make a difference', *Journal of Business Strategy*, **22**(4): 40.
6. Ibid. p. 41.
7. Op. cit. Crainer and Dearlove (1999) p. 81.
8. Op. cit. Crainer and Dearlove (1999) p. 81.
9. Op. cit. Greco (2001) p. 40.
10. Harvard Business School website, http://www.hbs.edu/mba/yourcareer/hbsnetwork.html, February 2007.
11. Op. cit. Greco (2001) p. 41.
12. See, for instance, Pfeffer, J. and Sutton, R.I. (1999) 'Knowing what to do is not enough: turning knowledge into action', *California Management Review*, **42**(1): 83; op. cit. Pfeffer and Fong, 2002, p. 79.
13. Op. cit. Greco (2001) p. 40.
14. Op. cit. Pfeffer and Fong (2002) p. 79.
15. Op. cit. Crainer and Dearlove (1999) p. 30.
16. 'But can you teach it', *The Economist*, 20 May 2004; see also Mintzberg, H. (2004) *Managers not MBAs* (San Francisco: Berrett-Koehler).

17. Crainer, S. (ed) (1997) *The Ultimate Book of Business Quotations* (Oxford: Capstone), p. 72.
18. Op. cit. Greco (2001) p. 40.
19. Op. cit. Greco (2001) p. 40.
20. Op. cit. Greco (2001) p. 40.
21. Op. cit. Greco (2001) p. 40.
22. Crotty, P.T. and Soule, A.J. (1997) 'Executive education: yesterday and today with a look at tomorrow', *Journal of Management Development*, **16**(1): 4.
23. Op. cit. Crainer and Dearlove (1999) p. 52.
24. Op. cit. Crainer and Dearlove (1999) p. 262.
25. Merritt, J., 'For MBAs, Soul Searching 101' *BusinessWeek* website http://www.businessweek.com, September 16, 2002.
26. 'The $100,000 question', *The Economist* (2002) **364**(8283): 56.
27. Op. cit. Pfeffer and Fong (2002) p. 84.

2 maximizing the MBA experience

A postgraduate qualification in management provides many benefits. These can range from broadening business knowledge, to increased self-confidence through to enhanced career opportunities. However, these improvements do not necessarily come automatically and some may never be realized.

There are two main reasons for this. One is that a business school may not provide a full range of learning opportunities. The criticisms of the previous chapter highlight that not all MBA programmes formally develop the 'softer' management skills. The other reason is that a student may fail to take full responsibility for their own progress and capitalize on the benefits available during their programme. As one student remarked: 'To get something from this, you really have to put in.' Indeed, 'putting in' involves more than a just a lot of effort. In order to fully benefit from an MBA, we believe students have to take control of their own personal development. If they do, they will be far more likely to benefit as both individuals and managers.

> In order to fully benefit from an MBA, we believe students have to take control of their own personal development. If they do, they will be far more likely to benefit as both individuals and managers.

This chapter describes the typical structure and objectives of MBA programmes. It also describes the style and educational approach many business schools adopt and the pressures that students are likely to experience. Additionally, it encourages readers to establish a sense of direction for their programme and think about the skills and knowledge they see the MBA providing. These three ingredients, MBA structure, MBA style and a sense of direction and the capabilities that can be gained from an MBA, are explored in this chapter.

the MBA programme: structure and aims

Advanced management degree programmes are usually divided into two main sections. The first part, often called the 'core course', concentrates on the major functional disciplines of management and takes up the first 6–12 months of the programme, depending on whether it is being taken full time or part time. During this period, students complete the compulsory subjects of the MBA. These ensure that students gain a firm foundation in fundamental disciplines such as finance, accounting, economics, operations and marketing. Here students learn about a common set of standards and techniques to help analyse and solve business problems. Although many schools now teach in an integrated way, the core subjects tend to be taught as separate disciplines. Cranfield School of Management, for example, which emphasizes the innovative, personal and applied nature of its MBA, still teaches the core as discrete subjects. The overall objective of the core programme, however, is to develop a shared language for describing business issues and developing a broader appreciation of different organizations and industries.

The second part of the programme typically consists of 'elective' subjects that allow students to specialize in one or more areas in greater depth. These electives build on the core subjects and allow for the integration and application of the skills learned in the first part of the MBA. This part of the programme is usually characterized by a greater degree of flexibility and personal choice and also more variety in the way it is taught. Thomas Steiner and Rebecca Wells identified at least 70 universities that describe their curriculum as integrative or cross-disciplinary.[1] Business schools can offer a considerable number of electives, either separately or in 'themes' depending on the size of the school. London Business School, for example, offers a diverse portfolio of over 70 electives, covering topics such as new venture finance, leading strategic transformation, international supply chain management, negotiations and project management. As with most schools, elective subjects can be used to either broaden management ability or concentrate on particular areas of interest.

> The reality is that many MBA degrees have for some time catered for a second category of student, which we call business professionals. These are students who want to concentrate on a specialist area, either to work in that discipline or become advisers or consultants.

MBA programme aims and objectives differ between business schools. However, while, as Julia Tyler argues, there is no such thing as a conventional MBA,[2] schools tend to produce three general types of graduate. The first of these (and most traditionally associated with an MBA), is that of general manager. These are students who are usually trying to move away from a previous area of specialism and move into more general management, usually in large corporations. In addition, the executive MBA tends to cater for students already experienced in general management, but who wish to enhance their abilities.

Producing general managers, however, is not the sole purpose of an MBA, despite some critics arguing that it should be. The reality is that many MBA degrees have for some time catered for a second category of student, which we call *business professionals*. These are students who want to concentrate on a specialist area, either to work in that discipline or become advisers or consultants. Schools now provide a broad range of electives that allow specialization in a particular functional discipline (such as finance, marketing or human resources) or industry area (such as hospitality, real estate or the public sector). Often these degrees are rebadged as MScs, but are very much in the MBA mould.

The third category caters for students with strong entrepreneurial aspirations. Schools like EM Lyon, for example, have entrepreneurial management as a central theme of their MBA and the *Financial Times* now regularly rates schools in terms of entrepreneurship. This third type of student, the *commercial entrepreneur*, seeks to create opportunities in the marketplace, often on his or her own or with a small group and usually at some risk. While this category is perhaps less formally acknowledged than the other two, many schools provide a range of electives, which give the student the tools to explore, develop and sustain a new product or explore market possibilities. These programmes often provide project-based electives allowing new service or product proposals to be reviewed. At the height of the dot.com boom, many entrepreneurial

MBA graduates started their own businesses hoping to exploit the new technological wave. In hindsight perhaps, not everyone got the feasibility studies correct.

On the surface, these three general categories of MBA seem to be different species. Indeed, much of the recent debate about the MBA has superficially divided the degree between producing 'hard-headed technocrats' or 'experienced people managers'.[3] However, while there is considerable variety in management degrees, the real difference is largely one of emphasis around different combinations of functional knowledge and management skills. Indeed, as Figure 2.1 highlights, there is an area of overlap that is critical to all three general categories and underpins the success of each, and this is the necessity to be an effective *business manager*. This is one of the reasons why all MBA programmes are anchored by a similar set of core subjects, which provide the fundamental business knowledge on which specialist or generalist ability is built or enhanced. However, being an effective business manager is not only about having the appropriate knowledge, but also about being able to use it effectively, requiring a range of additional abilities noted below.

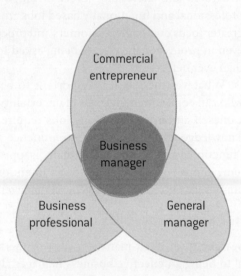

Figure 2.1 *MBA categories*

the importance of becoming a business manager

Being an effective business manager is concerned with having the core management skills and knowledge to operate effectively in whatever business environment one finds oneself. These skills are critical whether specializing as a business professional, general manager or commercial entrepreneur. Without having a strong grounding in the management fundamentals, success within the three groups will be severely compromised. Reflecting on the need to develop as a business manager is important for anyone embarking on an MBA and even those experienced as general managers will often benefit from revisiting this core area.

However, it is not unusual for new students to feel ambivalent about the development of business management skills. Ben's case, an MBA student and scientist by training and profession, illustrates the attitude. Prior to coming onto the MBA programme, Ben found himself being promoted into jobs, which meant supervising other technicians:

I recognized that there was a range of skills I would need to develop, but this recognition of inexperience and inadequacy did not motivate or inspire me, but rather froze me solid ... I can remember being with other scientists at management training courses and dismissing absolutely the importance and/or relevance of these classes.

Indeed, not only do some students dismiss the importance of developing management skills but also those who write about management can, at times, give the impression that it is a dying art. Radical organizational restructuring, as a result of competitive pressures and technological change, is said to be eliminating or marginalizing the manager as a distinctive organizational role.[4] However, while there may be fewer jobs around with the title of 'manager', there is no reduction in the need for managing the work environment. Rather, in many instances, management responsibility has merely shifted onto more shoulders.

The twenty-first century organization has become a more complex and demanding place in which to work. The trend towards flatter organizational structures and increasing levels of empowerment means that many professional and functionally based jobs are far more lateral, expecting a greater focus on people, customers and processes. As a result, employees even in professional roles are being asked to develop a broader skill set than ever before.[5]

> It is a question of being a little bit faster, able to spot an opportunity somewhat earlier, or reacting quicker to a new threat ...

Whatever the job, it is important to be a competent self-manager, who can cope with high levels of uncertainty and ambiguity and manage change both in oneself and in others. Many jobs require individuals who can blend their business knowledge with the capacity to influence and collaborate with others across different functional areas. Thus, rather than disappearing, business management skills have become more critical, whether one's intention is to major as a business professional, commercial entrepreneur or general manager.

the abilities needed to be an effective business manager

Strength in these three areas of self-management, business knowledge and collaborative ability is central to being an effective business manager. The MBA structure provides opportunities to develop these skills in different ways, although not necessarily equally. Most emphasis is usually placed on business knowledge. Its importance is highlighted by Arnold De Meyer of INSEAD when he argues that:

In reality, being a good manager is being marginally better than and different from your competitors. It is a question of being a little bit faster, able to spot an opportunity somewhat earlier, or reacting quicker to a new threat ... knowledge of management can provide this decisive advantage. A sophisticated manager, must, as a result, constantly update his or her knowledge of the latest concepts, insights and experiences in management thinking.[6]

For De Meyer, developing a 'decisive advantage' depends on knowledge of the disciplines of management. For example, the ability to segment markets and identify competitive threats, understand the financial consequences of a new investment or see the implications of long lead times for manufacturing a new product. These skills and knowledge will enable a good manager to make choices faster and with a greater chance of success than the untrained competitor. This is what all students learn during the core programme of their degree and what is explored in later chapters of the book.

However, being an effective business manager is also a product of a second area – being able to collaborate and deal with people. Well-developed interpersonal or 'softer' skills are critical in implementing business ideas, as their success will often depend on the support of other people who often report formally to others. It was noted in Chapter 1 that more business schools are starting to give softer skills airtime in the MBA curriculum. Indeed, Bob Joss, ex-Westpac banking CEO and dean of Stanford Business School, has argued that in future the greatest breakthroughs are likely to come from the softer side of management:

We know that when our students go out into the world, if they have to struggle, it will not be because they're not smart enough, or they don't have enough good ideas. It will be because they struggle over managing themselves and their relationships to other people.[7]

Some schools have developed programmes that formally help students to develop these skills. London Business School, for example, has several courses, some in the core programme, that enhance interpersonal skills. Wharton requires all MBA students to take their leadership course. However, overall, the formal provision of courses of this type among schools is inconsistent. Nevertheless, whether structured into the programme or not, on most MBA courses, there are opportunities for skill development. Clearly, a more conscious and self-directed effort has to be made by the student to improve if the skills are not formally dealt with during the programme. Later chapters provide guidance on how this might be achieved.

In addition, effective business management requires a third competency, also raised in the quote by Bob Joss above. This is the ability to manage oneself. It is not often formally taught on an MBA programme, although opportunities are often available to improve in this area. As with the development of interpersonal abilities, it also takes a conscious effort and high degree of motivation by the student to make progress.

Thus, while an understanding of the core functional areas is fundamentally important, students need to take advantage of opportunities to improve their ability to manage themselves and others effectively. How these opportunities present themselves on an MBA becomes clearer in discussing the typical style and pace of MBA degrees.

the MBA programme: style and pace

Given that the MBA is offered throughout the world and in an area, that is, business, that has many different potential applications, there will obviously be differences in the educational process and provision of postgraduate management programmes. However, degrees that are offered in university campus settings will usually have two main characteristics in common.

MBA programme style

The first of these characteristics relates to the educational style of the MBA. Despite some of the criticisms of the shortcomings of the degree raised in Chapter 1, the standard of most postgraduate management education is very high. While the traditional lecture style still plays a role in imparting information, it is also common for subjects to encourage student participation through case study discussion, group presentation or a range of other learning simulations, exercises and instruments.

However, while this participative style can be rewarding for many students, it can also be quite daunting, even for those who have some familiarity with such educational experiences. Often an MBA is quite competitive and the notion of getting the wrong answer in front of one's peers can be unsettling. Indeed, for students who have come from an educational system that places the professor in the central role and the student as the polite recipient of the lecturer's wisdom, it can be overwhelming and completely alien to their previous experience.

This emphasis on participation often extends outside the classroom and many schools expect students to work in small syndicate groups to prepare cases, presentation material and project work. Not only does this give additional insights into a subject and further encourage the application of concepts to practical business problems, but it also gives rise to other developmental opportunities. These can range from improved influencing skills through to more effective small group management.

While on the surface this seems an excellent chance to develop some of the business management skills noted earlier, the problem is that it provides a developmental opportunity without the support necessary to capitalize on the experience. Although the notion of having a personal coach or mentor to help improve one's management ability has become quite common in work settings, on most MBA programmes the expectation is that these skills will develop through some kind of personal osmosis. Ashridge Business School does provide one-on-one coaching, but this is rare. Most commonly, it is assumed that being put in the environment should lead to a personal transformation, when often these additional skills are neither identified and assessed nor do they attract feedback helpful to the student. Indeed, the lack of help in assisting students to manage and 'read' people was one of the major criticisms raised by Mark McCormack.[8] While the opportunity may be there, the formal guidelines may not, and it is often up to the students themselves to extract the maximum benefit from these experiences.

MBA programme pace

The second characteristic and an area that also provides opportunities to develop as a business manager comes as a result of what might be termed the 'pace' of the MBA. Unfortunately, this is also an area where personal improvement depends very much on the individual's own devices. Again, there will be differences between schools, but many programmes deliberately place pressure on the student. This is particularly true of the core part of the degree, which students often find very demanding. Indeed, several schools acknowledge that 'much of the first year is just plain tough'. The comments below give a flavour of what to expect:

The first six months of business school can be daunting. Chances are, if you're like most business students, you haven't been in a classroom for several years ... Once school officially starts; you're faced with unfamiliar subjects. There's a tremendous amount of work to do.[9]

> Often an MBA is quite competitive and the notion of getting the wrong answer in front of one's peers can be unsettling. Indeed, for students who have come from an educational system that places the professor in the central role and the student as the polite recipient of the lecturer's wisdom, it can be overwhelming and completely alien to their previous experience.

Amanda Sinclair's study of the way women MBAs learn highlights how overwhelming the experience can be. Some said it was like being hit by volumes of information and that coping with the process was challenging in many different ways and not always positive.[10] Often MBA programmes load the student with more material and tasks than they can thoroughly complete. Because so much has to be accomplished in so little time, getting an MBA is like living in fast forward, as the sample diary entry outlined in Box 2.1 illustrates.[11] This is a typical day for many full-time students completing the core requirements of a postgraduate management qualification. (For part-time students, the burden is heavier, given the additional requirements of holding down a full-time job.)

BOX 2.1 typical daily schedule

A.M.

7.00:   Review notes for my first class

7.30:   Eat some high-energy cereal; read the *Wall Street Journal* – professors like to discuss news items that relate to the class topics

8.00:   Read review for quantitative methods exam; do practice problems, reread case on control systems for organizational behaviour class

9.00:   Arrive at school. Go to 'reading room' to hang out with everyone. Check student mailbox for invitations to recruiter events

9.30:   Integrative management class: guest speaker from case study discusses how the company approaches problems

10.45: Hang out

11.00: Organizational behaviour class: get in a couple of good comments

P.M.

12.15: Grab some lunch and sit with friends. Talk about the lousy cafeteria food and who's dating whom

1.00:   Go back to reading room to review for 2.00 class

2.00:   Microeconomics class: listen to lecture on monopolistic competition

3.15:   Go home, change. Go running, lift weights, relax

6.00:   Eat dinner, watch the news. Read the next day's case

7.30:   Head back to campus for study group

7.45:   Discuss cases, help each other with homework problems on interpreting regression statistics: discuss how to account for capital leases versus operating leases

10.00: Back at home. Review more cases, read next class assignment in textbook, work on problem set

Midnight: Watch TV until I fall asleep

As a result of this continual intense pace, students will be 'time poor' on an MBA. Moreover, some students will be more 'time poor' than others depending on their time management skills, familiarity with the subjects taught and their other associated responsibilities including work and family.

A part-time student will need to incorporate MBA work into what is already a busy schedule. A full-time student may see the MBA merely replacing the previous time that was devoted to work. However, the sample diary entry indicates that this is not possible and a realistic assessment needs to be made of the number of hours that will be spent in the lecture room, the hours needed for preparation and the number of hours spent with colleagues, particularly if the programme requires syndicate groupwork. Preparation time will vary, but in some case study-based schools, this can be up to three times the amount of class contact time, that is, an hour and a half lecture can require four and a half hours' preparation.

In addition, an allowance needs to be made for assignments and exams. On some programmes the competition for grades is high. Moreover, some schools mark assignments and exams around a norm: if you are competing with extremely able colleagues, it is wise to expect some average scores. If the goal is to get higher grades, it will probably demand considerably more effort.

This pressure package usually ensures that study commitments take centre stage for quite some time. But there are other aspects of life that need to be managed. Students come on to the MBA with existing commitments and responsibilities and it is important to think through how these will be impacted by the workload of an MBA.

This is particularly important when completing the degree part time. Unfortunately, in some schools, the part-time MBA has been dubbed a 'marriage-breaker' or MBA reinterpreted as standing for 'Many Broken Alliances'. This can occur when a student becomes isolated from their partner and friends due to the pressures of trying to hold down a full-time job and continue part-time study. As one student explained:

I made an agreement with my partner on day one of this degree. But that started to wear very thin when, after 18 months, I continued to disappear off to study each evening. My children were, understandably, even less tolerant.

It can be just as tough for those taking an executive MBA. One student at Wharton joked:

One rough semester I slept about 11 hours per week ... Between work and school I was on my knees ... But I got through it. My family supported me; the other students on my team helped me.[12]

Family, friends, sport and leisure activities are, to varying degrees, part of daily life and they play an important role in terms of the individual's physical and psychological well-being. How important each of these 'personal domains' is will vary from person to person (see Figure 2.2). Some students choose to drop leisure activities or exercise in order to create more time for study. Others prefer simply to 'get through' the degree in order to keep other parts of their lives on track. When one of our graduating students was asked to list his achievements to date, he remarked: 'Life; surviving part-time MBA with sanity, relationship and job intact.'

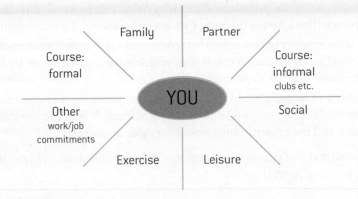

Figure 2.2 Personal domains

Surviving the programme and keeping sane are the bottom line requirements. But if that is all that occurs, then some of the major opportunities to develop as an effective business manager have been lost. The process should not be about short-term survival, but about developing skills that go way past graduation. The reason for this style and pace of programme is to simulate, to some extent, the pressures of a managerial environment. Harvard Professor Linda Hill's research into the trials and tribulations of first-time managers suggests similar baptisms by fire in a workplace setting. In *Becoming a Manager*, she tracks the rollercoaster highs and lows of 19 individuals during their first year in supervisory positions.[13] During that year, she witnessed a fundamental transformation in their identity and point of view – one in which managers moved from an intellectual understanding of the complexity of management to a hands-on appreciation of managerial work.

The pace and style of the business school environment has the potential to create opportunities for students to develop the core skills of a business manager. However, much of the responsibility is on the student to develop in these areas and without considerable thought, motivation and a continuous desire to excel, development could well be more by luck than design. It is all too easy to come out of an MBA knowing a lot, but having learned very little that is truly personally beneficial in the longer term. As Bernard Ramantsoa, dean of HEC Paris argues: 'An MBA is more than technical skills, it is also a once-in-a lifetime chance for personal and professional development.'[14]

the MBA participant: a sense of direction

As many choices have to be made on a management programme, it is important to have a sense of what you hope to get from the degree overall. Moreover, as David Campbell notes: 'If you don't know where you are going, you'll probably end up somewhere else.'[15] Thus, MBA students need to see themselves as active rather than passive participants in the learning and development process.

A way of helping to achieve your objectives is to produce a personal development plan. The plan provides structure, direction and a set of priorities. Creating a plan is the first step towards making sure that the development takes place. The principles involved are in having:

❶ *A sense of where you want to be*: This is concerned with understanding what you wish to get out of the programme and why. With this in mind, it is more likely you will finish with improved qualities that are critical for you.

2 *A sense of where you are now*: This requires an understanding of your current personal strengths and weaknesses. It also requires an awareness of which of these need attention in order to progress further.

3 *A sense of how you might progress*: An MBA provides many learning opportunities, but the learning process is not straightforward. A better understanding of how you learn and the opportunities available is also important.

These first two elements are explored below. A discussion of how we might progress is left to subsequent chapters.

an overall sense of where you want to be

The first step in producing a developmental plan is to have an overall sense of how you will benefit from an MBA. Many assume that this will 'somehow' appear during the course and then find it doesn't as they are buried by the volume of work.

Towards the end of their degree, some students emerge realizing that although they have had many excellent educational experiences, these remain as independent strands. For example, one may have a better understanding of finance or strategy, or can make great presentations, but how does this all come together as a personal package and for what purpose? One way of getting a handle on this is for you, at the start of the MBA, to picture yourself on graduation day and identify how you hope to have changed. You need to ask: In what ways do I expect to be different? How will I feel? What will I be able to do that I can't do now? The more specific you can be, the better.

One student tackled this exercise by choosing to picture herself in conversation with her old boss and mentor. Here's what she hoped she would be able to say about her experience on the MBA programme and the kind of job she would have after she graduated:

These past two years in the MBA programme have been a lot of work but extremely rewarding ... the MBA gave me the skills and confidence I needed to succeed ... I want my life to have some meaning and purpose ... I am now working as an HR consultant with an IT company in Vancouver. I formulate and introduce policies to improve the lives of my co-workers ... It's important to me that my personal goals be compatible with the goals of an organization ... This is a dream job for me. I crave variety and autonomy in a job. Every day is something different and I love that.

For this student, her longer term direction had to involve working overseas, in an organization and role that was consistent with her own strong sense of values and need for autonomy. But for any student, a sense of direction, or personal vision, improves the chance of making good choices about where to invest their energy during the MBA. They are also more likely to keep themselves focused and motivated as they work their way through the programme.

a sense of the capabilities required

Having given some thought to your broad aspirations for the course, the next step in producing a plan is to consider what knowledge and skills are needed to achieve this longer term vision. On an MBA, there is a vast array of potential developmental areas.

The most obvious of these is a range of informational and analytical opportunities, which include:

❶ A body of knowledge forming the basis of many business subject areas.

❷ The application of theories, models, methods and tools to solve critical problems that are typically found in these subject areas.

❸ A critical evaluation of the strengths and weaknesses of these models and tools.

However, there are also additional learning opportunities, including:

❹ The ability to think critically, not only about business issues, but also about the effectiveness of your thinking processes and problem-solving ability.

❺ The ability to manage people and the range of social skills and behavioural abilities required. Included here is the development of more complex leadership qualities needed to change situations and organizations.

❻ The ability to manage your emotions and understand how your beliefs and attitudes affect your view of the world. This also includes an ability to deal with ambiguity, stressful situations and the management of time.

❼ The ability to understand how to learn and what qualities and which contexts contribute to learning effectiveness.

While the MBA programme will certainly provide learning opportunities for the first three items above, the last four will not always be formally addressed and are often more dependent on student self-direction for their development. Nevertheless, these are critical areas of competency in the managerial world.

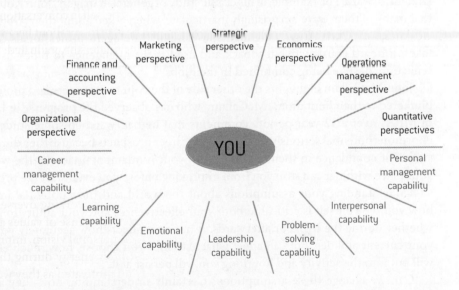

Figure 2.3 *MBA capabilities*

These seven items fall into two broad sets of capabilities mentioned in Chapter 1 and brought together in Figure 2.3. Those in the top half of the figure are key subject areas (usually covered in the core MBA curriculum), which act as the building blocks for longer term functional and professional development. These are the functional capabilities concerned with points 1–3 above.

The bottom half of the framework highlights the personal capabilities, that is, the personal and interpersonal skills and abilities that are also essential for effective business management, described in points 4–7 above. These are based on our original research into executive capabilities and the qualities needed to operate effectively at a high level of responsibility within an organization.[16]

The first of these qualities, a *personal management capability*, refers to the ability to take personal responsibility for setting direction and managing yourself effectively towards achieving your goals. An *interpersonal capability* encompasses the interpersonal skills and abilities required to work with others. A *problem-solving capability* refers not only to intellectual 'clock speed' and analytical ability, but also to the ability to think creatively, synthesize complex ideas and integrate them in solving real-world problems. A *learning capability* emphasizes the capacity to continue to learn and adapt in a changing business environment. An *emotional capability* is concerned with managing the pressures and emotional responses that affect our personal well-being and interactions with others. A *career management capability* is the ability to identify longer term work aspirations and manage critical transitions in one's career. Additionally, a *leadership capability* is concerned with taking ourselves and others forward, beyond the status quo, and achieving real change. All these areas are discussed in more detail later in the book.

a sense of where we are now and our mindset

However, in order to capitalize on such opportunities, some realistic idea is needed of current strengths and weaknesses. But reviewing these personal qualities is not straightforward. For example, in his classic study of general managers, John Kotter found that many of them were 'surprisingly inarticulate' when asked about their strengths and weaknesses.[17] Chris Argyris highlights how highly intelligent professionals could not take on board constructive feedback and used their intelligence to block useful self-reflection, despite being committed to their jobs.[18]

John McCallum highlights the other side of the coin to managers and professionals blinkered to their limitations. McCallum, who has observed the progress (or lack of it) of MBAs over a 32-year period, comments that he has 'watched some students with enormous potential seriously diminish their career prospects because they did not have sufficient confidence in themselves'.[19] Thus, your fundamental view of the world and your place within it can stop you from improving before you even start the process.

Understanding your assumptions about the world and their potential impact on how you see yourself is critical to both your effectiveness and your ability to improve, whether during the MBA or afterwards. It not only affects how accurately you review your current abilities, but can affect what activities you choose, how much effort you will put into the activity and how long you will persist at it.

Can we change these assumptions? Certainly understanding how they arise can help. A framework illustrating different mindsets and their potential consequences is illustrated in Figure 2.4. The four views of the world – *capable, closed, cautious* and *singular* – are the product of contrasting a positive (can do) or negative (can't do) mental attitude, with a mind open or closed to new information.

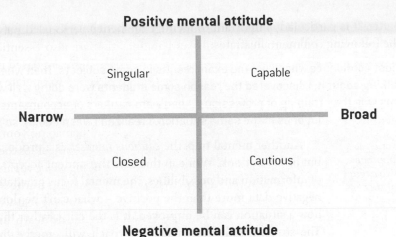

Positive mental attitude

Singular   Capable

Narrow   **Broad**

Closed   Cautious

Negative mental attitude

Figure 2.4 Mindset model

The mental set with the most potential for helping us to accurately review our current position and assist in moving us forward is a *capable mindset*. This combines a broad outlook with a positive mental attitude. This is not necessarily an easy mental state to be in, but is illustrated by the student who commented:

These past two years in the MBA programme have been a lot of work … I have to admit I initially doubted my ability to succeed … but by evaluating my strengths and weaknesses, taking on board realistic feedback and consistently working at ways of improving, I feel I gained in ways I never thought possible at the start of the degree.

This mindset involves accepting reality, looking at feedback objectively and exploring the important issues, while still maintaining a belief in your ability to succeed.

> Progress through an MBA will be a much less rich experience without a capable mindset.

It is the attitude that, when faced with critical feedback on a mid-term assignment, prompts the student to actively seek clarification on what went wrong and, if necessary, get advice. Progress through an MBA will be a much less rich experience without a capable mindset.

However, if we had this mental approach all the time, none of us would make the mistakes illustrated by Kotter, Argyris and McCallam above. It is possible to become trapped into other, less helpful mindsets depending on the circumstances. One of these is a *closed mindset*, where a negative attitude and narrow outlook is taken towards a circumstance, person or activity. This mental response to a problem is a variation of 'there's nothing that can be done'. On an MBA programme, some students adopt this mindset towards certain subjects. When the self-talk involves comments like 'I've never been good at numbers' or 'I'll never get to grips with formulae', the person is setting themselves up for potential failure in quantitative subjects. Self-fulfilling prophesies can, unfortunately, come true.

Regardless of ability, progress out of this mindset depends on the individual reflecting critically on the evidence that suggests they are going to underperform. Try to analyse the behaviour that may have given rise to the negative assumptions. If there are in fact weaknesses, then practical ways of overcoming these need to be assessed, for example maths refresher courses, or dissecting work patterns to identify the real causes better. It is particularly important to identify the benchmarks used for assessment, as the following comment illustrates:

I lost confidence when I got my exam results in some subjects. Then when I started talking about it, I discovered the reason some students were doing well was because this was their training or profession ... they were bankers or accountants. There were a lot of us in the same situation. I realized I wasn't doing so bad after all.

Another mental trap, the *cautious mindset*, is a product of a negative but broad outlook. While in this case the student accepts a broad range of information and possibilities, the mental focus gravitates towards the negative data more than the positive – what can't be done, rather than how a situation can be improved. It is the critic rather than the creator. The student with this mental approach will emerge from the MBA with the piece of paper and some additional knowledge and skills. But the preferred response of 'can't do' rather than 'can do' severely limits what can be achieved. It is not a lack of information, but an inability to take risks, which is the major problem. As one student commented:

> *Attitude and mental approach are vital to overall personal success, whatever the subject.*

I know I have a cautious mindset. For example, in class I know I can participate, but by the time I am ready, the discussion has moved on. I often take too much time to reach a decision which is an embarrassment to me. I know I can overcome my cautious approach by not worrying about how I compare with others.

Finally, while a positive mental approach is important, if it is accompanied by a narrow focus on limited and selective information, the resulting overall attitude can be a liability. This *singular mindset* is the one described by Argyris earlier. Having confidence, but a narrow focus at the wrong time, or at the wrong stage of the decision-making process, can lead to complacency or arrogance. Industrial history is littered with business 'leaders' who did not listen at the appropriate time and continued to drive their business into the ground. The arrogance of senior managers at companies like Enron, HIH and WorldCom are well documented. But, at a more mundane level, it can affect your performance on the MBA. As one student commented:

Attitude is vital to the success of a subject ... if you start with the belief that this will be easy and already know everything, then it is easy to stop listening and miss out on some of the complexities.

Attitude and mental approach are vital to overall personal success, whatever the subject. Consequently, it is important when reviewing any potential area of improvement that you adopt a capable mindset and a realistic belief in what you can and cannot achieve and the help required.

understanding the present and planning for the future

With a capable mindset, you can realistically begin to plan for the future. A plan is not the solution, but merely a framework within which to work. Producing any personal development plan has to be premised on the belief that personal progress is important and possible.

Box 2.2 is a capabilities checklist, which provides an opportunity to get a sense of your current position in relation to the capabilities described in the chapter. It is also

BOX 2.2 capabilities checklist

Instructions

1. Answer each question in terms of the extent to which the question characterizes you.
2. Answer each question twice. First put a circle ◯ around the number that best describes how you are *now*. Then put a square ☐ around how you *would like* to be after completing your degree.
3. Total the numbers in the circles and squares and create totals for A, B, C and D.

Functional capabilities

To what extent do you feel you have the necessary degree of knowledge and skills in:

	Very little			A great deal	
1. Economics	1	2	3	4	5
2. Finance	1	2	3	4	5
3. Marketing	1	2	3	4	5
4. Accounting	1	2	3	4	5
5. Operations management	1	2	3	4	5
6. Organizational behaviour	1	2	3	4	5
7. Strategic management	1	2	3	4	5
8. Quantitative methods/statistics	1	2	3	4	5

Total the numbers in circles _ + _ + _ + _ + _ A = ◯

Total the numbers in squares _ + _ + _ + _ + _ B = ☐

Personal capabilities

To what extent do you feel you are able to:

9. Understand your own strengths and weaknesses	1	2	3	4	5
10. Communicate and relate to people	1	2	3	4	5
11. Lead others	1	2	3	4	5
12. Learn effectively	1	2	3	4	5
13. Solve challenging problems	1	2	3	4	5
14. Manage your career	1	2	3	4	5
15. Manage yourself	1	2	3	4	5
16. Channel your emotions appropriately	1	2	3	4	5

Total the numbers in circles _ + _ + _ + _ + _ C = ◯

Total the numbers in squares _ + _ + _ + _ + _ D = ☐

Transfer your totals below   Scores

A   Your assessment of how well you rate currently on the *functional
     capabilities* (circled items 1–8).   ____

B   Your assessment of how you would like to be in terms of the *functional
     capabilities* after completing your degree (squared items 1–8).   ____

C   Your assessment of how well you rate currently on the *personal
     capabilities* (circled items 9–16).   ____

D   Your assessment of how you would like to be in terms of the *personal
     capabilities* after completing your degree (squared items 9–16).   ____

Interpreting your results

1.   Compare your scores for A and C. Do you feel your current strengths and interests lie
     more in one set of capabilities than the other?

2.   Take the difference between A and B, and then C and D. These two scores indicate the
     relative distance you feel you have to travel to develop your functional capabilities
     (A and B) and your personal capabilities (C and D).
     Are either of these scores of concern to you?

3.   It is likely you will make more progress by focusing on a few, rather than many areas.
     Consequently, look at your answers to the functional capability items and identify
     where the four largest gaps lie.

     _____   _____

     _____   _____

     Repeat the process with the personal capabilities.

     _____   _____

     _____   _____

4.   Which of these items are you most motivated to work on?

     _____   _____

     _____   _____

intended to prompt reflection on where you want to be at the end of the MBA and help you in focusing on your priorities. Consequently, as a result of completing the checklist, you should be able to answer four critical questions necessary for the first part of a development plan:

1 In what way do I see myself being different in the future?

2 What new knowledge and skills do I need in order to progress?

3 How great is the gap between where I want to be and where I am now?

4 Which are the most important gaps that need to be filled?

The second part of the plan then involves identifying what is needed to close the most critical gaps. This involves considering:

> What activities will allow me to develop the skill areas identified?
> What constraints or problems do I foresee?
> How could I minimize these?
> What resources are available to me?
> What help do I need from others and who might they be?
> What are my most likely constraints such as time or elective choices?
> How long are the improvements I want to make likely to take?

Help with these questions can also be found in subsequent chapters.

conclusion

While postgraduate programmes in management vary, they are largely at one in encouraging the development of effective business management skills. Where they differ is in the emphasis and opportunities provided to reach that goal. Moreover, even in schools where there is a broader range of formal development opportunities, incorporating both skills and knowledge subjects, the responsibility still remains with students to get the most value from their degree. We have argued that this can be helped by identifying a personal vision for the programme, clarifying which fundamental capabilities are required to achieve the vision and adopting the right mental approach to personal improvement. However, this is just the start of a complex process and even capabilities that seem straightforward can be quite challenging to fully master. One of these and one of the most critical, a learning capability, is explored in the next chapter.

references

1. Steiner, T.L. and Wells, R.M.J. (2000) 'Integration of the business curriculum: the case of finance and marketing in an MBA program', *Financial Practice and Education*, **10**(2): 149.
2. Tyler, J. (2004) 'The MBA strikes back', *People Management*, **10**(17): 23.
3. A typical example of the debate can be seen in Stern, S. (2004) 'MBAs with heart', *Management Today* (October): 4.
4. Hales, C. (2001) 'Does it matter what managers do?', *Business Strategy Review*, **12**(2): 50–9.
5. Hiltrop, J.M. (1998) 'Preparing people for the future: the next agenda for HRM', *European Management Journal*, **16**(1): 15–27.
6. Crainer, S. and Dearlove, D. (1999) *Gravy Training* (San Francisco: Jossey-Bass) p. 23.
7. Uren, D. (2000) 'Management', *Weekend Australian*, 22/23 January.
8. McCormack, M. (1984) *What They Don't Teach You at Harvard Business School: Notes from a Street-smart Executive* (New York: Bantam).
9. 'The first year', *Business Week Online*, 24 October 2001.

10. Sinclair, A. (1995) 'Sex and the MBA', *Organization*, **2**(2): 295–317.
11. Op. cit. *Business Week Online*, 24 October 2001.
12. Tyler, K. (2004) 'Getting value from executive MBA programs', *HR Magazine*, **49**(7): 105.
13. Hill. L.A. (2003) *Becoming a Manager: How New Managers Master the Challenges of Leadership* (Boston: Harvard Business School Press).
14. 'Visions from the dean', at www.topmba.com, 13 April 2005.
15. McCall, M.W. (1998) *High Flyers: Developing the Next Generation of Leaders* (Boston: Harvard Business School Press).
16. Dainty, P. and Anderson, M. (1996) *The Capable Executive* (Basingstoke: Macmillan). A more recent academic working paper building on this research and exploring the capabilities in an MBA context can be found at www.mbs.edu by clicking on the 'Faculty and research' button and searching under 'Faculty working papers'.
17. Kotter, J.P. (1982) *The General Managers* (New York: Free Press).
18. Argyris, C. (1991) 'Teaching smart people how to learn', *Harvard Business Review*, **69**(3): 99–109.
19. McCallum, J.S. (2004) 'Viewpoint', *Ivey Business Journal* (September/October): 1.

3   developing a learning capability

On the surface, the concept of learning, particularly for MBA students who have spent many years in the formal education system, would seem to require little elaboration. However, learning on many MBA programmes is not usually a straightforward process. This is for three reasons.

The first is that the MBA is usually a very different educational experience from a first degree. As one student commented: 'The MBA is a particular way of learning. It takes you a while to understand how it works and how you can benefit from it.'

The second is that students often come to an MBA with a view of learning coloured by their previous experience, which may not be appropriate for a postgraduate management degree. As another student commented after receiving his first term subject results: 'My understanding of learning has been limited to a formulistic approach of review, memorize and repeat. I now need to adopt more effective learning techniques.'

Thirdly, for many students, this may be their final shot at formal study and getting the most out it will usually be of prime concern. Another student commented: 'I realize that this may be the last chance I have for learning systematically for the rest of my life. In the future I will probably not go to school, so I have to gain a lot from this.'

Consequently, this chapter is about how you can gain as much as possible from the learning situations on an MBA. Two broad areas are considered. The first is concerned with the learning environment and ensuring that the systems you establish outside the formal MBA programme support your learning needs. The second looks at learning opportunities such as lectures, case studies, assessment processes (including exams and assignments) and research projects and how to maximize the benefits from these different formal contexts. First let us first consider the external learning environment.

external learning environment

On an MBA, learning occurs not only within the lecture theatre, but also outside it, particularly through private study. This external environment requires several processes to be in place to fully benefit from the range of MBA learning experiences. These aspects will be discussed under three headings: where to study; when to study; and how to study.

where to study

In order to learn efficiently, you need an environment where study can start quickly and continue for as long as possible. Most critical is the need to have a 'home base' – a room, or, at a minimum, a desk devoted to study. A room allows papers, books, notes and so on to be left undisturbed and to be returned to with minimum disruption. If only a desk or table is available to you, ensure that it is only used for study purposes. This should also contain your computer. Even if you have a laptop, still try to keep one desk for academic work. While laptops are largely self-contained, you will still need a place for books and papers that should be easily available. If the dining room table has to be cleared every time you wish to work and your papers are in a filing cabinet in the garage, then a radical rethink is needed.

What happens around the study area is also important. The fewer the distractions, the better. Concentrating on the material for some subjects can be hard (particularly after a full day's work if you are a part-time student). Obviously it depends on personal preference, but most people are distracted by background noise. Consequently, if you are serious about study, stay away from the stereo, hide the mobile phone and switch off access to the internet and any other potential distractions. This also applies if you are working away from your home base, which can be in the library, an area in the business school or a hotel room if travelling. Find places that get you into studying as quickly as possible and ones that keep you studying longer.

when to study

The next consideration is in scheduling appropriate times for study and managing time. This was raised in Chapter 2 and is a real challenge on an MBA. Part of the answer, as one student noted, is in having frameworks and tools that give some direction:

Certainly what is central in time management is actively mapping out an overall plan. The domains model [Chapter 2] was particularly significant to me as it allowed me to get a real feel for just how many hours there were to allocate in achieving my personal development goals while still covering all the basic requirements.

It addition to having an overall plan, more detailed day-to-day scheduling is also necessary. A diary or software program is a must. As well as identifying formal lecture sessions, the diary should show when you are going to study, what you will study and for how long.

The first step is to block out time periods in the diary that have been allocated to formal sessions. Next, make an estimate of the time needed to prepare for these sessions. Then include anything else that is likely to require study time, such as case preparation, subject readings, group meetings, assignment preparation and appropriate follow-up work (including time to complete a learning log, which will be discussed later). In the early days of the degree, it is often difficult to predict beforehand how much time might be needed on some tasks (particularly assignments). Consequently, it is important to build in overflow time. If you don't need it, you have lost nothing by including it in the schedule. If you are a part-time student, you clearly need to build this around your work commitments.

The development of a study schedule, however, is not only about time allocation. Several other factors need to be taken into account. You need to ensure that you study at effective times and for effective periods. Most of us have more energy at different times in the day and it is common to talk about being a 'morning' or 'evening' person. Thus, if you are not a morning person but are forced to study first thing in the day, limit the time and build in breaks that will help keep you refreshed.

It is also important to establish routines for study in terms of regular days and regular times of the day, such as Monday, Wednesday and Thursday evenings from 4 to 7pm for session or lecture preparation. This structure not only helps you slide into the task more easily, but also lets other people know when you are not available. Specific time also needs to be put aside for managing the other domains of life (family, friends, leisure) mentioned earlier. Learn to be flexible and realistic. It is probably best to have some core study times that are sacrosanct and also more flexible periods to cope with the unexpected or crises. If you do not think you can stick to the schedule you have written, then produce one that is going to work for you and the people around you.

how to study

Establishing where and when to study is relatively straightforward compared to deciding how to get the maximum benefit from studying. MBA study should always contribute to at least one of two fundamental objectives. One is towards achieving the development goals you have set and the capabilities you are trying to develop. The other is towards passing all assessed work at a satisfactory level (having defined what 'satisfactory' means to you). Hopefully, these two will be aligned, but sometimes they are not and it is important to think about where you stand in relation to both. Very different perspectives are taken by students on this issue. One end of the spectrum is illustrated by the following comment:

In undertaking this degree, I already had a very high benchmark to try and equal at least if not better my undergrad degree. I graduated top of my school. I slogged. I wanted to graduate cum laudae. That was my mission and that's what I wanted to do. I graduated cum laudae, and got the highest marks. Coming top of the school was just a bonus. But that's my benchmark, that's my starting point. So when I came to business school, my expectation was to excel academically.

An alternative approach can be seen from the student who stated:

It is not the grade that is so important. It is things that interest me and things that help my general abilities. I don't mean to say grades aren't important, it's just that I don't need to get 'A's to feel I am succeeding.

Whatever your perspective, it is important to clarify this early on. It affects your study patterns, how you approach different subjects and which learning opportunities you emphasize. It also affects how you approach your colleagues and how you deal with them, particularly in syndicate group activities.

study log

In approaching each study session, at a minimum, think about what you want to achieve and how each session contributes to the two fundamental objectives. Going further than this does require some additional work, but the effort can pay dividends.

Two activities in particular are worth considering. The first of these, keeping a study log, is aimed at consolidating the subject material and highlighting gaps. Sheila Cameron[1] suggests that a note should be made in the log of each study session, the date and also the length of time spent on the material. The significant points of the session should be listed and any relevant sources. Points requiring more immediate clarification, to be reviewed at a later date, taken up with the professor or raised in lectures should be noted. Also any major difficulties with the material need to be highlighted along with possible solutions.

Cameron also suggests that you should be clear about what you are trying to do with what is being studied. Are you aiming to learn this material by rote, or is it theoretical, needing evaluation, or a technique that you wish to become competent using? Is the material intended to change your perspective? Be clear about how this fits into course requirements. How much detail are you expected to absorb, what assignments does the material relate to, what other courses is it relevant to? If you plan your work for each session, noting in your study log your objectives and the extent to which these are achieved, together with any insights gained from testing the ideas against your experience, your study time will be more productive.

learning log

The second activity, a learning log or journal, is usually seen as more extensive than a study log and is concerned with capturing all relevant thoughts and turning them into learning benefits. The log should include notes on any attempts to apply the formal course material to the work environment, or in broader school settings (clubs and so on). But the log can also include significant learning experiences that occur as a result of activities other than formal study alone. The log can be in any form that works for you, although it is important to have some structure so that the comments can be reviewed and acted upon. Most writers suggest that the learning log should include the following elements:

❶ An account of what happened, outlining and analysing the activity.
❷ Learning points or conclusions drawn from the experience.
❸ A plan of action for next time, drawing on the learning from the experience.

If you want to go into more detail, then you would need to outline learning objectives, state the process you went through, analyse what happened, what you learned from it, how far the activity met your original objectives and what you could do to develop further. This process might be used, for example, with a research project where you wished to learn from how you went about investigating the subject (for example your interactions with stakeholders, or finding difficult data sources) in addition to learning from writing the project report.

The real benefit from keeping this kind of log is the chance to reflect on experiences and so develop a better understanding of the material and events. Few people seem to find this easy, but for most people there are tremendous advantages in at least attempting to reflect on the subject material and experiences. One student commented:

From a young age I have always used the analogy that, when learning, you must be a sponge and try and soak in as much as you can. Over the years I have realized that at times my sponge is too small, it doesn't retain enough water and I am unable to find it when I need it most. I now see the importance of knowing yourself and using your strengths to your full potential. I need to concentrate further on reflecting on events which happen to me and around me and to gain an insight on why they occurred, how they affected me and how I should deal with them in the future. Improvement doesn't occur automatically, but with plenty of work.

If these good intentions can be harnessed through a formal log or structure around which to reflect, it can make a difference both in the short and long term. As another student noted:

Sometimes before the class when I go through the reading pack, I will review the ideas myself. After that I reflect on whether the ideas are true or not and also whether what the lecturer says is true or not. During the term I will take notes – learning notes – and now I think I have about 40,000 words. These words are about things I am not so familiar with and things I have to work on. They help me with the exams but these notes will also help me after the MBA. In the future, I will use them to lessen my mistakes in my business or when I work for someone else.

The log can be applied to a wide range of experiences, including the development of interpersonal capabilities discussed later in the book. Clearly, to be successful, the exercise needs to be approached with a capable mindset, described in Chapter 2. But the log is also more likely to be successful if one can find support for the process either in terms of planning and identifying learning opportunities, or in reviewing and analysing experiences and events. A range of people can provide this support, which does not have to come only from a professor or manager. What is important is that the person is friendly and interested. On an MBA, there are many peers and colleagues with whom one can potentially develop a learning partnership.

formal learning opportunities

benefiting from lectures

Most people taking an MBA will have several years' experience of sitting in lecture theatres taking notes. At business school the lecture format is somewhat different and often more demanding.

For example, on an MBA, it is unlikely that you can walk into lectures without having done some preparation. It is important to check out the norm, but at many schools the rule of thumb is about two to three hours' preparation for every one-hour lecture. Clearly, this can vary, depending on the lecturer, the kind of lecture (for example presentation or case study) and the background of the student. This can be particularly challenging if English is not your first language. As one student commented:

There have been several problems at the beginning of the MBA especially for international students like me. English is one. In the first month I could only understand 60–70%. I couldn't catch many of the keywords and had to ask the other students. So the only thing I could do was prepare well, possibly doing it at night at one or two in the morning. So I have a very clear understanding and the next day I can understand more. Even today, at the end of the third term, some students still cannot catch what many of the other students say in class.

Lectures are often delivered using PowerPoint and slides are often downloaded from a central website or given out as hand-outs. However, this is a double-edged sword; the main points of the session may be captured, but they may not be fully understood. The personal benefits come if the material can be reviewed mentally and links made to past experience or future possibilities. Otherwise, the only real benefit of being in the lecture theatre is to get an attendance mark.

Lecturing styles vary, but at business school, lectures have usually progressed from an uninterrupted delivery of dense material to a more engaging process, often characterized by a two-way dialogue. Even if you are not involved in the dialogue, it is important to at least mentally engage in the interchange. If the lecturer asks questions, reflect on how the answers of others might relate to you, or how you might have answered the question posed.

Getting involved in class discussion, however, is not necessarily an easy process, even if English is your first language. This is because the process involves interjecting pertinent and succinct comments that add value to the discussion, at the right moment, but without dominating the lecture. For students not familiar with talking in class, or where they have been in an educational system that actually discourages two-way dialogue, this can be a daunting experience. One of our Asian students commented:

The traditional culture in Asia is not to be outspoken, so most of the time you just keep to yourself and if you speak too much, others will think that you are too aggressive, or too arrogant. So we need to be cautious, maybe because of the power distance with lecturers and also because of the seniority.

However, MBA classes generally encourage not only interaction, but also questioning of both the material presented and the person delivering it. This applies to both the lecturer and the student. For some students this may require a major change in thinking and approach.

Ultimately, the important thing is simply to have a go. This can be done by asking a relevant question. If others seem to disagree with you, don't be put off. Intelligent questioning can often help to develop the debate or provide additional insights into an issue. Often other students will have similar concerns or questions that they may not have been able to ask. Moreover, contributing in such group situations is a critical management skill, one that is important to develop.

It is also important to see the lecture in context. Often lectures summarize material and give an overview. Thus, the benefit comes from exploring the material further, particularly in the light of one's past experience and future needs. For example, a lecture, or even several lectures, on organizational change will only scratch the surface of the topic. So it is important to read about the subject in more depth, particularly relating it to your own experiences.

benefiting from case studies

An activity requiring a considerable amount of interaction both within the lecture theatre and outside it is the case study. The case study has been a staple of business schools ever since they were founded and has been made into an industry by Harvard Business School. The use of cases varies from school to school. In some schools, such as Harvard, they are used extensively, while in others their use is more selective.

Cases illustrate typical business problems and enable the student to explore and review potential actions and solutions in a 'safe' environment. There are few business topics not covered by cases, although their style and depth vary considerably. Cases can range from a single page to up to 90 pages in length. They can also be multidisciplinary, covering issues in, say, marketing, finance and organizational behaviour at the same time. They are, as Jeff Sampler of London Business School argues, a vehicle for 'finding different ways of bringing the business world into the classroom in a dynamic, realistic and lively way'.[2]

Cases do have their limitations. The major problems are that they can be too selective and narrow, imply that the ideal situation is the common one and play up the positive aspects of situations to the detriment of some of the downsides and realities of business life. However, some of the criticisms apply more to how cases are taught rather than their subject matter. Good case teachers highlight the weaknesses in the material as well as its strengths. As Harvard cases state on their first page, cases are a vehicle to be used for educational purposes and not as a model of good or bad practice.

Indeed, there are many potential learning benefits from case discussion. These include the opportunity to explore different business contexts, manage a large amount of sometimes complex information, recognize what is important and apply management models to provide better insights into problem causes and solutions. In addition to the problem-solving and analytical benefits, cases also often require effective teamwork, good time management and good advocacy and presentation skills. Indeed, as the following comment from a student indicates, cases can have tremendous benefits:

Going forward, I plan to use it [the case study] as a tool in my day-to-day life to improve my analysis of practical situations from multiple functional perspectives – marketing, finance, accounting and so on – where the data are often unstructured and incomplete. I believe that case learning is a very effective practical learning tool, which will assist me on the job to define problems, analyse them, take in different viewpoints and arrive at better managerial decisions.

However, getting to this degree of confidence in using cases takes time and practice. Deriving the best from cases is usually seen as a three-stage process. The first is as an individual process of digesting and analysing the information in the case. Secondly, cases are usually discussed in small groups outside the lecture room. Thirdly, the case is then discussed in the full class. Here we emphasize the first of these, working with cases individually.

managing case studies

While the objectives of cases vary, a generally accepted expectation is that they should be approached either as a consultant assessing and advising on the issues in the case, or from the perspective of a line manager or business professional dealing with one or several problems. Most cases are self-contained and while it is sometimes possible to get information on the company or case problem through the library or web searches, the focus should be on the information contained in the case. One of the aims of case studies is to learn how to deal with both information overload and data scarcity, challenges often faced in the business world.

becoming familiar with the case and the major issues

A starting point in managing all cases is for the individual student to clarify the purpose of the case and the learning objectives. Sometime cases have questions and these need to be addressed. If they don't, then ask yourself: 'What are the issues in this case, and what should be done about them?' Usually a fair amount of work is needed to come up with a credible set of answers.

Initially, the case should be read overall to get a feel for the kinds of issues it contains. If there is a surfeit of information, a judgement needs to be made about possible red herrings or less critical data. If the problems are not obvious, look for signs that might provide clarification through further investigation. Often market and financial data can provide clues to potential issues in the case (such as historical revenue figures or profitability).

Also bear in mind the subject the case accompanies. If it is part of the marketing course, then while, for example, people and financial aspects may play a part in the case, the priority is to ensure that the marketing issues have been identified. While some cases are interdisciplinary, unless the subject is interdisciplinary, then the issues need to relate, at least in the first instance, to the course subject. Additional problems can be written up in one's learning log if they are not covered in the lecture case discussion.

After first going over the case, subsequent readings should be aimed at exploring the case in more depth. Do not expect that the first reading will provide complete clarity. Often cases do not have clear themes. They may not even present the data in chronological order. Sometimes the information is incomplete or even contradictory. Often cases have so much detail that it can be difficult to pull out the essence of the problem, or see immediately the interrelation between events and causal factors. It is only by digging further and particularly in analysing the case that these issues become clearer. If you invest the time in preparing a case, you increase the opportunity to benefit from both small group and class discussion.

categorizing the data and analysing the case

Categorizing the main data in a case and performing an 'analysis' of it is essential. Writers and lecturers can have different views about what this means, so it is worth clarifying what your lecturer wants before working on the case. For instance, Sheila Cameron sees analysis as working out what is happening and why. However, Caroline Gatrell and Sharon Turnbull[3] see analysis as the application of conceptual tools and models. While management models can help, sometimes it is not obvious at this point which are appropriate. Consequently, a fall-back position is to first categorize the case data chronologically in terms of the past, present and future. This can be done whether the case is about an organization, a person or a set of events. Posing a number of questions can help in drawing out insights from this process. For example:

For the past:

> What has been the progression of the person/organization to date?
> What major events/actions have contributed to this performance?
> How has the person/organization dealt with these events?
> Have they squandered opportunities, or made the most of limited resources?
> How much have external factors, the economy, changes in technology and so on, influenced the progress of the person/organization?
> To what extent have internal factors, such as the culture or the degree of change, affected progress?

For the present:

> What are the major characteristics of the current situation?
> What dilemmas or problems does the organization/person currently face?

> How have events of the past contributed to the current situation?
> Are there particular problems/dilemmas that the person/organization must critically deal with?
> How are external events influencing the current situation?
> To what extent is the internal environment impacting on current progress?

For the future:

> What direction or objectives does the entity have for the future?
> What factors and forces are likely to have most influence in the future, particularly in terms of the person's/organization's objectives?
> Are these factors and forces likely to help or hinder these objectives?

applying course concepts and drawing out insights

Having clarified the major aspects of the case and categorized or grouped the data, it is then necessary to identify trends, particular themes or other insights. This is an investigative process concerned with trying to identify the critical clues that reveal a comprehensive picture of what is going on. It is at this point that the application of management models and concepts that may have been discussed previously (for example SWOT, Porter, Maslow, ratio analysis and so on) can accelerate the process. For example, Porter's Five Forces model might be used to help give insights into the strategic position of the company. Internally, change models may be needed, such as Kotter's model of organizational change, to identify how easily the company might adapt to the external environment. If the case has a web of interpersonal relationships, network analysis might be used, or models of power, to look at change possibilities in more depth.

If such models are not easily referenced, it is nevertheless important to try and cover all areas that look significant. The aim at this point is to identify the major problems in the case and have some understanding as to why these problems have arisen. But it is also important not to jump to conclusions too early and to constantly ask what evidence you have for your thinking, what assumptions you are making and how well founded these are. If you have identified several problems, it is worth prioritizing these. It is also important to bring the problems and underlying causes together to give as full a picture as possible of the overall situation.

identifying paths forward and recommendations

The next step is to look at how to resolve the problems. It is important to consider what you can influence and what you cannot change. Issues that a manager or consultant can do little about are aspects such as trends in international trade, although the impact of those trends on the firm is something that can be managed.

Problems that can be resolved should then be prioritized according to their degree of severity and importance. However, many managerial dilemmas do not have one solution. Consequently, in drawing up potential answers, it is important to think of alternatives. If these are not obvious, then using techniques such as brainstorming or reapplying some of the management models in terms of possible solutions (rather than problem identification) can help. It is also important to consider the timescale over which issues might be resolved and the resources, such as time, money and people, that may be needed. Additionally, thought needs to be given to how easy or difficult the potential paths forward are and the impact that changes in one area will have on others.

The next stage is to identify a preferred solution from the potential range identified. This may involve several recommendations, which should be justified in terms of importance, timescale, resources, degree of difficulty and potential returns. It is also important to think through the implementation process and what criteria might be used to assess whether the recommendations have been successful. Often, these aspects will not be asked for in the lecture theatre, but having given some thought to them, you may have more confidence that your recommendations are on the right path. Certainly, as a manager, you will have to think about these issues.

benefiting from assessment

As managers and business professionals, it is unlikely that you will have to go through anything that is similar to an academic assessment process. Managers are, of course, assessed, but performance appraisal processes are usually very different from the assessment process used on degree programmes. Assessment on degree programmes is continuous, with clear pass and fail criteria and a grading system that is often expressed in seemingly precise percentages. These are strong incentives to learn in a particular way.

While for the most part assessment procedures channel learning processes appropriately, it is nevertheless important to give some thought to the types of assessment used on a subject and their appropriateness to one's learning needs. With the core subjects on the degree, you will have little choice, but in taking electives, the form of assessment should also be reviewed as well as the subject matter. Moreover, in terms of personal development, assessment should not be considered in terms of its 'ease' or familiarity, but the extent to which it helps to meet your personal learning objectives.

Business schools have recognized that different forms of assessment have a place in academic programmes. Although traditionally the two or three-hour examination has been the core of most major schools' assessment process, this has broadened to include both different forms of examination, as well as different kinds of assessments in general, including project work and groupwork. Increasingly, schools are putting themselves through assessment processes run by external bodies such as EQUIS and the CSB to demonstrate their high standards. Below we explore individually based assessment processes.

benefiting from exams

An examination presents a standard, controlled environment and therefore is suited to measuring an individual's intellectual understanding of a subject. Possibly the major reason why examinations are still common is because the process provides a high degree of certainty that the work is the student's own. Three aspects are worth emphasizing; exam preparation, performance in the exam and reviewing the experience afterwards.

exam preparation

There are many ways to reduce tension in taking an exam, but perhaps the most effective way (and the one that potentially contributes most to personal learning needs) is to review the material as you proceed through the subject. Keeping on top of the material not only helps in retaining it more easily, but provides personal benefits through reviewing the ideas in the light of one's experience and future application.

A degree of learning by rote is probably necessary for an exam, whether it is open or closed book. Some formulas, concepts and techniques can only be retained through repetition. Even with open book exams, it may be necessary to learn by rote some concepts to minimize the time in having to look things up. However, as a regular strategy, it is of limited personal benefit. It is more likely to lead to greater anxiety as the material is unlikely to be embedded in personal experience and, even if you pass, it is unlikely that you will benefit further from the process as the material will be forgotten quickly. Thus, both personally and in terms of exam success, there is no substitute for thorough, reflective preparation. Moreover, this preparation does not need to be a solo activity. Going over the material with colleagues can not only help in remembering, but also add new personal insights through discussion.

Preparation may also involve looking at past papers, question spotting and thinking through what the examiner may want. There is some debate as to whether such practices are good or bad. They are bad if they are a product of desperation, but trying to predict the future and narrow the options or areas of vulnerability is a skill that most managers practise daily. If you have not thought about what the exam requires in terms of content, the potential application of the content and the additional techniques that might be employed to produce an answer (such as the use of statistical techniques), then a poor performance should not come as a surprise.

Thorough preparation is required for all forms of assessment, even if the exam is open book or involves a take-home case study. Indeed, in some ways, the open book variety can involve more work. This is because not only do you need to review the material beforehand, but you also have to decide what material (books, notes and so on) you will require in the exam room and how to access the material easily and quickly. Often the issue is deciding what to leave out.

Some schools allow the use of laptops for exams, but this is still not universal.

With case study exams, the most common approach is for the student to receive the case before the exam. Preparation is conducted privately prior to the exam, with the case questions given in the exam room. The best way to manage this is to follow the key steps for reviewing cases mentioned earlier. Again, if your preparation has been thorough, not only do you give yourself the best chance of success with the exam, but the personal learning is also greater.

It is also necessary to think through some basic logistics in taking the exam; venue, parking availability, exam times, what is allowed in the exam room, use of electronic devices and so on. Some schools allow the use of laptops for exams, but this is still not universal. Consequently, if your computer and keyboard are your closest study companions, then practise your handwriting skills and don't forget pens. Standing back, it all seems obvious, but under pressure you need to approach the day as a focused management task so that you can put your main energy into the exam itself.

exam performance

In taking the exam, it is important to be mentally focused. Some writers suggest that you should be relaxed, but in reality this is not easy and may not necessarily be in your best interests. Some tension is inevitable, although, clearly, panicking is not recommended.

Try to clear your mind as much as possible of extraneous thoughts and channel any nervous energy towards solving the task in hand. In essence, three things are critical; fully understanding what is required of you, delivering a quality answer(s) and doing this in the allocated time.

To establish what is required, it is necessary to read the exam paper carefully and completely once over. This includes the initial instructions as well as the specifics of each question. Imprint on your brain how many questions need to be answered and in what time frame. Then select your questions and, most importantly, read them again thoroughly.

Delivering a quality answer often requires more than regurgitating the course material, whether the exam is open or closed book. Examiners are looking for different things, depending on the subject, but most importantly they want to see that you have answered the question. If this requires the application of course concepts, then apply them. If it asks for examples, then produce them. If you are unsure, then reflect on the kinds of skills the subject has been emphasizing. If it has been things such as logical analysis, good judgement, clearly structured arguments, then it seems likely these will be expected in the exam. Just putting everything you know about the subject down on paper is never a winning strategy and rarely even a reasonable survival tactic.

> *Examiners are looking for different things, depending on the subject, but most importantly they want to see that you have answered the question.*

Delivering your answers within the specified time period seems straightforward. However, this regularly causes difficulties for many people. View this as a time management task. If you have to deliver four quality answers in three hours, you will need to plan the timing of each question. This should be flexible for the first question as you may have to read the paper and get yourself into exam mode. But, for each question, there should be an absolute time limit. If you reach it for one question, complete as much as you can, even using bullet points if necessary and move on to the next. This should not be a personal negotiation. You must ruthlessly force yourself to move on. Additionally, if you can leave time at the end to go over your paper, do so. People often write muddled sentences under pressure and many of them can be close to illegible if you are not used to writing for long periods of time.

exam review

Try not to walk away from the exam without giving some thought to the experience. Getting marks lower than expected, or even failing a subject, is, in our experience, usually due to one of two reasons. The most common one, ironically for management students, is the time management issue. They simply do not answer all the questions. If the paper states that you must answer four questions and all questions carry equal marks, then that is how it is marked. We have often been (and continue to be) completely mystified by students who believe that because they have written two brilliant answers, answering the other two half-heartedly, or sometimes not at all, does not matter. It is simple arithmetic. The examiner gives you marks for what you have written. If you don't write, you don't reap the marks.

The other reason for a substandard performance is that the student hasn't answered the question posed. It is like standing in front of someone and asking them to describe and evaluate the benefits of process re-engineering and for them to start talking about quality circles, or to describe process re-engineering but not evaluate it. In conversation, it is likely that the person would immediately see this as absurd, but it seems to be a blind spot in written exams. It doesn't matter how limited your knowledge of process re-engineering, you will gain a lot more from exploring what little you do know than a brilliant review and assessment of quality circles. Obvious, isn't it? Unfortunately, it does not seem to be so clear under exam conditions.

The feedback that you will get from an exam usually amounts to a grade and nothing more. If you fail, you will usually get feedback, but most students pass and move on to the next task. However, by doing this, you may be missing an opportunity to develop an important learning skill – the ability to reflect and learn from a performance with limited feedback. This is a real issue in a managerial environment and, with some thought during the MBA, can be developed into something that can help at work.

Exams are not arbitrary processes and most examiners can agree among themselves on what are good, middle of the road or exceptional answers. Consequently, while you may not be able to pick your exact mark, you should be able to identify where you did well and where your performance was weaker. Try to be realistic and calmly self-critical in looking at both your strengths and your weaknesses. Thinking about your exam will help to improve your ability to understand your performance in an ambiguous managerial environment. It may also help with the next exam.

benefiting from assignments

Possibly the most common forms of assessment, other than examinations, are written assignments and research projects. The boundary between the two can be blurred, but the major difference between them is usually in terms of the amount of primary data needed (data collected at the original source). Often, assignments require no more than reference to course notes or textbooks. In these instances, the aim is to discuss the application of a set of concepts or techniques.

Assignments of this type are often accompanied by clear instructions from the lecturer on what they want and possibly how the assignment should be tackled. Consequently, we will not dwell on them here except to emphasize a number of points.

If the assignment instructions are not clear, then do not make assumptions about what is required. Sometimes there can be cultural misunderstandings, illustrated by the following student comment:

Some of us are not always familiar with the format. A recent assignment had a word limit of 2,000 words which a friend of mine thought was the minimum, so he ended up with 3,000 words and was penalized. In China, we don't have a maximum word limit most of the time. If there is an instruction, it is a minimum limit.

However, it is important not to make assumptions whatever your previous experience. Although you may be used to providing written material in the form of executive summaries and pages of bullet points, if the assignment requires something different, such as an essay format, then this is what has to be produced. This is regardless of how much you feel that the executive style is an appropriate method.

You may feel that this is not what is normally expected at work, so why should it be expected at a business school? Clearly, this depends on what the task is, but often business school assignments will be aimed at getting you to understand and reflect on different management concepts and sometimes the best way to do that is through an essay. At work, the emphasis is often on producing the result. While this is true of business schools, in order to learn, there is also a high degree of emphasis on the process, including the approach you took and why, the way you argued your points, the concepts you referenced, the data you used as evidence and the way you arrived at your conclusions.

Consequently, in looking at any assignment, you need to consider:

> What is being asked of you? If you have a choice in what you do, relate this as much as possible to your learning needs.
> What are the logistics involved in terms of time, resources involved and completion date?
> What concepts, theories or techniques need to be referenced, discussed or included?
> To what extent are these to be applied? Is your own experience enough to do this, or do you need to get more information?
> How are you going to structure your answer? What headings or points do you need to specifically cover? What themes or arguments do you see running through the assignment?
> What kinds of conclusions do you need to come to?
> Has your final result answered the assignment task and demonstrated the knowledge and skills that the examiner is seeking?

MBA projects and research

MBA research projects vary tremendously both in terms of the methods used and the intended outcomes. They can range from library-based projects using secondary sources through to carefully researched investigations in field settings (for example visiting companies). They can also be aimed at producing general conclusions about broad issues, such as the impact of the internet on work practices, through to specific conclusions on a single issue. Consequently, in choosing a project, it is important to be clear about the potential benefits and pitfalls involved.

A desk-based project can develop secondary research skills. These are important management skills, as the issues facing managers today increasingly involve sifting through vast amounts of data and finding material that is both accurate and relevant. While anything can be found on the internet, it is equally easy to be overwhelmed by the vast quantity of data available. Moreover, the quality of the data varies tremendously. Development of both data-gathering and data evaluation skills is critical in the information age.

However, of potentially even greater benefit is the primary research project. Research projects on an MBA are usually practically oriented and often look at a problem or issue in one or several companies. The aim is to provide some resolution or insight into the problem. Some research projects are aimed at more general issues, or 'pure research'. If this is the case, it is worth consulting a specialized research handbook, particularly if the intention is to use the project as a precursor to possible PhD studies.

MBA research projects are often along the lines of consultancy interventions. This still requires, as any good consultant will emphasize, the use of valid and reliable research techniques to investigate and resolve the research questions. It will also call on one's ability to relate managerial concepts to the problems at hand and identify practical solutions. However, more importantly, and one of the reasons why projects have become more common in business school assessment, it will require a range of additional managerial skills to successfully complete the project. These include the ability to balance the different demands of the business school, the host organization and personal learning objectives; the ability to obtain information from different people, often at different organization levels; the ability to feed back sometimes contentious results; and the ability to deal with ambiguity.

selecting a project

The initial selection of a project is probably the most critical aspect of all. This affects the potential learning benefits, the potential benefits in terms of marks and the potential benefits to the external organization(s). Consequently, if there is a choice over the project, it is important to review the opportunities carefully. Thought also needs to be given to what is feasible and achievable within the constraints of the MBA. As a part-time student, one of the biggest problems with projects, gaining access, may be solved if it can be done in the student's organization. The downside, however, is that the common requirement to provide real benefits to a company may outweigh the chance to craft a project that will really develop your capabilities. Thus, there are several dilemmas in choosing a project, including the following:

> selecting a project that will develop the capabilities you feel are important
> choosing one that also meets the business school's requirements
> meeting the expectations of any host organizations
> being able to mange the project in terms of time, obtaining access and producing a quality result.

The major sources of ideas for selecting a project come either from discussions with tutors, or through looking at similar projects already completed, or as a result of a dilemma, problem or issue that has arisen as a result of your studies. Most writers suggest that the sooner your start thinking about the project and discussing possibilities with your lecturers, the better. They may know of organizations seeking help, or have knowledge of industries and companies that may be easier to access than others. It is also important to clarify whether you or the school has responsibility for obtaining a company's cooperation.

Other ways of selecting topics include reading the business press or web searches around areas of interest. These can include industries that are attractive, either to understand better or possibly work in at a future date. Also, targeting companies that have encouraged students in the past or have been highlighted in the media can yield results. However, do not expect companies that have had adverse publicity to open their arms to internal investigation. Some do, but many tend not to encourage unknown outsiders to look at problems they are uncomfortable about. You may learn a lot from politically sensitive projects, but gaining access to one and coming out of the experience relatively unscathed are both fairly remote possibilities.

Clarifying what you would like to investigate and why before approaching a potential organization or company is important. Even if a company has a ready-made research project, you need to have some idea of your own needs and capabilities to prevent taking on something that may be difficult for you to complete. If you are 'cold-calling' on organizations, it is particularly important to have an idea of the main elements you expect from a project. Clearly, you need to be flexible; often MBA projects are a compromise between you, the school and the host organization.

research design

Before approaching organizations, however, it is important to have some idea of what might be involved in the research process. Three things are important to keep in mind. The first of these, already discussed, is the objectives and aims of the study. The second is what data need to be collected and the possible methods employed. Third is analysing the data.

In relation to data collection, the first thing to consider is how much secondary data are needed in order to gain an understanding of the context of the research. This involves a literature review and is necessary in order to establish what has already been written on the topic or about the organization. With an MBA research topic, it is unlikely that the aim will be to contribute in any substantial way to management knowledge. But you will need to ensure that you use the knowledge that is already there to provide a context for your investigation. You will get no marks for reinventing the wheel or going over well-trodden ground that does not add any value to the research topic, the company or your own development. You will also not get much sympathy for ignoring research investigations in associated areas that could have helped with your own project. While a complete review of the literature is not expected, a reasonable understanding of the most relevant areas is.

Next to consider is the amount and type of primary data you will need. An important distinction is between quantitative (concerned with precision and replication) and qualitative (concerned with meaning and uniqueness) data. Understanding what is involved in collecting different types of data is important because there are trade-offs between different methods. Often quantitative data collection methods are easier to administer than qualitative methods and allow standardization, but qualitative data can provide more insights. Which method you choose affects your outcomes and must relate to what you are trying to do.

Quantitative methods include standard questionnaires, production schedules, market share data and financial returns. Qualitative methods include interviews, focus groups and observation techniques. Sometimes a research project may involve both methods. For example, in looking at a production system, in addition to the output numbers on a production line, the people involved in the production process may also need to be interviewed to understand what is happening with the system.

Some thought should also be given to how the data might be analysed. There are a range of different possible interpretations and unless consideration has been given to data analysis beforehand, the data collected may be in the wrong form. For example, you may need to know how to code data, particularly if you are contemplating interviews, or be familiar with software to analyse data statistically, before collecting the information. While some writers suggest going back to collect more data if there are gaps or problems, with MBA projects, time is often a limited commodity both for you and the host, so it is best to try and get this right first time.

With an idea of the type of project to be conducted, an understanding of the research context from published sources, the potential data collection methods available and possible ways of analysing the data, thought can then be given to specifying in more detail what is involved and what is needed to manage the project successfully.

The first step is to scope out a research proposal and plan of action that can be used as a basis for discussion by all the parties involved. This should include:

> an outline of the problem or research question to be investigated
> reasons why this as a valuable undertaking
> what data are needed and how they will be collected
> who will be involved and the other resources needed
> what meetings may be necessary with whom and when
> timelines for involvement with the organization and project completion
> suggested ways of communicating the results.

These steps may require a different emphasis for the various stakeholders involved. Also, the kinds of results and the way they are presented to a host organization (probably as a consultancy report) will often be different from the way they are presented to the school (as an assessed piece of work). In all cases, it is important to clarify expectations as much as possible before beginning the work. The organization may be more concerned with the results and recommendations, whereas the school may be more concerned with the methods you used, how you interpreted the results and whether you have used appropriate references. Having agreed on the proposal, it should be circulated and any misunderstandings rectified before you start.

In addition to outlining the parameters of the process, a range of management skills will be required for successful project completion. Most important is the ability to work to the timelines for various stages of the project and ensure that these are met. You also need to be prepared with a contingency plan if anything goes wrong. This is more likely for a project than taking a taught subject at the business school. Meetings can be cancelled, employees can suddenly be less cooperative than they first seemed, or the host company's expectations can change. Consequently, research projects of this type frequently involve practising influence and communication skills. It is important to keep everyone informed on a regular basis, to avoid committing yourself in a way not previously agreed and to manage less than helpful respondents in a way that leaves both you and them as positive as possible.

Finally, thought needs to be given to feeding back the research results both to the host organization and the school. If a presentation is involved, the principles outlined in Chapter 6 should be applied. Overall, it is important to keep in mind what you are trying to achieve, how you went about it and the outcomes. Targeting that information to the appropriate audience is the last step.

conclusion

This chapter has outlined the different learning opportunities on an MBA. However, in order to fully benefit from these, they have to be proactively managed. In approaching any learning activity, the particular skills and knowledge that a student wishes to develop overall should be identified. An environment that maximizes study outside the lecture theatre needs to be established, including creating the correct environment, use of study plans and learning logs. These devices can help in deriving the maximum benefit from both informal and formal learning opportunities on an MBA. Formal opportunities include lectures, cases and the major forms of assessment of exams, assignments and projects. Obviously, passing the MBA is critical, but this chapter also emphasizes that while assessment processes can be seen as hurdles to be overcome, their prime contribution is in improving management knowledge and skills. This will be enhanced further if personal learning needs are clarified both before and during the programme.

Nevertheless, whatever your learning needs may be, it is likely that you will have the ability to solve business problems high on your list of areas to improve. This is a vital and fundamental capability. However, as with a learning capability, developing a decision-making and problem-solving capability is not straightforward and, as the next chapter shows, it too needs a proactive approach to develop fully.

references

1. Cameron, S. (2001) *The MBA Handbook* (London: Prentice Hall).
2. Quoted in Crainer, S. and Dearlove, D. (1999) *Gravy Training* (San Francisco: Jossey-Bass) p. 36.
3. Gatrell, C. and Turnbull, S. (2003) *Your MBA with Distinction* (London: Prentice Hall).

4 developing a problem-solving capability

A well-developed ability to think through problems and make decisions is often a factor that distinguishes elite global managers from the rest. Indeed, at most levels in organizations and in most functions, highly developed cognitive skills are critical. This is one of the reasons why MBA programmes devote a great deal of time to developing these qualities. As one student commented:

It has become clear to me that a critical quality in a good manager is making decisions. Previously I had thought of managers more as evaluating performance, delegating daily tasks, increasing sales and profit, ensuring 'smooth sailing' of the company's various functions ... All these are facets of a manager's role, but really what a good manager does is make the big decisions, the tough decisions, before they need to be made.

But making tough decisions and, just as importantly, making good decisions in a continuously changing business environment has never been more challenging. There is no question that an MBA will improve your ability to diagnose business problems, look at alternative solutions and come up with workable solutions. As one student commented:

I am different from when I started [the MBA] ... I am able to see a broader picture, but within this I am more analytical, better able to solve problems, more critical, and less likely to just let assumptions pass by.

However, while the ability to make good business decisions is one of the most critical qualities developed by a postgraduate management degree, nevertheless, there are many facets to improving this capability. This chapter explores these and discusses both rational methods and more creative and intuitive approaches to problem solving. Often these approaches are not discussed formally on MBA programmes and a fundamental understanding of the problem-solving process will not only help with your MBA studies, but make you more effective in the real world. Whether it is dealing with a theoretical case in class or a real issue back at work, making the right decisions is important both for you and the people for whom you are responsible.

rational problem solving

The most dominant view of how managers make decisions and cope with complex problems, particularly in Western societies, is through the rational problem-solving model. Even if this is not familiar to you, it is the one most likely to be found during your MBA.

As shown in Figure 4.1, the problem-solving model generally consists of five parts:

> Identifying whether a problem exists and its importance.
> Clarifying assumptions and gathering appropriate information.
> Generating alternative solutions and selecting the best option.
> Implementing a chosen solution.
> Ensuring the solution is maintained and its effect monitored.

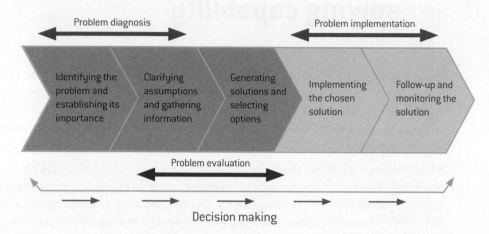

Figure 4.1 The problem-solving process

As Figure 4.1 also illustrates, problem solving can be seen in terms of three phases: *problem diagnosis* – identifying a problem, the reasons why it has occurred and its importance; *problem evaluation* – assessing alternatives and finding a solution, or course of action; and *solution implementation* – making things happen. Decision making occurs throughout this process, whether it is in deciding on the reasons for the problem, deciding on a course of action or deciding how to implement a solution.

The emphasis with this and similar models is on the need to act rationally and objectively. The more rational the process, the more objective and fair will be the outcome. Two of the most influential writers in this area, Irving Janis and Leon Mann,[1] argue that a high-quality decision results from a process that thoroughly gathers all the pertinent information related to a problem, carefully weighs up the positive and negative consequence of all known alternative solutions and makes detailed provisions for executing the chosen course of action.

There are considerable benefits in approaching problems in this way. This is often a good model to use in analysing case studies and one that can be transferred to many situations in the real world. For instance, when Xerox embarked on its drive for total quality in the 1980s, staff were taught a step-by-step problem-solving process to improve work processes within the organization. The training even helped the CEO at that time, David Kearns: 'I really learned from it [the training]. I don't have the most disciplined mind and I found the systematic process amazingly helpful.'[2]

However, the basic model has a number of limitations. For example, in ambiguous environments, identifying the real problem, considering all alternatives and making the 'right' decisions in a limited timescale are fraught with difficulty and may not follow the neat sequencing of the model. In its purest form, it assumes that problem solvers have clear objectives, have all the information they need and know what will happen as a result of their action. The model is particularly valuable for routine or operational problems, but may be less useful for non-programmed problems that require creativity and more lateral thinking.

Nevertheless, despite some limitations, the model is a useful starting point for exploring problem-solving approaches. This chapter discusses the issues around the areas of problem diagnosis and problem evaluation (leaving solution implementation until the discussion of leadership later in the book). Add in some understanding of how the mind works and why and when we need to deviate from the basic model, and our decision making can improve considerably.

problem diagnosis

mental frames of reference

In order to diagnose problems effectively (and also evaluate them), it is important to understand some of the factors that influence the way we think. We do not gather data as if we are blank sheets of paper. Managers, like everyone else, have a mental frame of reference, which is a product of their past experiences, assumptions, values and beliefs. These influence the way information about problems is gathered, distilled and what conclusions are reached. Making better decisions depends to some extent on understanding our frames of reference and why we choose to focus on some things and not others.

In many ways, our frames of reference are of great benefit as they help us cope with an overwhelming range of information. They enable us to make many and sometimes quite complex decisions seem straightforward. The automatic response patterns we developed to learn to drive, for example, enable us to take to the roads without having to think consciously about every action. Otherwise, we would be learners every time we got into a car, having to navigate roads full of equally confused drivers.

the shackles of the mind

However, while the development of such automatic responses helps in some situations, it can also limit us in many ways. Familiar and routine ways of thinking can stop us from looking at alternatives, even when those routines may not be helping. Indeed, students who worry incessantly about whether they are going to fail, whether something will go wrong and how they are going to get through their programme sometimes develop these mental patterns as a kind of 'thought' haven. This is not necessarily a happy state, but merely a mental shelter they resort to because 'worry' is what they have become used to.

Thus, we can become prisoners of our own thoughts. Mental routines are often a product of buried experiences and reinforced over many years, at school or at home, until they have become 'natural' to us. For example, if every time we try to express a different view about a topic we are told to keep quiet, it is likely that we will have developed a degree of reticence about speaking out. Equally, if by hassling everybody and everything we manage to get our own way, we may have become overly persistent. In themselves, there is nothing wrong with reticence or persistence. It is when one or two mental routines dominate everything that they become a problem.

A cold, hard calculating approach to decision making may be fine at work, but at home may not go down too well. Great creativity may be appropriate in developing an advertising campaign but not so smart when doing the accounts. These patterns often become habits that are rarely questioned. However, by thinking more about these routines, identifying what they are and how they may have developed, we can assess their usefulness and whether we should change them.

nature or nurture

The extent to which we *can* change, and the degree of choice we have in how we think, is a very contentious issue. The nature versus nurture debate (what we are borne with as against what can be developed) has raged for years with few clear conclusions.

However, we do have some idea of where our limits may lie. There are some aspects of our cognitive makeup that do not change easily and impact on how we gather and interpret data and make decisions. These are classified in different ways by different theorists. A popular categorization is the Myers Briggs Type Indicator™ (MBTI), which highlights how individuals can gather data through their senses in a factual, data-driven way, or through intuitive processes.[3] It also highlights the extent to which we make decisions either through logical, rational processes or based on feelings and principles (see Box 4.1).[4]

BOX 4.1 The Myers Briggs Type Indicator™

The Myers Briggs Type Indicator™ is a model of personality based on four preferences:

1 Where, primarily, do you prefer to direct your energy?

If you prefer to direct your energy to deal with people, things, situations, or 'the outer world', your preference is for **extraversion** – denoted by the letter (E).

If you prefer to direct your energy to deal with ideas, information, explanations or beliefs, or 'the inner world', your preference is for **introversion** (I).

2 How do you prefer to process information?

If you prefer to deal with facts, what you know, to have clarity, or to describe what you see, your preference is for **sensing** (S).

If you prefer to deal with ideas, look into the unknown, to generate new possibilities or to anticipate what isn't obvious, your preference is for **intuition** (N).

3 How do you prefer to make decisions?

If you prefer to decide on the basis of objective logic, using an analytic and detached approach, your preference is for **thinking** (T).

If you prefer to decide using values and/or personal beliefs, on the basis of what you believe is important or what you or others care about, your preference is for **feeling** (F).

4 How do you prefer to organize your life?

If you prefer your life to be planned, stable and organized, your preference is for **judging** (J).

If you prefer to go with the flow, to maintain flexibility and respond to things as they arise, your preference is for **perception** (P).

One of the implications of this is that it is unlikely that one person will be proficient in all aspects of the problem-solving process. Thus, teaming up with colleagues with complimentary skills can pay dividends. Another is that there is a limit to how proficient we are in some areas. But this is often overplayed. Some of us will never be able to perform complex mathematical calculations or read a classical music score by sight and so will have to give up on becoming theoretical physicists or concert pianists. But there is still a lot of choice even for those of us without these elite cognitive abilities. Indeed, if there is any consistent conclusion from cognitive studies, it is how little we use the potential brain capacity we have.

values and choices

Also influencing our choices, but potentially more susceptible to change, are factors arising from our social experiences, particularly our beliefs and values. Values, like truth, honesty, integrity and wealth creation, colour our view of the world. They can have a strong and positive influence on how businesses are managed. The direction of Anita Roddick's cosmetics business, The Body Shop, was determined in large part by her strong values about how businesses should be managed and the contribution that industry should make to society. In the early days, she argued:

> It is a business unlike any other: but we have no marketing department and no advertising department. We operate according to criteria which place more emphasis on human values than on strictly commercial considerations.[5]

But those views can equally cause us problems. It is easy to unconsciously discount data that are different from our beliefs or challenge our values, particularly under pressure. The impact of values is more pronounced in decisions where there is ambiguity and consequently a greater degree of subjectivity.[6] It is important, therefore, to have a sense of the values we hold and to recognize where they may be both helping and constraining problem solving.

Thus, the way we think is a unique and personal process that has both benefits and potential traps. However, greater awareness of our automatic responses and familiar mental patterns can help steer us away from jumping to wrong conclusions. We have considerable potential to develop how we think, how we analyse problems and how we produce creative solutions. We can also choose what we think about and how we think about it. At any point in time, we decide which problems we emphasize and how we view them. Our agendas are largely our own creation and we can improve our ability to deal with them.

symptoms vs causes

Being aware of how we think and the mental frames of reference we use are important in identifying and defining problems. Indeed, understanding what the 'real' problem(s) might be is an issue that will be raised frequently in discussing business issues and case studies on an MBA. Often core problems are not obvious either in real life or in cases. This is because in both circumstances there are often conflicting data and our frames of reference can inhibit us from seeing beyond what seems obvious. Indeed, most of us are not aware of the extent to which our mindset prevents us from clearly seeing the core problem or what is needed to solve the problem.

One common mistake is to address the symptoms of a problem rather than the causes. There are many examples of companies moving employees into open-plan offices to improve communication, when the real problem is poor interpersonal relationships and attitudes rather than the need to change the furniture, or introducing sophisticated IT systems to improve information sharing, when the issue is more to do with departmental rivalry than the inadequacies of the knowledge management system.

Indeed, even the biggest companies can fail to focus on the core problem or defer tackling it, hoping that other solutions might work. For instance, GM's answer to its considerable financial strife in 2006 and declining market share was to slash the price of its cars. But the problem may not have been the price of the car, but the cost of running it. With oil prices rising and consumers becoming more environmentally conscious, the decline in market share seemed to stem more from the kind of car the company partially relied on (big and fuel inefficient) than the initial price.

When reflecting on his time as CEO of Xerox, David Kearns illustrates the need to take time to explore the core problem and potential causes:

When they are confronted with a problem, American managers typically want it fixed fast – by yesterday. And this can be a deadly disease. I was very much the epitome of that school of thought. I felt I was decisive and impatient, and so I wanted problems solved as quickly as possible. But I didn't think enough about root causes. Rarely would I ask, 'What is the reason we are having this problem?' Now I think a lot about causes.[7]

Doing this is not merely an intellectual exercise; the consequence of not focusing on root causes can result in implementing the wrong solution, with considerable lost time and money. Indeed, 'getting it wrong' drives companies out of business. If consumers are buying GM cars because of their price competitiveness, then slashing the price may ensure GM will be around for the foreseeable future in its current form. If it is because consumers want smaller and more fuel-efficient cars, then GM could become a pale reflection of itself if it does not respond differently, as Japanese companies in particular eat into the American car makers' market position.

Even if it doesn't end in bankruptcy, not focusing on the real problem can still result in considerable strife. For example, it is a common mistake for organizations undertaking a merger to focus on the logistics of the merger and ignore employees' feelings about the process. While the physical assets may be in place and up and running fairly quickly, there have been numerous instances where employees have meanwhile been walking out the door. When IBM services merged with PwC in 2005, in some countries IBM had to resort to legal action to stop some of the PwC partners from leaving the merged entity. Such a course of action is unlikely to have got to the root causes of the defection.[8]

clarifying our assumptions

Having identified the core problem, the next challenge is to refrain from making assumptions about the nature of the problem and how to solve it. Unquestioned assumptions affect the kind of information that is gathered and how the issues are explored going forward. They may also lead to the wrong answer.

Edward de Bono illustrates our tendency to get trapped by our assumptions about the past with an exercise. A series of letters are presented one at a time and someone is asked to produce a word from the letters. The first word is A and the second T, producing AT. Then R is given, producing RAT. Next comes E, giving the word RATE. followed by G, resulting in GRATE. The problem arises with the next letter, which is T. It cannot be added to GRATE to make a new word and it is only when our assumptions about sequencing are challenged that the new word TARGET is produced.[9]

reframing

Many writers have suggested that a way around being trapped by one's assumptions is to reframe the issue. In thinking strategically, it is common to get organizations to rethink or reframe their assumptions about what business they are in. Viewing a trucking service as a logistics company gives rise to a broader range of possibilities. For years, sporting venues limited their opportunities because they assumed they were solely there to hold football or rugby matches. Reframing their purpose to specialists in large gatherings broadens the potential range of events from rock concerts to evangelical rallies.

What may also help us to clarify our assumptions is to look at a problem from different vantage points. Write down the problem, but then try to rewrite it in a different form, or imagine you are a specialist in the field (or from another discipline) and look at it from their perspective. Try to describe the problem using simple language and listen to how you are delivering the explanation. Try to explain it graphically. Keep asking questions about it until you can't ask, 'But why?' anymore.

Without doing this, one might still produce a terrific solution, but to the wrong problem. De Bono describes this dilemma in terms of vertical and lateral thinking. Vertical thinking is concerned with drilling down into an issue until an answer is found. Lateral thinking is concerned with trying to find where to drill in the first place by looking for different views of a problem. De Bono notes:

> Logic is the tool that is used to dig holes deeper and bigger, to make them altogether better holes. But if the hole is in the wrong place, then no amount of improvement is going to put it in the right place. No matter how obvious this may seem to every digger, it is still easier to go on digging in the same place than to start all over again in a new place. Vertical thinking is digging the same hole deeper; lateral thinking is trying again elsewhere.[10]

clarifying others' assumptions

But it is not only our own assumptions that can prevent us from exploring a problem fully. Managerial decisions are rarely taken in isolation. A range of external influences (including stakeholder expectations and peer opinion) affect both the data that managers receive and the decisions they make. Indeed, decision making is likely to be as much about persuasion and influence as it is a mechanistic process of gathering and assessing 'facts'.[11] Hence, this is one of the reasons why cases are discussed in class. Clearly, a class case discussion can never completely replace the real thing, but it can raise awareness of some of the pitfalls of real-world decision making.

Discussing problems with others can often lead to improved outcomes. But it can also result in restricted thinking. This can occur, for example, if we have a tendency to defer to others. In organizations, we may choose to defer to someone who is older, more senior, or just because they shout louder or are more aggressive. One of the most common reasons for this – particularly on an MBA programme – is because of someone else's expertise.

Clearly, experts have tremendous value in many situations. However, it is when we assume they *always* have value and are above being questioned that problems occur. This has cost some companies considerable amounts of money. There are numerous examples of senior teams deferring to IT experts when implementing new technological investments, only to have them ripped out a few years later. Westpac, one of the major banks in Australia, lost large amounts of money on an IT project called CS90. It was meant to revolutionize banking, based on the promises of 'experts', but was ignominiously wound down.[12]

Indeed, sometimes a whole industry, or at least part of it, can be held back because of deference to experts. For many years, all cars used to have a mechanical arm on either side of the vehicle indicating which way to turn. No other method was deemed possible or safe. Although drivers could often be seen leaning out of the vehicle (rather than driving it) and manually pulling a malfunctioning arm out of its socket, the danger was dismissed by experts. Eventually the assumption was challenged and the flashing indicator was developed.

> Often we do not challenge the assumptions of others, even when we may harbour doubts about what is being said.

Often we do not challenge the assumptions of others, even when we may harbour doubts about what is being said. The authors have been running group exercises with MBA students over many years. Some of these exercises are deliberately constructed so that nobody in the group has any more expertise or information about the group task than any other team member. Yet we have observed countless instances where the group decision making has been poor because team members failed to fully question the initial assumptions and reasoning of their colleagues, which were frequently wrong. Instead, the focus tends to be on avoiding conflict or saving time, which may feel good, but is only a short-term benefit.

problem evaluation

Clarifying assumptions is also important when evaluating alternatives, as well as in diagnosing problems. However, the emphasis will differ between the two stages. Important in evaluating problems is to first assess the degree of complexity of the problem. Clarifying assumptions here is concerned with providing direction for finding potential solutions, rather than continuing to identify the problem. But the effort in doing this should pay dividends. For Einstein, the activity that was most helpful in developing the theory of relativity was 'figuring out how to think about the problem' and the assumptions that underlie it.

David Casey illustrates the differences between problems by dividing the challenges faced by managers into three levels; simple puzzles, complex puzzles and 'real' problems. He sees a puzzle (such as the police tracking down a murderer) as distinct from a real problem (for example society trying to decide on capital punishment for murderers) by the fact that a solution to a puzzle exists somewhere, but just has to be found. A 'real' problem is so difficult that nobody knows what the answer is – there may not even be an answer.[13]

Although 'real' problems do not occur on a daily basis, they are nevertheless challenges that managers face. Trying to rescue two miners trapped nearly one kilometre underground with only a thin metal cage holding back tons of rock from killing them is a real problem. The rescue at Beaconsfield in Tasmania in 2006 had never been attempted before and involved careful planning, considerable engineering expertise and a fair degree of courage. But an even bigger problem is what happens now to the community that has grown up around the mine, if the mine closes because it is no longer safe to operate. As Casey points out, real problems cannot be neatly categorized as production, finance or personnel puzzles. Problems are large, ambiguous and unprecedented and some may be insoluble.

On an MBA, you will come across some real problems and we discuss below how these might be tackled. But the majority of challenges will be simple or complex puzzles, as defined above. This does not mean that they will necessarily be easy but that they will have a solution and usually can be solved sequentially with reasoning or logic, as illustrated below.

simple puzzles

Simple puzzles are found in numerous books and magazines. An example is the riddle where Henry looks at a photograph of a man and says, 'Brothers and sisters have I none, but that man's father is my father's son'. Who is the man in the photograph? The puzzle can be solved by simple logic. The answer is in the footnotes.[14]

Another example is a cryptarithm, which is a puzzle where each number has been replaced by a letter. Below, the answer to the sum is found by establishing which numbers corresponds to which letter.

$$
\begin{array}{ccc}
X & & Y \\
Y & & X \\
\hline
Z & X & Z
\end{array}
$$

The solution can be found by looking for clues and applying logic. The letter Z on the left-hand side of the bottom line must be a carry over from the previous column because there are no numbers above it. The sum of X and Y in the second column cannot be greater than 18 (9 plus 9), so Z must be 1.

If Z is 1, that means that the sum of the first column can be only 11 or 1. If it is 1, then X and Y would have to be a combination of 0 and 1. But as we know Z is 1, then neither X nor Y can be 1, so the first column must total 11. Consequently, X and Y must be 5 and 6, 8 and 3, or 9 and 2. In each case, with 1 carried over from the first column, the answer to the second column is 12. This means that X (as the number below the line in the second column) must be 2 and Y must be 9. Therefore the answer is 121.

The answer to the puzzle is reached by building up the clues step by step in a logical sequence. However, not all problems can be solved with this kind of process. Some issues are more complex and challenging and require going beyond the straightforward and the rational.

complex puzzles

Complex puzzles are challenges that are more involved or cannot be solved completely through reasoning. An example of the kind of thinking (rather than the degree of complexity) required for complex puzzles is illustrated by a set of problems that involve getting a number of items from one side of a river bank to another. The items involved in the exercise usually have the potential to consume each other and can include goats, foxes, cabbages and cannibals. The challenge is to get them from one side of a river to another in one boat, without any adverse outcomes. This kind of problem is well known in the field of artificial intelligence to illustrate the use of abstract concepts.

The least internecine example is where a family (consisting of a father, mother, daughter and son) needs to cross a river. The only means available is by borrowing a boat from a fisherman. The boat can only carry one of the adults or both children. What series of crossings need to be made to get the family to the other side and leave the boat with the fisherman?

Frustration with this problem usually comes from assuming that each family member only has to make the journey once, or that the boat cannot move with only one child, or that only the family is involved. The solution becomes more evident as one realizes that some members of the family have to make several journeys, the son or daughter can cross on their own and the fisherman can join in. A solution is found in the footnotes.[15]

Although this is a straightforward example, it illustrates the need to go beyond the 'obvious' logic to find the answer. Particularly important is the need to review one's assumptions, to keep questioning the approach being taken, and to try and see the problem from a different viewpoint. If, for example, you start with the question, 'How can the children get the family across the river?', then the problem is seen from a slightly different angle, which can help with the solution.

creativity and intuition

Solving more complex puzzles and real problems, however, may require completely different mental processes to the rational approach emphasized so far. Indeed, we are equipped with a greater range of mental abilities than we sometimes realize or are prepared to explore. In addition to our analytical processes, verbal reasoning and mathematical ability, we also have the capacity for visual imagery, creative synthesis, intuition, fantasy and associative processes. Historically, managers have been encouraged to use rational thinking. However, while useful and important in the right circumstances, this emphasis has its limitations. Indeed, Tom Peters and Robert Waterman blamed rational thought processes as a major reason for the problems US firms encountered when competing with foreign companies in the 1970s and 80s.[16]

Competition, uncertainty and ambiguity have increased considerably over the past 30 years, as has the need for more creative thinking. Developing a sense or vision of the future, generating new ideas and finding creative solutions to old problems are rarely a product of rational thought processes. Indeed, there are many circumstances where creativity and intuition are necessary, including:

> When a high level of uncertainty exists.
> When few previous precedents exist.
> When variables are less scientifically predictable.
> When 'facts' are limited.
> When 'facts' don't clearly point the way to go.
> When several plausible alternative solutions exist, with good arguments for each.[17]

creative techniques

As with some of the concepts discussed earlier, creative-thinking approaches can be used for problem identification, but they truly come into their own when looking for potential solutions. Typical creative problem-solving techniques include brainstorming and lateral thinking. Most techniques follow a similar sequence, starting with a problem exploration phase, followed by an idea generation phase and ending with evaluation and action planning. Central to these techniques is the aim of producing large numbers of ideas as well as variety and consequently surfacing a range of different possibilities.

In order for these processes to work, thought patterns that may have been with us since our secondary school years and have often been drummed into us as the 'true way', have to be suspended. When brainstorming, irrational and illogical thinking is not a sin, but is something that is deliberately emphasized and encouraged. Neither is thinking tangentially and taking time to mull over a problem, although these notions can be hard to leave behind, even if only temporarily.

It is also important not to harbour beliefs that thinking creatively is somehow beyond us. The comment from a student that 'I have found that I am not good at coming up with alternative solutions which comes from the fact I am not creative' is not uncommon and stems from a misunderstanding of our mental capacities and the various ways that creative thinking can occur. While some people do have blinding flashes of inspiration, many creative breakthroughs have come from painstaking trial and error, sometimes over many years. Picasso produced over 30,000 works of art, of which only a small percentage are considered masterpieces.

brainstorming

Fundamental to achieving success with brainstorming is to have a positive mindset and a willingness to refrain from being critical. This 'open mind' emphasis can be seen from the few, but important rules in brainstorming:

1. Suspend judgement.
2. Assume no one is 'wrong'.
3. Do not assess, evaluate or criticize an idea.
4. Try to 'free-wheel' in generating ideas.
5. Aim for quantity rather than quality of ideas.
6. Maintain a positive attitude.

In principle, the aim is to get an individual or group to mentally 'let go' and generate ideas that are original, even though they may seem improbable. Usually the ideas are written down as they are raised. Assessment takes place later. What is critical is to hold back from evaluating and particularly criticizing the ideas, before they see the light of day.

free association

In similar vein, the creativity technique of free association, used originally by Sigmund Freud, can help in making associations and links that might not otherwise be evident. In the business world, the technique most commonly involves taking a word at random (from a book or random word generator) and using that to come up with associations that may help with the problem in question. Sometimes, the word does not lead to very much and some writers suggest a modification of this, such as only using concrete nouns.

In *The Mind Gym*, there is a good example of how the technique was used to help better market a theatre, which had great plays but no audience. Traditional marketing methods include a marketing campaign, press coverage, telling friends and so on. However, by taking a random word, in this case 'out', from the script the cast was currently using, they used it to generate new promotional ideas. These included 'out' and exits and distributing leaflets at various venue exits; out and coming out – going to gay bars to advertise; out and outside – performances outside; out and patients – performing in hospital waiting rooms; outing – going on tour and so on.[18]

morphological analysis

A more structured technique for investigating associations and relationships is morphological analysis, developed by the astrophysicist Fritz Zwicky. It has been applied to everything from new product development to complex long-term societal challenges sometimes know as 'wicked problems'.[19]

Central to the process is a multidimensional matrix (or Zwicky box), which is used to bring together a range of potential solutions to a problem. The idea is to break the problem down into subunits and then bring these together to provide a more creative outcome.

The basic process is to first identify the attributes or component parts of a product, service or event and so on that is being reviewed. For example, if developing a new pen, the attributes might be casing material, ink colour, ink injection system, head (ball point, nib and so on), type of cap, length, width and so on. The attributes of an event, such as a conference, would be venue, subject, speakers, communication medium, audience and so on.

The next stage is to list as many alternate characteristics as possible under each attribute in a matrix. Both this and the attribute stage can be facilitated by brainstorming. When finished, the different alternates from each column can be combined to produce a new outcome.

Box 4.2 illustrates how the technique might be used to develop a new kind of holiday package. The three main attributes are shown – location, type and the potential audience. (More attributes could be added such as length of time.) Below these headings are lists of alternate possibilities. Combining alternates from the three columns can produce new ideas, such as a rafting holiday down the Amazon with university students. In the cold light of day, some of the outcomes may seem less than practical, such as parachuting over the Arctic with senior citizens. However, this is a creativity tool meant to generate ideas. If it triggers the seeds of a few new adventure packages or extreme holidays, it has served its purpose.

BOX 4.2 **Multidimensional matrix**

Location	Type	Main audience
Himalayas	Rafting	Anybody
Bermuda triangle	Boating	Teenagers
Africa	Climbing	Elite athletes
Above the clouds	Trekking	Senior citizens
Great Lakes	Swimming	Males in their forties
Mississippi	Parachuting	Females in their twenties
The Antarctic	Sailing	Civil servants
The Amazon	Biking	Stockbrokers
Kalahari Desert	Flying	Thrill-seekers
Black Sea	Motorcycling	University students

The matrix can also be used personally, for example in designing a house or room, or using Box 4.2 to identify the kind of holiday that would be appealing. I am sure there is a travel agent somewhere who can provide a sailing trip down the Amazon with thrill-seekers for those with an adventurous streak. In fact, the matrix can be developed to display thousands of possibilities on an endless number of issues.

creativity in groups

Many creative techniques and problem-solving approaches in general are shared activities. In MBA syndicate or study groups there will be many problems to be solved. In a later chapter we discuss how to get the best out of study groups, but it is worth outlining here a technique that can help with group problem solving. A technique called 'Six Thinking Hats'® was devised by Edward de Bono in the 1980s and has had extraordinary results. It is now taught in schools and in major corporations to improve the capacity to make productive decisions.

De Bono argues that we often create confusion by trying to think in too many different directions at once. We mix up logic, information, emotion, hope and creative thought, which is often more of a hindrance than a help in problem solving. In order to help members of a group to think along the same lines, de Bono devised the simple idea of using hats and colours to represent different types of thinking. So, when a group member is asked to imagine they are wearing a certain coloured hat, they have to think in a certain way – and only that way. Box 4.3 describes the different hats and what they represent.[20]

In Box 4.4, several sentences are analysed in terms of the hats.[21] Trying to analyse our own thinking in terms of the different hats can help us out of a mental hole or on to a new path, for example it can help us take off our black hat or judgemental view of an issue and put on the more creative green hat. As one student who had used the technique commented:

By using the Six Thinking Hats® technique I have learnt to move out of my habitual thinking style to have a more rounded view of situations.

BOX 4.4 **What Hat Am I Wearing?**

'If we did that, we would risk our reputation'
Black Hat. Black is to do with risk assessment, what could go wrong, or why something won't work. It points out potential problems and faults in design. A widely used hat.

'I am uneasy about all this borrowing'
Red Hat is concerned with feelings and emotions. Using this hat legitimizes people saying 'this is how I feel' – no need for explanations, reasons. Often used to 'take the temperature' of a group.

'We could save on packaging costs if we did it that way'
Yellow Hat, for the sun and optimism. This type of thinking seeks to show the benefits and values of the idea.

'Let's just double the price and see what happens'
Green Hat, the creative hat, is concerned with looking for alternatives, possibilities, and designs. Green Hat thinking pushes for many ideas without judging the workability of the ideas.

'Retooling would take a minimum of three months'
White Hat thinking deals with the facts. Under White Hat we ask three questions: What information do we have? What information is missing? How can we get the missing information?

'Here is a hats sequence that we could use to explore the issue'
Blue Hat manages the thinking process. With this hat you stand back and reflect on the thinking that is taking place or needs to take place. It helps to control the process and get the best out of every type of thinking.

However, while the technique can certainly focus group members, it needs practice to fully enhance more productive ways of thinking for everyone.

creativity and innovation

However, there are times when not even these processes can provide an answer to some problems. Increasingly, companies have to compete by going well beyond the practices and approaches that are current. One of the most innovative companies in the world, Apple Computer, used seven different types of innovation to launch the iPod. These included networking (a novel agreement among music companies to sell their music online), business model (songs sold for a dollar each online), branding (attractive and cool product and accessories) and use (simple iTunes software platform). But innovation isn't just an issue for high-tech industries. A 2006 *BusinessWeek*–BCG report found that 72% of the senior executives they surveyed named innovation as one of their top three priorities.[22]

> A 2006 BusinessWeek–BCG report found that 72% of the senior executives they surveyed named innovation as one of their top three priorities.

Innovation within companies is a bigger topic than can be discussed here, but at an individual level, an ability to think completely outside the box is an important quality to explore during the MBA programme.

breakthrough thinking

A process that might facilitate this is what David Perkins calls 'breakthrough thinking'. He notes that some of the world's most important innovations have had to overcome particular challenges, such as an overwhelming number of possible avenues to explore, or no clues at all to a solution, or having to move beyond the dominant paradigm to find a complete answer. For example, for many years, shipbuilders could only make incremental increases in the speed of ships because it was thought ships had to be made from wood. When they were able to think outside this restrictive notion and entertain the possibility that metal ships wouldn't just sink, a new transport era began.

Breakthrough thinking can help overcome these challenges and often involves the following elements:[23]

❶ *Long search*: Getting thoroughly acquainted with a problem enables the recognition of a precipitating event when it happens. Clyde Tombaugh reviewed thousands of photographic plates comparing minute specks of light representing endless numbers of stars. He eventually found one speck that turned out to be the dwarf planet Pluto.

❷ *Little apparent progress*: A breakthrough arrives after a period when there has been little or no apparent progress. Thomas Edison called invention 1% inspiration and 99% perspiration. He scanned large numbers of possibilities systematically in his search for a suitable filament for a light bulb.

❸ *Precipitating event*: Often external circumstances can trigger a breakthrough. Einstein was thinking about how fast light could travel between two clock towers, when his attention drifted to the clocks themselves. That moment triggered a realization that time might play a critical part in understanding light, speed and the universe.

❹ *Cognitive 'snap'*: Here the breakthrough comes rapidly, where things fall into place or a sharp cognitive awakening occurs. Unlike point 2, the breakthrough occurs relatively quickly.

5 *Transformation*: The breakthrough transforms one's mental or physical world in a generative way. The development of the computer and particularly the PC has had a transformational impact on most people's work lives.

Consequently, as implied in the first two points, persistence plays a much greater part in creativity than people often realize. But possibly of more importance is getting into the right frame of mind for developing creativity. This enables the mind to mull over ideas and generate paths forward that sometimes come outside the formal creative techniques noted earlier in the chapter. There are many examples of ideas coming to us when we least expect it, such as when walking the dog or reading the newspaper. For Einstein, taking a shower or staring into space seemed to assist in producing some of his best ideas.

incubation

Allowing our subconscious mind to mull over a problem while conducting unrelated activities such as going for a walk is called incubation. The idea is to leave the thought in the back of one's mind and for the mind to process the issue without its being constrained by assumptions about the 'correct' process or 'right' method of analysis. Hence we allow ourselves to think more broadly.

> Allowing our subconscious mind to mull over a problem while conducting unrelated activities such as going for a walk is called incubation.

A fairly common example of the kind of problem that incubation can solve is in considering what are the next three numbers in this sequence, 293 130 313. The answer to the problem cannot be found by any kind of mathematical calculation, which is why the solution is more likely to come through mulling over it. The solution is in the footnotes.[24]

A more challenging problem is one that Einstein used to present to his students. A walker carrying a gun came across a bear in open country. No one else was there. Both were frightened and ran away from each other. The bear ran to the west and the walker to the north. The walker stopped, aimed to the south and shot the bear. What colour was the bear?

Trying to work this out in some logical way usually ends up in tears. The idea is to try and come up with an association that gives clues to places where aiming a shot to the south can hit something to the west. I am not sure there is a definite answer, but one suggestion is that the walker must have been standing exactly at the North Pole when he shot his gun, so everything then is to the south. Although there are no bears at the North Pole, the closest possibility is a polar bear, so the bear must have been white.[25]

> In a study of nine creative individuals, they all said that insights occurred during idle time, and a number of them noted that they occurred while doing something else, during a 'repetitive physical activity', such as gardening, shaving, taking a walk or taking a bath.

However, getting a correct answer is not necessarily the aim of incubation, it is more about thinking differently and creating connections that will help in progressing a problem. Also important is the way this is achieved, which is largely through distracting and often mundane activities. In a study of nine creative individuals, they all said that insights occurred during idle time, and a number of them noted that they occurred while doing something else, during a 'repetitive physical activity', such as gardening, shaving, taking a walk or taking a bath.[26]

This does not mean that there is no hard work. But this usually comes from wrestling with the problem or getting all the necessary information pertinent to the problem in one's head, before putting it to one side. The problem is then left, with no pressure for an answer. Ideas can become clearer after a short break, or it may take longer, sometimes days or even weeks. But solutions, or part solutions, come if the subconscious is given a chance. I have faced several complete dead ends in writing this book. But in many cases, after a break and sometimes just a short break, perhaps doing some exercise or sleeping on the problem, ways forward present themselves.

> Overall, no amount of luck is going to help if your mindset is wrong in the first place. As Louis Pasteur said 'Chance favours the prepared mind'.

However, results do not always come without a helping hand and sometimes even a bit of luck. Indeed, David Perkins calls this 'lucking out'. He explains the idea using Gutenberg's invention of the printing press. Gutenberg couldn't work out how to impress print onto paper. This was solved unexpectedly when he went to a wine festival where he saw the press used to squeeze grapes and realized that the principle could be used in printing.[27]

But there are other examples. Philo Farnsworth was sitting on a hillside looking at the rows created by the objects of a nearby farm. This gave him the idea of creating a picture on a cathode ray tube out of rows of light and dark dots, which led to the invention of the television. Edward Land was taking pictures of his family when his daughter asked why she couldn't see the pictures there and then. He was blessed with the ability to listen and, instead of dismissing his daughter, he conducted experiments based on this idea. The result was the polaroid camera and the development of instant photography. And if you believe the story, probably the most famous example is Newton, with his falling apple and the discovery of gravity.

You cannot do much about luck, but you can prepare yourself for luck to play a part. Overall, no amount of luck is going to help if your mindset is wrong in the first place. As Louis Pasteur said 'Chance favours the prepared mind'.

flexibility and focus

As was pointed out at the start of the chapter, decisions will be made throughout the problem-solving process. However, some decisions will be more important than others and success in problem solving depends on making good decisions at three critical points. These are when deciding what the problem is, deciding on a solution and, as a leader, deciding on how to implement it.

> 'organizational effectiveness does not lie in the narrow minded concept called "rationality"; it lies in a blend of clear-headed logic and powerful intuition'.

In order to do this optimally, two things are important, flexibility and focus. While it has been suggested that a particular problem-solving approach is often more appropriate at certain stages, making decisions at critical points is often a product of several different approaches. Henry Mintzberg argues that effective decision making, particularly at the strategic level, requires the solid analytical input of management scientists, but also the need for 'soft' information and intuitive hunches.[28] In short, 'organizational effectiveness does not lie in the narrow minded concept called "rationality"; it lies in a blend of clear-headed logic and powerful intuition'. So it is important to be flexible in the way problems are approached and how they are solved.

In addition, while all the issues and pertinent facts have to be on one's mental radar screen, in making critical decisions it is also important to focus on what is vital. Isenberg, for example, found that, in addition to thinking about broader processes, senior managers also think about how to deal with one or two overriding critical concerns.[29] Similarly, Ford argues that elite decision makers have the ability to 'lock in on the important, crucial and relevant'.[30]

An example of this overall ability to take in the relevant data, synthesize them and then focus one's actions is illustrated by George Fisher, ex-Motorola chief, when he was hired in late 1993 to help lift Kodak from its bureaucratic ways. Essentially an outsider, Fisher had to quickly ascertain what were the major strategic issues facing the world's biggest photographic company. Within six months, he and his senior managers had completed an assessment of Kodak's complex environment. They moved swiftly in deciding to sell off some of Kodak's non-photographic businesses, announced a major initiative to re-engineer the organization from top to bottom and formed a new digital-imaging group to spearhead new business development.[31] Executives like Fisher exhibit the capacity to understand a complex environment and then focus their attention on the five or six most crucial decisions. As each of these is tackled, they then distil the next handful of important issues to keep both themselves and their staff clearly focused.

conclusion

Thus, improving our thinking involves building on the core aspects of the rational problem-solving model of problem diagnosis and problem evaluation in several ways. These include ensuring that:

❶ All the pertinent factors in a situation are brought together.

❷ Those factors are sifted through and the most relevant identified. This may mean discarding some items or prioritizing others.

❸ Linkages are made between the various items. Can we group them? If a decision is made about one set of data does it affect another and if so, how?

❹ Perceptions and assumptions on which our decisions and those of others are based are questioned. This can involve rethinking even the most 'obvious' and accepted modes of operating.

❺ An assessment of the complexity of the problem is made that will influence the way we go about solving it.

❻ There are many ways to diagnose and evaluate a problem and both rational and creative techniques have their place.

❼ Ultimately, it is important to be flexible in reviewing problems but focused in making critical decisions at each stage.

Focusing on these principles will certainly enhance your problem-solving ability. However, as we noted earlier, problem solving does not occur in a vacuum. In this chapter, cognitive abilities have been emphasized, but to be fully effective in a business environment, it is necessary to understand how emotions also affect performance. This is explored in the next chapter.

references/notes

1. Janis, I.L. and Mann, L. (1977) *Decision Making: A Psychological Analysis of Conflict, Choice and Commitment* (New York: Free Press) p. 11.
2. Kearns, D.T. and Nadler, D.A. (1992) *Prophets in the Dark: How Xerox Reinvented Itself and Beat Back the Japanese* (New York: Harper Business) p. 210.
3. Nutt has used the MBTI with senior executives to understand their decision-making processes. He argues that despite a wide number of instruments developed to measure decision style, only the MBTI has both conceptual and empirical support as a decision style measure. See Nutt, P.C. (1990) 'Strategic decisions made by top executives and middle managers with data and process dominant styles', *Journal of Management Studies*, **27**(2): 173–94.
4. *'Myers-Briggs: A complete guide and questionnaires'* (2006) at www.teamtechnology.co.uk.
5. Roddick, A. (1992) *Body and Soul* (London: Vermilion) p. 23.
6. Organ, D.W. and Bateman, T. (1986) *Organizational Behaviour: An Applied Psychological Approach* (Plano: Business Publications) pp. 142–3.
7. Op. cit. Kearns and Nadler (1992) p. 210.
8. 'IBM goes ballistic as PwC partners take off', *Australian Financial Review*, 12 July 2004, p. 15.
9. Cited by Polster, R. 'Escape thinking' (1996) at http://members.optusnet.com.au/ charles57/Creative/Techniques/escape.htm.
10. Quoted in Adams, J.L. (2001) *Conceptual Blockbusting: A Guide to Better Ideas* (Cambridge: Perseus Books) p. 34. Also see de Bono, E. (1990) *Lateral Thinking* (London: Penguin).
11. Dunford, R.W. (1992) *Organizational Behaviour: An Organizational Analysis Perspective* (Sydney: Addison-Wesley) p. 271.
12. Dow, D. (2000) *Westpac & the Bank of Melbourne: The Anatomy of a Bank Merger* (Melbourne: Melbourne Business School) p. 9.
13. Casey, D. (1985) 'When is a team not a team?', *Personnel Management*, January, pp. 26–30.
14. The photograph is of Henry's son.
15. One solution involves the boat crossing the river 13 times. The children cross first and the daughter returns. The father then crosses alone and gets out. The son then returns to pick up his sister, who then cross to their father who are all now on the far bank. The daughter comes back and gives the boat to her mother who crosses on her own. She gets out, and the son then returns to pick up his sister and they both cross so all the family are on the far side. However, they have to return the boat. The son gets out and his sister returns to the near bank. The fisherman then takes the boat to the far bank where the son comes back to pick up his sister and then return to the far bank. The fisherman then rows the boat back to the starting point.
16. Peters and Waterman, cited in Behling, O. and Neckel, N.L. (1991) 'Making sense out of intuition', *Academy of Management Executive*, **5**(1): 46–54.
17. Agor, W.H. (1986) 'The logic of intuition: how top executives make important decisions', *Organizational Dynamics*, **14**(3): 5–18.
18. The Mind Gym (2005) *The Mind Gym: Wake Your Mind Up* (London: Time Warner Books) pp. 268–9.
19. See Ritchy, T. 'General morphological analysis', at www.swemorph.com/ma.html.
20. de Bono, E. (2000) *Six Thinking Hats®* (London: Penguin) pp. 14–15.
21. Six Thinking Hats® was created by Edward de Bono and is copyrighted and trademarked by The McQuaig Group Inc. on his behalf. For information on professional training and certification in Six Thinking Hats®, see www.debonothinkingsystems.com.
22. Quoted in the *Australian Financial Review*, 9–12 June 2006, p. 46.
23. Perkins, D. (2001) *The Eureka Effect: the Art and Logic of Breakthrough Thinking* (New York: W. W. Norton) pp. 10–11.
24. The answer will probably come when looking at a calendar, as the answer lies in the number of days in each month, starting with February and assuming the year is a leap year. Putting the numbers into pairs also helps. The next three numbers are 031 – 0 for the last number of the days in June and 31 for the number of days in July.
25. 'Brainteasers', at http://hlavolamy.szm.sk/brainteasers/einsteins-riddles.htm.
26. Csikszentmihalyi, M. and Sawyer, K. (1995) 'Creative insight: the social dimension of a solitary moment', in R. Steinberg and J. Davidson (eds) *The Nature of Insight* (Cambridge: MIT Press) p. 348.

27. Op. cit. Perkins, 2001, p. 45.
28. Mintzberg, H. (1976) 'Planning on the left side and managing on the right', *Harvard Business Review*, **54**(4): 49–58.
29. Isenberg, D.J. (1984) 'How senior managers think', *Harvard Business Review*, **62**(6): 80–90.
30. Ford, C.H. (1977) 'The "elite" decision makers: what makes them tick', *Human Resource Management*, **16**(4): 14–20.
31. 'Picture imperfect', *The Economist*, 28 May 1994, pp. 59–60.

5 developing an emotional capability

Emotions can help to sustain performance at high levels, drive us to overcome the most daunting hurdles and develop creative responses we may never have thought possible. They can also have an unfavourable impact, particularly on our ability to make good decisions and operate effectively. Therefore, learning how to recognize, understand and respond to our own and others' emotional responses is critical in order to get through the MBA and to manage successfully in the future. However, this capability is unlikely to get much airtime on a management programme. Despite the extent to which emotion pervades our lives, a discussion of the subject is more frequently seen as an aberration to be ignored rather than embraced.

One of the reasons for this is because emotions are sometimes difficult to predict and hard to understand. They can arise from a multitude of circumstances and can be interpreted in many different ways. What may be cool-headed forcefulness to one person may be interpreted by others as barely contained anger. Indeed, often we may not even be able to label our emotions, which can be a concoction of feelings driven by our traits, past experiences and current hopes and fears.

Nevertheless, despite their complexity, it is critical that attempts are made to understand their impact. They are an essential part of creative problem solving and developing long-term objectives. They affect our motivation, work performance and commitment. They play an important role when it comes to leading and managing others. An ability to keep calm in difficult situations, to show passion in advocating an important proposal and to understand the emotional responses of colleagues are qualities needed in most work environments. On an MBA, they can have a more immediate impact. As one student commented:

I feel my attitude and emotional responses have been hindering my ability to learn. There is no doubt that my fear of taking risks, my worry about what others will think, and an emotional dread of taking feedback have prevented me from developing.

This chapter explores some of these issues. While the space is not available to review all aspects of work-based emotion, two topics in particular are covered here. The first is stress, increasingly found in many occupations and not unusual on an MBA. The second is in coping with conflict, often emotionally charged, and important in dealing with others. However, before exploring these issues, it is worth providing a general understanding of emotions and their implication in the work environment and on an MBA programme.

understanding emotions

the nature of emotions

Emotional competence has long been seen by Edgar Schein, an eminent management guru, as one of three basic qualities for managing effectively.[1] But emotions are complex. Robert Plutchik argues that the subject is one of the most confused areas in psychology, with more than 90 definitions of 'emotion' having appeared in the last century. However, there is agreement on a distinction between primary and secondary emotions. Primary emotions include joy, sadness, acceptance, disgust, fear, anger, expectation and surprise, while secondary emotions are a combination of these.[2]

Emotions have a genetic base. Two traits, *positive affectivity* (PA) and *negative affectivity* (NA), predict general emotional tendencies in people. If you are high on positive affectivity, you tend to be lively, sociable and often in a positive mood. If you are high on negative affectivity, you tend to be unhappy, possibly distressed at times, and focus on negative outcomes.[3] These tendencies can influence the work environment. If you are positive at work, you are more likely to be rewarded for good performance by your manager.[4] Highly positive people are seen as better leaders, have higher management potential and are more satisfied with their work and their life.[5]

However, it is wrong to conclude from this that having these traits condemns us either to a life of despondency or to one of continual elation. A high affective trait predisposes us to experience higher levels of emotional intensity under certain conditions. Someone with high NA is more likely to react more strongly to negative events when they happen, but feel relatively calm in their absence. For example, a research study showed that teachers high on NA placed in a stressful environment experienced more stress than teachers low in NA. However, in less stressful environments, stress levels were similar, regardless of the teachers' level of NA.[6] Medical students prone to negativity suffered from stress in the weeks before an exam. But, at other times, their level of negativity was the same as their colleagues.[7] Similarly, one of our students commented:

I have found that, generally, negative attitudes tend to surface when I am tired or under a significant amount of pressure from my studies. Once my workload has been drastically reduced and I have an entire week's holiday, I realize that I enjoy the challenge and excitement of my job and like the people I work with.

This is an important point in dealing with emotions. While our traits predispose us to react with different degrees of emotional intensity, it is the event that is critical. As Nico Frijda[8] points out: 'Emotions have an object, they are about something ... One is happy about something, angry at someone, afraid of something.' Thus, we are not passive emotional recipients of whatever happens around us, but can manage circumstances and events to our own and others' benefit if we understand how we are likely to respond in various situations.

managing emotions

An event-focused approach to managing emotions involves identifying the event that gives rise to an affective response and working out a strategy to deal with it. There are many emotionally challenging events on an MBA, from meeting deadlines through to syndicate discussions, that can be dealt with by changing the event or circumstances that cause the problem. Potential solutions to such situations are discussed below and in other parts of the book. However, in addition to this external approach, emotions can also be managed by focusing on our personal internal response. Anger management is not just a topic for popular films, but something that we can do something about.

emotional intelligence

The idea that we can do more to manage our emotions is one that underlies the concept of emotional intelligence (EI). The EI movement has probably done more than any other set of ideas to make it acceptable to explore how emotions manifest themselves in the workplace and their personal implications.

In general, EI is concerned with internal self-awareness and regulation and external empathy and interpersonal skills. The emphasis is on managing emotions intelligently. The concept has been introduced into companies ranging from American Express to Woodside Petroleum. The *Harvard Business Review* article by Goleman, linking EI to leadership, is among the most requested reprints in the journal's history.[9]

Having high levels of EI can be useful in interviewing and selection processes, career development, staff appraisal and coaching, and managing diversity. David Poole suggests that Ernest Shackleton, the great Antarctic explorer, had considerable emotional intelligence (see Box 5.1).[10] Although very few of us will experience the kinds of challenges Shackleton did, his personal approach and the way he managed others are a good example of the mental resilience that may be needed to get through challenging experiences.

BOX 5.1 Ernest Shackleton in the Antarctic

The great explorer Sir Ernest Shackleton appears to have possessed considerable quantities of EI. During the 1914–16 *Endurance* expedition, Shackleton led a team whose aim was to travel 3,000 kilometres across the Antarctic on foot. Unfortunately, Shackleton's ship *Endurance* was stuck fast in polar ice just a day's sail from its destination, coming to rest some 2,000 kilometres from the nearest sign of civilization.

Pack ice dragged the ship for 10 months and then crushed it completely as the crew watched helplessly from their tents pitched on nearby ice. They lived in winter darkness for four months before the Antarctic summer arrived, but the thawing of the ice forced Shackleton and his men to sail for a week aboard three small lifeboats to a stinking, manure-covered island, where they lived, huddling under their upturned lifeboats. Shackleton later took five men and a lifeboat and sailed a further 1,300 kilometres to a whaling station, first crossing a frozen mountain range to get there. He immediately turned back and led a rescue operation to retrieve his men.

Unlike most of the other early twentieth-century Antarctic explorers, Shackleton did not lose a single man. A born optimist, Shackleton believed that the creature comforts of his men were critical; he gave them meaningful work to do during the long periods of boredom; he selected the crew carefully; he believed in providing a healthy diet and exercise, and keeping up the morale and spirits of his men. Even when things were at their toughest, he would celebrate the good work of his men and their ability to survive. Shackleton's approach was summarized in his famous saying, 'better a live donkey than a dead lion'.

Fundamentally, the message of EI is that the ability to understand emotions and their potential impact is within the grasp of everyone. While traits may predispose us to react in certain ways, there is much we can do to manage the situations we find ourselves in and cope better with affective responses.

This is particularly important in dealing with stress and conflict. Neither are certainties on an MBA programme, but they are common experiences. A better understanding of the nature of stress and conflict and your potential responses to them can make a significant difference in managing their impact. First we will explore these issues in relation to stress.

understanding stress

the nature and consequences of stress

Stress can be interpreted in several different ways, but typically it is seen as an abnormal reaction to accumulated pressures. Not all pressure is bad. As one student commented:

I have personally found times when being under pressure from impending deadlines does raise my effectiveness and overall ability to produce results.

Many people need added pressure to perform effectively. But pressure can have negative consequences. The same student continued:

However, I have also experienced occasions when prolonged pressure 'builds up' and my motivation wanes. I recall times when I have sat in front of my computer and, feeling completely overwhelmed by stress, have simply 'stared through' the screen … wondering what on earth I am going to do next.

Indeed, many of the negative outcomes of pressure and stress are costly. In the UK, 40 million working days are lost each year due to stress-related disorders. A survey of EU member states found that 28% of employees (41 million workers) reported stress-related illness or health problems and in the US it is estimated that over half the 550 million working days lost each year due to absenteeism are stress related.[11]

At an individual level, symptoms of stress include an inability to concentrate, headaches, backaches, anger, anxiety, depression, nervousness, fatigue and irritability, as well as major illnesses such as ulcers, high blood pressure, heart attacks and possibly even cancer. At an organizational level, they can lead to high absenteeism, high labour turnover and industrial accidents (Figure 5.1).[12]

Some aspects of the MBA environment can potentially cause considerable stress and hence influence success on the programme. High stress levels can affect the ability to learn new things and to concentrate. Stress also impedes one's ability to listen, make good decisions, solve problems effectively, and plan and generate new ideas.[13] Indeed, it can dull our capacity to realize when we ourselves are under stress. This and the need to understand stress better is highlighted by the following student comment:

I found myself sitting in the waiting room of the local GP, sweating profusely and shaking all over. I had absolutely no idea what was happening, but as I discussed things with the doctor, an emerging picture began to develop. I had been under a great deal of stress in the previous six months. While a new personal relationship contributed significantly to my situation, increasing long and demanding hours at work, coupled with part-time MBA studies, also placed excessive strain on both my physical and mental fitness. While I had an intuitive understanding of my problem, an unwillingness to actively address the causes meant I remained unable to construct any meaningful plan for remedying the situation.

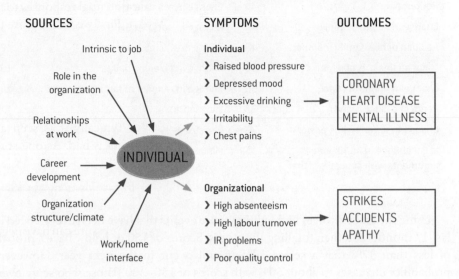

Figure 5.1 *Sources and symptoms of stress*

causes of stress

Different events have different consequences as illustrated by the social readjustment rating scale developed by Thomas Holmes and Richard Rahe (Box 5.2).[14] They found that some changes are more stressful than others and produced a scale which assigns different levels of importance to each event. Clearly there are differences between individuals, but in general the relative weightings of each event hold true regardless of culture, age or occupation.

BOX 5.2 Holmes and Rahe's social readjustment rating scale

Life event	Mean value	Life event	Mean value
Death of spouse	100	Taking on a large mortgage/loan	31
Divorce	73	Change in work responsibilities	29
Marital separation	65	Trouble with the in-laws	29
Detention in jail/institution	63	Outstanding personal achievement	28
Death of close family member	63	Starting/leaving school	26
Major personal injury/illness	53	Major change in living conditions	25
Marriage	50	Revision of personal habits	24
Being fired	47	Trouble with boss	23

Life event	Mean value	Life event	Mean value
Marital reconciliation	45	Change in working conditions	20
Retirement	45	Change in residence	20
Change in health of family	44	Change in social activity	18
Addition of new family member	40	Taking on a bank loan	17
Major business problems	39	Change in sleeping habits	16
Change in financial state	38	Change in number of family reunions	15
Death of a close friend	37	Vacation	13
Change to different line of work	36	Christmas	12
Major change in number of arguments with spouse/partner	35	Minor violations of the law	11

Using the scale involves highlighting those events that have been experienced in the last 12 months and then totalling the scores. Scores of 150 or below have a probability of less than 37% that a serious illness will occur in the next year. However, the probability increases to about 50% with scores of 150–300. Those who score over 300 have an 80% chance of serious illness.[15] Research indicates a significant relationship between having high scores, and illness and injury among the population in general,[16] and a range of different groups, including managers.[17]

personality and stress

A high score does not definitely mean that a major injury or illness is just around the corner. This depends on a range of factors including one's personality and ability to manage these events. The most commonly used model to explain the relationship between personality and stress is the type A and type B typology developed by Meyer Friedman and Ray Rosenman.

Some of the characteristics of the two types are listed in Box 5.3. Friedman and Rosenman's studies found that a type A profile correlated highly with many of the unhealthy consequences of stress. Although this varies between individuals, the kinds of behaviours exhibited by type A personalities are more likely to have a negative impact on well-being. In particular, anger, impatience, hostility, competitiveness and feelings of urgency have been seen to be particularly conducive to producing potentially harmful outcomes.[18]

However, as with positive and negative affectivity, these types only *predispose* us to react in certain ways. In a study of senior executives, Charles Cox and Cary Cooper found a predominance of type A personalities. But the executives also tended to avoid stress by developing good coping mechanisms.[19] Knowing our personality type helps us to better manage stressful situations, rather than condemning us to negative experiences.

BOX 5.3 **Type A and B characteristics**

Type A	Type B
Competitive	Relaxed
Achiever	Easy-going
Aggressive	Seldom impatient
Fast worker	Takes more time for hobbies
Feels under pressure	Not easily irritated
Restless	Works steadily
Hyper-alert	Seldom lacks time
Explosive of speech	Moves and speaks slower
Tense facial muscles	

situational stressors

The events listed in Box 5.2 above are often described in terms of situational stressors (arising from the environment) and social stressors (having to deal with people). Situational stress is a product of unfavourable working conditions, including a lack of time, long working hours, lack of control and lack of resources.

Some of these are particularly relevant to MBA programmes. Time pressure and meeting deadlines are two of the most common causes of stress for MBA students and managers alike. Many MBA programmes (either intentionally or otherwise) involve an overwhelming amount of work. This in itself is not necessarily a problem and indeed pressure can be motivating, as mentioned earlier. It is when constant deadlines have to be met (for example assignments), the deadlines are important (miss one and it affects a grade) and the pressure continues for some time (12 months and beyond) that stressful symptoms are most likely. As one student commented:

As an IT professional from one of the world's fastest growing economies, I have invariably encountered stress in my personal and professional life alike. When I started working I used to relish tight deadlines as it gave my ego the kick that was needed. However, over a period of time, especially after proving myself under strenuous conditions, my productivity declined and I was getting more frustrated and unhappy. It was also affecting my personal life and I was unable to spend qualitative time with my loved ones. Further, I used to get irritated and lose my temper, resulting in increased worries and fear. What made it worse was that I had got into a chain reaction where the stress was feeding my frustration.

This cumulative effect comes from the frequency, intensity and duration of potential stressful situations. Thus, long hours on a regular basis need managing. Research indicates that working for 10–15 hours a day can often lead to stress, which is not uncommon on some MBA programmes. Also important is the extent to which we feel in control of the situation. Many studies show that stress is experienced if employees have little (or no) control over their work environment. While MBA programmes often allow choice in the latter stages of the programme with elective subjects, the core subjects are usually inflexible, with relentless requirements.

Stress can also be caused not only by what we do, but also what we think might happen in the future. Anticipating events that might be uncomfortable or threatening, such as failing an exam, not getting the desired job, or losing something precious, can have a detrimental impact. Indeed, the event does not have to be overly onerous to be stressful. Quite trivial incidents can cause stress for those with high personal expectations or a desire not to 'lose face'. This fear of failure is one form of 'anticipatory stress' that frequently afflicts MBA students. Driven to succeed in almost every circumstance, the thought of missing one's footing, even only slightly, can cause enormous pressure. Thus, in terms of the environment, an MBA has many stressful possibilities.

social stressors

Few people have escaped the experience of a strong disagreement with a partner, colleague or friend and the resulting emotional after-effects. Except for purely online programmes, MBA courses are not 'people free'. Nor should they be, as the opportunity to engage with people, warts and all, is an important training ground in managing others. Moreover, even though MBA programmes tend to emphasize individual performance, students are often expected to work effectively in groups and increasingly are assessed through group assignments.

But it is not just the MBA environment that harbours social stressors. There are many lurking outside the mainstream programme. Particularly for those completing their degree part time, not only does the MBA have to be managed, but also the interpersonal environment at work. Often there is considerable stress caused by clashes between what employers want and what the business school demands. If you have a young family as well, you could be in for an emotional roller coaster.

Again, the fact that the environment is conducive to stress does not necessarily mean that an individual will have a stressful experience. But it is seriously worth thinking about it. Social stressors have significant negative effects on productivity and satisfaction and have also been identified as a major cause of burnout.[20]

managing situational stress

Before looking at ways of coping with stress, it is important to stand back and review how effective you are at managing the challenges you face currently. As one student commented:

I often respond to stress by working harder at the task, procrastinating or hoping the problem will go away by avoiding it, by losing patience, skimming detail, rubbing my forehead, bouncing my leg and clenching my shoulders! I tend to try and cope with stress by daydreaming about nice situations, by drinking with friends and sharing 'war stories' about work or by littering my desk with reminder Post-it notes. I incessantly jot appointments into my Palm-Pilot to give me comfort that things are under control. Despite this, I do not feel as though my responses to stress have ever been effective in reducing stressful situations, not do I believe that I generally cope well with stress.

Improving situations like this starts with clarifying your objectives for the MBA. These not only provide a focus for your learning, as discussed in other chapters, but help in managing stress by reducing fear of the unknown and putting issues into a manageable context. But please don't see this as a routine or straightforward exercise. As one student commented:

> As I sat in the lecture, I felt great resentment towards many of my colleagues …
> I felt as if I was the only one who had failed to set goals for myself. However, as I looked around the lecture hall, I was shocked by what I saw. The discomfort felt by a majority of students in that lecture was plain to see … although the setting of goals is regarded as an integral part of personal development, clearly, many of my colleagues were being challenged by what was being discussed. The situation reinforced something I already knew from personal experience: actively addressing aspects of self can be a complex, challenging and extremely uncomfortable task.

An overall sense of direction provides a framework within which a more detailed set of short-term plans can be developed. Short-term planning can help to reduce situational stressors, particularly time pressure. The issues related to time are discussed in Chapter 2, so they will not be revisited here. However, it is important that the infrastructure is in place for managing time. Clarifying priorities, putting in place diary techniques and setting up good study practices may take time to establish, but will provide an environment that can reduce a lot of the potential stress on the MBA.

In establishing short-term plans, try to highlight events that are likely to give rise to emotional and potentially stressful outcomes. For example, what has been your experience of exams, or the way you have worked in groups, or managed presentations and so on? In doing this, it is important to try and base your assessment on the actual evidence. If presentations are stressful, why is this? What objective feedback have you had in terms of both the strengths and weaknesses of your performance? Similarly with exams. Have you actually failed any exam or is it a general dread of the process that causes anxiety?

Where you have limited choice, as with the core course of an MBA, having good information about what is wanted can help to reduce situational stressors. It is important that you are fully aware of what is required of you for all subjects. This involves being clear about when sessions are scheduled, particularly additional sessions, what preparation is required, when and what assignments are required and what the performance expectations are. Reviewing previous exam papers may also help in reducing exam stress.

By identifying possible difficulties, fears can be reduced. A plan gives a sense of purpose and reduces anxiety by putting the activities into context. It also helps by reducing anticipatory stress and focusing the mind. As a study of CEOs found,[21] planning strategies can help in getting through difficult times by:

1. Focusing on the future through planning and goal setting.
2. Focusing on areas where constructive action is possible.
3. Recognizing the optimum time to make decisions and then acting.
4. Not making major decisions alone during a period of high uncertainty.
5. Maintaining an active and regular schedule during difficult periods.

Good information and planning can help in managing stress, but possibly more important is the way we reflect on potentially stressful situations. Indeed, some writers have summed up the overall mental approach that is needed to operate in demanding managerial environments, and arguably on an MBA, in terms of a 'hardiness disposition'.[22]

Suzanne Kobasa found that 'hardy executives' had a lower rate of stress-related illness.[23] This stemmed from three things: a feeling of involvement in what they were doing; seeing change rather than stability as normal; and feeling they could influence events around them. Overall, they viewed change, good or bad, as an opportunity for growth and an inevitable part of life's experience. Although they could not always control the changes that occurred, they could, and did, control their responses to change. Additionally, Charles Ford found that elite executive decision makers were 'positive thinkers', self-confident and tough-minded.[24]

> A tough-minded approach does make a difference in difficult circumstances.

A tough-minded approach does make a difference in difficult circumstances. Particularly in public life and at more senior levels of management, the ability to cope with media scrutiny and sometimes public criticism is a fundamental part of the job. But mental resilience can make a difference in a range of circumstances. For example, often the real difference between elite sportspeople, who have the same level of skill, is the ability to fight back from a losing position or keep their nerve until the end of the game. Whether it is the football World Cup or a Grand Slam tennis final, the difference between success and failure often depends on mental as well as physical strength. Although not as pressurized as elite sports events, demanding work environments, including business schools, also require individual mental strength.

self-talk and small wins

How do you develop mental resilience? One way is to examine your mental patterns and whether you tend to encourage self-defeating thoughts. Condemning yourself for incompetence in delivering a presentation is unlikely to take you anywhere but downwards. Replacing such self-talk with more specific and helpful assessments can make a difference, such as 'I just need to make sure I project my voice', 'Don't look down: keep eye contact with the audience', 'Whatever happens, I know I can learn from the experience' or 'I will get someone who can help me through this'. Persistence is critical when the chips are down and the MBA is a good training ground for developing this ability.

Reviewing the way we talk to ourselves can help us through immediate difficulties. Moreover, done regularly and consciously, it can form the basis of a more powerfully embedded set of thought processes that are longer lasting and protect us from stressful environments. More can be found on these issues in Chapters 2 and 7. However, it is worth noting here that on its own self-talk is usually not enough. Success has to be reinforced. One way of doing this is through 'small wins'.

A 'small wins' approach involves making small but concrete changes towards a desired outcome. Start with something that is relatively easy to change. When successful, make another small and relatively easy change. As each win mounts up, optimism increases. A sense of momentum builds and the success encourages more steps to be taken. The confidence gained from achieving one desired overall outcome gives us the strength to take on other challenges.[25]

Success through small wins also reduces fear from anticipatory stress. We feel a greater sense of control as each win reinforces the feeling that we can influence events. However, it is also important that we reward ourselves for our change attempts as well as our achievements. This is described more thoroughly in Chapter 7, but it is important that the process is reinforced. Done consistently, a small wins approach can certainly help in developing mental hardiness.[26]

It is also helps if we are in an environment where small wins and acknowledgements are liable to occur on a regular basis. For example, research shows that 'well-being' may depend more on the frequency of positive events than their intensity. An environment that gives rise to daily, although small, positive experiences is likely to provide greater overall satisfaction than one that has major, but infrequent events such as yearly awards and bonuses.[27]

visualization and rehearsal

Also helpful are rehearsal and visualization. Rehearsal involves walking yourself through a potentially stressful situation and trying out different scenarios and alternative reactions in a safe environment. Working through the situation and potential reactions can help an individual regain control and reduce the immediacy of the stressor.

Visualization is a similar mental process. The technique has long been used by athletes, for example, to visualize themselves performing a high jump, pole vault or running a race. In this case, the emphasis is on the correct way of performing the act, rather than looking for any pitfalls or challenges in the performance. Mental preparation of this kind increases the chance of success. In fact, research suggests that effective visualization helps with goal achievement in all aspects of life, while poor visualization reduces success.[28]

Desensitization, another mental technique aimed at reducing stress through mental imagery, is a little more involved. The process entails thinking about a scenario, breaking it down into stages and imagining what success feels like at each stage. For example, in giving a speech to a large audience, we first imagine presenting to a colleague. If this is manageable, we then imagine presenting to a small group. If this is stressful, however, positive self-talk is used to help us relax to reduce the stress. By working with the image and calming ourselves when we feel tense, we become less sensitive to the situation. When we feel comfortable in presenting to the small group, we can then move up to imagine more challenging situations.

An example of using these different mental approaches to overcome a potentially stressful situation is described in Box 5.4.[29] This also illustrates that the use of several techniques is more likely to pay dividends than any one technique alone.

physiological approaches

Box 5.4 suggests that in addition to our mental approach, stress is also affected by our ability to reduce physical tension and our overall physical state. Sometimes we fail to pay enough attention to these factors. As one student noted:

As I reflected on my own state of disrepair, I realized how easy it is to neglect one's physical well-being. I had placed work, university and other social commitments before my own physical well-being, and was suffering the consequences. I was constantly tired, lethargic, and lacked a general enthusiasm for life … I realized two things: first I had neglected one of the most important aspects of well-being: physical fitness. Second, physical fitness is inextricably linked to overall emotional well-being.

There is overwhelming evidence that physical condition affects an individual's ability to cope with stress. Two areas are particularly important – diet and exercise, and relaxation.

diet and exercise

Most people are well informed about healthy foods and eating habits, but on a busy management programme, these may be ignored. The key principles are:[30]

❶ Eat a variety of foods, maintain optimal weight, eat sufficient whole foods and consider vitamin and mineral supplements.

❷ Avoid excessive quantities of fats, sugar, sodium, alcohol and caffeine (which, ironically, given its use by many students to help study for longer to reduce exam anxiety, is a stimulant that exacerbates stress).

It is unclear whether exercise directly reduces the likelihood of heart problems, but it certainly helps in coping with stress, either through the physical benefits of exercise or as a result of using exercise as a mental distraction to stressful situations. Regular exercise helps to increase psychological well-being and improve the cardiovascular system. It increases self-esteem and helps with depression. It also makes individuals less prone to anxiety, less susceptible to illness and reduces work absenteeism.[31]

Improving the cardiovascular system can be achieved through brisk walking, jogging, cycling or climbing the stairs. So long as the target heart rate is sustained throughout the exercise and the exercise occurs for 20–30 minutes, three or four days per week, then improvement occurs. Since cardiovascular endurance decreases after 48 hours, it is important to exercise at least every second day.

relaxation

Relaxation can help in both eliminating short-term stressful situations and managing longer term challenges. There are many ways to relax, ranging from reading a good magazine or watching television, through to more demanding relaxation techniques such as meditation. Many writers advocate a balance of activities across cultural, spiritual and general entertainment pursuits as a means of managing stress. These also include breaks and holidays. On the MBA, there may be fewer opportunities to pursue these on a regular basis. However, as pointed out in Chapter 2, despite the potential pressure of the programme, it is still important to devote some time to other pursuits. This is not only to alleviate stress, but also to ensure that, in gaining a degree, you don't lose your life. Friends, social groups, sporting skills, fitness and so on are unlikely to stay neatly on hold for us while we complete our educational programme. As one student said:

If I knew then what I know now about the MBA, I would not have given up sailing. The only time I ever felt truly at peace and at one with myself was when I was in a boat. But at the start of the MBA, I saw it as a luxury. I now realize how much my hobby anchored me – literally, physically and mentally.

Deeper relaxation techniques such as meditation, yoga, self-hypnosis and biofeedback take time to develop and the results may not be immediate. Nevertheless, if practised regularly, the long-term benefits in reducing the negative effects of stress can be considerable.[32]

Deep relaxation techniques have to be practised over a period of time to develop fully, but they are not difficult to learn. Most involve the following conditions:[33]

❶ A quiet environment with minimal external distractions.

❷ A comfortable position to reduce muscular effort.

❸ A mental focus – a word, phrase or object. Focusing on a word or object helps to rid the mind of all other thoughts.

❹ Controlled breathing with pauses between breaths. Thoughts are focused on rhythmic breathing, which helps to clear the mind and aids concentration.

❺ A passive attitude, so that if other thoughts enter the mind, they are ignored.

❻ Repetition, as both physiological and psychological results depend on consistent practice. The best results occur when such techniques are practised for 20–30 minutes a day.

Muscle relaxation involves systematically reducing the tension in each muscle. A muscle group is tightened for about 10 seconds and then completely relaxed. Starting with the feet and progressing to the calves, thighs, stomach up to the neck and face, one can relieve tension throughout the entire body. All parts of the body can be included in the exercise.

Thus, there are many ways to manage stress. How you do this is your choice. But it is a choice and one that should not be ignored. As one student commented:

The implication of thinking about these things for myself is primarily as a wake-up call. This has energized me to review my current behaviours and implement proactive stress prevention strategies. Stress, I feel, can be managed if I make a conscious effort in that direction. I understand that although stress at times cannot be prevented, its effect can be minimized if I can prioritize activities, maintain a balanced professional and personal life, and accept my limitations. I strongly believe that I must enjoy the small milestones that I conquer.

BOX 5.5 Stress Management Plan

Date plan made _____   Review date(s) _____

Personal perceptions of stress
- Recognize stressors   1 _____
- Understand self-talk patterns   2 _____
- Identify type A behaviours   3 _____
- Assess hardiness   4 _____

Work/school environment
- Conducive work space   1 _____
- Time management   2 _____
- Overload strategy   3 _____

Lifestyle choices
- Work/life balance   1 _____
- Leisure time use   2 _____
- Social support   3 _____

Relaxation
- Traditional methods   1 _____
- Deep relaxation   2 _____
- Meditation/yoga   3 _____

Physical outlets
- Aerobic exercise   1 _____
- Recreational sports   2 _____
- Gym/systematic training   3 _____

Emotional/spiritual paths
- Talking with others   1 _____
- Talking with religious guides   2 _____
- Prayer   3 _____

Professional help
- Counselling   1 _____
- Medical assistance   2 _____
- Psychotherapy   3 _____

Box 5.5[34] summarizes some of the major areas discussed above. It may also help in developing a stress management plan. First identify those approaches in the left-hand column that may work for you. The right-hand column can then be used to itemize some specific action items that are relevant and helpful. The plan should be ongoing and reviewed from time to time. But just completing the plan once may help in thinking about the issues and possible solutions. It is not the plan in itself that is important, but what you do to improve on the stressful circumstances.

managing conflict and social stress

Poor interpersonal relationships and particularly conflict are also a major source of stress. While conflict does not characterize all social interactions by any means, a quick glance through any newspaper will highlight its pervasiveness. Conflict is a natural part of life and exists in politics, work organizations and in our personal lives. It is a major problem for managers due to the interpersonal nature of the managerial role.

On an MBA programme, it is most likely to occur in syndicate groups. Although syndicate work can be great fun and provide many positive learning experiences, there is always the potential for conflict. Conflict can arise from unclear role responsibilities, disagreements over the aims of the group, group processes or the way members interact. Throw in a few assessed group assignments with some tight deadlines and the result can be a potent brew.

However, while conflict is fairly common, the ability to deal with it is less widespread. The emotional feelings of frustration, hostility, anger and the potential stress that conflict generates often make it a difficult subject to tackle. But it is important to have some understanding of how to manage conflict effectively, as the following comment illustrates:

I reflected on those events that had stood out ... most of these situations inherently involved some level of conflict. For example, for many years, my work in product development has necessitated frequent struggles between my production staff and their priorities on one side, and marketing personnel and their often very different priorities on the other, with my staff and myself trying to find the balance in between. I felt it was partly this conflict, and my lack of skills and confidence to handle it effectively, that were hampering my overall influencing capability. I knew that these would be skills that I would continue to need for the rest of my working and personal life – that having them would help me to feel more confident and capable as a manager.

Conflict arises from the pursuit of incompatible goals. Not all conflict is negative. Conflict can motivate us to find different solutions, review problem solving approaches and improve our bargaining techniques. However, conflict is more often associated with undesirable outcomes. It can give rise to stress, disruptive behaviour and use up large amounts of time in resolution attempts.

The causes of conflict are usually categorized into two main areas. One is 'substantive conflict', which arises from disagreements over external factors like the distribution of rewards, allocation of resources, time frames, overlapping responsibilities and different goals. The other is 'personal conflict', which arises from internal personality differences and perceptions. This includes different attitudes, values and beliefs, feelings about what is right and wrong and different personal styles. If you are an intense type A achiever and you have to work with a more easy-going type B colleague, it is probable that you will have different views about how a task should be achieved and conflict is highly likely.

Both types of conflict involve emotions, but emotional responses are usually greater with personal conflict. However, the two overlap and it is not unusual to find personal antagonism expressed through substantive issues. If you are arguing over something that seems trivial, it is probable that there are additional personal issues involved. Moreover, conflict is more likely in ambiguous situations that contribute to misperceptions and incorrect judgements.

Ambiguous situations, however, are not the only thing that can exacerbate conflict. Ambiguous behaviour can also be an issue. Although shouting and heated arguments may be unpleasant, at least you know there is a problem. Often the signs that conflict exists are expressed through missed meetings, blocked projects or sniping behind an individual's back, which makes it much harder to deal with. As one student commented:

If I have to face a difficult confrontation, I will try to put it off for as long as possible. Even if there is little more than a chance that I will face conflict, based on my past interactions with an individual, I will do all that I can to avoid the individual concerned … I've come to understand that avoidance is not the answer.

Indeed, avoidance can result in no one benefiting, illustrated by the Abilene paradox in Box 5.6.[35]

BOX 5.6 The Abilene paradox

The paradox was suggested by Jerry Harvey as a result of his experiences on a trip to Abilene. Sitting together on a very hot (104°F) Sunday afternoon, Jerry's father-in-law suggested that the family, who were at that point quite relaxed, all travel to Abilene to have dinner. This would involve a round trip of over four hours in a car without air conditioning. The family set off across the desert in blasting temperatures, to eat an unpalatable meal, only to return home exhausted. What was significant about the event was that nobody in the family wanted to go in the first place, even Jerry's father-in-law. They had assumed that each of the others wanted to go. Nobody had raised doubts about the journey because they wanted to keep the others happy. In fact, everyone had done exactly the opposite of what they really wanted to do.

While not 'rocking the boat' may have the short-term advantage of keeping everyone happy, the longer term consequences need to be thought through. The key White House staff involved in the Watergate scandal all agreed later that the plan to burgle the White House was inappropriate, but implemented it despite their misgivings. The downfall of a US president is quite a long-term consequence. Thus, it is important to recognize that the ability to voice one's concerns in a productive way is an important skill in dealing with conflict situations.

diagnosing conflict

Whether manifest or not, thinking about the possible preconditions that might give rise to conflict can at least prepare you for potential difficulties. For example, a syndicate group with strong personalities, different ways of working and faced with tough deadlines has all the hallmarks of a potential conflict situation.

If faced with conflict, it is important to try and map out some of the key issues. First, establish what is causing the conflict. Conflict arising from substantive issues such as scarce resources or data is usually easier to solve than personal conflict stemming from issues of principle or personal style. As one student noted:

I have found that when conflict moves from task-based issues (revolving around an activity or object) to personal-based issues (such as personality or cultural differences) positive outcomes can be much harder to achieve. It becomes important then to have the right attitude and skills to avoid these negatives and increase the chance of a positive outcome.

Next consider the contextual factors. Are there aspects of the environment that need a particular focus? For example, different cultures deal with conflict in different ways and understanding this is important not only in diagnosing the conflict, but also resolving it. If individuals have to maintain an ongoing relationship, then how the conflict is dealt with has longer term consequences. Moreover, resolving conflict between peers is often harder than if the group has a clear leader, unless, of course, it is the 'leader' who is the problem.

resolving conflict

Two areas are usually emphasized when looking at ways of resolving conflict. One is through the procedures and controls that can be used to manage disagreements. These include formal dispute procedures, agreements on the conditions for discussing certain topics and by reducing interaction between individuals. The other is through behavioural approaches. On an MBA, conflict resolution often depends more on having the appropriate skills than in establishing structural solutions. Consequently, we will concentrate on behavioural responses.

However, before pursuing any of the skills presented below, it is worth standing back and making an assessment of how difficult the conflict may be to resolve and consequently what conflict resolution approach might be beneficial. This is not easy if you are part of the conflict situation. However, try to distance yourself emotionally. You need to understand who is involved, what the issues are and what everyone's needs and concerns are before considering an appropriate resolution style. A process like this can clarify the extent to which the disagreements are personal or substantive. The process can also clarify misperceptions and reduce the personal element of the conflict.

Interpersonal skills development is dealt with in more detail in the next chapter. But good interpersonal skills are important in managing social stress and so conflict resolution skills are worth discussing here. Kenneth Thomas and Ralph Kilmann's conflict model describes five of the major skill styles. Figure 5.2 illustrates these styles.[36] It contrasts an emphasis on getting one's own way (concern for self) against allowing others to get theirs (a concern for others). A brief explanation of each style is given below.

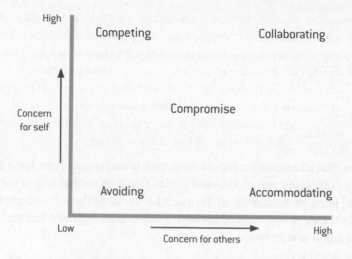

Figure 5.2   Thomas–Kilmann conflict handling styles

avoiding

Avoiding, positioned in the bottom left-hand corner of Figure 5.2, is a strategy where neither your goals nor the goals of others are being satisfied. As mentioned earlier, avoidance can have dire consequences if important issues are not addressed. However, avoiding has some benefits. Not every issue is important and therefore worth getting involved in. Sometimes withdrawing until a better time presents itself can be more effective than fighting against the odds. Moreover, the pain and effort involved in resolving some conflicts may outweigh any benefits and warrant avoidance. It is when avoiding becomes your preferred style that other approaches need to be considered.

competing

Competing is a style aimed at achieving your goals at the expense of others. This style involves using whatever you have at your disposal to win. It could be an ability to argue, a forceful personality or control over resources. With MBA colleagues, it may be a style that could be used effectively in emergency situations, for example when a group cannot agree and there is an imminent deadline. However, it is not a style that works effectively if used on a regular basis, particularly with peers. Pushing your own agenda is a long-term strategy that is unlikely to bring anyone with you and if anything leads to increased conflict.

At the other end of the spectrum is accommodating, a style where the individual forgoes their own concerns, for the concerns of others. This style has an element of self-sacrifice and resolves conflict by giving in or giving something up. There are positive aspects of this style. Never giving in or yielding a point or position is likely to give others the impression that you are inflexible, which can stop discussion before it even starts. Often by giving in on smaller issues, progress can be made later or on more important issues. However, accommodating on a regular basis means that others are obtaining their objectives at the expense of your own. As a manager this is untenable.

compromise

The aim of compromise is to find a mutually acceptable solution that partly satisfies both you and others. It is halfway between competing and accommodating, giving everyone an outcome they can live with, rather than feeling someone has been beaten. You usually lose something when you compromise, but not enough to feel none of your objectives have been met.

While the style can result in 'splitting the difference', it often involves a degree of negotiation. Thus, both parties do engage in communication and sharing views. It is also typified by exchanging concessions, but the style emphasizes tactics and bargaining, rather than joint problem solving. Thus, while good for short-term solutions, used on a regular basis, it may mean that the fundamental issues driving the conflict are never resolved. It is good in seeking a middle ground position, but the danger is that it produces a superficial result rather than one with any lasting outcomes.

collaborating

Collaborating involves an attempt to work with the other person to find a solution that substantially satisfies the needs of both. This does not mean that everyone will necessarily completely meet their objectives. But it does mean that by exploring an issue to identify the underlying concerns and possible solutions, a greater outcome than would be obtained by compromise is possible. In some cases, the outcomes may be even greater than expectations, but this requires considerable skill, willingness and patience in trying to explore the issues.

Collaboration is a communication and influence process that requires sharing views about the conflict, confronting the differences between the people involved, identifying options for resolving these differences and developing an outcome beneficial to all. Described like this, it sounds straightforward, but collaboration is far from emotion free and requires management of the emotional content to be successful. Even if the conflict is centred on substantive issues, there will be emotions that have to be dealt with. This is not easy, as the following student comment indicates:

Several of us were uncomfortable with the way the meeting had gone so far. However, instead of expressing our concerns, we merely resorted to joking, cynicism and procrastination ... But one more selfish comment became the 'final straw' for the team that day and several got angry. Everyone then put their cards on the table and we began to discuss how much latitude we were going to grant each other ... We tried to stick to the issues, but frustration regularly showed through. But we got through and after we had discussed it, it had the effect of making constructive disagreement 'OK' for future meetings.

Consequently, space should be provided for people to express their feelings about the conflict situation. Indeed, in some cases, it is not until people have 'got things off their chest' that they are ready to move on and address the substantive issues. A way of doing this is to reflect back the feelings that have been expressed. For example, if another person says that they're sick and tired of you not pulling your weight in group projects, your response should not be to launch into a tirade of their inadequacies. A more appropriate response would be to reflect back their feelings by saying 'You're obviously angry about the way I have been working with the group. Is that so?' This may be difficult to do from an emotional viewpoint, but if you are serious about trying to find out what is happening you have to be prepared to explore the issues empathetically.

Empathy is crucial in conflict resolution. It means stepping into the other person's shoes and seeing the conflict situation through their eyes. This is why trying to paraphrase what the person has said and reflecting back their feelings is important. This does not mean that you have to completely agree with everything they say. The idea is to get the other person to say what is troubling them and for you to listen. Your aim is to identify as objectively as you can where they are coming from and their issues and then explore how the current situation could be changed. No, it's not easy. But if you can develop this skill, it will be invaluable in the future.

Also, do not forget the possibility of getting someone to mediate. In general, the involvement of third parties increases the chance of a negotiated outcome. This is because they are likely to see the situation more objectively as their emotional involvement will be less. Moreover, never see asking for this kind of help as 'failure'. Even some of the most skilled counsellors will ask for assistance from a third party when they are embroiled in their own personal conflict. Indeed, one of their skills is also in appreciating their own strength and limitations both in terms of their skill set and their emotional competence.

Finally, remember that, as with all the personal competencies, development is not an overnight experience. As one student commented:

I realize this is not the end of the journey – I feel that I have a long way to go before I reach the ideal I have set myself ... some of the things that I would like to keep working on ... include developing more assertiveness, understanding my sources of power and preparing for conflict beforehand so I know what I want and I don't get 'thrown' by the other party's comments or actions.

conclusion

As the last comment suggests, developing an emotional competency can sometimes be a lifelong quest. This chapter has focused on stress and conflict and clearly there is more to developing an emotional competency than these two aspects alone. Nevertheless, the chapter is a starting point in understanding the impact that emotions can have. They can influence not only performance on the MBA and at work, but also affect our overall well-being. Understanding the consequences and possible sources of stress, and the need for different approaches to managing stress can reduce their negative impact and help us to understand how to manage our emotions personally. Understanding how conflict arises and how we might deal with it can also help us to understand and manage our emotions in social situations.

If there is one aspect worth emphasizing in developing an emotional competency, it is the need for mental resilience. How you develop this is your choice and will fit your own personality and style. Whether you take an optimistic mental approach to life, develop the ability to turn worries into problems, ensure you are decisive, continually give yourself recognition, savour achievement, always look for something to enjoy each day, or all these things, the need to have emotional strength is critical. Even if you do not naturally take an optimistic view to life, you can still make choices and take actions that alter the odds in your emotional favour. Separating out issues, biting off what you can chew and then working at them systematically can turn an overwhelming situation into a manageable one. Staying focused on the end game can stop you being sidetracked by peripheral and unnecessary worries. You can manage these situations, no matter how difficult they may look at first.

This is particularly important if you intend leading others. If you can't keep yourself on an emotional even keel, the challenge of helping others to do the same is that much greater. If good habits and effective methods of dealing with the pressures of the programme can be developed now, those behaviours and ways of thinking will be truly beneficial after graduation.

references

1. Schein, E.H. (1993) *Career Anchors: Discovering your Real Values* (San Francisco: Jossey-Bass).
2. Plutchik, R. (1994) *The Psychology and Biology of Emotion* (New York: HarperCollins).
3. Weiss, H.M. and Cropanzano, R. (1996) 'Affective events theory: a theoretical discussion of the structure, causes and consequences of affective experiences at work', in B.M. Staw and L.L. Cummings (eds) *Research in Organizational Behaviour*, **18**: 1–74.
4. George, J.M. (1995) 'Leader positive mood and group performance: the case of customer service', *Journal of Applied Psychology*, **25**(9): 778–95.
5. Tosi, H.L., Mero, N.P. and Rizzo J.R. (2000) *Managing Organizational Behaviour* (Malden: Blackwell) p. 44.
6. Parkes, K.R. (1990) 'Coping, negative affectivity and the work environment: additive and interactive predictors of mental health', *Journal of Applied Psychology*, **75**: 399–409.
7. Bolger, N. (1990) 'Coping as a personality process', *Journal of Personality and Social Psychology*, **59**: 525–37.
8. Frijda, N.H., ' Moods, Emotion Episodes and Emotions', in M. Lewis and J.M. Haviland (eds) *Handbook of Emotions* (New York: Guildford Press, 1993) p. 381.
9. Poole, D. 'Managing emotional intelligence', in P. Murray, D. Poole and G. Jones (eds) (2006) *Contemporary Issues in Management and Organizational Behaviour* (Melbourne: Thomson) p. 341.
10. Adapted by Poole, D. from Morrell, M. and Capparell, S. (2001) *Shackleton's Way* (London: Nicholas Brealey); Poole, D. 'Managing emotional intelligence', in P. Murray, D. Poole and G. Jones (eds) (2006) *Contemporary Issues in Management and Organisational Behaviour* (Melbourne: Thomson) p. 347.
11. 'What is workplace stress?', *International Labour Organization*, at www.ilo.org, March 2006.
12. Adapted from Cooper, C.L. and Marshall, J. (1976) 'Occupational sources of stress: a review of the literature relating to coronary heart disease and mental ill health', *Journal of Occupational Psychology*, **49**:12.
13. Carlopio, J., Andrewartha, G. and Armstrong, H. (1997) *Developing Management Skills* (Melbourne: Longman) p. 108.
14. Holmes, T.H and Rahe, R.H. (1967) 'The social readjustment rating scale', *Journal of Psychosomatic Research*, **11**: 216.
15. Holmes, T.H and Rahe, R.H. (1967) 'The social readjustment rating scale', *Journal of Psychosomatic Research*, **11**: 213–18.

16. Jenkins, C.D. (1976) 'Recent evidence of psychological and social risk factors in coronary disease', *New England Journal of Medicine*, **294**: 1033–4.
17. Kobasa, S.C. (1979) 'Stressful life events, personality and health: an inquiry into hardiness', *Journal of Personality and Social Psychology*, **37**. 1 12.
18. Freidman, M. and Rosenman R.H. (1974) *Type A Behaviour and Your Heart* (New York: Knopf).
19. Cox, C. and Cooper, C.L. (1988) *High Flyers: An Anatomy of Managerial Success* (Oxford: Blackwell) p. 155.
20. Op. cit. Carlopio et al. (1997) p. 115.
21. Quick, J.C., Nelson, D.L. and Quick, J.D. (1990) *Stress and Challenge at the Top: The Paradox of the Successful Executive* (New York: John Wiley) pp. 45–67.
22. Maddi, S. and Kobasa, S.C. (1984) *The Hardy Executive: Health Under Stress* (Homewood: Dow Jones-Irwin).
23. Kobasa, S.C. (1982) 'The hardy personality: towards a social psychology of stress and health', in J. Suls and G. Sanders (eds) *The Social Psychology of Health and Illness* (Hillsdale: Erlbaum) Part 1.
24. Ford, C.H. (1977) 'The "elite" decision makers: what makes them tick', *Human Resource Management*, **16**(4): 14–20.
25. Op. cit. Carlopio et al. (1997) p. 142.
26. Weick, K. (1984) 'Small wins', *American Psychologist*, **39**: 40–9.
27. Diener, E., Colvin, C.R., Pavot, W.G. and Allman, A. (1991) 'The psychic costs of intense positive affect', *Journal of Personality and Social Psychology*, **61**: 492–503.
28. The Mind Gym (2005) *The Mind Gym* (London: Time Warner Books) p. 239.
29. Adapted from Grasha, A.F. (1987) *Practical Applications of Psychology* (Boston: Little, Brown) p. 159.
30. For more on this, see, for example, Crofton, K. (1998) *The Healthy Type* (Toronto: Macmillan).
31. Op. cit. Carlopio et al. (1997) p. 137.
32. Cooper, M.J. and Aygen, M.M. (1979) 'A relaxation technique in the management of hypocholesterolemia', *Journal of Human Stress*, **5**: 24–7.
33. Op. cit. Carlopio et al. (1997) pp. 143–4.
34. Adapted from Quick et al. (1990) op. cit. p. 190.
35. Harvey, J.B. (1988) 'The Abilene paradox: the management of agreement', *Organizational Dynamics*, **17**(1): 17–43.
36. Thomas, K.W. and Kilmann, R.H. (1974) *Conflict Mode Instrument* (Tuxedo: Xicom).

6 interpersonal capability

One of the fundamental requirements of professional and managerial jobs is the ability to relate to other people. It is an essential element of all jobs and can have major benefits for companies who encourage best practice. Richard Branson, for example, considers that direct communication is essential for keeping good staff.[1] In addition, an interpersonal capability is a fundamental platform on which good leadership skills are built.

However, the importance placed on developing this capability on MBA programmes has been patchy at best. Indeed, criticisms of the MBA are rarely about the lack of intellectual rigour but frequently about the lack of formal programmes to develop the 'softer' or people skills. Some schools have responded by incorporating skills-related subjects into the curriculum, but this is not universal.

Nevertheless, developing an interpersonal capability is critical and whether or not the formal subjects are available, it is imperative to seek ways to improve this capability in a proactive way. Moreover, the opportunities are certainly available on management degrees, particularly on campus-based programmes. By looking at ways to contribute better in lectures, giving presentations, through experiential exercises and working in syndicate group activities, an interpersonal capability can be improved. Identifying how this can be done is the concern of this chapter.

Fundamental to any ability to deal with people is the ability to communicate. Although interpersonal communication is often considered to be straightforward – a generic skill that does not seem to need special attention – it has nevertheless been seen as one of the route causes of many problems within organizations. Whenever an employee survey shows dissatisfaction among the workforce, poor communication, particularly between a staff member and their immediate supervisor, often tops the list of reasons.

the nature of communication

At one level, there have been massive improvements in communication methods over the past few years. The ability to transmit messages and gather information through a wide range of sophisticated technological devices, from the internet to video conferencing, has become part of everyday life. But how much of this has actually improved the quality of communication between individuals is unclear. Indeed, the assumption that more information transmitted to more people, more quickly, means a substantial improvement in understanding between people is highly debatable. While there has been a massive increase in the volume of information available, technology has not overcome many of the difficulties of interpersonal communication. This is because the communication process has several characteristics that are only marginally affected by technological improvements.

A characteristic of communicating between two or more people is the use of symbols (and often very imprecise symbols). These range from the words we use, through to our facial expressions and gestures. Symbols are part of a communication process that often has a high degree of ambiguity, involves several stages and has many possible pitfalls between what is sent and what is received.

The dangers are highlighted in Figure 6.1.[2] Any messages that are sent, such as a set of instructions, have to reflect what the 'source' intended to say. But there is no guarantee that those statements will be clearly received by the other person and even less certainty that they will be clearly understood. If the aim is then to gain acceptance of the instructions, or indeed to get someone to take action based on the instructions, quite sophisticated communications skills are needed, particularly if there is any degree of reluctance by the receiver.

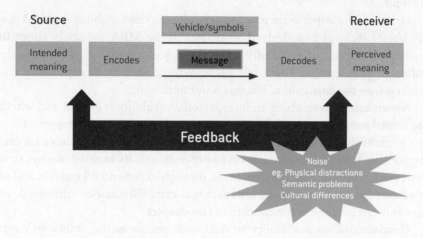

Figure 6.1 The communication process

A breakdown in this process can have massive implications. In 2006, the demands by the international community for Iran to freeze all activities relating to the 'enrichment' of uranium were seen, on the surface, to be very precise. However, the real meaning of 'enrichment' was disputed, both in terms of its definition and the intentions behind the actions of different counties. This lack of clarity had the potential to produce outcomes that ranged from economic disruption to global conflict.

Even in routine situations, communication difficulties can occur, but the chance of misunderstanding increases considerably in ambiguous situations, where emotions are heightened, or where people's backgrounds or cultural experiences are very different.

barriers to communication

One of the primary reasons for these difficulties arises from our different mental frames of reference, discussed in Chapter 4. Consequently, we tend to listen to what we want to hear, largely dismissing information we feel uncomfortable with. As Carl Rogers has argued: 'The major barrier to interpersonal communication is our very natural tendency to judge, to evaluate, to approve (or disapprove) of what the other person is saying.'[3]

The tendency to judge, however, is just one of several potential barriers to effective communication. Barriers to receiving messages can range from the listener's values, anxieties, needs and expectations through to distortions from environmental effects, such as noise and distractions. Barriers to understanding what is being said include differences in language, the use of jargon, prejudices and status differences. Our values, our logic, our assumptions and our feelings are all potential barriers to communication because they can stop us from exploring differences, illustrated further in Box 6.1.[4]

BOX 6.1 Six peculiarities of human communication

1. Words have different meanings for different people and are imprecise vehicles of communication. Terms such as 'anger' or 'love' evoke very different responses.
2. People often 'code' messages so their real meaning is masked. We have been trained from early childhood to express ourselves indirectly on many topics and feelings. Guesswork is often needed to understand the speaker's code.
3. People rarely begin a conversation by communicating the things that are of greatest concern. They 'beat around the bush' because the real problem may be too difficult to discuss and they need a way of getting there.
4. Many people have trouble getting in touch with and constructively handling their feelings. People may be blind to their emotions or blinded by them.
5. When listening, we can be easily distracted. We can think much faster than we can talk, which gives us ample space to reflect on our own agendas while the speaker is talking.
6. Filters distort what we hear. There are a whole host of emotional filters that impede our listening ability, including prejudice, expectations based on past experience, our self-image and lack of esteem.

---

improving communication

There are many subtleties in the communication process, particularly in unfamiliar environments and cultures, which can take years to fully comprehend. But it isn't only in these circumstances that an improved awareness of communication methods can be of benefit. Even in everyday surroundings, communication can be vastly improved if attention is given to three particular areas. These are having clear objectives, a capable mindset and comprehensive skills.

clear objectives

In delivering a message, it is important to be as clear as possible about what you want to say. This might sound obvious, but there are many examples where not fully thinking this through has caused unnecessary problems.

For example, when Ben Bernanke was appointed as the new chairman of the American Federal Reserve Bank, the financial world dissected his every word, trying to establish whether interest rate increases might end in June 2006. After 16 successive monthly increases, the hope was that inflation had been contained and the world's biggest economy would have the monetary shackles eased. At a White House dinner, a reporter asked Bernanke whether he thought the media had interpreted his recent testimony to Congress accurately. His response to her, 'No it's worrisome that people would look at me as dovish and not necessarily an aggressive inflation fighter' (subsequently publicly broadcast), sent world share markets tumbling for the next eight days, wiping billions of dollars off equities around the globe. He later admitted to Congress that the comment was a mistake.[5]

Thus, it is important to think about the outcomes you want from a situation. If the aim, for example, is to convey some facts or ideas, then the communication techniques used will be different from trying to gain commitment and acceptance of those views. Going further and trying to change someone's behaviour requires a greater degree of checking out, discussion, persuasion and possible negotiation. This is very different from putting a few bullet points on a PowerPoint slide and hoping everyone gets the message.

Achieving your communication objectives is also aided by how you deliver the message. Within 10 days of his communication lapse, Bernanke had recovered and 'with impeccable timing his mild remarks about inflation set the markets roaring ahead'.[6] Consequently, it is particularly important to reflect on:

> When to deliver a message – timing is often important to effective reception.
> How to deliver it – be aware of the language used. Will the receiver understand the words and phrases? Will they have any emotive connotations?
> Where to deliver it. Privately? On the sender's or receiver's ground, or in a group setting, on or off the premises?

In receiving a message, clear objectives are also important. Is your aim to sit and look attentive, or to understand what is being said? This may be easier said than done, particularly if what is being said is disturbing to your ideas and values. Thus, it is important to clarify the extent to which you are prepared to listen and commit to what is being communicated.

Both as a sender and as a receiver, having a capable mindset, with a positive attitude and a willingness to listen (as discussed in Chapter 2), is clearly critical to the communication process. This does not mean that our minds should be blank sheets or that we will not have biases. However, understanding what these might be and trying to reduce them will help to improve communication. This is particularly important in conflict situations, where progress often depends on trying to see issues from the other person's point of view. This does not mean that we have to agree with their position, but it does require us to keep an open mind long enough to hear what they are saying. An MBA student illustrates the problem as follows:

I believe that the most crucial thing in understanding people processes is the importance of keeping an open mind when engaging with people for the first time. It has always been my initial response to judge those in a group and benchmark my background and skills against theirs. This has been a huge issue for me in the past. My layers have prevented me from being objective. I have always tended to stereotype on simple character traits. A good example of this was in a group exercise, where I had a sales person in the group, who had immediately provoked stereotypes of the iconic real estate worker. My natural response was to automatically discredit almost all his opinions. However, when I forced myself to look outside my narrow reference points and try to be objective, I noticed that he was actually bringing quite a lot of order and direction to the group and had a much better understanding of the issues than I did.

The space is not available here to review all the skills needed for effective interpersonal communication. However, a useful distinction, and one that makes the area manageable, is between 'fundamental' and 'complex communication skills'. Complex skills include activities like interviewing, appraising, negotiating and coaching. Fundamental skills include behaviours such as listening, assertiveness, questioning, the use of silence and reading body language. They are the building blocks for the effective use of complex skills. If fundamental skills, such as listening, are weak, it doesn't matter how much training is given in a complex skill like coaching, its overall effectiveness will be limited.

Thus, at this early point in your management programme, it is worth reviewing your fundamental communication skills. Skills like the ability to listen and demonstrate assertiveness are important management skills and not everyone, even in senior executive positions, always has these to a high degree. Moreover, there are many opportunities on the MBA to develop more complex communication skills, which is discussed later. But, without strong fundamental skills, it is harder to capitalize fully on the opportunities. Two critical fundamental skills are discussed below.

listening

Listening is a skill that for most people needs to be addressed proactively. Even among the highly intelligent, it can be lacking, as Chris Argyris pointed out with professional groups and their proclivity for defensive reasoning.[7] One of the problems with listening is that because we have been doing it from birth, it is assumed that it no longer requires any attention. But because of our tendency to interpret information in a way that suits us and the ease with which we become distracted, it is a skill that requires conscious effort. Indeed, research suggests that 75% of vocal communication is ignored, misunderstood or quickly forgotten.[8] As one student noted:

One of the biggest challenges for the students I've observed recently is in achieving balanced listening and contribution. With such a competitive group of high performers, the tendency to outdo each other is significant. Listening is critical both at business school and in the workplace.

Consequently, in improving listening skills, it is important to be conscious of the following:

1. Recognize that listening needs a proactive approach.
2. Use body language, such as posture, eye contact and gestures, to encourage the speaker and show attention.
3. Suspend judgement and take an objective approach to what is being said.
4. Use words to encourage the speaker and check for misunderstanding.
5. Reflect back facts and feelings.
6. Use silence. Mozart said, 'silence is the most profound sound in music'.[9] Silence can also provide the space for profound comments.

Another important fundamental skill is the ability to give and receive feedback. It is vital to personal development both on the MBA and at work. Without constructive feedback, it is difficult to progress, whether as an individual or a company. Businesses spend large amounts of time and money in gaining feedback from customers as it is critical for business survival. While feedback may not be so important to personal survival, it certainly is critical to personal development and plays an important part in many interpersonal processes (as in Figure 6.1).

Feedback helps us to become more aware of the impact we may, or may not, have in different circumstances. As one part-time student commented:

I have learned a lot about giving feedback as well as receiving it on the MBA. On some occasions previously, even though I have meant well, I haven't taken into account personal emotions when giving feedback in a work environment. I will now utilize this at work, resulting in better management.

However, the feedback process is far from straightforward, which is one of the reasons why helpful, constructive feedback is not as common as it should be. There are challenges both for the individuals receiving feedback and for those giving it (Box 6.2).[10] We all have egos and receiving feedback that highlights weaknesses can be difficult to accept. We may react defensively and not be prepared to explore the possibilities. As another student commented:

I must admit that at times I do not take criticism in a constructive way. I don't critically analyse myself in the way I should be doing and hence the learning does not happen in a progressive manner.

BOX 6.2 **Feedback**

Effective feedback	*Ineffective feedback*
1. Intended to help the individual	Intended to belittle the individual
2. Specific	General
3. Descriptive	Evaluative
4. Useful	Inappropriate
5. Timely	Untimely
6. Considers feedback readiness	Makes the individual defensive
7. Clear	Not understandable
8. Valid	Inaccurate

SOURCE: From Luthans, F. (1995) *Organizational Behaviour* (New York: McGraw-Hill) 7th edn, p. 42. Used by permission of The McGraw-Hill Companies.

Thus, both giving and receiving feedback are skills that need practice. Some of the important points to remember in giving feedback are that it:

> Should be as specific as possible.
> Should describe the behaviour or action, rather than evaluate it (that is, good or bad).
> Should be concerned with behaviour that the person can act on.
> Is given at an appropriate time, usually close to the behaviour occurring.
> Is given in an appropriate environment, a private room, rather than the corridor.

❯ Is given when the receiver is more disposed to be listening.

In receiving feedback:

❯ Listen and acknowledge the other's viewpoint.
❯ Ask questions if necessary.
❯ Check feedback with other sources.
❯ Try not to react defensively.
❯ If positive, acknowledge and give thanks.
❯ If negative, acknowledge, explore and end with understanding for future action.

Box 6.2 outlines some further characteristics of the feedback process. The MBA provides the opportunity to develop this skill in a less threatening environment than is found in many work environments. Practice in developing this skill and communication skills overall can be facilitated by using the communications skills audit in Box 6.3. The audit should be given to people who know you well enough to give you a reasonable assessment of how you communicate. They fill in the 'other's rank', while you fill in the 'own rank' column on a separate audit.

BOX 6.3 Communication skills audit

For each of the items listed below, rank your view of your level of effectiveness in that skill from 0 (low) to 5 (high). Get someone else to rank your skills as well.

		Own rank	Other's rank
1.	Making a good first impression		
2.	Picking up underlying feelings from others		
3.	Getting ideas across to others		
4.	Communicating even when things are tough		
5.	Not talking too much		
6.	Drawing others out		
7.	Staying open to others' ideas		
8.	Giving instructions to others		
9.	Ignoring hostility when necessary		
10.	Speaking up for your view		
11.	Giving a clear presentation to a group		
12.	Staying silent when necessary		
13.	Listening constructively to criticism		
14.	Persuading others to do what you want		
15.	Giving clear specific feedback to others		
16.	Understanding others' ideas		
17.	Leaving discussions that don't involve you		
18.	Interviewing others effectively		

		Own rank	Other's rank
19.	Collecting information from others		
20.	Putting people at ease		
21.	Letting others know how you feel		
22.	Contributing effectively in meetings		
23.	Coming over well when being interviewed		
24.	Building rapport with others		
25	Getting others to accept your views		
26.	Picking up audiences' reactions to your presentation		
27.	Helping a meeting to progress		
28.	Conveying your feelings to others		
29	Understanding when someone is upset		
30.	Finding out about other people's interests		
31.	Making conversation		
32.	Communicating your emotions clearly, when you choose to		

The audit can be completed by one person or several colleagues (in a 360°-type feedback process), either openly or anonymously. Comparing your scores with your colleagues gives some indication of your strengths and weaknesses. However, much greater benefit can come from discussing the scores and the reasons behind them. This is what makes feedback valuable but challenging. But there is little doubt that the effort can pay dividends. As one student noted:

The positive independent feedback I received from the team leader that I had integrated well with the team and had made a positive contribution was a significant confidence booster for me. As a normally introverted person, I now have the confidence to participate fully as a syndicate member.

A summary of some general guidelines for improving communication is provided in Box 6.4.[11]

BOX 6.4 **Guidelines for preventing communication problems**

> Define terms that seem to be troublesome and check your meanings with those of the other person.
> Deal with facts rather than interpretations or inferences.
> Take the other person's and your emotions and feelings into account as being important and, if appropriate, recognize them.
> Restate issues as the other party sees them to test your own understanding.
> Test or check out your understanding of the message.
> Share openly, but sensitively, any perception and/or feelings engendered by the message.

> Observe non-verbal behaviour that can help in confirming what is being said.
> Where there are discrepancies between verbal and non-verbal behaviour, examine more closely what is going on.
> Ask for clarification or repetition if necessary.

communication opportunities on the MBA

This understanding of fundamental communication skills is important in discussing some of the opportunities on the MBA programme to develop an interpersonal capability. Below, presentations, lectures, experiential exercises and working in syndicate or study groups are reviewed.

presentations

Making a presentation is a skill that is not only important on most management programmes, but also at work. Although presenting has become commonplace, being able to do this at a high level is not quite as widespread. Nevertheless, good presentation skills are expected in most corporate environments and an ability to present well cannot be underestimated.

The main factors in producing a good presentation are discussed below in terms of preparation, process, planning and practice. In reviewing these, it is important to also keep in mind the communication challenges discussed in the first section (Figure 6.1).

preparation

There is nothing inherent in the presentation process that prevents an MBA student from presenting to a high standard. However, if there is one key to presenting successfully, it is preparation. The skills can be learned, but many fall down either because they underestimate the time needed to present well, or they are complacent, based on past performances. You are only as good as your last performance. Even if you are experienced in this area, it is still likely that improvements can be made. One student highlighted the dangers as follows:

I present regularly as part of my job. My enthusiasm for the presentation exercise was not what it should have been, as only two months earlier I had attended a four-day presentation course, so I believed I had little to learn. That course had highlighted my voice as my main weak point as I tend to talk in a monotone. Unfortunately, during this exercise, I only recalled my weakness when I had finished presenting and received my first piece of feedback. It seems overconfidence restricted my learning opportunity and other weaknesses came to light. I received feedback to say I seemed wedded to my notes at all times and lacked confidence as a presenter. It seems a four-day presentation course fails to make you an expert.

process

There are a number of important aspects to the presentation process, from being clear about your overall aims to ensuring that the message is delivered at the end. In order to do this effectively, it is important to consider to whom you are presenting and what for.

On an MBA, this could be an academic audience or it could be a corporate group, or with project work, it could be both. One student commented:

Upon reflecting on a presentation delivered to senior managers and directors from 10 European countries, I should have clarified the objective for the first topic with the seniority of the audience in mind – this would have also influenced the development of content and ensured it was relevant. I should have done it, but I didn't, with unenviable consequences.

Consequently, being aware of your audience's needs and expectations and meeting these is critical. To do this effectively, the following should to be taken into account:

Presentation objectives and the audience:

❭ Consider what knowledge the audience has of the topic.
❭ Be clear about what you want them to have as a result of the presentation.
❭ Assess what elements should be included and the depth of coverage required for each. Academic assignments tend to require more emphasis on process. Corporate assignments may favour conclusions.

Start and structure:

❭ Begin by saying who you are, what you are going to do, how long the session will take and how questions and comments will be handled.
❭ Outline a road map of your presentation, signposting the major elements.
❭ Make sure the structure is evident, with a clear start, middle and end.
❭ If you are nervous, learn the first few minutes of the presentation off by heart.

Delivery:

❭ Aim for clear diction and vary your tone.
❭ Use word pictures (verbal descriptions or examples) to illustrate points.
❭ Ensure the pace of your presentation matches your audience's understanding.
❭ Maintain eye contact with the audience and do not speak to the screen.
❭ Use gestures and space to engage your audience but don't try to be a performing seal, unless you aspire to work at Disneyworld.
❭ Watch irritating mannerisms, such as playing with pens or using unnecessary sounds (ums and errs).
❭ Use brief cards or overheads to prompt you; do not read through a written script.

Visual aids:

❭ Aids (such as PowerPoint, videos, props, music) enhance audience understanding and maintain interest through variety. Too many aids can be distracting, but it is hard to maintain audience interest with only your voice.
❭ Ensure written slides are readable.
❭ Don't use the presentation to demonstrate your knowledge of the intricacies of PowerPoint or the amount of detail you can fit on to the slide.
❭ Limit the number of slides to what you can explain comfortably and the audience can bear.
❭ Read through the slides beforehand for errors and clarity.

Ending:

> At the end, summarize the key points. Leave the audience with a message.
> Allow time for questions. Try and anticipate what might be asked.
> Don't be defensive in answering questions. Answer honestly. If you don't know, say so. Don't waffle. It is unlikely you will improve your credibility by talking for longer if you don't know the answer.

It is important to review the presentation after the event. Honestly consider what you did well and what areas need to be improved. Try to get feedback from those who heard you and try to get beneath comments like 'Yes that was fine'. Why was it fine and is 'fine' good or mediocre?

If you are nervous of presenting, try and present early on in your degree. If you avoid it, it makes it much harder if you have to present under assessed conditions later when there is more pressure. Take every possible opportunity to present, so you will gradually build up your ability and confidence, as demonstrated by the following comment:

No matter how many times I rehearsed the introduction, I kept getting more and more nervous. The stress was overwhelming. On stage, I fumbled at the beginning, my voice was extremely shaky and nerves were really setting in, but as I kept talking, I got more confident, knowing I had the audience's undivided attention. I fed off them. By the time I had finished, I had covered all the points I needed, wrapped it up and felt great. It wasn't as bad as I had anticipated and has given me the confidence to present more often.

planning and practice

A presentation does not need to be learned verbatim, however, you do have to know the key points, the messages you want to send in relation to each point and the order in which you want to send them. Consequently, planning is important.

Additionally, doing a full dummy run beforehand and in the location where you will present, or one similar, helps to iron out potential difficulties. This is particularly important if it is your first presentation, or a presentation that is significant. However, even if you are experienced, be careful of becoming too blasé, as illustrated below:

You would think third time lucky I would do it well, when delivering a small presentation on a topic I know quite well to a small audience. But no! I had the framework in front of me as a checklist, and yet still didn't get around to performing a full rehearsal. My issue seems to stem from attitude or confidence towards the presentation content and a general failure to realize that practising is also about quality of delivery. Going forward, I am going to ensure adequate practice.

participation in lectures

Participation in lectures is an interpersonal skill that is also relevant to operating successfully in the outside world. In the business world, it is quite common to have to defend one's position without being briefed beforehand. Both as a manager and an MBA student, a question can be deflected by agreeing to reply later, but this cannot be done on a regular basis without losing credibility. Both students and managers need to be able to defend their position or argue their case. As one student commented:

I intend to consciously force myself to talk in public, such as being more vocal in class. I will be working on my emotions, which have prevented me from seizing opportunities. These steps are important not just on my MBA but also as a manager, where I have to take calculated risks and seize opportunities whenever they present themselves.

As this student indicates, the ability to speak in class may not just occur 'naturally' and may require some effort to develop successfully. Indeed, participation in lectures can be more demanding than making presentations. In class, there is much less structure and less individual control. Although in lectures it may be possible to make only a few comments, timing is critical. Also, a greater degree of listening skills are required in order to hear the points appropriately and react accordingly.

While it is usually not possible to prepare for a class discussion to the same depth as a presentation, nevertheless, being prepared is essential. This is particularly important in case study discussions. It is unlikely that all the angles of a case can be anticipated, but potential discussion areas and questions can be identified. Similarly, with meetings at work, there may be an agenda, but often the discussion will take different paths. Giving some thought to what these might be beforehand can improve your contribution.

However, the leap from anticipating to contributing can be a big one for some students. Unfortunately, there is no substitute for having a go. Asking a relevant question is one way to ease into the process. The next stage is to make statements that contribute to the debate, even if only brief ones. It is important in doing this that you do not expect everyone to stop and applaud your brilliant input. Often students will not contribute because they are looking for the 'show stopper', the comment that will demonstrate to everyone their true brilliance. But it is rare for anyone to be able to do this. Sometimes, even when a good answer is produced, it may still be challenged either by the lecturer or by other students. Frequently, it is more important to be able to defend your initial position with additional examples or comments than deliver the knockout blow. Indeed, even if others seem to disagree with your statement, this does not mean that what you have said is not valuable. It can still assist in developing the debate, or provide additional insights into an issue. One student overcame the participation issue by setting himself objectives:

I set a goal for myself. I needed to participate. In the past, in the Chinese education system, we never have this experience. There, everyone listens to the lecture, but here it is different. Here I said to myself that to learn English is one goal, another is to gain learning from the other people and at the same time to contribute my own experience, or bring some of my own examples to the class to benefit others. In the beginning, I understood very little but I still tried very hard. First of all I set a quantitative goal for myself. I managed to participate at least once in each class. Now I regularly participate in class.

Even if you are not able to contribute, it is still important to follow the discussion. Often fellow students have experiences and insights that you could easily miss if your mind is on 'hold' until the lecturer starts talking again. Moreover, either at work or in the lecture theatre, if you are 'cold-called', you do not want to miss the opportunity to shine.

Experiential exercises, such as simulations and role plays, provide the opportunity to develop an interpersonal capability further. The emphasis in these activities is learning by doing and some of the learning principles involved are outlined in Chapter 7. The responsibility for learning outcomes in these exercises lies with the student rather than the instructor.

Experiential exercises in business schools usually involve the student taking the position of a manager or a stakeholder of a firm and acting out scenarios within set parameters. For some students, this kind of experience can be problematic because of self-consciousness, or the difficulty of taking on a fabricated role. However, there can be considerable benefits in overcoming this reticence. In these kinds of exercises, the student often has to face confronting consequences. The exercise might involve being a purchasing manager having to buy critical raw materials, or a general manager cutting budgets and having to make people redundant. As a result, the student can learn not only about managerial decision making, negotiation, power, tactics and strategy and so on, but also their possible emotional response to certain situations. One student commented:

I think I learn better from experiential learning. The simulation classes were phenomenal and I learned a lot from them. In the class, you really had to critically examine yourself and how you behave and how you interact with others. I think this improved my abilities tremendously and I have learned a lot about myself. But it is so easy not to do as it is often very confronting. It's uncomfortable to look critically at yourself.

While experiential exercises are a depiction of events and not the 'real thing', trying to act as if they are can pay dividends. There will always be caveats with such exercises. However, if you are seeking, for example, insight into how you might react in an interview situation, how you might discipline a staff member or negotiate a new contract, a simulation or role play is a good way to identify potential weaknesses. There must be many career counsellors and indeed employers throughout the world who have seen potential job candidates flounder miserably because they have not taken the time to put themselves through a simulated interview scenario (see Chapter 8).

syndicate groups

A particularly rich learning opportunity for developing a broad range of interpersonal abilities is in syndicate groups or learning teams. Most MBA programmes, particularly campus-based programmes, provide opportunities to work in small groups and many make groupwork an integral part of the programme. The ability to work successfully in syndicate groups has tremendous potential benefits after the MBA has finished. Many corporations emphasize teamwork and some consultancy groups such as McKinsey see it as essential for providing a high level of service to clients.

The kinds of skills that can be developed through groupwork include practising team management skills, influencing skills, presentation skills and improving case study discussion skills. Indeed, the more forgiving environment of the MBA syndicate, in contrast to the world of work, allows much greater experimentation and risk taking with less damaging consequences. As one student noted:

Certainly syndicates are hard, but it's more or less a safe environment to make mistakes, to learn how to work with other people. I've had mostly positive experiences and some challenging times. But they have definitely made a difference to my development.

However, despite these opportunities, and despite the fact that, in general, groups can produce a better outcome than an individual, syndicate groups are not without their challenges. One of the most significant issues is that a group of peers in a non-hierarchical context with no formal authority is potentially one of the hardest groups to make work well. As another student noted:

In syndicate work, as opposed to working in my team at work, there are no clear lines of hierarchy and responsibility, making it potentially harder to form a structured group with everybody aware of what their different role is. If you are lucky, lines of responsibility can be allocated without a problem, but you could easily run into some bother with this. The groups have been different each time at business school, with new dynamics, requiring different ways of behaving and different input each time.

Consequently, if one can make a syndicate group perform successfully, it is possible that one can make almost any type of group succeed. But it is also worth emphasizing that to a large extent the success of a study group is in your control. A dysfunctional group, which can waste time and energy, is not a burden anyone wants, particularly on a pressurized course. Nevertheless, while it may not be easy to change, a broken group can be mended and a mediocre group can be improved. Moreover, while outside help may be necessary, it is something that you and your group colleagues can do something about.

Below are outlined the major areas on which to focus in order to improve group functioning. While there has been a tremendous amount written on groups, there are some fundamental principles that are important in solving group problems, both at work and on the MBA. These can be categorized under three headings: group purpose, group process and group design.

group purpose

The first issue in developing group effectiveness is in ensuring that there is clarity around the group's goals and purpose. Groups can have an overall purpose, with additional specific objectives for completing individual tasks. A group's overall purpose, for example, might be to help everyone get through the MBA, or maximize the group's learning. Such broader overall aims can help lift the group above day-to-day worries, giving a sense of overall direction and helping with longer term motivation. The limitations of not doing this are illustrated by the following comment:

The discussion on group purpose has highlighted a deficiency in how I go about leading teams. I have not previously developed a collaborative group purpose before, preferring either to have no clear direction or set it unilaterally. I recognize that performance has been limited in my teams because of this lack of strategic objective and my failure to successfully communicate this, let alone get the agreement of others.

Whether or not the group has a strategic purpose, it is still important to clarify the objectives for each group task undertaken. Is the aim of a group meeting, for example, to discuss a case study, complete a group exercise, make a group presentation or complete a group assignment? Each of these tasks is different and evokes different degrees of commitment and energy. Many groups fail because this requirement has not been consistently addressed.

However, in addition to the formal group objectives, it is also important to clarify the needs and objectives of each group member. At work and on an MBA programme, it is unusual to find individuals completely sublimating their personal objectives for the group. Consequently, individual and group objectives are unlikely to align perfectly all the time. However, if there are discrepancies between an individual's personal objectives and that of the group, it has to be ensured that they are made manifest. Otherwise, hidden agendas (covert personal agendas) can debilitate the group. Groups that have individuals with divergent personal objectives will not function very well, or in some cases not at all, as illustrated by the following comment:

My expectation initially of working in syndicate groups was that because people were here because they wanted to be, everyone was motivated by the same things, to achieve at the highest possible level and to commit themselves to everything they put their names on. How very naive. We had real difficulties because we failed to understand we were driven by different things and had a real mismatch between people in the group, with vastly different levels of contribution and intent.

group process

The group's internal processes also impact on group effectiveness. Usually group processes are divided into two categories; those concerned with achieving the task (task processes) and those concerned with the relationships between team members (people processes).

Task processes are the working infrastructure or 'ground rules' by which groups operate. These include developing a group agenda, assigning tasks and meeting deadlines. This is usually relatively straightforward and on an MBA course with limited time, it is essential that task processes are established in order to get through the work. They include procedures for:

> Deciding on roles, for example whether a chairperson is needed
> Allocating preparatory work
> Establishing the criteria for success
> Defining a problem
> Identifying knowledge resources
> Analysing the available information
> Agreeing the most appropriate action
> Evaluating outcomes
> When and how ideas are recorded
> When procedures are reviewed.

People processes are concerned with the activities to do with people's feelings about working in a group and their interactions with each other. They include:

> The way the group is handled
> Who tries to influence
> Who really influences

> Who contributes
> Who does not contribute (and why)
> Who talks (or does not talk) to whom, how often and why
> Who encourages others
> Who tries to reduce tension.

A group will not perform effectively unless the people processes are addressed and there is an open, balanced and objective dialogue between members. Without this, ideas cannot be pooled and problems cannot be solved. Groups with poor people processes are characterized by frequent interruptions between team members, aggressive promotion of one or two ideas, domination of the group by a few individuals, overly emotional reactions to opinions, poor listening, and opting out.

While most groups ensure they have adequate task processes in place, the people processes are less frequently tackled. Often this is because it involves conflict. As one student commented:

While I've endeavoured to purposely set objectives for teams and been clear in setting task processes, I don't think I've been as perceptive about the people processes. It is clear now that I haven't sought to address people process issues. This is more than likely because of a preference to avoid conflict and hence avoid difficult conversations.

However, often the short-term pain of dealing with conflict is better than the long-term consequences of avoidance. Once entrenched patterns take hold, they can be much more difficult to rectify. As another student noted:

There were a few groups where we had a bunch of like-minded people and that was great. But the rest were a bit of a battle. We generally found that two of us would do the work and the rest would coast. The true leaders deal with it and those who aren't so good do it themselves.

group development

The group development wheel (Figure 6.2) provides an illustration of the factors that affect a group's success and the points of intervention.[12] The precise sequencing of the stages of the wheel is debatable. Nevertheless, the model highlights the main elements that need to be addressed in developing an effective small group.

stage 1

The first stage, *forming*, is concerned with ensuring that the group's objectives are clarified, each individual's areas of contribution are understood and there are enough operating structures in place to enable the group to function adequately. The wheel highlights the common tendency when groups first form, for individuals to be polite, watchful and guarded. This is quite common, but the danger is that politeness becomes the main objective and the group gets stuck at this stage, illustrated by the following comment:

We tended to be very polite with each other, but it was often not very effective. For example, I would say to someone they were doing a good job even when it was poor.

I felt I didn't want to argue with them, we were just doing a project, and it was not worth having an internal quarrel. But this didn't work. Some students got marks they shouldn't have because I did not want to complain. I did not want to damage the relationship, but this is not good for learning about the business environment.

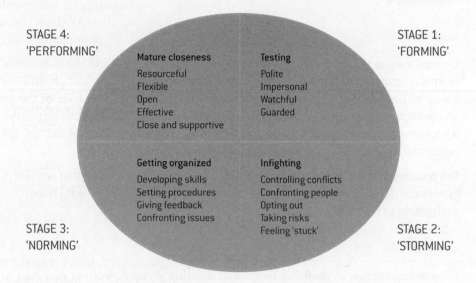

STAGE 4: 'PERFORMING'

Mature closeness
Resourceful
Flexible
Open
Effective
Close and supportive

Testing
Polite
Impersonal
Watchful
Guarded

STAGE 1: 'FORMING'

Getting organized
Developing skills
Setting procedures
Giving feedback
Confronting issues

Infighting
Controlling conflicts
Confronting people
Opting out
Taking risks
Feeling 'stuck'

STAGE 3: 'NORMING'

STAGE 2: 'STORMING'

Figure 6.2 Group development wheel

Stage 2

While many groups overcome their initial politeness, there is no guarantee that they will do so without some effort. The second stage, *storming*, is where problems, like those illustrated in the previous comments, should be sorted out. This, as the label suggests, can give rise to some tough discussion and challenges. To what depth and for how long varies considerably. Indeed in some instances, particularly where the team members have well developed team skills and are prepared to work through their differences, this stage can be relatively painless. However, in many instances, the storming stage is hard work. As one student commented:

The groups prepare you for dealing with different people and for different problems. We had a group that couldn't communicate. There were a lot of misunderstandings and different expectations. From the start you have to go beyond just being pleasant when you get in the group. The problems have to be confronted. It is at your expense if you let things go.

This is the period when individual and group objectives need to be aligned, hidden agendas surfaced and leadership issues resolved. Not exploring these issues to an adequate depth and resolution can lead to continual tension within the group. This may not surface all the time, but is most likely to be problematic when something critical is at stake, for example when a deadline is looming or the group has to complete a significant task. Another student noted:

I managed this situation by bringing the differences to the table and getting an understanding that we are driven by different things and we had a mismatch with this project. So we agreed on a way each of us could contribute. I would basically run the project and bring it all together in a way that we were happy with, which satisfied everyone else because they had contributed and the output was to my level of expectations.

stage 3

Groups vary in the extent to which they are able to resolve all the issues raised in the storming stage. At a minimum, there needs to be enough common ground for the group to proceed to the *norming* stage. This is the basic operating level of the group, where each person is able to contribute appropriately, difficult issues can be confronted with some hope of resolution and an open discussion can be held about the group's performance. A student illustrated this with the following comment:

The process stage of the framework was also revealing as it showed that without concentrating on both task and people processes, the team is less likely to be performing at its full potential.

stage 4

Continuing success in resolving issues and meeting group objectives may lead to the group operating at the level of *performing*. This is where groups can be very satisfying to work in. However, achieving this state is not necessarily automatic or permanent and the group needs to be aware of potential problems. Success can sometimes breed complacency. Major changes in group objectives or in team membership may require the team to revisit earlier stages and re-establish the ground rules in order to operate at an optimum level. This is also true when new groups form. New groups need a fresh makeover, regardless of the past experience of the individuals in them. As one student commented:

Because we had all been prepped so much about syndicates in the first term, I think we were all very careful about how we handled them. But my second term syndicate was a disaster. I think that was because we had all come from successful syndicates and we all thought we knew how to handle these things. But there were issues raised in this group that we thought we knew about, but hadn't really worked through properly in the past.

group design

The third major area that affects group effectiveness is the design of the group. Three aspects are particularly important – group composition, group environment and group rewards.

Group composition involves a number of considerations. One is group size. Research on groups indicates that five to eight members are optimum, while higher than eight makes the group harder to manage, particularly in terms of participation. A second issue is group membership. At work one may have more control over this than on the MBA. But if the opportunity to choose group members arises, give consideration to what the group has to achieve before teaming up with someone merely because they are known to you. Individuals bring a range of skills and knowledge to a group. For an MBA, which involves tackling a range of topics and subjects, a diverse group with a range of skills is probably best. Individuals also bring different degrees of motivation and commitment to a group. There is a big difference between someone who sees the group assisting them to get high assignment marks, in contrast to someone who sees the group as a vehicle for developing their interpersonal skills. Congruent motivation and goals, as mentioned previously, are as important to group success as the skills that individuals bring to the group. As one student commented:

I know we can't change who is in our group, but we can make sure we know what each other's strengths and weaknesses are and thus the roles and responsibilities of everyone. In the past I did not undertake team-building activities initially that would have highlighted the ways in which people prefer working. We later discovered this through trial and error – a long and difficult way to learn.

Group environment is concerned with the setting in which the group operates. An important aspect of this is the proximity of group members to each other and the opportunity to meet. This is not usually a problem if individuals are based around a business school campus, but it can be disruptive for the group if team members are scattered across a number of locations. The ability to meet frequently is important. While it may not guarantee success, it is a prerequisite for it. Indeed, one of the major reasons why groups do not progress beyond the forming stage is because they do not have the opportunity to meet frequently enough to iron out the difficulties they may face.

In addition, the physical location where the group meets needs to be conducive. This includes making sure that the meeting room and its facilities are adequate and the group can work uninterrupted.

Group rewards are the third main component of group design. Both at work and on the MBA, reward systems often favour individual performance. As a consequence, one needs to think through how rewards can be constituted for achieving group outcomes. This may not be a problem for assignments that receive a group mark. However, there are many tasks that do not attract formal marks and it is worth developing the group's own reward system for tasks executed successfully. This might be a dinner celebration, or at the very least, verbal acknowledgement for jobs well done. This is also where having an overall group purpose and rewarding the group for fulfilling it can contribute to maintaining group morale and motivation.

However, while the emphasis here has been on some of the challenges that groups face and how these might be overcome, whatever your experience of syndicate groups, it is more likely that the benefits will outweigh the difficulties. When asked to reflect on their MBA, many students highlight their syndicate group activities as being some of their most memorable experiences and the lifelong friends they made their most rewarding.

conclusion

In this chapter, some of the major opportunities to develop an interpersonal capability on the MBA have been reviewed. The development of this capability is critical for operating successfully in the business world. While the MBA has been criticized for not emphasizing this area enough, there are nevertheless many opportunities available to develop an interpersonal capability on most management degree programmes. The challenge, however, is that the help and responsibility for developing these skills lies to a large extent with the student rather than the lecturer.

Increasingly, students are being given more structured support in this area. Several business schools now provide formal programmes in team building and a range of interpersonal skills. Additionally, through selecting various kinds of project work, a student can also use this to enhance their influence and communication skills. Moreover, many schools have extracurricular activities and clubs where interpersonal skills can be further improved. It is not that the opportunities are not available on MBA programmes, but that the learning has to be largely personally driven.

However, while very important to operating effectively in all work environments, an interpersonal capability is only part of what is needed in today's business environment. Also critical are leadership skills, which require the student to go beyond what has been discussed here. The increasingly important, but also challenging, issues related to leadership are discussed in the next chapter.

references

1. *Australian Financial Review*, 14 March 2006, p. 47.
2. Bailey, J., Schermerhorn, J., Hunt, J. and Osborn, R. (1991) *Managing Organisational Behaviour in Australia* (Singapore: Jacaranda Wiley) p. 395.
3. Rogers, C. (1961) *On Becoming a Person: A Therapist's View of Psychotherapy* (Boston: Houghton Mifflin) p. 330.
4. Bolton, R. (1979) *People Skills* (Englewood Cliffs, NJ: Prentice Hall) pp. 65–76.
5. Isidore, C. (2006) 'Bernanke admits a "lapse"', *CNNMoney.com*, 23 May.
6. 'Fed chairman sends market soaring', *RWE Business News*, 16 June 2006.
7. Argyris, C. (1991) 'Teaching smart people how to learn', *Harvard Business Review*, **69**(3): 99–109.
8. Op. cit. Bolton (1979) p. 30.
9. Eales-White, R. (1998) *Ask the Right Question* (New York: McGraw Hill) p. 31.
10. Luthans, F. (1995) *Organizational Behaviour, 7*th edn (New York: McGraw-Hill) p. 426.
11. Tagiuri, R. (1972) 'On "good" communication', *HBS Case Services* No. 9-475-013.
12. Tuckman, B.W. (1965) 'Developmental sequences in small groups', *Psychology Bulletin*, **63**: 384–99.

7 developing a leadership capability

A vast amount has been written, both in the academic and popular press, about leadership. Almost every popular magazine regularly features articles that directly or indirectly cover the subject, whether in business, politics, war, sport or entertainment. The academic literature contains numerous leadership theories, from the strategic and charismatic varieties through to supervisory and transactional leadership. There are also theories on leading from behind and leading from afar. You name it, there is probably a leadership theory that covers it.

Despite the amount that has been written, there seems to be as much confusion about leadership as there is clarity and obviously it is not possible to cover here many of the wide-ranging views on the subject. Nevertheless, it is important to cover some of the issues. The reason why so much has been written about leadership is because it is considered to be a critical capability for those wanting to be successful not just in the business world, but in many walks of life. Indeed, most of you will go back into the workforce and be expected to take on leadership roles, while many of you, completing your degree part time, will be struggling with the concept on a daily basis. Consequently, it is an issue that can't be ignored.

> The reason why so much has been written about leadership is because it is considered to be a critical capability for those wanting to be successful not just in the business world, but in many walks of life.

It is highly unlikely that you will pass through your management degree without being exposed to many leadership theories. However, no matter how much you read, you will find that two of the most important questions remain controversial. The first is what is 'leadership' and what do 'good' leaders look like and the second is whether you can develop leadership skills on an MBA, or indeed at all.

There are no definite answers to either question, but there are ways forward. With regard to the first question and despite the controversy, there are several principles of leadership on which most people agree, which can form the basis for building a leadership capability. In essence, leadership is about having a vision or sense of direction, being able to communicate that direction and then moving towards it. How you move or change yourself and other people is a matter of style, which is a concern of much of the leadership literature. As many different styles, both directive and consultative, have been successful in bringing about change, it is possibly one of the reasons why there is so much debate and confusion surrounding the concept. Yes, some people seem to be born leaders, such as Winston Churchill or Nelson Mandela, but there are many ways of making an impact, even by people without their characteristics.

While some critics question whether management degrees can develop leadership skills, the reality is that there are many opportunities to do so on MBA programmes, regardless of whether there is a formal leadership subject. This can be done by participating in the clubs, societies and student programmes that are available during the MBA. But it can also be done in other ways. You may not yet be in a position to lead an organization, but you can be a syndicate group leader, a social leader or thought leader. Many situations will arise where you will be able to put forward alternative views, take risks and take others along with you. The principles of leadership can be applied in many different ways – but they have to be applied – which is why it is easy to miss, or even dismiss, the opportunities available to develop leadership skills.

This is the real problem with leadership, regardless of the debates in the literature. For most of us, leadership requires a proactive approach. While you may not become a great leader, you can certainly become a better leader. However, this requires both thought and action about what skills you want to develop and how you might go about doing this.

Consequently, this chapter focuses on the opportunities available on management courses to develop leadership skills, rather than reviewing the leadership literature. It focuses on two areas in particular. These are *personal leadership* (leading oneself) and *public leadership* (leading others).

personal leadership

The vast weight of the leadership literature concentrates on public leadership, concerned with leading others or the broader organization. However, an equally critical ability is personal leadership, the ability to lead oneself.

Public and personal leadership are inextricably linked. An individual's personal qualities determine how well they lead others. Warren Bennis, one of the foremost authorities on leadership, has argued that a lack of self-knowledge is one of the most common reasons for failure to lead others successfully.[1]

However, leadership is not only an outer-directed activity. The principles of leadership can be applied to oneself in the sense of establishing a set of personal aspirations and moving towards them. In exploring self-leadership, Charles Manz has argued that leadership is an internal as well as an external process, and involves managing ourselves and our environment so that we can reach our full potential and meet our personal goals.[2] Moreover, if we cannot change ourselves, why should we think we have the leadership ability to change others?

Indeed, personal leadership is critical to really benefiting from an MBA and developing the capabilities outlined in this book. An MBA is an opportunity to lay the foundations for becoming an effective and capable businessperson. This entails a learning and change process that goes beyond bolting on a few pieces of additional knowledge. It involves improvement in both functional and personal capabilities and potentially becoming a qualitatively different person. However, as we explore below, exercising a high degree of personal leadership can involve challenges as great as any found in leading others.

personal leadership and the mind

Some writers play down the part that cognitive and thought processes play in leadership. This is understandable to some extent as leading others is ultimately an interpersonal process and a strong intellect does not necessarily translate into good leadership.

However, leadership does require a lot of thought and it is important not to lose sight of this in leading oneself and others.

The knowledge gained on an MBA is essential for formulating an organization's vision and mission. Without an understanding of different markets and products, competitive forces and organizational realities, a firm is more likely to be led into bankruptcy than financial success.[3] Moreover, particularly in leading at the top, the ability to solve complex puzzles and problems (raised in Chapter 4) is a vital capability. Indeed, Elliot Jacques and Stephen Clement, for example, have criticized the emphasis on interpersonal skills at the expense of the intellectual capacities of the executive. They argue that the scale and complexity of the world requires a leader to employ increasingly complex mental processes and, in particular, the capacity to deal with uncertainty and abstract concepts.[4]

The ability to analyse oneself, identify individual strengths and weakness and produce a realistic personal vision (discussed in Chapter 2) is a cognitive process that is the starting point for personal leadership. Our propensity to take risks and move into the unknown influences the progress we can make in changing ourselves and others. Our values, and particularly the values of trust and integrity, are also important. Additionally, our mental resilience and ability to deal with stress and change, discussed in Chapter 5, are also critical to successful leadership. On the flip side, Manfred Kets de Vries highlights how top managers' neuroses can also be related to various organizational dysfunctions.[5] These are all cognitive issues.

Our creativity and mental imagery (discussed in Chapter 4) influence our ability to produce credible pictures of the longer term. The way we talk to ourselves affects our confidence and our willingness to engage in difficult events. Our whole mental thought patterns affect the problems we see and the choices we make. Indeed, we cannot exercise personal leadership at all without a capable mindset and the willingness and motivation to learn and change. If you thought leadership was all about taking action, then you need to think again.

personal leadership and behaviour

Having a desire to develop and a willingness to review strengths and weakness is the starting point in personal leadership. In addition, action and a different set of skills to those discussed above are required. But it is a mix of the two that is important.

The need to be mentally as well as behaviourally responsive to change is illustrated by Kurt Lewin's model (Figure 7.1), which has been successfully used by companies such as GE for many years as part of their change programmes.[6] Lewin suggests that learning consists of unfreezing current approaches, moving to new learning (including review and practice) and refreezing the learned behaviour (through the application of reinforcement and feedback). Without a preparedness to unlock or unfreeze the mind to new approaches, behavioural skills courses or leadership roles will have little impact on one's actual ability to lead. As one student said:

I was aware that there are both external and internal factors that influence my own leadership development. But I had never explored what they were or the actual influence they had. I have had ample learning opportunities, but have discovered that it is my attitude towards learning that has failed me. I knew attitudes played a part in learning but I had never reflected or explored how they affected me personally.

Going forward, I will recognize my attitudes are my greatest hindrance in learning, specifically my attitudes towards taking a risk and learning from mistakes.

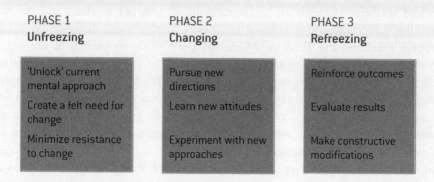

PHASE 1
Unfreezing

'Unlock' current mental approach

Create a felt need for change

Minimize resistance to change

PHASE 2
Changing

Pursue new directions

Learn new attitudes

Experiment with new approaches

PHASE 3
Refreezing

Reinforce outcomes

Evaluate results

Make constructive modifications

Figure 7.1 Lewin's model of individual change

Changing, Lewin's second phase, is unlikely to occur without the right attitude. But this second phase is not straightforward and involves an interplay between thought and experience. This is illustrated by Kolb's learning cycle, which emphasizes four aspects: having an experience, reflecting on it, drawing conclusions and then trying new ways (Figure 7.2).[7]

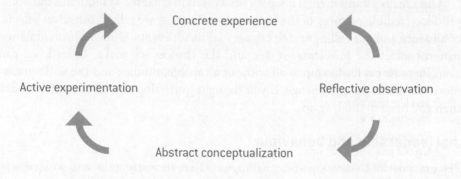

Concrete experience

Active experimentation

Reflective observation

Abstract conceptualization

Figure 7.2 Kolb's learning cycle

For example, the first aspect of having a 'concrete experience' might involve your making a substantial contribution to a case study discussion. The next stage of 'reflective observation' involves reviewing this experience. You may feel that many of your comments in the discussion fell on deaf ears. This provides you with information for the next stage of drawing conclusions and creating tentative mental models, called 'abstract conceptualization'. As a result of the experience, you might conclude that you will not be listened to unless you order your facts logically and deliver them succinctly. In going to the next stage of 'active experimentation', you try out this conclusion and prepare yourself better for case discussion. It is at this point that the cycle starts again. If you are still being ignored (concrete experience), then you now have new data on which to reflect and form new theories about how you contribute to case study discussions.

The model highlights that both action and reflection are critical in the learning process. Developing new behaviours requires attention to each stage. Most people have preferences between the various stages of the cycle, illustrated by the learning styles outlined in Box 7.1.[8] Each stage has strengths and weaknesses, and in general we do not naturally progress through each stage, but become comfortable in our preferred style. Thus, if we emphasize 'active experimentation', we may fail to reflect in enough depth or consolidate our experience. If our preference is for 'abstract conceptualization', we get into analysis paralysis and not act, or not act often enough. Thus, there are benefits in assessing one's learning preferences and how one can progress through the cycle, as one student commented:

Kolb's learning cycle made me aware that I have a tendency to get caught partway through the cycle. I spend little time reflecting and quickly move on to the next thing to do in my day. I take little time to look introspectively, to reflect and analyse experiences to allow myself the chance to move forward. Now that I understand this process and the benefits of completing the 'full cycle', I will try to achieve this in the future.

BOX 7.1 Learning styles

> **Activists** (concrete experience) involve themselves fully in new experiences and enjoy the here and now. They are open-minded and gregarious. They tend to act first and then consider the consequences afterwards. They like excitement, to tackle problems through brainstorming and they thrive on new challenges.

> **Reflectors** (reflective observation) like to stand back and look at things from different perspectives. They are cautious and thoughtful. They are thorough in collecting data and analysing them and will postpone decisions as long as possible. They tend to take a back seat in meetings and discussions and act only after listening and observing others.

> **Theorists** (abstract conceptualization) prize rationality and logic. They like things to be tidy and fit into a rational scheme. They think problems through in a methodical way and like to analyse and synthesize. They tend to be detached and dedicated to rational objectivity and feel uncomfortable with subjective judgements.

> **Pragmatists** (active experimentation) are practical and down to earth. They are keen to try out new ideas, theories and techniques to see if they work in practice. They like to experiment and get on with things and ideas that attract them. They are impatient with open-ended discussions and respond to problems and opportunities as a challenge.

Thus, this model emphasizes that behavioural learning comes from trying things out, learning from what works and what does not, thinking about what was learned, and trying again. It emphasizes that behavioural learning and change do not occur without taking a leap and getting involved. Personal leadership is not a purely intellectual process.

However, while the need for both reflection and experience is fundamental for achieving personal goals, alone they are usually not enough. Many of us reflect on our experience and conclude that we need to be different, but even then do not change.

Indeed, on one celebrated day of the year, millions of people around the world resolve to be different, and then more often than not fail miserably to make any progress with their New Year's resolutions. While being resolute is a good starting point, in order to change behaviour and refreeze (Lewin's second and third phases), additional factors need to be taken into account. These are explained by behaviouralist and social theories of learning and change.

Of all the theories of learning and change, behaviourally based models are possibly the most pervasive. They can be found underpinning most work organizations, early child development activities, teaching methods in schools and management degree programmes. The theories have their routes in operant conditioning and the principles of using positive reinforcers (rewards) and negative reinforcers (punishment) to change behaviour. Managers frequently use positive reinforcers in the form of money, recognition programmes, time off and so on to get employees to behave differently. Often, grades (both rewarding and punishing) are used to direct effort on an MBA programme. Behavioural principles help us to understand our current behaviour and show us how to change and learn new behaviour.

behavioural self-management

Behavioural self-management uses these principles to help us reach our personal goals. Much of our behaviour is based on patterns and actions that are rewarded in various ways. For example, switching on the TV is based on an initial (or antecedent) stimulus (the need to be entertained). If the TV programme provides the solution to our need (for example a compelling thriller), then the behaviour of switching on the TV is reinforced and will continue in the future. These three elements, antecedent stimuli, behavioural response and consequent reinforcer, are called the ABC of behaviour.

Individual behaviour is, of course, more complicated than this and is a combination of our traits, the immediate environment and our previously learned repertoire of potential responses. But the ABC sequence often underpins patterns of behaviour that solve many everyday problems successfully and often automatically. Thus, driving a car is a pattern of behavioural responses to get us from place to place. If our behaviour is reinforced positively each time we drive (that is, we have no accidents or no criticism from passengers), we will continue to drive in the same way.

However, while these patterns can be effective in ensuring success, they can also prevent us from learning new behaviours or changing easily. For example, we rarely question our driving patterns and it is usually only after a few accidents (negative reinforcers) that we may rethink our driving behaviour. To understand how we might change before disaster forces our hand, the following need to be considered:

> Identifying the problem
> Assessing the extent of the problem
> Selecting change goals
> Being aware of behavioural patterns
> Developing reinforcement strategies to change behaviour
> Accounting for the environment and its impact on learning
> Using contracts to monitor and review progress.

identifying the problem

Identifying possible problems and areas for improvement is the first step. At this stage, you may have broad concerns, for example that you are not very approachable, lack confidence or are overly arrogant. The next step is to try and identify the general contexts in which the behaviours do or do not occur. For example, if you feel you are 'not a confident person' or 'not very approachable', you need to identify in general where this might be a problem. Someone may not be very confident in giving speeches to large groups, but in small groups they may feel quite comfortable. An individual may not be very approachable because of the pressures of work, but quite open during leisure time. Thus, it is first necessary to think of behaviours in the situation in which they occur.

If the problem is not clear cut, providing two or more examples of the suspect behaviour will indicate the situations in which it happens.[9] Thus, if you feel you are too aggressive, look for examples in your life where you feel the problem occurs. It may be that it only happens when you are working, or are under pressure from deadlines. Moreover, what does the 'aggressiveness' consist of? Is it abrupt, but polite behaviour, or do you turn into a tyrant? Trying to label the behaviour correctly helps in changing it in the future.

assessing the extent of the problem

To assess the extent of the problem, more specific data on what is or is not happening currently is then needed. Having accurate information, for example on the nature of the behaviour – when, how often and for how long it occurs, and under what circumstances – is necessary if change attempts are to have an impact.

To do this, you need a simple and convenient measuring system, such as a diary. Noting how many and what kinds of comments you make in a syndicate group discussion, or in the lecture theatre, can be made on a notepad. While this may seem awkward, one of the most common reasons for the failure of behavioural change programmes is inadequate data. Box 7.2 is a sample diary that illustrates how the process can help in highlighting the real issues. Indeed, in some cases, just going through the process of recording what you actually do, rather than guessing, can provide new insights. Even better is audio or video feedback. Feedback from peers may also help, but this has to be accurate and specific.

BOX 7.2 Example diary

This is an example from the diary of a student who was underperforming. He was not sure why, as he said he was studying for three hours a day and thought he was bright enough to pass the degree. He was asked to keep a diary of what he did when he studied including the times spent studying. These are some examples of his entries.

Time p.m. Activity

Time	Activity
4.00	Got to library to study.
4–4.10	Find a desk, open books, settle down.
4.20	Realize I am worrying about the forthcoming exam. Only a few pages read.
4.25	David comes to say hello. Only talks for a few minutes, but I have lost my train of thought.
4.35	Find myself staring at the material. Have read the last page three times.
4.40	Realize I am worrying about my relationship with my father, who I haven't seen for some time.

| 4.50 | Managed to read 10 pages by forcing myself to concentrate. Realize that I am in a noisy part of the library. This may not be helping. Decide to find a new location. |
| 5.00 | Resettled. Open books, start reading. |

The student found that the new location did not help very much. After completing his diary for several days, he realized that a lot of 'study' time was spent doing something other than reading the material. Sometimes, it was spent staring at the material, worrying about a range of issues apart from his father, looking around the library at more interesting events and so on. He was putting himself in a location to study but not studying efficiently. He realized that he had to sort out some of the issues that were bothering him before he could make real study progress.

selecting change goals

Having identified possible issues and their impact, the next step is to set goals for improvement. In doing this, select behaviours to change that are important and manageable. Setting goals that are too high or attempting to change too much is likely to lead to failure. Success is more likely to come from concentrating on one or two behaviours, rather than trying to make many changes at the same time.

For example, you may have identified that you are not confident when working in syndicate groups and wish to contribute more to group discussions, or spend more time studying in the evening. In terms of the syndicate group, you might initially aim to contribute more on strategy discussions (rather than attempt the full range of subjects). But even here the input should be broken down into manageable chunks. In the first week, the objective may be to make at least two comments on the material under discussion. Then the number of comments can be increased by two per session. The next step might be to lead the group in analysing a strategy case. Similarly, with increasing your time spent studying, while the goal might be to study for two hours extra each night, it is best to start off by studying for, say, half an hour extra and then build up the study time. Examples of change goals are shown in Box 7.3.[10]

BOX 7.3 Identifying change goals

These are some examples of how general aspirations can be broken down into behavioural goals.

1. **I need to learn to study better:**
   > I want to spend two hours a day reviewing lecture notes.
   > I need to stop studying with the radio and TV on.
   > I need to allocate clear periods during the day for study.

2. **I want to learn to contribute to the study group more:**
   > I will ensure that I never miss study group meetings.
   > I will ask two members of the group for three ways that I can contribute more.
   > I will volunteer to lead a case discussion each week.

3. **I want to become better informed about international events:**
   > I will spend an hour a week reading *Time* magazine.
   > I will read the world section of my daily national newspaper.

> I will watch at least two international current affairs programmes each month.

4. **I want to improve my leadership skills:**
    > I will identify two specific behaviours that I feel show leadership, such as taking a stand on an issue, motivating someone or bringing people together on an issue.
    > I will identify specific environments where these opportunities may arise, such as at work, in a school society or during the formal programme.
    > I will identify what I did well and what I could have done better after each event.

5. **I want to learn to give better presentations:**
    > I will look for occasions where I can volunteer to give more formal presentations.
    > I will identify and apply the main principles for presenting to all presentations I give.
    > I will give at least two presentations a month using these principles.

6. **I want to learn to be less aggressive:**
    > I will identify three occasions where I feel I have been too aggressive each week and which are likely to occur in the future.
    > I will stay calm in at least two of those situations and if necessary say nothing.
    > I will review my actions at the end of each week and identify new ways to reduce my aggression.

7. **I want to learn how to manage my own share portfolio:**
    > I will read a book on share trading each week for the next month.
    > I will attend at least one seminar on portfolio management in the next month.
    > I will arrange a meeting with my bank to identify what help they provide.

being aware of behavioural patterns

When setting change goals, remember that often our behaviour is not just a single isolated action but is part of a sequence or pattern of behaviours, like our driving. These patterns and the context in which they occur need to be understood in order to change the behaviour in question. This can sometimes make even quite small behavioural change difficult, as attempting to change one behaviour is likely to affect others. Thus, if the aim is to increase your study time by two hours a night, this will have implications for other aspects of your life and what will have to disappear as a result. To be successful, these secondary changes also need to be taken into account.

Understanding that there are usually critical points in a sequence of behaviours can also help in making change more effective. Learning to do something different quite often involves locating the problem at the point in the sequence where the behaviour necessary to move to the next step is impeding progress. Usually this is best done early on in the sequence rather than at the end. For example, if you are having difficulty in studying in the evening, then break down your typical sequence of behaviours. If you tend to relax as soon as you get home from business school or work, try to change your early evening behaviour. It is easier to study if you can get yourself out of the lounge at the start of the evening, rather than motivate yourself to switch off the TV at 9 p.m., having been riveted by the latest crime drama, and attempt to tackle a list of accounting or statistics problems.

While goal setting and a greater awareness of behavioural patterns are important, the factor most likely to affect whether change occurs is the impact of positive and negative reinforcers. Behavioural experts assert that most habitual behaviours – including undesirable ones – are maintained by some form of reinforcement. The aim is to identify what reinforcers maintain our current pattern of behaviour and how these, or new reinforcers, can be used to encourage different behaviours.

Whenever possible, positive (rather than negative) reinforcers should be employed to change behaviour. Negative reinforcers are usually seen as less effective because their outcome is not as predictable, is less permanent and creates negative attitudes because we feel we are being punished. Constantly giving ourselves verbal admonishments for not achieving the right grade, studying at the right time or making the right contributions in class does little to help our self-confidence, which itself may impact on us negatively. Anthony Grasha has identified six positive reinforcement types (Box 7.4) as follows:[11]

❶ Social interactions with others, for example praise from others
❷ Things to reduce physiological needs, for example food
❸ Attractive environmental stimuli, for example going to a movie
❹ Personal verbal reinforcement, for example 'you did well'
❺ Use of mental images, for example receiving your degree at graduation
❻ Doing enjoyable things to help modify problem behaviours.

BOX 7.4 **Six types of positive reinforcement**

1. **Social**

| Approval of another person's behaviour | 'That was a nice job you did' |
| | 'I appreciate the time and energy you took to do this' |

| Paying attention to another person | 'That is a good analysis; you must have worked hard to achieve that result' |
| | 'I'd like the rest of the group to see how well you have performed on this' |

2. **Physiological needs**

Food: crisps, chocolate bars, favourite meal
Liquids: soft drinks, wine, milk shakes, beer
Physical: sleeping in, getting a massage

3. **Pleasant or attractive environmental stimuli**

Going to the cinema, attending a concert, taking a drive in the country, sunbathing, buying new clothes

4. **Verbal self-reinforcement**

'I did very well on this problem'
'I think I am doing well in difficult circumstances'
'I know I can get through this'

5. **Mental images**

'I can imagine myself presenting to a large group of people. They are smiling at me and seem pleased to see me. They listen attentively and as I present, I relax and

---

feel more confident. I am getting my points over. The group claps at the end of the presentation'

'I imagine looking John in the eyes and ask him calmly why he is so dismissive of my ideas. He looks at me as if he does not know what I am talking about. But I persist and give him two examples where he ignored me. Although I feel anxious, I tell him how this made me feel. He looks shocked, realizing what he has done. He genuinely wants to know how he can improve our relationship'

6. Responses we enjoy

'I like to jog a lot. I will only allow myself to run if I have completed the case studies for classes the next day.'
'I like watching a good DVD on Friday nights. I will only watch the DVD if I have completed any assignments due that week'

Reinforcers have to be strong enough to stop you doing one thing and start learning the desired behaviour. If they are not, little change will occur. Just hoping you might make a bigger contribution in study group discussions, or work longer of an evening, is unlikely to be enough on its own. Looking at the list above, group contributions might be rewarded with personal verbal reinforcement, such as personal praise for making an attempt to contribute. It could also include giving yourself a small luxury item at the end of a period if the syndicate contribution goals have been met (such as a visit to the cinema or a new CD). Additionally, positive reinforcement may come from the group itself through positive verbal comments about your contribution.

James Gibson and his colleagues note that properly timing reinforcers is extremely important. You are more likely to perform a new behaviour if the reinforcement comes regularly and immediately after performance, rather than having to wait a long time.[12] It is no use giving yourself a night out at the cinema, if it does not come until the end of term several weeks away.

Reinforcing the desired behaviour each time it occurs is particularly important when trying to learn new behaviours. Intermittent reinforcers, given after periods of time (intervals) or after a certain number of responses (ratios), are better when the goal is to maintain new behaviours. For example, it is not necessary to reward yourself constantly once new study patterns have been established, but you do need to ensure you are reinforcing the new rather than the old habits from time to time. This is what Lewin meant by refreezing (Figure 7.1).

It is not necessary to only reward yourself when the new behaviour is perfectly executed. Much of our learning, particularly learning new behaviours, takes place gradually over time, in small steps, and we are unlikely to get things right first time. Consequently, rewarding behaviour that is close to what is desired rather than always waiting for the perfect response is an important principle called 'behaviour shaping'. It is particularly effective at the start of learning something new.

In learning new behaviours, clearly it is important to take the environment into account. We frequently modify our own physical environments inadvertently in order to make desirable things happen, for example setting aside an isolated area or room for study so that environmental distractions, such as the TV, are removed.

This can also include modifying the social environment, such as not going to a social event or inviting friends around when we know we have to work. However, the presence of others, as well as being a temptation, can also be a positive help in achieving our goals. Friends, family and other respected people can help with advice, particularly those who know us well or understand the personal objectives we may have set for ourselves.

Indeed, social leaning theory argues that the social environment is indispensable to our learning. Albert Bandura points out that we acquire much of our behaviour by observation and imitation of others in a social context. He argues that, with complex behaviours, modelling is an indispensable aspect of learning.[13]

Thus, observing others, particularly those who are successful at what they do, can help in giving us a picture of what 'good' looks like. How do those who get their points across in syndicates groups do it successfully? What do they do particularly to influence the other group members? Do they show they are on top of all the information, speak in a certain way or listen particularly well before intervening?

This approach can be broadened to help us in other areas. We can learn a lot from observing successful CEOs, for example how they run their company or demonstrate leadership ability. The aim is to look for the principles they adopt. By observing good role models, we can unravel complicated behaviour patterns, which give us ideas on what might be done differently. However, to be successful, observation of others is not enough on its own. This just gives an overall picture. We then have to identify and incorporate the particular skills into our own repertoire by using the reinforcing techniques outlined above. According to behaviouralists, only by rewarding what we actually do will our behaviour change or improve.

using contracts to progress

An important aspect of attempting to learn new skills and behaviours is to do this within a framework or structure, which guides attempts to improve. Something that helps with this is a contract – an agreement with oneself about the rules to follow in the learning and change process.

Having a contract helps in tracking progress and making judgements about whether your learning programme is working or needs to be modified. Moreover, often people fail in their attempts to improve, because they feel they are not making progress, when in fact they are. Change can be slow, so it is important to record information on what you are actually doing.

According to Arnold Goldstein and Leonard Krasner, a behavioural contract should have short-range goals and be written.[14] It should have seven elements as follows:

1 A clear and detailed description of the target behaviour and achievement goals
2 A time period over which the contract lasts
3 The means by which the behaviour is observed, measured and recorded

4 The specific positive consequences of meeting the goals

5 The timing of reinforcements following the new behaviour

6 Provision for what happens if the contract is not fulfilled

7 A bonus clause indicating the rewards obtainable if the requirements of the contract are exceeded.

Those who are successful at obtaining behavioural change use more techniques for a longer period of time, rate themselves as more committed to personal change, generate more plans and schedules to facilitate change and use methods more frequently and consistently. Research suggests that the chances of success of self-modification increase if a project is chosen that is really important to the person. But be flexible. Change the plan if you are not getting the results aimed for.

Thus, personal leadership involves developing a personal vision or set of aspirations, experimenting and reflecting on experience and using rewards and the environment to reinforce the adoption of new behaviours. If you can stick with these principles, then change can occur.

personal leadership and development

However, while the principles outlined above can certainly help to achieve some of our goals, they may not be enough for significant personal improvement. This is because more fundamental personal change – development that involves transformation to a substantially higher level of ability (similar to a butterfly breaking free from a chrysalis) – is sometimes not something we can control and rarely arises from the structured approaches discussed so far.

Michael Lombardo and Robert Eichinger found that the experiences with the most potential for personal development are things like challenging jobs, working with exceptional people, coping with mistakes and enduring hardships (see Box 7.5).[15] The writers concluded that a developmental experience usually involved five or more of these challenges. They saw work assignments largely providing these, but the challenges can equally be found on a demanding management programme. An MBA will not contain all the items on the list, but it certainly has many of them to varying degrees of intensity.

BOX 7.5 **Eleven challenges common to developmental experience**

Experiences with high potential for personal development have the following characteristics:

1. Success and failure are both possible and will be obvious to others
2. Require aggressive, individual, 'take charge' leadership
3. Involve working with new people, a lot of people, or both
4. Create additional personal pressure, such as that caused by tough deadlines and high stakes
5. Require influencing people, activities and factors over which one has no direct authority or control
6. Involve high variety, including working at a hectic pace, needing to get large amounts of information
7. Will be closely watched by people whose opinion counts

---

8. Require building a team, starting something from scratch or turning round an operation
9. Have a major strategic component and are intellectually challenging
10. Involve interacting with a specially good or bad boss
11. Something important is missing, such as support, key skills or knowledge.

While personal development can result in high gains, the challenges can also be great. Indeed, in some instances they can be quite frightening. Edgar Schein suggests that radical change is characterized more by frustration than achievement. He dismisses the popular notion that such processes are fun, but more a process of guilt and anxiety. Indeed, he does not believe radical change can be achieved without blood, sweat and tears.[16]

While this may sound extreme, Schein is not alone in his views on personal development. At the very least, some degree of tension and sometimes a degree of distress is involved in these processes. As Bill Braddick notes, when some individuals face new and difficult circumstances, they may have to deal with shock, anger, bargaining and depression during the transition process.[17] For some, this description fits well with the MBA. It also demands a particular kind of personal leadership to benefit from the experience.

transitions

The impact of these kinds of experiences is illustrated by the transitions curve described in Figure 7.3.[18] It highlights that often an emotional adjustment has to be made when going through the three stages of change described earlier by Lewin. Unfreezing (or letting go of old ways), finding new ways and refreezing (or making a new beginning) are not detached experiences. For some people, finding new ways can feel like crossing a desert, with little support and no clear sense of direction.

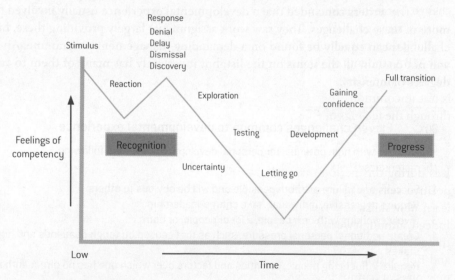

Figure 7.3 Transitions curve

The transitions curve consists of two axes, contrasting feelings of individual competency with the dimension of time. The curve can be applied to any major change in one's life, such as taking on a very different job, starting a new management degree, living in a new country, or radically changing one's personal relationships, such as getting married or moving away from family and friends. Each of these alone can be very challenging. So if you are pursuing an MBA in a different country and without friends or family, careful thought needs to be given to how you manage yourself through the process.

The model has two important aspects. The first of these, the *recognition* stage, is concerned with coming to terms with the kind of change that is needed. The second stage, *progress*, is then concerned with moving forward.

first stage: recognition

With many new situations encountered for the first time, our feelings of competency tend to go down. Things are not what we expected. The new job we took has more conflict than we thought, or we may find the MBA is more pressurized than we expected. Most people react to this by working harder at what they know best. So the new GM from the finance department takes refuge in the numbers; MBA students may cope with the pressure by adopting the same learning patterns they used as undergraduates. While these strategies may make us feel more competent in the short term and so the curve goes up, in neither case has there been any development. In order to progress, both the manager and the student have to learn to work smarter and differently, rather than longer on familiar things.

At the top of the curve, the individual needs to take a deep look at what they are doing well and what they are not doing well. In very different circumstances, such as working in a new country, new ways of thinking, behaving and working have to be found. But these cannot be picked up immediately. Not only do the subtleties of the culture have to be learned, but just coping with day-to-day activities has to be mastered. Consequently, as we really look at what we don't know and how much we have to change, our feelings of competency can go down. As they do, we can feel out of control, isolated, stressed and fearful.

But it does not require relocation to a new country to engender these feelings. Many new MBA students on receiving the marks for their first piece of assessed work can feel the same way. Certainly feeling overwhelmed and anxious by these first experiences is not uncommon. This is where true personal leadership is necessary to take oneself through the feelings of gloom and on to better things.

second stage: progress

It is during this period that giving ourselves positive self-reinforcement (particularly positive self-talk) for making progress, no matter how small, is critical. In order to learn new skills, it is necessary to take risks, experiment and accept some mistakes. Indeed, although we may feel least like it, taking risks and accepting that we will not get things completely right first time and rewarding close tries is important. Jeffrey Pfeffer and Bob Sutton argue that whether we are enhancing our skills or radically learning new ones, it cannot be done without making mistakes.[19] Indeed, Warren Bennis and Burt Nanus assert that all learning involves some 'failure' and requires practice in a supportive environment.[20]

The temptation is to go back to what is familiar or quit altogether. But that will not result in any kind of personal development. While there will be mistakes, there will also be successes. One of the reasons why making a personal contract is so important is that our progress can be recorded, we can reduce feelings of being overwhelmed and we can reflect on successes and why these occurred. As we get runs on the board and find that the new ways of working are yielding results, improvement gains momentum. As confidence returns, development often accelerates, and as we begin to master most aspects of our new situation, we move to the top of the curve.

The importance of the transitions curve is not in highlighting the potential difficulties involved in radical change, but that big gains in personal improvement may not come easily. It also reminds us that when the going gets tough, this is not an indication that the wrong decision has been made in taking on a management degree, but that one may indeed be on the path to real personal improvement. As one student noted:

> The curve helped me understand more about transitions and change. I feel I am now better prepared to cope with the rollercoaster of the next few months. The idea that there is a common pattern of emotional responses to periods of change will help me retain my confidence in meeting the challenges of the degree.

public leadership

Developing personal leadership skills will assist in becoming a better public leader. Understanding the personal change process will help you to understand change in others. However, the skills required for public leadership are different in several ways. With public leadership, you are no longer concerned with achieving the task alone, but working through other people. While Hollywood often portrays the lone warrior as a heroic leader, in most organizational contexts it usually leads to inglorious failure. Indeed, this shift from doing everything yourself to genuinely helping others to improve their contribution is possibly one of the hardest to make in improving public leadership skills.

There are, however, many opportunities on an MBA programme to practise public leadership skills. In doing this, it is important to keep in mind the following principles:

❶ Leadership is concerned with change, which involves risk.

❷ A picture of the future has to be created and communicated.

❸ It is the leader who motivates others to achieve the vision.

❹ Leadership doesn't work without understanding others.

❺ There are many different leadership styles that can be effective.

Let us deal briefly with each of these.

leadership is concerned with change and risk

Our discussion of personal leadership has centred on personal change. In leading others, change is also involved. Both you as the leader and your colleagues as followers have to be prepared for this and be given the appropriate support. For some people, this can be a challenging process, as the transitions curve indicates and is illustrated by the following comment:

I have become conscious of the fact that while I thought I had a good approach to change, I exhibit many non-learning behaviours. These include blaming others for my shortfalls, not wanting to be challenged for decisions I have made. Being cautious, guarded and at times defensive. I don't want to take risks, I justify what I do, I like being in control and in my comfort zone.

a picture of the future has to be created and communicated

Reducing the risk of change can be assisted by giving people a sense of direction and a sense of what the outcomes of changes might be. On an MBA, many of the activities will be fairly short-term exercises and often in syndicates. While this may not give you the opportunity to provide grand visions on a regular basis, it does give you the chance to practise showing your colleagues a way forward.

However, the opportunity should not be missed to also provide something more inspiring than clear task goals. Most syndicates are together for at least a term and helping to find an overall sense of purpose for the group is an important leadership skill. If a syndicate group has a broader purpose, such as the overall achievement of high standards or the aim to build a strong group that can overcome any challenges, then this can help in providing focus when the group may be going off track.

How you communicate task goals and a broader mission, however, is crucial. No group of peers is going to go along with you merely because you stated your views. In order to lead in these circumstances, you have to be a perceptive listener, good at one-on-one communication and also in small groups. In order to do this effectively, you need to think about the communications skills discussed in Chapter 6.

A critical aspect of the communication process as a leader is not only what you say, but also what do. Leaders quickly lose credibility when they say one thing and do another. On the MBA, there are many opportunities to practise what you preach. If you suggest that your colleagues should meet deadlines, then you must meet them also. If you encourage sharing materials and ideas, then you have to do it. Not being aware of behavioural symbols and their impact is a major issue in leadership and one that can be easily practised on an MBA.

the leader motivates others to achieve the vision

Because you are dealing with a group of peers, with no formal authority or the rewards normally available in the workplace, MBA environments are an excellent opportunity to develop genuine motivational abilities. Indeed, if you can learn to motivate your peers on a management programme, you are more likely to be effective in many different environments.

However, peer environments can be challenging. Motivating other management students to follow your path involves more than just pushing your point of view. This is where the ability to listen, empathize and provide a way forward that appeals to other people, as well as you, is critical. Moreover, while the rewards at your disposal may be limited, you still have motivational tools, such as praise, helping others overcome their own personal hurdles, giving others confidence, hope or the will to succeed. Indeed, some people will follow leaders because they embody certain ideals or values, not because they offer pragmatic rewards.

Don't underestimate the impact of being enthusiastic, positive and dynamic. People will follow you if you demonstrate that you know what you are doing, are confident in yourself (and them) and credible in your belief that you will lead them to somewhere better.

leadership doesn't work without understanding others

However, doing this does not come from some sort of telepathy, but from empathy. In addition to working out what rewards you can provide, you also have to work out what motivates others and the kinds of leadership actions that will get them to respond. This is not straightforward, but is a skill that can be developed on an MBA, as one student illustrated:

What comes out of the MBA for me apart from the business skill sets, theories and frameworks is more about the subtleties, relating to people, situations, learning how to draw more of the best out of people. All my positions in the past have come to be team leader positions, but I realize what I was doing was more transaction management than people management. The MBA helped me to understand people better.

However, understanding others often has to be taken a step further. The real test is to use this knowledge to reconcile different aspirations and viewpoints. Lynda Hill suggests that among all the challenges facing new managers, the need to reconcile different constituencies' expectations and interests is probably the most difficult.[21] Thus, if you can practise these skills with your MBA colleagues, this should help considerably in leading in the workplace.

different leadership styles can be effective

How you take people forward varies considerably. The current literature tends to suggest that charismatic and inspirational leadership approaches are the answer. If you have this ability, then that is terrific. But there are many ways of moving people and helping them to excel. Indeed, a large part of the leadership literature, called 'contingency studies', suggests leadership style depends on the circumstances. One style rarely fits all situations. Even Winston Churchill, the popular example of a charismatic leader, was not right for all circumstances. While he excelled during the Second World War, his approach was not appropriate for reconstructing postwar Britain.

Two things are particularly important in considering your style. The first is that public leadership is about motivating others, helping them to achieve their goals (which will also be partly yours) and finding answers to their challenges. If your starting point is other people, then you are in with a chance of making a difference.

The second is that while leadership emphasizes motivating others, it does not require a leader to become a chameleon. The key is in working from a position of personal strength. It requires you to assess your own preferred style and to work from that starting point to enhance your skills. Yes, you may have to develop your communication skills, or your ability to empathize, for example. But do this in a way that brings out what you have already and use your personal raw material to your advantage. If you are never going to be a great orator, then do not worry about it, but focus on developing your leadership skills in small groups or one on one. Box 7.6 outlines some of these skills.

leadership opportunities on the MBA

There are a number of different contexts in which you can practise these skills. In addition to the different formal group situations frequently found on an MBA, there are also many opportunities outside the formal programme, or at work if you are a part-time student. The range of clubs, societies and social activities at business school provides many informal opportunities to develop public leadership skills. As one student noted:

I ran for the Student Representative Council to be more involved and I am a much better leader of people now. This is because I have had to interact with different people and the diversity of the student body and interact in so many different situations and work with so many different people. The extracurricular activities have been an important part of the experience and really instrumental in my leadership development.

global leadership

An additional opportunity found on an increasing number of MBA programmes is in laying the foundation for developing global leadership skills. This has become particularly important over the past few years, with more companies looking for people who can function effectively in a global environment.[22]

Global experience can be gained in several different ways, for example by taking an MBA in a foreign country or getting involved in an exchange programme run by some of the top schools. However, inherent in most MBA programmes are opportunities for global learning. Subjects exploring the global business environment, ranging from global marketing to international finance, are often found on management degrees. But in addition to the functional knowledge, there are also important opportunities of a different kind. These are in understanding how to lead people from different cultures and nations.

multicultural opportunities

The wide range of backgrounds of students on most management degree programmes provides a wealth of opportunity to explore different views and ways of thinking. As one student commented:

One of the things that surprises and delights me every day I go to class is that here I am in a syndicate group with an Indonesian and there I am having lunch with a Norwegian and then I might be discussing a problem with someone from Peru. The people I am meeting from around the world and who I am learning from is of tremendous value.

The opportunities to develop real skills in understanding others, a leadership principle noted above, is provided through such multicultural opportunities. Taking time to explore individual expectations, assumptions and values can give insights into the needs and motivations of people from divergent backgrounds in a way which may not be possible in many other situations, even from working in different countries. Many multinational companies provide cultural immersion programmes and work experiences from which you can learn. But the work environment is often different to an MBA degree and assumptions can remain hidden from view (such as beliefs about gender, leadership, authority, age and etiquette). The reason for this is that while an MBA often has the same intensity as the work environment, it also provides the space and developmental opportunity to explore problems, misunderstandings and hopes and fears that are often not available in a work context. As one student noted:

Even though my previous work was on a global multinational project, in a multinational team and with a multinational client, the interaction I had was superficial. As a result, I made a very bad mistake, where I basically had a stand-up argument with a Japanese colleague. While in the end everything was fine, I realized, based on what I have learned on the MBA, that however broad-minded I thought I was about international issues, this is not sufficient. Cultural background is more important than I gave it credence and I am now more mindful of that and more insightful of the amount of preparation I need to do before going into a cross-cultural interaction.

It is in syndicate groups that the best opportunities to practise global leadership skills present themselves. Multinational syndicate groups are the rule rather than the exception on many internationally accredited MBA programmes. Here a real understanding can be gained of how people from very different perspectives think and act. However, such groups also have challenges as well as benefits and the learning does not always come easily. Individuals from different national cultures bring with them different mental views of the world and the outcomes can be exceptional or disastrous. While multicultural groups can perform highly on complex decision-making tasks, have higher creativity and develop better solution alternatives when compared with culturally homogeneous teams, the downside is that they frequently fail to realize their potential.[23]

Thus, the leadership principles outlined earlier have to be applied with a great deal of sensitivity and skill. It is important in leading a multicultural group that we recognize our own cultural assumptions, the differences of others, and that diversity is an opportunity to learn rather than a barrier to completing tasks quickly.

Several things can help with developing this kind of group. Informal time spent face to face can be especially valuable in understanding colleagues' preferences and assumptions. Getting team members to explain cultural differences also helps in learning, as highlighted in Box 7.7.[24] Understanding will not occur overnight. But a purposeful, open and patient approach to understanding cultural differences is an invaluable contribution to developing a global leadership ability.

BOX 7.7 Explaining cultural differences

Martha Maznevski and Lena Zander illustrate how, when conducting a training programme with members of an American-Japanese-German joint venture project, ignorance of culturally related different courses of action can be identified and addressed. When, for example, Americans, Japanese and Germans exchange information, make presentations and discuss issues in order to reach a common decision, they are unaware that their suggestions are based on different 'culturally programmed' courses of action, which remain hidden to the participants. One's own ethnocentric expectations and practice remain the unquestioned benchmark against which others' actions are considered 'not normal': thus, the Japanese are 'not logical', Americans 'not credible' and Germans 'meticulous'. They encourage participants to exchange their intuitive assessment of critical situations, and so express their tacit intercultural knowledge explicitly. Then, erroneous assessment can be corrected, respect for different courses of action can be instilled and effective ways of dealing with differences can be learned.

---

conclusion

This chapter explores leadership from two vantage points. In developing personal leadership, the chapter outlines the different opportunities for learning and change that can help the individual to fulfil their aspirations on the MBA. Personal leadership is a combination of thought and action, which has both challenges and benefits. The development of these skills may lead not only to personal goal achievement, but also help in understanding the challenges involved in public leadership.

Public leadership, the ability to lead others, is a complex skill that will not occur overnight. But there are many opportunities on an MBA programme to at least prepare the ground for developing this capability. Even if the opportunity to take leadership subjects is available on your programme, it is nevertheless critical that you also pursue some of the ideas in this chapter. Leadership is not about taking a subject and ticking it off, but a daily challenge, which without a proactive approach, is unlikely to develop to any real depth. But despite the effort needed, this can pay real dividends. Indeed, the potential to understand and potentially lead people from different cultures, backgrounds and perspectives may be a tremendous advantage offered by some MBA programmes. Developing real depth in this area may give you an advantage in the international arena that truly puts you above the rest.

references/notes

1. Bennis, W. (2005) 'What leaders allow themselves to know', in P. Michelman, *Becoming an Effective Leader* (Boston: Harvard Business School Press) p. 171.
2. Manz, C. (1992) *Mastering Self Leadership* (Englewood Cliffs, NJ: Prentice Hall).
3. John Kotter in his seminal work on senior managers (1982) *The General Managers*, New York: Free Press) emphasized the need for knowledge of the industry, job and business environment. In looking at leadership potential, Morgan McCall et al. (McCall, M.W., Spreitzer, G.M. and Mahoney, J. (1994) *Identifying Leadership Potential in Future International Executives*, Boston: ICEDR) highlight the need to 'know the business', which is concerned with having a strong technical base, understanding how the business works and how the 'parts fit' together. The importance of this knowledge should not be underestimated in leadership.
4. Jacques, E. and Clement, S.D. (1991) *Executive Leadership: A Practical Guide to Managing Complexity* (Oxford: Blackwell).
5. Kets de Vries, M.F.R. (1995) *Life and Death in the Executive Fast Lane* (San Francisco: Jossey-Bass).
6. Kurt Lewin's ideas on individual change were developed in the late 1940s. His work has been appraised by many academics. For a recent review, see Burnes, B. (2004) 'Kurt Lewin and the planned approach to change: a reappraisal', *Journal of Management Studies*, 41(6): 977–1002.
7. Kolb, D.A. (1984) *Experiential Learning: Experience as the Source of Learning and Development* (Englewood Cliffs, NJ: Prentice Hall) p. 42.
8. Honey, P. and Mumford, A. (1992) *The Manual of Learning Styles* (Maidenhead: Peter Honey) pp. 4–5.
9. Watson, D.L. and Tharpe, R.G. (1972) *Self-directed Behaviour: Self-modification for Personal Adjustment* (Belmont, CA: Wadsworth) pp. 66–104.
10. Adapted from Grasha, A.F. (1987) *Practical Applications of Psychology* (Boston: Little, Brown) p. 166.
11. Adapted from Grasha (1987) op. cit. p. 142.
12. Gibson, J.L., Ivancevich, J.M. and Donnelly, J.H. (1994) *Organizations: Behavior, Structure, Processes* (Burr Ridge, IL: Irwin) p. 178.
13. Bandura, A. (1971) *Social Learning Theory* (New York: General Learning Press).
14. Goldstein, A.P. and Krasner, L. (1991) 'Self-management methods' in Kanfer, F.H. and Goldstein, A.P. (eds) *Helping People Change: A Textbook of Methods* (New York: Pergamon Press) pp. 305–60.
15. Lombardo, M.M. and Eichinger, R.W. (1989) *Eighty-eight Assignments for Development in Place*, Report 36 (Greensboro: Centre for Creative Leadership) p. 2.
16. Schein, E. (2002) 'The anxiety of learning', an interview by D.L. Coutu, *Harvard Business Review*, **80**(3): 100–9.
17. Braddick, W.A.G. (1988) 'How top managers really learn', *Journal of Management Development*, **7**(4): 55–62.
18. Adapted from Parker, C. and Lewis, R. (1981) 'Beyond the Peter principle: managing successful transitions', *Journal of European Industrial Training*, **5**(6).
19. Pfeffer, J. and Sutton, R.I. (1999) 'Knowing "what" to do is not enough: turning knowledge into action', *California Management Review*, **42**(1): 83–108.
20. Bennis, W. and Nanus, B. (1997) *Leaders: Strategies for Taking Charge* (New York: Harper Business) p. 60.
21. Keller, Johnson, L. (2005) 'Debriefing Linda A. Hill: accelerating the new manager's start' in *Becoming an Effective Leader* (Boston: Harvard Business School Press) p. 124.
22. For more on this, see Dainty, P. (2006) 'Developing global business competencies', in P. Murray, D. Poole and G. Thomson (eds) *Contemporary Issues in Management and Organisational Behaviour* (Melbourne: Thomson) pp. 222–45.
23. Maznevski, M.L. and Zander, L. (2001) 'Leading global teams: overcoming the challenge of the power paradox', in M.E. Mendenhall, T.M. Kühlmann and G.K. Stahl (eds) *Developing Global Business Leaders* (London: Quorum Books) pp. 157–74.
24. Ibid.

8 developing a career management capability

The MBA is one of the few qualifications that opens up career paths in many sectors, ranging from management consultancy and investment banking through to manufacturing and public administration. As one student commented:

The MBA will definitely help me make the change I want to. From a résumé point of view, I will have better credentials, but from a confidence standpoint, I will know what jobs I can handle. Before I would have shied away from some areas as I felt underqualified. But now I have a lot more confidence that I can do many things and I can convince people of my ability.

However, while the MBA may bring real meaning to the notion that 'the world is your oyster', it can also lead to the dangerous assumption that the MBA on its own is the solution to all employment-related problems. It isn't. In addition to the qualification, a career capability, as with the other capabilities discussed throughout the book, requires considerable thought and application.

There are several reasons for this. One is due to the changing nature of the work environment. Downsizing, dislocation and personal dissatisfaction mean few people now stay with the same company for life. The changing nature of the employment contract, discussed in Chapter 14, indicates that this may not just mean having several different jobs, but pursuing several different careers (and up to seven according to some estimates).

A second reason is that while many companies put a lot of effort into developing and retaining their staff, many also accept that careers are ultimately the responsibility of the individual. Indeed, some writers refer to the career of the twenty-first century as the *protean* career, driven by the person and not the organization and requiring periodic personal reinvention (Box 8.1).[1] No matter how well meaning a company may be, it is up to the individual to develop the skills, find job satisfaction and monitor potential opportunities to achieve long-term career success.

BOX 8.1 **Characteristics of the protean career**

> Focus on *psychological* success rather than vertical success.
> Lifelong series of identity changes and continuous learning.
> Career age counts, not chronological age.
> Job security is replaced by the goal of employability.
> Sources of development are work challenges and relationships, not necessarily training and retraining programmes.

> ❯ The new career contract is not a pact with the organization, rather, it is an agreement with one's self and one's work.
>
> ❯ Focus on learning *metaskills* (learning how to learn), that is, how to develop self-knowledge (about one's identity) and adaptability.
>
> ❯ Adaptability and identity learning is best accomplished through interactions with other people (reflected in interdependence, mutuality, reciprocity and learning from differences).

A third is that this is a long-term process. For many, it spans over 40 years and cannot be taken lightly. Work has a major impact on our quality of life and many people define themselves by what they do. A positive job and career experience can provide intellectual challenge, emotional satisfaction, financial remuneration and social interaction. A bad experience can give rise to misery, stress and depression, illustrated by the following student comment:

One of my greatest fears is waking up one day, perhaps 10 years down the track and asking myself what exactly it was that I had done with my life. To date, I have accepted opportunities as they have arisen. Approximately half the time I have had some general goals in mind, while at others I largely ignored my short-, medium- and long-term objectives. My worry is that such a short-term focused behaviour pattern could eventually lead to frustration later about missed opportunities, pointless but demanding commitments and a feeling of meaninglessness.

Consequently, managing one's career is a critical, long-term exercise requiring careful thought, good skills and ongoing dedication. But this exercise cannot be left to the end of the MBA. This chapter encourages you to consider career issues early on and is an aid to developing a career capability. It does not try to address areas where there is already a wealth of material, such as résumé writing or salary negotiation. Explored here are the key career development principles most pertinent to the MBA student not only at the end of their studies, but also at the start of the MBA and long after graduation. These include having a career direction, understanding personal aptitudes and preferences, knowing the work environment and accessing career opportunities. Let us start with planning a career direction.

planning a career direction

Planning anything that lasts a lifetime is, of course, going to be less than precise. Like life itself, work experiences will have unpredictable lows and opportunistic highs, both of which add to the richness of our experience. A sense of direction, however, increases the chances of finding a satisfying career. As Ed Holton notes, a direction is a broad plan, not a narrow path.[2] It should be detailed enough for you to be able to identify jobs that will be potentially satisfying, but flexible enough for you to explore a variety of jobs and accommodate any real opportunities that come along. One student sees it as follows:

The aim of my career plan is to build a better understanding of my strengths and weaknesses and to use this understanding to establish a more effective framework for making career choices. In the past, I have been more reactive than proactive in many of my employment decisions, which has resulted in me continuing my previous career for longer than I should have. I feel that I might have been able to make a change much earlier if I had had a clearer idea of where I wanted to be and what was really important to me.

It is not unusual to be confused about career goals. Some people have a clear career vision and achieve it. But, for most, the process is challenging and changing for several reasons. Many people lack a clear understanding of their full range of personal characteristics and preferences. There are numerous potential employment opportunities but often information on their benefits and drawbacks is not readily available. Social and family pressures can complicate career choices. Changing interests can make the once perfect job now feel like a millstone.

This complexity is all the more reason for developing a sense of career direction well before graduation – not only because the process requires thought, but also because it can affect what you do during your degree. Career considerations should not preclude you from taking elective subjects for pure enjoyment, but they need to be taken with the potential trade-offs in mind. A combination of certain subjects may place you in a better position to get a finance or operations job. Indeed, on some MBA courses, you can obtain additional professional qualifications (such as in marketing or HR) by taking specified electives. You can also gain valuable career insights, for example, from internships (whether self or school generated) or extracurricular activities and clubs, such as those exploring entrepreneurial ventures.

Consequently, in finding a career path, it is important to think systematically around the model highlighted in Figure 8.1, which emphasizes two main areas. The first is concerned with analysing where you are now. The aim here is to identify, as much as possible, what motivates you (and the rewards you value), what you are able to do (your skills and abilities) and what interests you (the types of work activities you find engaging).

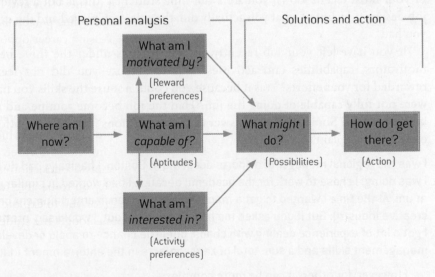

Figure 8.1 Career development

The second area is concerned with what you might do and the range of possible areas and potential occupations that can provide you with a fulfilling career. It also considers the different avenues for achieving career goals. Several paths may be possible with different implications. Let us start by reviewing where you are now.

where you are now: understanding aptitudes and preferences

The earlier chapters in the book have encouraged you to explore your aptitudes in terms of personal capabilities. The second part of the book will give you an idea of the functional capabilities that most interest you. This will help you to think about the kinds of skills and abilities that will form the foundation of your career choices. Additionally, your preferences, in terms of what motivates you (and the rewards you value, such as salary and promotional opportunities) and what job activities interest and engage you, need to be taken into account when thinking about careers. This is illustrated by the following student comment:

In order to develop a better framework for managing my career, I need to have a greater awareness of what is important for me both in the short term and the long term. This not only requires understanding strengths, weaknesses and values, but also developing the tools that will enable me to enhance my level of self-awareness.

Two broad approaches (used both together and separately) are typically taken in helping us to understand these career-influencing factors better. One is through an analysis of our work and educational experiences. The other is through profiling and psychometric testing. Let us deal with occupational analysis first.

occupational analysis

most recent or current work role

Occupational analysis usually involves two slightly different approaches. The first requires you to think about either your current work role (if you are in employment) or your most recent job (if you are a full-time student). This is not a review of your job description, but of what you actually did, the roles you played and the experiences you had.

If you have left your job recently, list the reasons under the three headings of motivators, capabilities and activities. Was it because you did not feel suitably rewarded for your efforts? Was it because you could not use the skills you had, or you were not fully capable of doing the job? Had the job become routine and no longer interested you? Sometimes the answer to these questions is quite straightforward, as one student explains:

I was the regional manager of a sports academy in Boston. I basically had no idea what I was doing. I chose to work for the academy because I had worked in similar jobs while at uni. At the time I wanted to get a management position in entertainment or another creative industry. But if you asked me how this worked out, I would say 'pretty bad'. I got a lot of experience dealing with chaos, but little chance to apply or develop my management skills and a sum total of zero contacts in the entertainment industry.

However, for others it can be more complex:

As a national manager of a large and vital team of design professionals, I had reached a long-term career goal prematurely by the age of 29. My goals included financial success, an interesting career and the attainment of power. But I hadn't expected to achieve these until my late thirties at the earliest. Since that point, while I appeared to be successful in the eyes of other people, my job increasingly lacked any meaning.

Consequently, careful thought may be needed to understand what may have prompted recent job changes. The reasons listed below may help:

Motivators:

> you did/do not get paid enough
> opportunities for promotion were/are limited
> the hours of work do/did not suite your lifestyle
> the culture of the organization is/was not right
> relationships with your boss or colleagues are/were problematic.

Capabilities:

> you lack/lacked the skills or knowledge needed to do the job now
> you lack the skills or knowledge needed to do the job in the future
> you were not able to develop the skills to change occupation
> the job did not utilize your skills fully enough
> there were limited opportunities to develop new skills.

Interests:

> there seemed to be nothing new to learn
> the days had become routine
> the challenges seemed the same
> the job felt too easy
> other jobs/occupations/industries seemed more interesting
> you were doing activities you dislike, such as selling or report writing
> the work no longer felt satisfying.

historical work-related experiences

The second approach, although using the same principles, involves a more detailed historical analysis. It is particularly applicable to those of you who have not recently left a job (entered the MBA from university) or continue to be in employment (part-time students).

In this case, you go back (usually to when you left school) and identify any career-related decisions. Some writers suggest you focus on your educational choices or the critical work experiences you have had, for example going to university, significant vocational jobs, or the reasons for taking and leaving subsequent jobs. Having located each event or career decision, you then identify the factors that had most influence on the decision in terms of the three categories above.

Other writers suggest you look at all events and experiences that could help in understanding career decisions. This involves looking not only at activities directly related to work, but any significant experiences or projects, whether it was in the Girl Guides or through the local car enthusiasts club. In each case, you again try to identify the activities that motivated you, interested you and allowed you to apply or develop your skills. Even if you had a bad experience, for example during a summer job, identifying what was distasteful about the experience can add to your personal career knowledge.

The main aim of all occupational analysis exercises is to look for patterns. Are there any consistencies in terms of the three categories? Have you moved jobs because of motivating factors or because your interests were not being met? Other patterns may show themselves in terms of external or internal factors. For example, external factors like status, prestige or power may have driven your choices more than internal factors such as work variety, project work or working with people. There is nothing inherently wrong with any pattern so long as you are aware of it. As one student commented:

In reviewing my career decisions, I found I had been driven by the prestige of moving up the ladder. But in doing this I had lost sight of some important needs. This helped to explain the increasing sense of malaise I'd been experiencing in my job. My performance reviews and customer feedback indicated that I was successful, but it did not feel like success to me. The roles I had taken had lacked the opportunity for creativity and the chance to use other abilities that were important to me. I had been deluding myself into thinking that what others wanted was what I wanted.

personal profiling

Profiling is a process of using questionnaires and tests to give you greater clarity around your career interests. Most business schools offer career services with expert help. Although the profiles have different labels, they usually provide information around the areas of motivations, capabilities and interests. The career instruments most widely used with MBA students are the Birkman Method[3] and CareerLeader,[4] although there are several others. Some can be taken online, but they often need the help of a professional adviser to help interpret the results.

Nevertheless, it is important to remember that you are ultimately responsible for your career, not the counsellors. You still have to spend time reflecting on your aptitudes and preferences. Moreover, outside help is not always necessary to make progress. This book is concerned with helping you understand your capabilities better, both personal and functional. The self-assessment encouraged in Chapter 2 is an aid to contributing to this self-understanding. This should also be used, along with any other questionnaires you may use on your MBA, to provide you with a more rounded personal profile. You are essentially building a three-dimensional picture of yourself (of motivators, capabilities and interests) but some of the parts may be missing. As you progress in your career, you will be able to add to the picture, but it may only be in later stages of your career that you can see all sides of the profile.

However, the picture is more than a static personal image. It is the key to slotting yourself into an appropriate career. There are many potential slots. Three general areas were highlighted at the start of the book: the general manager (emphasizing managing people and resources), the functional specialist (largely using expertise and knowledge) and the commercial entrepreneur (concentrating on finding new paths and exploiting ideas). These are good but broad starting points. The more you can add to your understanding of these areas and your preferences towards them the better.

An exercise that helps to do this and uses both occupational analysis and personal profiling has been developed by Edgar Schein.[5] His approach combines an interview exploring career-influencing factors with a questionnaire. The aim is to identify career direction in terms of eight categories or career anchors. The anchors are outlined in Box 8.2.[6] Particularly valuable for MBA students is that the career anchors address managerial, functional and entrepreneurial career paths. Also important is Schein's description of a general managerial anchor. This consists of having abilities in three areas – analytical skills, interpersonal and group skills – but also emotional resilience to handle power and responsibility. Having an emotional capability as a general manager is particularly important, as we have emphasized in Chapter 5.

BOX 8.2 Schein's career anchors

Technical/functional competence: With this anchor, you would not give up the opportunity to apply your technical/functional skills and develop those skills to a higher level. Your sense of identity comes from exercising these skills. You are willing to manage others in your functional area, but are not interested in management per se, and are unwilling to go into general management if it means you would have to leave your own area of expertise.

General managerial competence: With this anchor, you would not give up the opportunity to climb higher in the organization to enable you to integrate cross-functional activity and take responsibility for a unit's output. You want to be fully accountable for total results and identify with the success of the organization. Working in a technical/functional role is viewed as a learning experience in order to move to a generalist job as soon as possible.

Autonomy/independence: With this anchor, you would not give up the opportunity to define your work in your own way. In an organization, you remain in jobs that allow you work flexibility. If organizational rules are too restricting, you seek occupations that allow you considerable freedom, such as teaching or consulting. You refuse promotion or advancement opportunities to retain autonomy.

Security/stability: With this anchor, you would not give up employment security or tenure in a job or organization. The main concern is to have a sense of having succeeded. This shows up in concerns for financial or employment security. Such stability may involve accepting whatever is asked of you by an employer in exchange for job tenure. Everyone is concerned with security at some time, but as a career anchor, security and stability are always a primary concern.

Entrepreneurial creativity: With this anchor, you would not give up the opportunity to create an organization or enterprise of your own, built on your own abilities. You want to prove that you can create an enterprise that is the result of your own effort. You may work for others in an organization to learn and assess opportunities, but you will go out on your own as soon as you can manage it.

Service/dedication to a cause: With this anchor, you would not give up the opportunity to achieve something of value, such as making the world a better place to live, solving environmental problems, helping others and so on. You pursue such opportunities even if it means changing organizations. You do not accept transfers or promotions that do not enable you to fulfil your values.

Pure challenge: With this anchor, you would not give up the opportunity to work on solutions to seemingly unsolvable problems, to win over tough opponents, or overcome difficult obstacles. Some people find this challenge in intellectual kinds of work, such as engineering. Others find it in complex, multifaceted situations such as in being a strategy consultant and others in interpersonal competition such as being a professional athlete. Novelty, variety and difficulty are ends in themselves.

Lifestyle: With this anchor, you would not give up a situation that permits you to balance and integrate your personal needs, family needs and the requirements of your career. All the major sectors of your life have to work together and need a career situation that provides enough flexibility to achieve such integration. Your identity is tied up more with how you live your total life and success is defined more broadly than career success alone.

where you might go: understanding possibilities and actions

What you are capable of doing, what motivates you and what interests you are three different factors that have different implications for the kind of work you do. Ideally, your career should consist of job experiences that are high on each of these three factors. If you are to find what Doug Hall calls a 'path with a heart', it is important that it is driven by these fundamental needs.[7] However, your career path does not need to be linear, as this student explained:

If anyone ever asks me what would be my dream job, I would say it should include food and wine, helping people be happy and performing the lead role in these activities. Reading Doug Hall's article helped me to understand that it is appropriate to want to be working in an area you are passionate about even if it is not what would be traditionally seen as a high-flying business career. It also made me realize that I don't have to do it right now if it doesn't feel right.

Consequently, our road to success can take many different turns and may also involve compromise. For example, a career is not necessarily always onwards and upwards. It can be a move up in the hierarchy, but it can also entail a lateral move or even a step backwards. Such moves can be strategic (when it necessary to break into a different industry or functional area) or permanent (the need for a different lifestyle). A career is a sequence of different job opportunities aimed at fulfilling your varying needs at different times in your work life.

Indeed, we may well have different needs at different points in our life and it is important to understand what our motivators are in order to maintain drive and energy. As one student said:

Certainly for me this has been the case. Initially in my career I was more concerned with promotions than earning a lot of money. However, I am now more focused on financial reward, probably due to my mortgage.

realities of the work environment

In addition to understanding changing motivations and interests, the second critical component of career management is in understanding the changing nature of the work environment. While the MBA is probably the most portable degree in the world and can open up many doors, the degree is not a guarantee of anything and its attraction can vary between countries, industries, employers and over time. If your dreams are to come true, you also need to understand some realities.

The first reality is that attitudes towards the MBA, by both employers and business commentators, can range across the full spectrum. At one end, there are still many employers who do not regard an MBA as a particularly important qualification. A few are antagonistic, some are sceptical, some are ignorant and others wait to be persuaded. So the notion that an MBA graduate can walk into a job and be received with open arms in all circumstances is erroneous.

However, at the other end of the spectrum, the attitudes can be very different, particularly from employers who themselves have completed an MBA. They and those who have knowledge of the MBA will understand that you will have put a lot of effort into getting the degree and, in the right circumstances, will make a valuable contribution to their organization. However, the point is you that cannot assume anything about the way employers will view you or the MBA. In some circumstances, it will speak for itself, in others you will have to speak for it.

A second reality is that there has been a considerable increase in the number of MBA and associated postgraduate management degrees over the past decade or so. Despite the constant prediction of a business school shake-out, the likelihood of the popularity of the MBA diminishing is slim. Certainly, its form and content may change, but the need for qualified management professionals will be strong if the predictions of population growth, particularly in the Asia Pacific region, are realized. However, this does mean and will continue to mean that there are more qualified people on the market. For many jobs and particularly the most attractive jobs, you are likely to be in competition with equally talented MBA and professional applicants.

A third reality is that while the MBA opens up many doors because of its general nature, there are few areas where an MBA is a prerequisite for employment. Some professional jobs, most notably in the medical and legal profession, require certain qualifications to practise, but this is not the case in business and management. Some industries are seen as more supportive of MBAs than others, particularly management consulting and some jobs in the financial services sector. But even here other realities are taking hold, with an increasing trend in both areas to hire undergraduates and/or people from non-business disciplines and other professional fields.

A fourth reality is that there are broad economic trends, sometimes regional and sometimes international, which impact on your employment opportunities. Several Western economies, for example, have experienced the following changes:

> a reduction in employment in primary sectors such as agriculture and fishing
> relatively fewer jobs in manufacturing industry
> relatively more jobs in the service sectors, such as retailing, financial services, health and personal services
> an increase in the relative importance of employment in smaller organizations and self-employment
> outsourcing some work (such as IT and payroll services) from larger organizations to smaller companies or the self-employed
> a growth in cutting-edge, but often high-risk technology companies, such as biotech
> a growth in temporary and part-time employment.

These trends will differ between regions and highlight the need for monitoring the changing nature of the employment scene on a regular basis. The realities vary between markets and countries and also with time. For example, while the resources sector worldwide was for many years either static or in decline, the massive growth in countries like China and India has given rise to a resources boom and a major skill shortage in many parts of the mining industry. While new technology, and IT in particular, was seen as an international growth industry in the late 1990s, within a few years, opportunities changed dramatically. It is only now, five years after the 'tech wreck', that the IT industry is modestly growing again in some countries.

narrowing your career focus

Within this general employment context, it is important to identify those areas that are most likely to provide you with a satisfying career. This involves targeting the kinds of industries and sectors that you might work in. Your aim is to get a better picture of the jobs, general work environment and the skills, knowledge and experience required to succeed in an industry. This does not exclude other areas, but it will be more fruitful if you focus on what seem to be the most appealing areas first and discount these before moving on to other possibilities.

information gathering

Obtaining information about the job, the environment and the opportunities available can be gained from several sources. These can be divided between the general and specific.

General sources include:

> people known to you who know something about an industry or occupation type
> press and journal articles on job and career issues
> reference books, career directories and library material
> government career services
> recruitment agencies and search firms
> professional and industry organizations – literature and websites
> employee organizations and trade unions – literature and websites.

Specific sources include:

> company brochures, annual reports and company websites
> job adverts in newspapers
> job vacancies on notice boards
> a company's human resource function
> special libraries in some larger companies on careers and training
> discussions with people inside the organization
> people who have worked for the company either as employees or contractors
> customers of the company.

As you gather information, draw out areas, companies and jobs that appeal to you. You do not need to find the complete answer at this point. In these early stages, you are trying to find a direction in terms of industry sector, types of employer and possible companies. As you go through the process, it is likely that you will get a better understanding of your own needs and be able to narrow down the areas where these can be best met. The student comments in Box 8.3 illustrate how you might integrate the data with your personal needs.

As you get closer to graduation, or closer to moving positions, you will need to think more about the following:

> the precise nature of the job role and the activities involved
> what is involved in a typical working day
> what is expected in terms of performance
> what does success look like on the job
> what other opportunities exist in the organization either vertically or laterally
> the external motivating factors, including remuneration, promotional opportunities, geographical location, work environment, training opportunities
> what kinds of work colleagues and culture typify the organization.

Gather the information systematically. From time to time (and particularly as you get closer to changing careers), structure and summarize what you have learned, both in terms of your aptitudes and preferences and career potential and direction. Use the following headings:

> *Personal qualities*: capabilities, motivations, interests
> *Career paths*: general management, business professional, commercial entrepreneur
> *Occupational areas*: industries, companies, positions

These headings will help give you an overview of where you are now, where you want to go and where the possible starting points are. You can add or subtract from this as new data come to light, either about yourself or possible occupations and opportunities.

Having identified career paths and potential jobs, the next step is to consider where you go from here. Be careful of believing, however, that you must make a change. The process described above may confirm, for a part-time student, that you are in the right job, but open up future possibilities. For full-time students, it may support a return to the industry you came from or the company sponsoring you.

Moreover, even though you may be uncomfortable in your current job, this does not mean a full-scale career or even job change. It may encourage you to rethink several aspects of your current job to make it more compelling or satisfying. You may need to set new objectives, expand certain areas of work or deal with a festering problem that is making an otherwise attractive job become a grind. Having a career capability is concerned with getting the best out of your work environment throughout your life, which can result in radical, but also incremental changes. Indeed, for some part-time students, the knowledge gained from the MBA can provide new insights on how you can be more productive and extract more from your current job.

However, perhaps the biggest danger and dilemma is that you will stay too long in an occupation or on a career path that has run its course. One part-time student reflected:

I feel as if I have been wandering or stagnating from a professional perspective. Yes, I had the energy or single mindedness to pursue an MBA. However, on the professional front, I feel as if I have been drifting, cruising and performing at a non-challenging level. I know I need to address this issue with more determination.

For full-time students, one of the most difficult steps in career change has already been taken. You have moved on. Staying in a job until it becomes unbearable poses several problems. Not least is the likelihood that you will not make good career decisions if you are desperate, or be able to mask your dissatisfaction when meeting potential employers. That is why personal reflection and job analysis should be done regularly and honestly. You shouldn't need to be reminded that you only get one life, but many people seem to forget this when it comes to career management.

Some moves are easier than others. Changing the content of your current job is different from moving to a similar job in another company, which is different to moving to a similar job in a different industry, which is different again from moving into a new job, new company and new industry at the same time. All these are possible, but the latter is usually a much bigger task than the former. However, what you should not do is go back to a sector or company because that is the easy option. If it is right for you, then fine, but if it's wrong, and this is where the analysis is so important, then try that little bit harder, search that little bit further and persist that little bit longer.

There are, however, two caveats to this advice. The first is that you may have to go back to a previous occupation or position, or stay in the same job, for tactical reasons. For some career transitions, and particularly trying to move into general management positions, you may have to return to a functional role to prove your capabilities. Indeed, in some cases, you may even have to take a step backwards. Moving into a completely new area with little experience can be challenging and risky both for you and an employer. Consequently, a more junior role, or a job that does not pay the high salary you had originally expected, may be the only way to make the transition.

The second caveat is that you can only go so far with analysis and planning. Indeed, some writers argue that the notion that careers can be planned at all is questionable. For instance, Herminia Ibarra found through her research that the most successful career transitions involve a messy trial and error process of learning by doing. It was experience that shaped an individual's ideas about what was plausible and desirable.[8]

Most career experts argue that some form of planning is essential. However, there is no substitute for experience and no way that you can fully know whether a job or industry is right for you until you actually perform in the job. Consequently, there will always be an element of risk in career moves. The risks can be minimized by taking a structured approach to career development. They can also be reduced, for example, by taking internships to see what similar jobs might entail. You may be able to structure project work or subject assignments to get a better feel for a sector. Voluntary work may also be a possibility. Your MBA classes and case studies will give you insights into different industries and their challenges. But ultimately you have to take a leap. We encourage you to plan your career, but this will not give you all the answers. So, if the chance comes to role the career dice from time to time and you have worked out the worst-case scenario, go for it. If you dream but never act, you will need to be comfortable with the haunting words, 'if only'.

networking

Whether an offer comes through planning or good fortune, your chances of success will be greatly enhanced by networking. Susan Cohn and Donald Hudson, for example, argue that 85% of the jobs in the market are found through internal networks,[9] while Robert Gardella notes that most people find jobs through friends, relatives, colleagues, classmates and other acquaintances, despite the increasing use of the web for job searches.[10] Certainly, networking is not the only way of finding a job, but it is important in managing your career over the longer term and particularly as you go higher.

Feeling uncomfortable about networking is not uncommon. The notion of grilling people for information, fawning around them, or giving acquaintances the hard sell at every interpersonal opportunity seems abhorrent to some, and so it should be. This is not successful career networking. Networking is not about a short-term gain, but about developing long-term relationships that will be of mutual benefit both now and in the future. As the following student comment shows, this requires a change of thinking:

Importantly, I was able to discard my bias against networking on the basis of the Machiavellian connotations I perceived. I forced myself to reframe my attitudes to appreciate that it is an important mechanism to achieving favourable outcomes in an increasingly interdependent society.

In general, networks are interpersonal relationships largely concerned with getting and giving information in order to achieve more effective outcomes or decisions. Networks take different forms and often have different purposes. The most common networks are social. But whatever form they take, they are not sustainable as one-way interactions where only one person benefits. Important in all forms of networking is reciprocity. Most people accept that to be part of a social network they have to give as well as take, but seem to forget this when trying to establish career networks. Even though it may not be easy to immediately repay those who might help you, by keeping in mind the notion of mutual benefit it will make you aware of the need to manage the relationship carefully. As one student noted:

I believe very strongly in networking. I don't have all the answers. The more people I talk to the better. But I know it's about giving as well as receiving. I would much rather feel that I have a better understanding of situations and people and they of me, than have gained an immediate and probably very small win.

As this student suggests, networking is not a sequence of one-off encounters. It is a longer term process. Often contacts yield nothing at first. It is in being able to go back to them, or in their remembering you positively when something useful comes up, that the benefits occur. However, as the student below shows, this needs some work:

The payoff from a network is dependent on the ongoing investment made. This, in turn, depends on creating an ongoing climate of mutual giving and sharing of information and other resources. This requires a conscious effort. Successful networking requires a wide range of contacts to nurture, and nurturing effectively requires finding ways to offer support to network contacts.

For those who find network building a challenge (and even if you don't), the easiest place to start is with family and friends. Introductions are easy, friends are likely to want to help and, while they may not have a job up their sleeve, they will often give you additional insights on careers and may act as a sounding board that would not normally be available with casual acquaintances. Also, do not forget your colleagues on your management degree. They will have a wealth of experience that is easily accessible. In the longer term, MBA alumni are one of the most valuable resources you will ever have.

However, family and colleagues should really be only the start. Indeed, if you are completing your MBA away from home, you will have no choice but to approach people who may not be familiar to you. It is important that you begin to do this early on in your MBA as it time-consuming. First, list anyone who may be able to help, even people who you would not normally approach. You can make a decision later about whether you contact them, but at least get all potential help on your radar screen. This may trigger ideas about other people who may be more accessible.

Try not to only include people who you feel you will get on with. People you feel comfortable with may also think the same way you do. While this has some benefits, if you are trying to move into new areas, you need to talk to people who have different perspectives. Additionally, you may also consider attending events you may not have considered previously, such as Rotary clubs or public seminars. These kinds of experiences may not only give you new insights, but also give you information that can help you build your network with others.

Examples of the events and groups that can help broaden your thinking include:

> professional organizations in disciplines you are interested in
> other business organizations or pressure groups
> campus recruiting programmes
> job search support groups
> company open days or promotions
> presentations on areas of interest

> writers in trade and professional magazines
> alumni of colleges or institutions you have been part of
> religious and social organizations.

managing networks

Having identified potential networking opportunities, you then need to think about how you approach each situation. Think about what you want to achieve. This will often be different, depending on the events you go to and the people you meet, as illustrated by the following comment:

My first attempts at networking were with close colleagues. They suggested that I seemed unclear what I was seeking from them. Did I want a job, a referral or just general advice? Of paramount importance, I discovered, is to be explicit as to the purpose of the contact from the outset.

Thinking explicitly and tactically about each encounter is important. For example, your overall aim may be to get a job, but this should not be your primary objective in making contact initially. Indeed, while you may make your longer term intentions clear, asking directly for a job, particularly in the early stages of networking, is unlikely to help you realize your goal. You may strike lucky, but you are more likely to put people off. One of your objectives should be to be able to return to any contacts you make for advice or help in the future. If your contacts believe your only aim is to hassle them for a job, it should not surprise you how unavailable they will suddenly become. As the following comment illustrates, you should aim to approach each contact professionally:

Prior to contacting anyone, I research the company based on information in the public domain, particularly financial and strategic data and analysts' appraisals. I establish specifically what information I require from them and examine how I might reciprocate, based on my research and understanding of the particular organization.

This also highlights the need to think about how interactions should proceed, as they will often be different depending on the individual. This is not about scripting each event perfectly. There will be some spontaneity in every interaction. However, and particularly if you are making contact for the first time, you need to consider your initial introduction, the questions you ask, how you will do this, the information and impression you will give about yourself and how you might add value to them. This may be no more than telling them how helpful they have been, or keeping them informed on how the information they gave you may have helped. But you need to keep others in mind as well as your own agendas. Remember, they are not going to give you leads if they feel your actions will reflect on them negatively.

Further down the track, you may need to be more direct in your encounters. But in doing this you also need to have refined whom you contact. The information you should have gathered should help you to identify the gatekeepers and how to get around them. If you have strong career credentials, you need to present them to people in a strong position to help. If the decision makers do not figure somewhere in your networking strategy, then you need to rethink your contacts. As one student commented:

I have identified a number of organizations and have targeted several individuals in each. Some of these I already know, while I require a referral from others. I have found that I need to contact those who can create employment opportunities. As a result, I have refined my approach, aim to articulate my goals clearly and, where appropriate, present a plan to enable them to assess my value to them.

As you proceed, keep notes on who you met, what was discussed and who else you might contact. Maintain your current network and keep contacts informed of any progress you have made because of their help. Even if you are not changing careers in the short term, think of ways of adding to the network. This is a long-term activity that yields real benefits from regular investment and a structured approach, illustrated by the following student:

An effective system for organizing data is imperative. In addition to enabling ready retrieval of details of network contacts, a database provides the central focal point for enhancing a network and facilitating the strategic objectives over time. I have developed a contact management system based on the Microsoft Access database. Multiple fields reflect not only professional information but also personal data. Of particular importance is a field to inform me of areas of interest the person has as a prompt to enabling me to provide assistance to them, and hence emphasizes the reciprocal nature of the networking process.

personal marketing

Like networking, for some students the idea of personal marketing can send shivers down the spine. Although many people have no difficulty in promoting a product or service, when it comes to promoting themselves, they are often less than compelling. Again this is partly because of a misunderstanding about what personal marketing involves. Yes, you are going to have to sell yourself, but if you have thought more broadly about how you might market yourself (and early on in the MBA, rather than at the end), it becomes a lot easier and more effective.

Personal marketing is concerned with being clear about your portfolio of capabilities, understanding how these relate to the employment market and promoting yourself successfully. Thus, the subjects discussed so far in this chapter form part of personal marketing and hence can be developed early on in the MBA.

However, personal marketing also involves personal promotion and demonstrating to an employer how your portfolio of talents will benefit them. While this part of the process should not overly concern you at the start of your MBA, nevertheless it should not be left until the last few weeks of your degree. This is not a two-minute exercise that can be completed overnight. It is a planned, strategic and often targeted process that involves more than sending out your CV like spam email. Large companies receive speculative CVs on a regular basis and few take any notice of them. Consequently, it is important to think about:

> the portfolio of talents you have
> the benefits you will bring to an employer
> how to position yourself in the market
> identifying potential customers (that is, employers)
> identifying their needs and requirements

> promoting your services effectively
> selling your strengths.

Underlying this is a clear understanding of your value proposition. If an employer is going to hire you, what are the five or six major attributes or benefits that he or she will receive? You should be able to communicate these succinctly, both verbally and in writing. They should play a central part in any interview and in covering letters; hence the reason for customizing all your employment communication. This is about synthesizing your talents and services and using them to achieve a good fit between you and an employer. It is not about pressing an electronic button that distributes a standard CV to a speculative list of recipients.

Thinking in marketing terms does two things. First, it should make you focus on your unique attributes and the things that make you different from the crowd – what gives you a personal competitive advantage. Second, it should make you think about how you communicate these distinctive qualities. If you do not know what they are, or cannot clearly outline them, it is unlikely an employer will have the motivation to tease them out for you. Few of your competitors will be so trusting. While you may not need a hard sell, you certainly need to put in the hard yards to encapsulate who you are, understand what an employer is looking for and confidently position yourself as the stand-out candidate.

> *This is about synthesizing your talents and services and using them to achieve a good fit between you and an employer.*

The analogy with marketing can only go so far, however. While it is important to consider your career development partly as a personal marketing process, there is another side to the coin – you. You are not only a service to be consumed by others. Your needs also have to be met and the best organizations know this. However, the reality is that unless your skills and abilities are in very short supply, employers have the power. Telling an interviewer what you want, before having outlined what you can do for them is not a good strategy, marketing or otherwise.

interviews

The last sentence highlights the importance of interpersonal communication skills in the career management process. Communication skills are important in many of the areas discussed so far, particularly in networking. However, they come into their own in interview situations. Despite a great deal of research highlighting the limitations of interviews and the general acceptance that they are blunt instruments, it is improbable that you will go through your career without being interviewed on many occasions.

The fact that they are blunt instruments should not give rise to the belief that they do not matter. There are still many things you can do to reduce their variability. Moreover, while interviewing well is no guarantee of success, interviewing badly is pretty much guaranteed to wreck your chances before you even start. This is a skill that is usually used in circumstances where the stakes are high. So get some practice in developing good interview skills while on the MBA.

interview preparation

The starting point to interviewing well is good preparation. Obtain as much information as possible on the position, company, situation or person you will be talking to. Next, be clear about the purpose of the interview. With a formal job interview, the primary aim is to promote yourself and demonstrate why you are the best candidate for the job. But it is also an opportunity to get more information on the company, the culture, the job, performance expectations in relation to the job, training opportunities and so on. Make sure you have seen a job specification before starting the interview.

The next step is to think through the best way to achieve your purpose. Consider the kinds of qualities the interviewer will be interested in and the questions likely to be asked. Some of the more common questions include:

> Tell me about yourself – past history and experiences.
> Why did you leave (or want to leave) your past/current job?
> Why do you want to work for this organization?
> Why do you want the position?
> If you got the position, what do you think you would bring to it?
> What do you see as your strengths and weaknesses?
> What excites you at work?
> What causes you apprehension at work?
> Where do you see yourself in the future?
> Describe a work situation where you had to make changes. How did you go about it?
> Describe a work situation where you did not succeed. What did you do about it?
> How did you get on with your previous manager/work colleagues?

managing the interview

During the interview, be conscious that interviewers will be considering not only what you say, but how you present yourself and particularly your body language. They will assess how you think, your attitudes and enthusiasm. They will also make an assessment about how you will fit into the company or department. Everything you do in an interview leaves an impression, because sophisticated interviewers are looking at everything you do and weighing up everything you say. You are painting that three-dimensional picture of yourself, but on their canvass. So you have to think about whether you are painting a delicate and subtle picture, or splashing the paint all over the canvass and on the walls as well. The difference is illustrated by Susan Cohn and Donald Hudson, who highlight the need to look for the underlying meaning of interview questions and respond to what is really being asked.[11] Consequently:

> 'How was your trip?' is an icebreaker, not a chance to complain about public transport or parking in the city.
> 'Tell me about yourself' is an opportunity to explain your core attributes for the job, not regurgitate your CV.
> 'Why did you change jobs?' is meant to see if you have thought the changes through, not to criticize you for making a bad call.
> 'Summarize your strengths and weaknesses' is meant to test your ability for self-evaluation, not to pick holes in your persona.
> 'Describe a difficult situation and what you did about it' is meant to extract your interpersonal and problem-solving abilities, not to listen to how dysfunctional your last organization was.

In answering any question, even if your previous job or work relationships were terrible, do not leave the interviewer with a negative impression of you. This does not mean dishonesty, but it does mean that if you highlight difficulties at work (and you would be a unique candidate who has not faced some hurdles), you need to show how you overcame them or what you learned from them.

Always keep calm and try to respond clearly and succinctly. Don't talk for the sake of it. There is nothing wrong with silence in thinking of a response. But there is a lot wrong with unstructured replies that neither answer the interviewer's question, nor convey your personal strengths. Answer what the interviewer asks you and then stop talking. If they need more from you, they will prompt you. If you are unsure whether you have replied appropriately, ask if you have answered the question.

The only real exception to this is to make sure you have conveyed what you see as the major reasons why the organization should employ you. Having thought about this beforehand helps to focus your mind on what is critical. If you have not had the chance to make these points and the interview is coming to an end, make sure you get them over. If you can deliver them in the context of a summary, even better, as you can then put your overall skill portfolio into context.

You will also usually have the chance to ask questions. While this is an opportunity to get information about the job and company, remember you are still being interviewed. Asking questions that you could have easily read in the annual report is not particularly smart. Asking questions about the company literature that applies particularly to the job is smart, as it shows you have read the material and thought about the issues.

At the end of the interview, find out what the next steps are. When will the company give you an answer and what form will that take? This is to stop you worrying if you have not heard anything and also to manage the process afterwards.

After the interview, make notes about the experience. What did you do well and what not so well. Try and recall the events as these will also give you clues about the company and the people you might work for. Did you get interrupted, was the questioning aggressive, were you put under pressure, and if so, how, were there trick questions, did the interviewer listen attentively? These may be signs of a bad or good interview, but they may also be indicators of the company culture more generally. If so, check them out with other sources.

> *Underlying everything is the need to have a degree of self-belief and a capable mindset. Confidence is essential.*

Don't forget to follow up by writing or emailing the people you met and thanking them for the meeting/interview. If you hear nothing, then give the company a call. Be careful to draw a line between persistence and petulance. If you failed to get the job and feel it is appropriate, ask for feedback. However, do not see this as another chance to continue the interview, or the feedback will invariably be unflattering.

Our final comments relate to both developing a career capability and the other capabilities explored in this book. Underlying everything is the need to have a degree of self-belief and a capable mindset. Confidence is essential. This is not about being arrogant and selling a false promise. But it is about being professional and assertively demonstrating what you have to offer, which for MBA graduates is considerable.

Career changes have the potential for many setbacks. Some employment environments can be difficult and, with some career moves, short-term rejection is inevitable. If you intend to make big changes, keep in mind the transitions curve outlined in Chapter 7. Be conscious of asking for support when necessary, celebrating small wins when you make progress, and focusing on your long-term goals when things get tough.

conclusion

This chapter has outlined several career principles that you should keep in mind in pursuing a journey that lasts nearly a lifetime. Be aware of your aptitudes and work preferences, but also be aware that these will change as you grow. Be knowledgeable of the work environment, but also know that there are no certainties, either today or tomorrow. Set a career direction, but not one so rigid that when the big opportunity comes along you will be unable to steer a slightly different course.

The MBA can provide you with the potential to develop several highly desirable capabilities. But in order to do this you have to work with the opportunities provided to develop your own unique range of skills. This is also true after the MBA has finished. The MBA is a starting point in providing you with a fulfilling and satisfying career, but it also needs your own blend of focus and passion to succeed, reflected in this student comment:

If I was writing my eulogy, I guess what I would hope others would learn from me is that life is pretty simple – figure out what you love and do the things you need to make it happen. It's a short life and it's getting shorter.

Whether your journey is long or short, if the MBA equips you with a range of personal capabilities and a set of functional capabilities (explored in the second part of the book) that enable you to achieve and grow, it will have been more than worth the sacrifice.

references

1. Hall, D.T. (1996) 'Protean careers of the 21st century', *Academy of Management Executive*, **10**(4): 8–16.
2. Holton, E. (1989) *The MBAs Guide to Career Planning* (Princeton: Peterson's Guides) p. 51.
3. More on the Birkman Method can be found at www.birkman.com.
4. More on CareerLeader can be found at www.careerdiscovery.com.
5. Schein, E.H. (1993) *Career Anchors: Discovering Your Real Values* (San Francisco: Jossey-Bass).
6. Ibid pp. 76–9.
7. Op. cit. Hall (1996) p. 10.
8. Ibarra, H. (2004) 'Changing careers, changing selves', in HBSP, *Managing Yourself for the Career You Want* (Boston; Harvard Business School Press) pp. 52–61.
9. Cohn, S. and Hudson, D. (2000) *Finding Your Way With an MBA* (New York: John Wiley & Sons) p. 22.
10. Gardella, R.S. (2000) *Guide to Finding Your Next Job* (Boston: Harvard Business School Press) p. xix.
11. Op. cit. Cohn and Hudson (2000) p. 19.

core topics in business

2

introduction

While many business schools offer capstone or integrative subjects at the end of their MBA degree, few try to give students an overview of what lies ahead at the start. As we explained in Part 1, the first few months of business school can be fairly daunting, if not overwhelming. Students are expected to 'hit the ground running' and work their way through, literally, volumes of information. Many hours will be spent trying to build a picture of what a core subject is about and, just as important, where it fits into the overall scheme of management. This part of *The MBA Companion* has been written to accelerate this process. In our experience, it is much easier to synthesize new material into your thinking if you first have an overview of a subject and an understanding of some of the key concepts likely to be covered.

It has not been possible, within the confines of this book, to cover all the core courses that might be offered on an MBA. Instead, our intention has been to focus on those general areas that tend to be a platform from which other disciplines are built. Similarly, we are not trying to replace the content of any one subject nor suggest how it might be taught. Rather, we are trying to bring together, in one book, a series of chapters that map out and introduce the functional content that underpins an MBA.

Each of the authors who contributed chapters to this part of the book recognizes the need to make a subject discipline accessible to MBA students. Several of them have written textbooks that are now into their 5th or 6th editions – testimony to their capacity to translate complex ideas into understandable concepts. Others have an outstanding track record of teaching MBA students; they truly understand those aspects of their discipline that students find hardest to grasp. As you will read, each of our authors conveys a passion for his or her subject and clearly explains its importance to business and management.

structure and content

Below is an overview of the chapters that make up Part 2. They don't follow a predetermined format or style – just as in the classroom, individual lecturers present their material in very different ways. We suggest you pick and choose between chapters as you go through your MBA, rather than attempting to read Part 2 as a complete whole.

Professor Paul Dainty wrote 'periods and perspectives in management' (Chapter 9) to give students an overview of the management discipline and how it has developed. It looks back in time at some of the major milestones in management and identifies some of the most influential management thinkers. He traces the emergence of the major management disciplines in the second half of the twentieth century and the growth of the 'management ideas industry' today. He argues that MBA students need to develop a critical and discerning eye when trying to distinguish between the latest management fad and important management principles.

In their chapter 'operations management' (Chapter 10), Professors Kannan Sethuraman and Devanath Tirupati review those processes and activities that are used in business to transform raw materials (labour, material, capital and other 'inputs') into finished goods. The authors trace the evolution of operations management from a function largely focused on manufacturing to one that emphasizes services, with extensive applications in financial services, insurance, hospitality and healthcare, to name but a few. They provide a flavour of some key themes that are often covered in a core operations subject. In so doing, they draw attention to the strategic nature of the discipline today and its potential to strengthen a company's competitive ability.

Chapter 11, 'quantitative methods in business: making the numbers work for you' by Professor Clare Morris, is designed to calm the nerves of the less numerate MBA students. The term 'quantitative methods' (QM) refers to a broad range of mathematical and statistical techniques, which are often used across a variety of business operations. On MBA programmes, these techniques are often taught as an integral part of the subject area – but the techniques themselves are often portable, hence the reason we provide this chapter early on in Part 2. Students are encouraged to read this common-sense explanation of some of the major quantitative techniques used in business, before tackling, for example, the ensuing chapters on accounting, finance or international finance.

Managers need to understand the way in which accounting numbers are produced and used – which is why 'accounting' (Chapter 12) is a core subject on an MBA programme. Professor David Trende argues that knowing the procedural aspects of accounting is, for an MBA student, less important than being able to question and understand the assumptions underlying the numbers. This distinction is critical. Accounting, like several other disciplines in management, has its own terms and definitions that take time and effort to understand. In the process of learning these, it is important not to lose sight of the end objective. For those who hunger for a layperson's guide to key accounting concepts, this chapter has been written for you.

Many business schools set prerequisites for their basic finance course – typically, economics, accounting and/or quantitative methods. At the start of his chapter on 'finance' (Chapter 13), Professor Rob Brown explains the reasons for this by showing how finance relates to other subject areas on an MBA. For example, finance and economics share a similar approach to modelling and reasoning. The principal assumptions in both basic finance and economics subjects are that people act in a rational and self-interested way and transact in competitive markets. Similarly, the student of finance will benefit from having some basic knowledge of accounting, because accountants provide data relevant to financial decisions. Some of the fundamental concepts in finance are statistical in nature. So, the ability to think statistically is invaluable to the financial student, which is why a working familiarity with quantitative methods is of help. In the rest of his chapter, Professor Brown examines the main ideas that tend to dominate MBA courses in finance.

In Chapter 14, Professor Paul Dainty takes a critical look at one of the more controversial areas of management – managing people for competitive advantage. Often labelled as the 'soft' side of management, the ability to understand and predict human behaviour is, in practice, one of the hardest things a manager has to do.

'Organizational behaviour' (OB) is also a subject that every student will have direct experience of – working with people in an organization – and preconceived ideas about how this should be done. Professor Dainty describes the major areas explored in OB at the individual, group and organizational levels. The field of OB provides insights into how individuals view the world and what drives them. It explores the dynamics of groupwork, conflict, stress and leadership. Culture, structure and change are just some of the macro-issues that are also addressed.

In Chapter 15, Professor Michael Baker looks at the role of 'marketing' in the modern organization and its contribution to the strategic direction of all organizations – be they public or private, for profit and not-for-profit, large or small. He shows how the concept of marketing has evolved over the years and the various ways it has been defined and codified. He ends by examining some of the challenges faced by this 'synthetic' discipline, arguing that if marketers are to meet and resolve these challenges, they need to be customer-focused, build long-term relationships with customers and think of their lifetime values as opposed to their short-term profitability.

The final three chapters examine the broader operating environment of the firm. In Chapter 16, Professor Mark Crosby explores 'macroeconomics and public policy'. Macroeconomics tries to understand the forces shaping the 'big picture' in an economy. In particular, understanding how public policy may impact on local economies and businesses is key. He starts by describing some trends in the global economy in the past 30 years and uses this historical lens to illustrate the type of questions addressed in the discipline of macroeconomics. His chapter includes a description of the central principles that economists use to analyse the economy.

In Chapter 17, 'international finance', Professor Gonzalo Chavez builds on the information presented in earlier chapters by exploring the financing decisions associated with international investment. How should managers measure, forecast and manage the risks when investing at an international level? The good news is that most of the conceptual structure used in finance is applicable in an international context. However, other building blocks need to be introduced to help cover country risk and the impact of currency volatility. Students considering a specialist degree in finance, or wishing to pursue a more financially oriented elective will find this chapter of particular interest.

'Business strategy' (Chapter 18) occupies a central place in the MBA curriculum, and in some programmes there may also be electives relating to various specialized aspects of strategy. In this chapter, Professor Colin White argues that it is no accident that, in the area of management studies, strategy has been the focus of the greatest attention in recent years. In his view, strategy 'provides a, if not the, unifying framework in which other management functions must place themselves'. As a discipline, strategy raises all sorts of issues about what an enterprise is trying to do and its interaction with the various environments in which it operates. Professor White gives the reader a flavour of what these are and how managers can choose to respond.

the need for integration

These chapters will give you a foundation on which you can build as you progress through your MBA. One of the enduring dilemmas that you will face, however, is how much of the material you need to digest and learn in detail. The answer to this, in part, lies with you. Nevertheless, these subjects are dealt with in some depth on an MBA, so that you will feel confident of being able to tackle the management issues that may confront you. However, how the subjects relate to each other is just as, if not more, important. In most managerial and professional jobs, you will need to draw on several disciplines to solve many of the problems you face. For example, operational issues are often solved using principles from organizational behaviour. Marketing issues often need to take financial considerations into account. A strategy for the enterprise can't be pursued without analysing the economic environment.

Additionally, you need to relate whatever you study to your own personal development. Understanding the various subjects and making the links between each discipline is not simply an intellectual exercise. It should be done in the light of how you, as an individual manager, wish to progress. As you read about the subjects in the chapters that follow, try to also think about them in light of the integrated model presented in Figure P2.1. It serves to remind us that the personal and functional capabilities are meant to do one thing – make you a better and more effective businessperson.

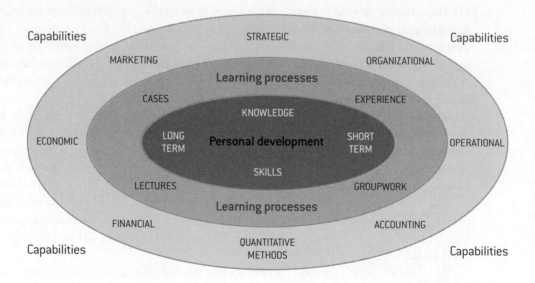

Figure P2.1 Integrated model

9 periods and perspectives in management

professor paul dainty

Before exploring the individual subject areas, it is important to have some knowledge of the management discipline as a whole and how it has developed. The discipline is unique in several ways and without some context in which to place current management thought, discerning rigorous ideas from the ridiculous and the useful from the useless will be much harder.

This chapter provides a historical overview of some of the major milestones in management thought and some of the most influential management thinkers. The chapter does not identify every major contribution to the discipline, partly because of space, but also because the critical ideas are covered in subsequent chapters. However, it does give you a flavour for the development of management thought, some of the challenges the management discipline faces and a way of assessing the importance of these ideas in the current context. Understanding the strengths and weaknesses of any discipline is critical if the ideas are to be of any real use.

the management ideas industry

An MBA provides participants with a vast wealth of knowledge on the leading issues in business and management. Indeed, there is now so much material available that trying to keep up with the continuous output of management ideas is a major challenge. Jeffrey Pfeffer and Bob Sutton point out that, even in 1996, more than 1,700 business books were published in the USA.[1]

Moreover, it is not only through the public domain of books and journals that management ideas are promulgated. They are also pushed heavily by private consultancy firms. For example, McKinsey, one of the top consulting firms, views 'thought leadership' as an area of competitive advantage and now spends up to US$100 million a year on 'knowledge building'. The company claims to spend more on research than Wharton, Harvard and Stanford business schools combined. London Business School, one of the top European schools, spends £4.5 million annually on research, a mere trifle in comparison to McKinsey.

Additionally, ideas are also developed and disseminated through training and other management development activities. More than US$60 billion each year is spent by organizations on training, particularly management training.[2] There are also many formal educational programmes in management, such as the MBA, which are financed privately. Not all these programmes will add anything new, but the 'management ideas industry', including both the development of ideas and their dissemination, is now a global business.

Taking a management degree exposes the individual to a comprehensive selection of these ideas. Indeed, management ideas, and the development of analytical processes, are the major currency of most MBA degrees. While there is an increasing emphasis on skills development, management ideas and cognitive tools are still a critical part of most programmes. However, while management writers have made a tremendous contribution to the practice of management over the last half century, the ideas found on an MBA are not written on tablets of stone, nor do they have the certainty and benefits that some advocates claim. In fact, the MBA student faces two problems. One is extracting information, which is relevant to the problems faced, from the sheer volume of material. The second is then deciding which information will provide the best solution to those problems. Unfortunately, this is not just a process of picking between several equally commendable alternatives, as the value between the solutions may vary considerably.

Questioning the value of management ideas is a relatively recent phenomenon, but it is growing. Articles in the popular press, dismissing management ideas as 'fads', are becoming more common. Indeed, some claim that there is widespread cynicism in business circles towards these ideas. This is a result of recent corporate collapses and scandals such as Enron and HIH, outrage over CEO salaries and the failure of many of the promises made for the IT revolution.

> The Holy Grail of management does not exist, but there are some ideas that are more likely to move us closer to management heaven, rather than managerial hell.

Information technology and internet-based commerce are not the only areas where some of the promised benefits have failed to appear. Process re-engineering, for example, which swept the world in the early 1990s, now rarely gets a positive endorsement. TQM, an integrated set of ideas for improving quality and dominant for nearly two decades, is rarely mentioned. The learning organization, which spawned whole departments geared to developing and applying the concepts outlined by Peter Senge in *The Fifth Discipline*, is certainly not the force it was. Indeed, there is a long list of ideas that have seen the same fate, from JIT to the forceful management principles of Al Dunlap, the downsizing doyen.

To suggest that the reasons for the disappearance of these ideas from the global spotlight are similar would be wrong. Indeed, one of the increasing challenges is to understand which of the vast range of ideas are of value and under what circumstances. The Holy Grail of management does not exist, but there are some ideas that are more likely to move us closer to management heaven, rather than managerial hell, even if we experience periods of organizational purgatory in the process.

Which ideas are these? Unfortunately, like the search for the Holy Grail, there is a degree of ambiguity involved in picking the most appropriate conceptual path. Considerable help will be provided on an MBA by the professors of the subjects taken and, indeed, one of the reasons for attending business school and taking a rigorous academic degree is to get help in identifying the most appropriate ideas.

However, students also have to make their own choices about which ideas they explore and use. This is partly because each individual is on a personal journey. For example, if the intention is to work in manufacturing, then understanding how the hospitality industry works may have limited relevance (not, please note, no relevance as there will be issues that cross both environments). But it is also partly because the wealth of information experienced on an MBA programme is rarely neatly sifted and rated in terms of its advantages and disadvantages. Thus, it is important, as the barrage of information continues throughout your working life, to develop techniques for identifying the benefits and pitfalls of management ideas, so that at least the path towards the Holy Grail, rather than its attainment, remains squarely in focus.

the management discipline

One aim of completing a management degree is to graduate equipped with management concepts that can be applied to different industries, are relevant to different time periods and useful in different circumstances. How well equipped depends on a number of factors, including the quality of the teaching and the dedication of the individual student. This will be enhanced if you as a student have developed some insights into the context in which management ideas have been developed overall and continue to be shaped.

Management is a collection of different subjects. Some of these subjects are relatively straightforward (at least in terms of what constitutes the subject, rather than how easy they are to understand). For example, the ideas, concepts and tools that make up subjects like statistics or accounting are largely controversy free. It is true that in areas of accounting there are disagreements about some accounting rules or how these are applied, and the accounting 'language' has to be understood. But, in essence, the principles are accepted by the profession in the geographic region where the rules apply. The body of knowledge is robust, enjoying general support.

In other areas, there is less agreement, particularly in some of the behaviourally based subjects. For example, in the area of leadership alone, there are over 15,000 studies published in serious academic journals on the topic. In addition, there have been countless articles in books and magazines that have added to the leadership debate. And it is a debate, both in terms of what good leadership looks like and the extent to which one can develop as a leader, as discussed in Chapter 7.

An additional problem is that of defining what management encompasses. Over the years, what constitutes 'management' has changed, becoming broader and more complex. Partly because of this, management is still a long way from coming close to having an overarching, integrative framework that brings even a few of the subjects together. If one then stops to consider the angst found in many business schools about which, if any, of the subjects are more important (and consequently should be given most teaching time and explored in the most depth), then some of the limitations of the management discipline become clearer.

> Management is still a long way from coming close to having an overarching, integrative framework.

As a consequence, some argue that management has had a bad press. 'Because it is multifaceted, pinning it down is like nailing a jellyfish to a wall. Is it marketing, is it strategy, is it inspiring people, is it budgeting? Given this complexity, it is not surprising that the historical and theoretical strands which make up contemporary management thought are many and varied.'[3]

Nevertheless, it is important to have some knowledge of these historical and conceptual strands. The issues that have influenced the development of the management discipline still affect the ideas promoted today and will continue to affect the ideas of tomorrow. Hence, understanding some of the reasons and driving forces behind these developments is particularly important if judgements are to be made about their relevance and importance. If, as Churchill suggests, 'the further backward you can look, the further forward you can see', an understanding of the historical development of the discipline should help with those judgements.

early developments

One of the major driving forces behind management ideas and practice, like many disciplines, has been necessity. Indeed, the practice of management has a long history dating back to the earliest times. Record keeping was developed about 5000 BC and problems of administration were written about during the Greek and Roman Empires.

Developments have occurred at various times throughout history, as Table 9.1 highlights.[4] For instance, Pacioli is credited with the development of double-entry bookkeeping in the fifteenth century. Machiavelli provided many leadership and political insights in his work *The Prince*. However, it was not until the rise of the capitalistic system and the Industrial Revolution that serious attention was given to management issues.

In 1776, Adam Smith's *Wealth of Nations* was published, in which he emphasized the division of labour. Some of the first factory owners concentrated on improving methods of production and introduced concepts that proved fundamental to modern manufacturing methods. For example, Eli Whitney and Simeon North developed the concept of the interchangeability of parts in the manufacture of pistols and muskets. Before then, each gun was unique. If a part did not work, a soldier on the battlefield could not pick up an abandoned pistol to provide a replacement for his own firearm. Under fire, this became a matter of life or death, which was a compelling necessity for developing interchangeable parts.

In the early nineteenth century, the need for larger amounts of financial capital to support factory operations resulted in more specialized legal forms of organizing a business. In particular, the development of the corporation as a separate legal entity allowed shares to be sold to many individuals to raise large sums of capital. But shareholders then became numerous. They could not all actively manage the business, so a distinction between the function of owners and managers arose. This distinction set the stage for management processes as an identifiable and separate activity.

In most cases, these changes came about as a result of trying to solve the commercial challenges of the time. But there were also by-products, which could not be ignored. For example, the social evils of the Industrial Revolution received widespread attention. In England, social reformers sought legal regulation of employment practices in the Factory Acts of 1802, 1819 and 1831. Robert Owen became a pioneer of people management. As the manager of a large textile mill in New Lanark, he concentrated on the improvement of working conditions and the development of a model community. However, Owen, along with a handful of other reformers, was in a minority and the main focus of management centred on finding ways to produce industrial products with little thought given to the social or environmental consequences.[5]

twentieth-century developments

frederick taylor and scientific management

While the foundations of contemporary management were laid in the eighteenth and nineteenth centuries, it was only in the twentieth century that a formal process of investigating and communicating management ideas began. The starting point for management as a separate and distinct field of endeavour is usually attributed to Frederick Taylor and the 'scientific management' movement. Joseph Massie notes that Taylor stressed that the core of scientific management was not in individual

Table 9.1 *Early streams of managerial ideas*

Dates	Sources	Ideas	Situational demands	Relevance to management today
5000 BC	Sumerian civilization	Written records	Formation of governments and commerce	Recorded data are esential to life of organizations
4000–2000 BC	Egyptian	Planning, organizing, controlling	Organized efforts of up to 100,000 people for constructing pyramids	Plans and authority structure are needed to achieve goals
2000–1700 BC	Babylonian	Standards of responsibility	Code of Hammurabi set standards for wages, obligations and penalties	Targets of expected behaviour are necessary for control
600 BC	Hebrews	Organization	Leaders organized groups to meet threats from outside	Hierarchy of authority is a basic idea
500 BC	Chinese	Systems, models	Commerce and military demand fixed procedures and systems	Patterns and procedures are desirable in group effort
500–350 BC	Greeks	Specialization, scientific method	Specialization laid foundation for scientific method	Organizations need specialization. Scientific method promotes progress
300 BC–AD 300	Romans	Centralized organization	Far-flung empire required communication and control by Rome	Effective communication and centralized control are necessary
1300s	Venetians	Legal forms of organization	Venetian commerce required legal innovation	Legal framework for commerce serves as foundation for ventures
1400s	Pacioli	Double-entry bookkeeping	Effective classification of cost and revenue demanded by increased trade	Accounting systematizes record keeping
1500s	Machiavelli	Pragmatic use of power	Government rely on support of masses. Expectations of leader and people must be clear. Survival and the use of power	Realistic guidelines for the use of power are key
1700s	Adam Smith	Division of labour	The competitive system resulted from specialization	Specialization and profits are key to private enterprise
1800s	Eli Whitney	Interchangeability of parts	Mass production is made possible by availability of standard parts	Modules, segments and parts are building blocks for organizations
1900s	Western nations	Corporation	Large amounts of capital required by entity with long life and limited liability	Owner/manager separation increases demand for professional managers

techniques, but in the new attitudes towards managing a business enterprise. Four areas in particular underpinned this approach:[6]

> The discovery, through the use of the scientific method, of basic elements of work to replace rules of thumb.
> The identification of management's function of planning work instead of allowing workers to choose their own methods.
> The selection and training of workers and the development of cooperation, instead of encouraging individualistic efforts by employees.
> The division of work between management and the workers so that each would perform those duties for which they were best fitted, with the resultant increase in efficiency.

In observing the ways in which workers tackled jobs and then finding the 'best way' to perform the task, Taylor's first step to improving efficiency was to match people to the task. The next steps required supervising, rewarding and punishing them according to their performance. His ideas were taken on enthusiastically by Henry Ford and other managers. However, it was the husband and wife team of Frank and Lillian Gilbreth who developed time and motion studies to improve the efficiency of individual jobs. While writers such as Henry Gantt emphasized the psychology of the worker and the importance of morale in production, it was the mechanical aspect of production, exploited by efficiency experts, which predominated in the 1920s and 30s.

In addition to scientific management, another major set of ideas that influenced how managers thought about work and workers during the first half of the twentieth century was known as 'administrative management'. The movement was dominated by a French engineer, Henri Fayol, who focused on what managers do (and therefore the elements that make up management) and how to manage effectively. This helped promote the idea that managerial work should be separated into different functions, such as accounting, production and marketing.[7] Administrative management also led to functional structures in organizations. It formalized the notion of authority as an essential component of management. Meanwhile, in Germany, Max Weber was the first to try to define different types of organizational structure, predicting that bureaucracies would become the most prevalent.

elton mayo and the human relations school

The ideas underpinning both scientific and administrative management had little place for the workers themselves and their needs were largely ignored. Such mechanistic thinking was challenged by the Hawthorne studies of Elton Mayo and his Harvard colleagues at the Western Electric Company between 1927 and 1932. There, a team of social scientists worked with management at the plant to explain variations in productivity in the factory. Physical factors such as lighting and working conditions were the first aspects to receive attention, but psychological factors emerged as the more important.

These studies ushered in the 'human relations' era. According to Margaret Brindle and Peter Stearns, the emphasis here was on ways to increase productivity rather than on understanding the needs of the workforce.[8] However, the ideas did broaden our understanding of work performance beyond the mechanistic approach of scientific management. Others followed. Mary Parker Follet, for example, made contributions to the psychology and sociology of management. She offered a process for resolving conflict and pursuing integrated outcomes. Kurt Lewin studied small group dynamics and developed ideas on individual change still in use today, such as 'force field analysis'.

What is significant about these early movements is the impact the underlying ideas continue to have. The principles of scientific management are still pervasive and, indeed, so are the potential downsides. 'Process re-engineering', popularized by James Champy and Michael Hammer, had a considerable impact on management ideas and practice in the 1990s. Re-engineering was concerned with encouraging managers to look again at how best to organize their companies in the most efficient manner. The approach emphasized organizational processes rather than functional reporting relationships, but as Stuart Crainer notes, while it was

a simple process, the blank sheet of paper ignored the years of cultural evolution. It appeared inhumane – echoing Taylor. For re-engineering purists, people were objects who handle processes. Depersonalisation was the route to efficiency. Re-engineering became a synonym for redundancy and downsizing.[9]

Despite the problems with ideas like time and motion studies and affiliates like process re-engineering, trying to find more efficient production methods using principles first highlighted by Taylor will continue to be pursued. Equally, finding better ways of managing the workforce (from a psychological as well as a skills viewpoint) is also a human relations issue that will continue to challenge managers. Indeed, these ideas are so pervasive that some popular writers argued that the dominant management ideas of 2003 divided into two camps; those stemming from the human relations school and those from the 'school' of measurement, with roots in scientific management and Taylorism.[10]

The current range of management ideas is much broader than two schools of thought established at the start of the century. However, there are two significant aspects about these developments. The first is that these (and later) themes reoccur (which are sometimes repackaged and redelivered) because the problems they are meant to solve continue to challenge managers. The second is that solving problems in one area may have negative consequences in another. For example, ideas that solve production problems may clash with the requirements of employees, or the aims of marketing. Thus, ideas in management are driven not only by necessity but by a range of enduring dilemmas and the difficulty of solving problems at the interface between disciplines and needs. As we proceed, we will see that these drivers and dilemmas have become more complex over time.

immediate postwar period

While the themes discussed above still have an impact, it was not until the Second World War and the immediate postwar period that management as a relevant, teachable and coherent discipline came into its own. It was during this period that many managerial activities, from leadership through to planning and production methods, were identified as areas that could be consistently developed and improved. The driving force was not only the need to rebuild a war-torn world, but also a growing confidence that the systematic investigation, analysis and communication of management issues, problems and solutions could actually make a vast difference to the way organizations were run.

the growth of management disciplines

While business schools had been around since the turn of the century, the appointment of Peter Drucker as professor of management at New York University in 1950 was a symbolic one.[11] As Crainer notes, he was 'the first person anywhere in the world to have such a title and to teach such a subject'.[12] The 1950s and 60s saw a massive growth in executive education and the development of new business schools. They also saw the growth of already well-established subjects like finance and economics and the development of new management disciplines, such as marketing and strategic management, and many new ideas in the areas of leadership, organizations and operations management.

Some of the major driving forces that gave rise to the ideas that came to the fore at this time are illustrated in Table 9.2, which also highlights some of the main thinkers at various times and some of the ideas that developed in the different disciplines. After the war, for example, 'customers' and the notion of 'marketing' began to take on a new meaning. Crainer argues that the concept of marketing is considered to have been started by Peter Drucker in 1954, when he wrote in *The Practice of Management*, 'there is only one definition of business purpose: to create a customer.'[13]

Customers became important, but only up to a certain point. For example, in 1960, E. Jerome McCarthy offered the concept of the marketing mix consisting of the '4 Ps'. But as Philip Kotler notes, these represented a sellers' rather than a buyers' mix and the 1950s was a sellers' market. Nevertheless, marketing began to take hold and while the ideas were subject to the economic conditions of the time, and the balance of power lay more with companies than consumers, the importance of having an external focus became established in the management literature. In 1960, when Ted Levitt wrote about 'Marketing myopia', he basically argued that companies should be market led, rather than production driven. He also distinguished between marketing and selling – the notion of a short-term hit in exchanging cash for a product – and encouraged more sophisticated strategies in relating to the consumer.

This development of an external focus was also reflected in the development of strategy as a subject. 'Strategic planning' emerged in the 1950s and 60s, drawn from the military strategies of the war, and also the fact that products were generally produced to be distributed. The postwar shortages and the relative lack of competition meant that dealing with the external environment was more an allocation process than, in many cases, a fight for survival between companies. Consequently, strategic planning dominated the subject for some time. The first instalment in the modern understanding of strategy came with Alfred Chandler's *Strategy and Structure* in 1962. However, particularly influential was Igor Ansoff who produced *Corporate Strategy* in 1965 and also introduced us to the concept of 'synergy' (2 + 2 = 5). Indeed, it was not until the publication of Henry Mintzberg's *The Rise and Fall of Strategic Planning* in 1994 that Ansoff's ideas were strongly challenged.

The same postwar influences can be seen in the development of leadership and the management of people. The democratic fervour evident in parts of Europe and the USA

Table 9.2 Management periods and perspectives

	1900–20s	1930–40s	1950–60s	1970–80	1980–90	1990–present
Functional perspectives	*Operations* Scientific management Efficiency	*Organizations* Administrative management Hawthorne Studies	*Leadership* Traits HR school *Marketing* Marketing mix Market-led companies *Strategy* Strategic planning	*Organizations* Matrix management MBO *Operations* Quality circles *Leadership* Behavioural *Strategy* Portfolio management	*Organizations* Excellence Culture *Operations* TQM JIT/kanban *Leadership* Contingency Team-based work *Marketing* Customer focus *Strategy* Competition	*Organizations* Learning Restructuring *Operations* Six sigma Re-engineering *Leadership* Empowerment Transformation Charisma *Strategy* Strategic intent Competency
Ideas industry	Tuck, Harvard and major consultancies established	Management seen to be a discipline with a body of knowledge	Exec. educations 50s New B schools 60s	From society to self	Andersen Consulting established 1989	650 US B schools. By 1994 AC has a turnover of $4.2b
Management movers	Taylor, Fayol	Weber, Mayo	Drucker, Maslow, McGregor, Levitt	Demming, Ansoff, Mintzberg, Handy	Peters, Porter, Kanter, Bennis, Juran, Hersey	Senge, Champy, Hamel & Prahalad
Business background	Industrialization Mass production First World War	Urbanization Great Depression Second World War	Postwar rebuilding Impact of military democratization	Start of uncertainty Internationalism	International competition Service sector growth	Globalization IT revolution

coloured the way thoughts were developing on how people should be managed. In the early 1950s, Douglas McGregor highlighted two sets of general assumptions in the form of 'theory X and Y'. These two concepts contrasted beliefs about individuals in terms of whether they needed to be controlled (theory X) or whether people were largely capable of self-motivation and working autonomously (theory Y). These ideas are still relevant and underlie managerial assumptions about the workforce and the kinds of structures and processes that are implemented today. McGregor's idea of paying greater concern to the needs of workers was reinforced by others, such as the 'motivation' theories of Abraham Maslow and Frederick Herzberg. These highlighted the need to look beyond basic motivators when managing people and to build more opportunities for self-realization into jobs, ideas which built on the earlier human relations themes.

In the same way that ideas were developing about the way people should be viewed and managed, leadership was also being viewed differently, particularly in the way leaders were developed and chosen. There was a move away from the military-based approach of identifying leadership traits, to exploring the kinds of behaviours that were needed for leadership. The assumption that leadership was a product of an individual's genetic make-up gave way to the belief that leadership could be learned. The development of behavioural theories of leadership, like those of Robert Blake and Jane Mouton and their 'managerial grid', occurred at this time.

Developments were occurring in several other areas. For instance, in the 1970s, new organizational structures developed such as 'matrix management' pioneered by NASA. This was born out of internationalization and attempts to get people to relate across functions to more than one manager, group or products. In the operations management area, a focus on quality began to gain momentum, first with 'quality circles' and then spurred on by Deming and 'total quality management'.

There are many more ideas, but in general these changes were a product of several underlying influences. Some reflected the changing competitive circumstances. Some reflected the changing views on the way people should be managed. Some highlighted the emergence of the dilemma between an external focus (whether through an economic, strategic or marketing lens) and a focus on the internal management of the corporation. All three influences continue to drive the development of management ideas today.

the development of rigour in management ideas

These approaches highlight another issue that is currently relevant. That is, few of the early postwar ideas were generated in any exacting way. However, this changed during the 1960s, and particularly after reports of the Ford and Carnegie Foundations in the USA placed an emphasis on achieving precision using quantitative methods (mathematics and statistics) or the more rigorous approaches of the behavioural sciences (psychology, sociology and anthropology).[14]

Consequently, a more critical and questioning approach emerged in the 1970s. Some of the ideas that had been accepted for years were now being challenged in a more vigorous way and with more reliable evidence. Notable was Mintzberg, who challenged the predominant assumptions about management. In *The Nature of Managerial Work*, he demonstrated that Fayol's ideas on managerial work, topical since the turn of the century, were a long way from reality.[15] But others were also questioning the picture of a rational world assumed by previous writers. Donald Hambrick, who pioneered research on top teams, also found a very different set of dynamics in the workplace. In researching top executives, rather than finding grand plans and brilliant strategies, he was confronted with the human realities of bounded rationality, limited search, information overload, biases and coalition dynamics.

However, this more critical approach to management ideas, like many of the trends in the management discipline, has proceeded in fits and starts. What have emerged are several types of ideas with varying degrees of empirical support. These ideas can be loosely categorized as:

> *Speculative*, based on assumptions and untested conclusions
> *Provisional*, based on some testing, but with limited empirical support
> *Rigorous*, based on a scientific approach to data collection and analysis.

All three can provide insight into more effective ways of operating, although to varying degrees. Speculative ideas may fill a gap where no research has been done and solutions are needed. However, such ideas, with little empirical support, have to be viewed with the most scepticism. Provisional ideas, based on best practice, limited testing, or case studies over time, are potentially more reliable, such as ideas on time management. However, they still have limitations. Rigorous ideas, that is, those with a solid research base, are largely the preferred option, but even here there are caveats. In some management subjects, rigorous depth can be difficult to achieve and in others, the research focus may be so narrow as to be of interest to only a handful of specialists. Theories that are of most use for the practice of management have to be both rigorous and relevant. Thus, it is important to view the current and continuous outpourings in the management literature with a degree of care.

the start of the contemporary era

The 1980s and 90s saw some continuing themes, but also many developments, as Figure 9.1 illustrates.[16] The later decades of the twentieth century saw the emergence of new influences on management thought and laid the foundations for the new millennium. Some of these ideas have resulted from changes in technology and, in particular, changes in information technology. The growth and exploitation of IT, with the development of the microchip and home computing in the 1970s, created a whole new subject area and influenced most other subjects on the MBA curriculum. If one reflects on the impact of the web and the astounding developments in computing software and hardware since the mid-1990s, it seems likely that IT will continue to have an impact on management thought and action.

However, it was possibly broader macroeconomic factors in the late 1970s and early 1980s that, initially at least, had the most influence on the take-up of management ideas. The Japanese were the first nation since the Second World War to challenge American economic dominance.

This gave rise to *In Search of Excellence* by Tom Peters and Robert Waterman in 1982, which spawned a new energy and interest in management issues. The competitive threats were now real and many people were prepared to listen, particularly to a message that had a combination of legitimate criticism of corporate America, but demonstrated a new hope in doing things better.

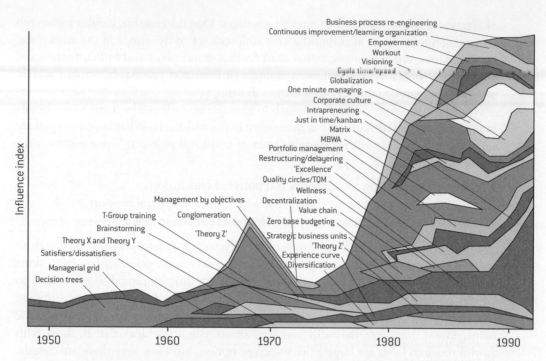

Figure 9.1 *The ebbs and flows of business techniques 1950s–1990s*

With these economic and competitive challenges as a backdrop, other subjects became more prominent. Strategy, for instance, developed into something more than an elaborate planning process. The resurgence of strategy in the 1980s and 90s was greatly influenced by Michael Porter and the economists' view of strategy. Porter's *Harvard Business Review* article 'How competitive forces shape strategy' in 1979 and *Competitive Strategy* in 1980 had a major impact on strategic thinking worldwide. But a new generation of strategy was born with Gary Hamel and C.K. Prahalad's *Competing for the Future*. In some ways, this interest in external factors was reflected in the resurgence of marketing as a discipline, which had also gone through a hiatus for several years.

> The resurgence of strategy in the 1980s and 90s was greatly influenced by Michael Porter and the economists' view of strategy.

The increase in international competition and the popularity of the 'excellence' movement also led to exploring new ways to manage internally. In particular, attempts to improve 'quality' took on broad dimensions during the 1980s, including ideas on different ways of managing people as well as new production methods. W. Edwards Deming, Joseph Juran and Philip Crosby led the corporate world in the quality movement with TQM, JIT and other techniques. In 1988, Joseph Juran laid down his quality gospel in *Juran on Planning for Quality*, adding to a worldwide trend that has continued with companies like Motorola and subsequently GE and their 'six sigma' quality campaign.

There have been many more influential concepts, from the 'learning organization', to the 'balanced scorecard', through to 'economic value added'. Indeed, there have been significant developments in most subjects and the following chapters on the core subject areas elaborate on some of those current themes.

However, while ideas abound, it is not necessary to know every twist and turn in management thinking. But it is important to keep in mind the lessons from history and to be conscious of both the underlying dilemmas that have characterized management throughout time and the fragmented nature of the discipline. While the commercial environment has become more complex, the management ideas industry may, in some ways, have added to the chaos rather than helped to cope with the complexity. There are few barriers to entry to an industry that includes business schools and management faculties, a host of training organizations, numerous consultancy firms, business journalists, freelance writers, government officials and businesspeople themselves, all publicly suggesting how businesses should be run. Thus, a reason why management can be so challenging is not only because managers are faced with complex problems but also because they are bombarded with many and varied solutions, some of which may not just be unclear, but not even helpful. This needs to be borne in mind in understanding how management ideas relate to the contemporary business environment.

the challenges of a complex environment

The current business environment is indeed complex. We are in an unprecedented era of globalization and international competition. Few domestic companies and environments now escape the pressure from international competition. Not only has the number of competitors increased in many industries, but so has their sophistication. The quality and reliability of many products today bear little resemblance to what many consumers experienced just 20 years ago. 'Mass production' no longer carries with it a perception of second-rate merchandise. Methods of taking products to market have also changed remarkably, while speed, whether it is speed of communication, speed of response or even speed of obsolescence, is something that most people experience on a daily basis.

But the changes have not just been in improved production and marketing techniques. In the past two decades, the whole structure of many economies has changed dramatically. For example, in the late 1970s and 1980s, especially in the USA and the UK, the emphasis began to shift from manufacturing to service activities. By 1990, service companies dominated both economies, with 73% of American and 70% of British businesses in the service sector.

Consumers have unprecedented access to information on products and services and universal communication opportunities to voice their disapproval.

Coupled with this have been increasing demands from a whole range of stakeholders, including consumers, governments and employees. Consumers have unprecedented access to information on products and services and universal communication opportunities to voice their disapproval. Whether governments overall have become more interventionist is debatable, but in some areas, such as tax and product liability, the demands on managers are much greater. Certainly, the expectations of employees and how they should be managed have generally increased. Even in those organizations where enlightened leadership ideas have failed to penetrate, the 'safety' bar has been raised, with more stringent legal requirements to provide a healthy, safe workplace and to take a responsible position towards the environment. Whether or not one agrees with the mounting legislation and societal pressures, the demands are very real.

In terms of ideas and solutions, it is easy to see from this how management ideas have grown to reflect the vast range of problems arising from the unprecedented change and increased complexity of the economic environment. But while many of the ideas have had a beneficial impact and continue to do so, there is also an increasing dissatisfaction with some of these ideas and their failure to meet expectations. Moreover, it is unlikely that the deluge of ideas will diminish with easy distribution, lucrative opportunities and a receptive managerial audience. Instead, we are likely to witness an age of confusion – an age where it becomes even more important that one develops a critical and thoughtful approach to the ideas presented.

One of the reasons for the confusion is the nature of the management discipline. As our brief history has shown, it has evolved over time, but in a disjointed fashion rather than as a continuous progression; it is a subject faced with growing pains. These pains result from the continuous process of having to accommodate new ideas that spring from many new sources. Management thought, therefore, constantly requires restatement and consolidation. Given this, there will be times when there will be gaps in our understanding of management and some of the issues.

However, these gaps can sometimes be quite large. For example, Richard Mahoney and Joseph McCue, in reviewing strategic management, argue that one of the reasons for the struggle this subject has had in gaining respect from other major disciplines (social science, mathematics, medicine, engineering and so on) is that, unlike those fields which build on history and precedents, in strategic management, the recent fad is usually the new 'truth'.[17] Old ideas never seem to be captured, even as useful history or building blocks, to develop a coherent body of knowledge on which to draw.

> *The need to build on evidence and concepts that have gone before is basic to developing a robust subject.*

The need to build on evidence and concepts that have gone before is basic to developing a robust subject. Without a serious history of measuring long-term progress, it is hard to know if a field is making gains. If previous ideas are dismissed by the next 'hot' author as being naive or misguided rather than useful in their time, or even important steps on a learning continuum, then it is not possible to get any sense of progress. The continuum of progress is what makes for a solid body of knowledge that can be passed on to aspiring managers in a coherent way.

However, this is not just a problem that affects strategic management, but also one that plagues other management subjects to varying degrees. Increasingly, there has been a tendency for authors in many subjects to proclaim that their ideas outshine anything that has gone before, with no sense of how their work progresses the topic. The leadership area, for example, has a plethora of concepts, many of which are based on questionable assumptions. In fact, in some areas, quick fixes have become the order of the day and speed and simplification have became virtues (as the popularity of books like *The Ten Minute Manager*, *MBA in a Box* and *MBA for Dummies* testifies).

Of course, all the management subjects have areas that are built on evidence and precedent, particularly academic research. However, many of the ideas that have become popular have not necessarily been thoroughly scrutinized, nor have they positioned themselves in the historical building process of their subject. This has been compounded by the fragmented nature of the discipline overall, which, with the growing ahistorical bent, has reduced the chances of some ideas being successfully implemented in a management context. Solutions frequently require an understanding of the broader environment for success. An example of the problem is highlighted by Margaret Brindle and Peter Stearns, who point to Peter Drucker's article, 'The discipline of innovation', which outlines seven places to look for innovation opportunity and turn them into advantage.[18] However, no mention is made of economic context, government or legal issues, structure, operations, accounting or finance, just the enthusiasm for innovation and its wonders. The same criticism can also be aimed at many other ideas, such as MBO, empowerment and boundarylessness, which have faltered on implementation, often as a result of failure to take into account broader issues, whether they are culture, cost or strategic need.

The great benefit of completing a postgraduate management qualification is that the ideas are put into context and reviewed in some depth. Nevertheless, anyone approaching the management literature still needs to do so with a critical eye. One way to bring clarity to the confusion of ideas is to approach them with a schema that helps in focusing on some of the strengths and limitations of the concepts presented. A framework that does this is outlined in Figure 9.2. It builds on the earlier suggestion that management ideas are based on varying degrees of empirical support and can be speculative, provisional or rigorous. These different degrees of 'certainty' of an idea can also be contrasted with how broadly 'applicable' the idea might be. Thus, some ideas may be limited to only one context or period of time (narrow), while others may be more broadly applicable over a long period of time and/or a range of different contexts (universal).

	Applicability	
Certainty	Narrow	Universal
Rigorous	Focused research 'Excellence' ideas	Statistical principles Personality tests
Provisional	Six sigma Process re-engineering Boundarylessness	Quality principles Scientific management Team-building approaches
Speculative	Managing dot.com companies Share management models	Fayol and managerial work Boston Box

Figure 9.2 Management ideas

speculative ideas

Speculative ideas (at the bottom of Figure 9.2) with minimal support have the lowest degree of certainty. *Narrow speculative ideas* include some of the glamorous ideas and predictions for managing dot.com companies during the internet boom, or some of the current theories on how to manage share market volatility, both applicable to particular points in time. *Universal speculative ideas* include concepts like 'the Boston box'. The box possibly did and still does provide insights into markets and positioning, but its questionable empirical base should instil considerable caution in its use. The same is true of Fayol's ideas on managerial work, which had universal appeal for many years but were largely speculative.

provisional ideas

Provisional ideas generate more trust and confidence, but still have pitfalls. *Universal provisional ideas* seem to hold true, because many companies or individuals have demonstrated that the ideas generally work either in different contexts, or over time. There is more evidence for their success than speculative ideas, but they do not have empirical certainty. For example, scientific management ideas which provide general principles on improving efficiency would come into this category. Many of the models on team building and quality would also be universal provisional ideas. In general, while the principles underlying good teamwork or quality improvements are far from being universal laws, in general their application in most circumstances adds value.

Narrow provisional ideas are those that are often based on universal principles, but are unique to a particular time or context. For example, process re-engineering, with leanings towards scientific management, boundarylessness based on teamwork principles, and the principles of the learning organization have much merit. But the successful application of the ideas depends on distinct circumstances or conditions.

rigorous ideas

Rigorous ideas have strong empirical support. They can be based on traditional research methods, or result from practice over many years demonstrating reliability. *Universal rigorous ideas* include statistical concepts, based on mathematical principles, and some personality tests, based on thorough research. However, reliable judgement still has to be exercised in relation to their application. All these concepts can be used or abused and it is not unusual to hear of the misapplication of personality tests or statistical techniques. The ideas are more certain and applicable, but they also have their limitations.

Narrow rigorous ideas are applicable to a particular set of circumstances, such as management research aimed at investigating certain types of consumer products, or production techniques. This is also true of some types of popularized field research such as *In Search of Excellence*. Based on rigorous data, much of which came originally from academic sources, the book was largely appropriate to a particular time period. However, as with many of the ideas in all six categories, the concepts can still provide considerable insight, so long as their limitations are understood.

enduring dilemmas

All management ideas have strengths and weaknesses and we have focused here on two aspects in particular – certainty and applicability. The aim is to encourage a thoughtful approach to management ideas that goes beyond polarizing them as either in vogue or not viable. In order to complete the process, we need to return to the drivers that give rise to the need for the ideas and solutions in the first place.

New economic circumstances will give rise to different challenges requiring fresh solutions. Some of the challenges are unique to one point in time. However, there are also issues that have continued to challenge managers throughout history. These issues do not have 'the' one solution, but pose a dilemma. In each case, there may be several solutions, which depend on time and circumstance. Some dilemmas resurface in slightly different ways, but in essence pose the same problems. Hence, some ideas will always have universal applicability over time and always, at least, partly solve the problem, because the issues themselves are enduring. Some of these universal dilemmas for a company include:

> Should the *guidance* on what behaviours are expected in the organization be communicated through clear rules (regulations) or general principles (values)?
> Should the overall *focus* be on the organization (internal and efficiency) or the market (external and flexibility)?
> Should *control* of the organization be centralized or decentralized?
> Does *productive* advantage lie in our hard resources (machinery/systems) or our soft resources (people)?
> Should the organization *structure* be complex (layered) or clear (flat)?
> Should the *future* be based on expansion (the unknown) or continuity (the familiar)?

Each of these dilemmas should be viewed flexibly. In some cases, the solution will be an equal blend between the two extremes. For example, when reviewing a company's productive advantage, attention may be paid to both people (soft resources) and production systems (hard resources) in equal amounts. In other cases, time will change the emphasis. For example, in relation to control, centralization may be appropriate at one point in time, but decentralization at another, as a result of, for example, changing consumer demands requiring more diffuse decision making. Additionally, the focus in terms of the future may differ. For example, some parts of a business may emphasize expansion by taking new products to new markets, while another may succeed through continuity (in Peters and Waterman's terms, by 'sticking to the knitting' and doing what you do best).

Thus, in considering the ideas you are presented with, you always have to relate them to the problem you are trying to solve. Any repackaged theory that pronounces that decentralization is the answer to your company's problems, or a flat structure, or clear rules, is only a viable solution if you know what the problem is in the first place. Yes, the cutting-edge theories are vital and you will learn many of them on the MBA. But if you haven't also developed a capability to understand and identify the type of problem you are faced with (Chapter 4), you will eventually end up throwing most management ideas into the 'unviable' rubbish bin.

conclusion

The chapter has given a brief overview of the development of management ideas. Management is better seen as a collection of disciplines at varying stages of progress than a coherent body of knowledge that has been developed in an integrated way. This knowledge has also to be seen in relation to an increasingly complex environment. It is not surprising that there are gaps in the extent to which management theories and ideas can solve the problems facing practitioners.

We can go a long way in solving managerial problems by being clear about the dilemmas faced. If time has been spent in understanding the underlying problems, then better judgements can be made about which ideas are most likely to provide effective solutions. There is no Holy Grail among these ideas, but many have been rigorously developed and many are relevant to solving the management issues of the day. What is truly beneficial about completing an MBA is that you will have the time and will be given the professional guidance to understand the strengths and weaknesses of the major management concepts and how and when they can be best applied.

references/notes

1. Pfeffer, J. and Sutton, R.I. (1999) 'Knowing what to do is not enough: turning knowledge into action', *California Management Review*, **42**(1): 83.
2. Ibid.
3. Crainer, S. (2000) *The Management Century: A Critical Review of 20th Century Thought and Practice* (San Francisco: Jossey-Bass) p. xix.
4. Based on George, C.S. (1972) *The History of Management Thought* (Englewood Cliffs, NJ: Prentice Hall); reproduced by Massie, J. (1987) *Essentials of Management* (Englewood Cliffs, NJ: Prentice Hall) pp. 12–13.
5. Ibid. Massie, p. 15.
6. Ibid. Massie, p. 16.
7. Brindle, M.C. and Stearns, P.N. (2001) *Facing up to Management Faddism: A New Look at an Old Force* (Westport: Quorum Books) p. 21.
8. Ibid. p. 23.
9. Crainer, S. (1998) *Key Management Ideas: Thinkers that Changed the Management World* (London: Financial Times Pitman) p. 187.
10. Fox, C. (2003) 'From fad to curse', *AFR BOSS Magazine*, January, pp. 22–5.
11. The first business school, the University of Pennsylvania's Wharton School, was founded in 1881. The first postgraduate degree in business was awarded by the Amos Tuck School of Business at Dartmouth College in 1901 and Harvard's first MA in business administration came in 1910.
12. Op. cit. Crainer (2000) p. 91.
13. Op. cit. Crainer (2000) p. 99.
14. Op. cit. Massie (1987) p. 26.
15. Mintzberg, H. (1973) *The Nature of Managerial Work* (New York: Harper & Row).
16. Curves shown are for illustrative purposes. Pascale, R.T. (1994) *Transformation* (London: BBC Enterprises). Simon & Schuster from Pascale, R.T. (1988) *Managing on the Edge*.
17. Mahoney, R.J. and McCue, J.A. (1999) 'Big ideas of the past three decades: are they fads or enablers', Center for the Study of American Business, CEO Series 29.
18. Op. cit. Brindle and Stearns (2001) p. 62.

10 operations management

professors kannan sethuraman and devanath tirupati

The operations function is responsible for the physical and business processes that transform labour, material, capital, energy and other inputs into finished goods and/or services that are of greater value to society. It encompasses a number of activities and processes from procurement and managing suppliers to converting raw materials into products and services and delivering them to the end customer. The breadth of these tasks and the range of skills required to manage operations make it an exciting and demanding area for aspiring managers. In today's fiercely competitive global and dynamic markets, companies increasingly recognize the critical role that a well-run operation can play towards achieving sustainable competitive advantage. An effective operation has the potential to reduce the costs of offering products and services through improved efficiency, increase revenue through good quality, and act as a basis for future innovation. Hence, whether or not you intend to pursue a career in operations, it is essential that you understand the concepts that underlie operations and the key role that operations plays in achieving the firm's short- and long-term objectives.

> In today's fiercely competitive global and dynamic markets, companies increasingly recognize the critical role that a well-run operation can play towards achieving sustainable competitive advantage.

We begin this chapter with a brief history of the field and how the field of operations management has evolved over the years, as we believe this is essential for understanding and appreciating the main themes or concepts that follow.

the evolution of operations management

The early evolution of operations management can be traced back to the work of Adam Smith in *Wealth of Nations* (1776) in which he articulates the benefits of the division of labour for efficient production. In the late nineteenth and early twentieth centuries, a number of professionals from industry contributed significantly to our understanding of managing operations in large businesses. Most notable among these contributions was that of Frederic W. Taylor who, at the turn of the twentieth century, emphasized the need to replace subjective management by 'objective management' based on scientific principles.[1] He developed ways to improve the performance of individual workers. Peter Drucker remarked that Taylor's valuable insights were a greater contribution to America's industrial rise than stopwatch or time and motion study'.[2] The other pioneers of scientific management included Henry Gantt (1861–1919), who is best remembered for the Gantt charts used in project management, and Frank and Lillian Gilbreth who, through the analysis of work, developed the concept of time and motion study to eliminate wasteful effort.

Henry Ford, keeping in touch with the ideas of Taylor, transformed his Highland

Park plant from a poorly equipped job shop to a highly efficient moving assembly line in 1913. Although Ford is given credit for developing the notion of mass production, others who worked with him at the time argued that the process simply evolved. As one observer remarked:

Henry Ford had no ideas on mass production. He wanted to build a lot of autos. He was determined but, like everyone else at that time, he didn't know how. In later years, he was glorified as the originator of the mass production idea. Far from it; he just grew into it, like the rest of us. The essential tools and the final assembly line with its many integrated feeders resulted from an organization which was continually experimenting and improving to get better production.[3]

Through scale economies and standardization, Ford achieved market leadership. Interestingly, Ford made his share of mistakes and his famous quote, 'you can have any colour so long as it is black', essentially highlights his failure to see the need to offer a variety of cars to satisfy the diverse needs of customers. His focused plant made Model T cars in large volumes, which achieved low cost and offered zero flexibility. Alfred P. Sloan (1875–1966) capitalized on Ford's mistake and pioneered the restructuring of General Motors (GM) as a collection of autonomous operating divisions coordinated through a general office. Each of GM's divisions targeted specific markets (for example, Cadillac was positioned to cater to the high end of the market) to achieve Sloan's goal of 'a car for every purpose and every price'.[4] This essentially highlights the classic productivity dilemma that manufacturers face between choosing a strategy that achieves low cost and economies of scale through standardization and elimination of variety and a strategy that aims to gain market share by achieving scope economies by offering variety and flexibility.[5] The challenge is in achieving high-volume production (scale), while providing products/services suited to the specific requirements of the consumer (scope).

Taylor's work on scientific management inspired Shewart at Bell Laboratories in the 1930s, who laid the foundations behind statistical quality control. The USA maintained a strong hold on the worldwide postwar market. Japanese firms slowly began to build up their reputation around the reliability and quality of their products. In the 1980s, following the popularity of Toyota's production system, other philosophies and practices such as total quality management (TQM), the theory of constraints (TOC), time-based competition and business process re-engineering (BPR) started gaining more prominence.

During the past quarter century, the operations function has evolved from a manufacturing focus to emphasizing services, with extensive applications in banking, financial services and insurance, logistics, transportation and the hospitality sector, healthcare, outsourcing and offshore operations, e-commerce and so on. Furthermore, capabilities in managing operations have emerged as being critical for success in today's environment, with growing competition and globalization. Wal-Mart, Toyota, Dell and Southwest Airlines are well-known examples of firms that have succeeded through excellence in operations. We believe that an appreciation of the role of operations and its contribution to the firm's competitiveness is essential for the modern manager, irrespective of his or her responsibilities. Our aim in this chapter is to present an overview of the operations function and provide a flavour of some key themes that are part of the core in most MBA programmes.

operations strategy and strategic fit

'Strategic fit' is defined as the process of aligning organizational activities so that they reinforce one another and the configuration of one activity raises the value of other activities.[6] Skinner was perhaps one of the first to recognize multiple dimensions of manufacturing performance and to conceptualize and articulate the notion of operational strategy. Some of his pioneering articles, written more than three decades ago, are amazingly prophetic and relevant today.[7] He argued against the traditional, reactive role that operations plays in an organization in which many operations executives wait for product, service and market-related decisions to be made and then respond to those requirements reactively. He stressed the importance of aligning operational strategy with other functional strategies and the overall business strategy to achieve sustainable competitiveness. Skinner argued that 'too often top management overlooks manufacturing's potential to strengthen or weaken a company's competitive ability'. The kernel of his argument was that if managed properly, the operations function can contribute as much towards the competitive success of a business as any other function in the corporate arsenal.

Furthermore, Skinner argued that the conventional factory attempts to do too many conflicting production tasks within one inconsistent set of manufacturing policies, and it was not possible for a factory to excel on every yardstick.[8] For example, according to his thesis, a plant could either be a low-cost producer focusing on efficiencies or a responsive supplier, but not both. Skinner advocated a 'focused factory' approach, in which he stresses the need to choose a competitive position first, defining the key performance characteristics consistent with the overall business strategy and other functional strategies. It is important to note that the choice of focus needs to be made through a comprehensive analysis of the firm's resources, strengths and weaknesses, position in the industry, assessment of competition, and forecast of future customers' needs. Operations strategy and operational function should then be geared to meet these objectives.

> *If managed properly, the operations function can contribute as much towards the competitive success of a business as any other function in the corporate arsenal.*

Hayes and Wheelwright expanded on this idea and developed a framework called the product–process matrix for classifying and understanding manufacturing systems.[9] In this framework, the basic premise is that the product mix (number of products, volume and degree of standardization) determines the process choice. This choice can be made from five classic types of processes – projects, job shops, batch flow processes, line flow systems and continuous flow processes – together with a number of hybrid processes. A model of this matrix is shown in Figure 10.1.[10]

We provide a brief description of these five classic process types below:

> *Project*: This represents the process to do one-of-a-kind jobs like building a cricket ground or making a movie. It typically requires several inputs to be coordinated in line with a customer's requirements and will often require resources to be taken to the location where the product is to be built or the service is to be provided. In terms of the level of customization demanded, projects represent the most unique and highly customized products or services. (Project is excluded from Figure 10.1 as it typically exists to do a particular, unique job.)

> *Job shop*: This represents a highly flexible process consisting of flexible machines

and/or people, capable of producing a wide range of products in significant quantities. Machine shops, tool and die shops, auto repair shops and general hospitals are classic examples of job shops.

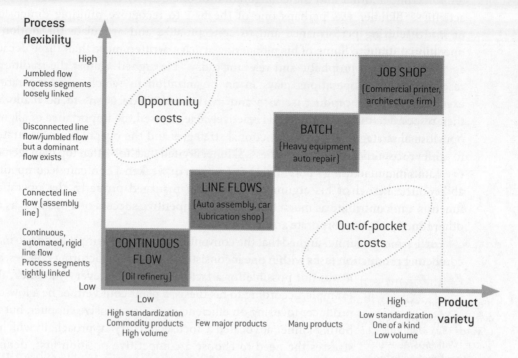

Figure 10.1 The product–process matrix

> *Batch flow process*: This process shares a lot of features with that of a job shop. Similar to job shops, they are organized by function and not by products. They typically have a set menu of standardized products that are produced in 'lots' or 'batches' consisting of a long run of a single product. While the job shop operates in a make-to-order environment to fulfil a customer's order by a given due date and in the requested quantities, the batch flow operation produces goods stored in inventory from which customer orders are satisfied. Industry examples of batch flow processes include clothing and white goods, such as refrigerators, air conditioners, dishwashers and so on.

> *Line flow systems*: As the sales volume of each individual product increases, processes are typically designed to support high-volume production of the standardized product or service at minimal cost. The design of such a process would involve dividing the production into a series of steps to be performed in sequence. The different steps are set out in a line and hence the name. This process is most commonly exemplified by car assembly lines.

> *Continuous flow process*: Typically, high-volume consumer goods and commodities are manufactured by continuous flow processes. They are characterized by higher levels of capital investments and automation in comparison to line flow processes. Given the high costs associated with stopping and restarting these systems, they are run all day and every day with minimum shutdowns. Paper mills and oil refineries are excellent examples of continuous processing.

The product–process matrix is a powerful concept with many implications for manufacturing:

❶ It recognizes that, technically, most products can be made in more than one type of process and thus the choice of process type is really a business decision.

❷ It identifies performance measures best met under different processes. For example, while continuous flow and line flow processes focus on cost efficiency, reliability and predictability, job shops focus on flexibility to both product and volume changes. (Note that this is consistent with Skinner's 'focused factory' concept.) Hence, the choice of the process will have implications for the firm's operations in terms of its cost and flexibility.

❸ Most importantly, the matrix explicitly brings out the linkages between product and process choices. Hayes and Wheelwright argue that for continued success and maintaining competitiveness in the long run, it is critical that the firm aligns its product and process choices and any mismatch is likely to result in unnecessary costs and/or inability to satisfy customers' needs. In fact, alignment between product and process choices would position a firm on the diagonal of the matrix and a position off the diagonal would indicate a mismatch and result in either out-of-pocket costs or opportunity costs.

❹ The framework is also useful in identifying the key manufacturing challenges associated with different process and product choices.

In order to provide a flavour of how this framework might work in practice, we present an example of how process choice has direct implications for a firm's performance in terms of its cost and flexibility. Diecraft, a fully owned subsidiary of Tupperware supplying moulds, has aligned its manufacturing strategy with its corporate mission of meeting Tupperware's needs for customized moulds in a responsive manner. Typically, the orders are small and require an initial design effort. Processing is order specific and varies widely. In addition, demand is seasonal and uncertain. Diecraft has adopted 'flexibility' as its core strategy to cope with these requirements and invested in sophisticated, state-of-the-art, general purpose equipment. The factory is organized by process, to provide pooling benefits. It relies heavily on overtime (up to 40%) and limited unattended operations during the third shift to meet customer deadlines in the presence of demand uncertainty and fluctuations. Clearly, Diecraft's strategy results in higher costs – both in equipment and labour. However, improved service and capability results in higher prices that adequately compensate for the higher costs.

Analogous to the product–process matrix is the matrix of service processes introduced in the early 1980s[11] and later refined by Roger Schmenner (Figure 10.2).[12] Services are classified along two dimensions that significantly affect the character of the service delivery process. On the vertical axis, industries are classified based on 'the degree of labour intensity', which is defined as the ratio of labour cost to capital cost. Airlines and hospitals would be classified as industries with a low degree of labour intensity due to their heavy investment in buildings and capital equipment relative to their investment in labour. Examples of labour-intensive services would include schools and legal services. The horizontal dimension represents 'the degree of customer interaction with and customization of the service for the consumer', which describes the ability of the customer to affect the nature of the services provided. Barber shops and hairdressers are classic examples where customer presence is required during service production and represent a high level of customer interaction. Similarly, hospitals also require high levels of customization. Standardized services, on the other hand, are often characterized by little interaction between customer and service provider in comparison. In this framework (see Figure 10.2), services are categorized into four distinct types – service shops, service factories, mass services and professional services. Schmenner uses the framework to identify key challenges and managerial issues and derives strategic and operational implications of different types of service processes.

Degree of customer interaction and customization

	Low	High
Low	**Service factories** Airlines Trucking Hotels Resorts Recreation	**Service shops** Hospitals Auto repairs Other repair services
High	**Mass services** Retailing Wholesaling Retail aspects of commercial banking	**Professional services** Doctors Lawyers Accountants Architects

Degree of labour intensity

Figure 10.2 The service–process matrix

process analysis

The foregoing discussion should make it clear that manufacturing and service systems are diverse and complex, and decision making involves trade-offs between different performance measures. Developing an understanding of the process dynamics and the interrelationship between the different performance measures is a prerequisite for effectively managing operations. Typically, this involves capacity analysis, determination and assessment of bottlenecks,[13] determination of resource and capacity utilizations, lead time analysis, quality, flexibility and so on. While simple processes can be analysed without any special tools, complex processes require more sophisticated techniques. For example, line balancing techniques are useful in understanding the impact of work allocation in an assembly line and its implications for capacity, labour utilization and production costs. Similarly, critical path and network methods can be used to address scheduling and resource allocation problems in managing projects. Today it is well recognized that poor planning is responsible for cost overruns and delays in project completion. For example, Federation Square in Melbourne, a project scheduled to be completed by 2001 at a budgeted cost of AUS$150 million, was finally completed five years later with costs exceeding AUS$600 million. Much of this escalation in costs and delay in completion date were attributable to poor planning and continuous change in the scope of the deliverables.

Process analysis tools are equally useful in analysing service delivery systems. For example, line balancing principles have helped shape patient flow for boutique hospitals like Shouldice Hospital in Thornhill, Ontario, which focuses on the treatment of inguinal hernias. Similarly, the concept of bottleneck management is useful in the design and operation of service systems. Simulation and waiting line analysis (queuing theory) are other examples of process analysis tools that are useful in performance assessment of both manufacturing and service processes.

Process analysis goes well beyond the tools for assessing system performance and determining relationships between various performance measures. It actually provides a framework (sometimes referred to as a 'process perspective') for taking a systemic view of the entire process and making operations decisions based on business considerations. Sometimes this may necessitate going beyond organizational and functional boundaries.

Process perspective is not limited to operations and production processes and the tools of process analysis are applicable to other business processes as well. Order processing, accounting procedures and customer service systems are some examples of business processes that could benefit significantly by applying the tools of process analysis. Similarly, process analysis is typically one of the basic building blocks of many business process re-engineering efforts that focus on the redesign of business processes to improve their effectiveness. For example, process analysis is a basic component of well-known initiatives by Wal-Mart, P&G and others in improving their logistics, inventory management and distribution systems.

lean production aka toyota production system

The term *lean production*[14] has been used in OM literature to signify a broad philosophy of continuous improvement that helps achieve better quality products at lower costs through the elimination of waste in all forms.[15] It is essential to note that waste is not just scrap and rejects (as understood in common parlance), but is defined as any element of production not contributing directly to meeting the demand when it is required, with minimum effort. Thus, waste includes all forms of excess production leading to inventories, excess movement, redundant operations and so on.

The term 'lean' was used to characterize the minimalist approach to manufacturing that Toyota pioneered. The Toyota production system (TPS) had its origin in the factory shop floors of Toyota Motor Manufacturing. Postwar Japanese auto manufacturers faced a heterogeneous market that exhibited slow growth and economic uncertainty. Also, in 1950, the Japanese auto industry produced only 30,000 vehicles comprising a number of different models of cars and trucks, which was equivalent to about one and a half day's worth of output of the US industry.[16] Satisfying such a small but fragmented market required a different approach to manufacturing. It necessitated systems that could operate efficiently in a small lot, high variety environment. Some Japanese manufacturers, most notably at Toyota, quickly realized that imitating US methods of manufacturing was not the most appropriate course of action and pioneered an alternative manufacturing management system that emphasizes the smooth flow of work – accomplished through the mapping of various processes and eliminating unnecessary steps, and using teamwork to identify and fix problems as and where they occurred. This has been hailed as the source of Toyota's outstanding performance as a manufacturer of quality automobiles and experts consider these principles to have sparked the second industrial revolution.[17] After Womack et al.[18] popularized the lean production principles and attributed their adoption for the impressive performance differential between Japanese and Western auto manufacturers, scores of US and European manufacturers responded by experimenting with and adopting lean practices, and reported impressive improvements in their operational performance.[19]

Lean production comprises a number of tools, techniques and systems spanning a range of planning and operational activities driven by the TPS philosophy. TPS implementation involves gearing the entire organization towards the objective of continuous improvement by appropriately empowering employees at all levels and securing their buy-in. The aim of lean manufacturing is to go beyond superficial symptoms and eliminate different forms of waste by addressing the root causes by asking the 'five whys'.[20]

It is interesting to contrast the treatment of quality in the TPS vis-à-vis its treatment in the traditional (Western) approach. Conventional practice is to make workers responsible for quantity through production quotas and worker incentives. Quality is addressed through inspection and handled by a quality control group. The TPS approach is diametrically opposite, with workers responsible for quality. They are empowered to stop the line in the interests of quality and disrupt production if necessary (thereby leading to loss of production). Achieving production targets is the responsibility of management that needs to resort to overtime to make up for lost production and is held accountable. This approach has the effect of shifting the focus for quality away from workers to other key elements – design of products and processes, worker training, tools provided and so on. It is worth noting that this philosophy is consistent with that of Deming, who argued that 85% of quality problems are due to management.

> The aim of lean manufacturing is to go beyond superficial symptoms and eliminate different forms of waste by addressing the root causes by asking the 'five whys'.

It is critical to note that the TPS is not a quick fix to problems in manufacturing, producing instantaneous results. Rather, it is an organic process of improvement that is time-consuming and often laborious. For example, even after 50 years of success, it is still evolving at Toyota, a live example of continuous process improvements. Half-hearted attempts, with the adoption of a few elements such as kanban systems, are likely to yield only limited benefits.[21]

It is important to recognize that, in its basic form, the tools and techniques of the TPS have been developed and are suitable for discrete manufacturing systems with relatively stable environments. However, the TPS philosophy is more general and the approach can be extended to other environments and beyond manufacturing. Hence, implementation of JIT to other situations needs some adaptation of the tools and techniques.

theory of constraints or synchronized manufacturing

The theory of constraints (TOC) was first developed and popularized by Goldratt in his landmark book *The Goal*, and was targeted initially to a hybrid of job and batch shop environments.[22] It is an approach that focuses its attention on the bottlenecks of the operation that determine the pace of output. The TOC is fairly comprehensive and integrates a variety of tactical planning and operational issues. It considers the entire system: all internal functional areas as well as all external suppliers and customers.

Essentially, the framework is an adaptation of many of the lean principles for a hybrid of make-to-stock and make-to-order situations, enhanced by the incorporation of planning features such as capacity planning, product mix choice, synchronous scheduling and so on. By emphasizing the business objective of making money as the primary goal, Goldratt establishes the business implications of operations and has made a significant contribution towards the recognition of operations as a business function.

Similar to TPS, the TOC approach requires a systemic view of operations, and typically involves the following five steps:

❶ *Identify* the system's constraint.
❷ Decide how to *exploit* the system's constraint.
❸ *Subordinate* everything else to that decision.
❹ *Elevate* the system's constraint.
❺ Don't allow *inertia* to become the system's constraint. When a constraint is broken, go back to step 1.

Clearly, these elements constitute the planning component of synchronous manufacturing, necessitated by the job/batch shop characteristics with dynamic demands. Consistent with the TPS, the TOC approach involves flow-based planning with system bottlenecks determining the flow rate.

Scheduling in a multiproduct, multistage environment is recognized as a difficult problem, which has attracted attention in operations management for several decades. Goldratt's approach essentially is based on the bottleneck resource driving the plant schedule. The schedule at the bottleneck is determined by plant performance considerations such as costs, resource utilization, cost of inventories and customer measures, such as on-time delivery, cost of delays and so on. Once the schedule at the bottleneck is determined, it is used to develop the schedule at other stages of the plant (upstream and downstream of the bottleneck).

The approach to quality likewise combines the TPS philosophy with conventional wisdom, and is guided by the bottleneck. For example, in order to conserve bottleneck capacity, the TOC suggests inspection and control practices to ensure that only good quality inputs are processed at the bottleneck. Unlike the TPS, the TOC does not emphasize quality at each stage. Instead, it provides for product inspection at intermediate stages.

To summarize, the TOC philosophy can be interpreted as a hybrid of conventional and TPS principles that combines philosophy of waste elimination with short-term considerations for improving performance, adapted for job and batch shop environments. The approach has also been extended to other types of systems such as projects.

total quality management

A product or service must meet the requirements for the customer's use, or else it is of no value. The quality of products and services remains fundamental to the success of organizations and the evolution of quality spanned the entire twentieth century. In the early 1900s, quality control was mostly reactive and limited to product inspection and after-the-fact detection of defects. Initially, sampling plans were developed for product inspection in situations involving purchase (by consumer) and delivery (by producer) in lots. Clearly, acceptance/rejection decisions based on such acceptance sampling plans are subject to statistical errors (rejection of good lots and acceptance of poor lots) and the objective is to devise plans that minimize the total cost of quality control while maintaining the risks of incorrect decisions to within prespecified levels.

The next phase in the evolution was the quality control phase, in which the focus shifted towards controlling the processes to minimize the production of defective units. In this context, statistical process control (SPC) has witnessed a tremendous surge in applications during the past 25 years, particularly in North America.[23] The primary motivation for SPC derives from the notion that after-the-fact product inspection, while protecting the consumer, is not particularly helpful to the producer. Instead, by shifting control to the processes involved in production, the producer benefits by preventing defects from occurring, thereby avoiding the costs of rejects, scrap and rework. The basic premise is that with capable processes that are suitably designed for the product, operation in the desired or 'in-control' state will result in good production that will make product inspection unnecessary. This philosophy is widely accepted today, and a large number of firms routinely waive product inspection of incoming material and rely on self-certification by the supplier based on their SPC systems. For example, shipments from suppliers (located nearby) are delivered directly to Toyota's assembly lines without any additional check. Such practices have become common and followed by other auto assemblers such as GM and Volvo and firms in other industries. IBM, Dell and Motorola are examples of companies in the semiconductor and computer industry that implemented such schemes several years ago. Besides improving quality and significantly reducing inspection costs, this practice reduces inventory requirements at the customer end and provides additional benefit.[24]

Understandably, the first two phases focus on the operational level and emphasize conformance of product to specifications. The evolution of quality beyond the operational level is attributable to the work of Feigenbaum who introduced the concept of total quality management (TQM), which seeks to integrate all organizational functions, including marketing, design, engineering, production and finance, to focus on meeting customer needs and organizational objectives.[25] It represents a holistic framework, aimed at continually improving not just the products or services but also the processes associated with developing them, through a company-wide commitment to quality. More recently, the approach was extended to introduce the notion of strategic quality management to fully tap the competitive potential of quality.[26] In this context, it is useful to note that each phase in the above framework subsumes the phases that preceded it and incorporates elements from those phases. For example, the process control phase will incorporate elements of quality control and product inspection.

From an application perspective, the basic principles and tools of quality are relatively well accepted and widely adopted globally. These developments are partly due to the influence of the three leading 'quality' gurus – W. Edwards Deming, Joseph Juran and Philip Crosby. While commitment to quality remains a common theme across their philosophies, their respective approaches and focus vary considerably.

In the early 1980s, Deming argued that if management followed the new line of thinking, productivity and quality would simultaneously improve:

Improvement of the product increases uniformity of product, reduces rework and mistakes, reduces waste of manpower, machine-time, and materials, and thus increases output with less effort. Other benefits of improved quality are lower costs, happier company.[27]

Joseph Juran defined quality as 'fitness for use', which had five dimensions: quality of design, quality of conformance, availability, safety and field use.[28] He developed detailed approaches to quantify the impact of different areas that spanned the product's entire life on the different dimensions of fitness for use. He also advocated a cost-of-quality (COQ) accounting system to attract top management attention towards quality issues. Juran argued for investments in prevention and appraisal as long as these costs are less than failure costs (on a per unit basis). When prevention was prohibitively expensive, he suggested that it is better to maintain quality rather than attempt to improve it further.

Philip Crosby, an advocate of the notion that quality is free, advised that every company should tailor its defect prevention programme towards the ultimate goal of achieving zero defects.[29] He firmly believed that the savings accruing from this pursuit for zero defects will more than offset the costs associated with it. He emphasized the vital leadership role that top management played in the achievement of this goal.

Although the above three philosophies differ in their approaches to achieving quality improvement, they all strongly emphasize the role of top management in this pursuit and the importance of everyone in the organization believing and supporting this mission. It is interesting and instructive to note that, together, they capture the requirements for achieving excellence – systemic approach, broader firm-level goals, tools and techniques, and the leadership and management of human resources/people. This philosophy is nicely captured in a report prepared for the 1983 White House Conference on productivity:

Managing the quality dimensions of an organization is not generally different from any other aspect of management. It involves the formulation of strategies, setting goals and objectives, developing action plans, implementing plans and using control systems for monitoring feedback and taking corrective action. If quality is viewed only as a control system, it will never be substantially improved. Quality is not just a control system; quality is a management function.[30]

inventory management

Mismatch between demand and supply is inevitable and inventory provides a powerful and often efficient mechanism to manage this gap. Many process and environmental factors, some of which are not always within management control, contribute to the discrepancy between demand and supply. Some of the more common and important factors that lead to demand and supply mismatch are listed below:

1. To manage uncertainty and prevent shortages or lost sales, firms hold excess inventory.

2. To cope with seasonality in either demand and/or supply, firms choose to produce during periods of low demand and hold inventory to meet demand during peak times. This is motivated by their desire to avoid changing capacity levels with changes in demand.

3. Economies of scale in production or procurement encourage overproduction in order to reduce setup or order costs, resulting in inventory for later use.

④ Since production is not instantaneous and customers are often unwilling to wait, firms hold inventory to provide immediate supply and improve their service.

While inventory serves many useful purposes in meeting demand, it involves investment and other associated holding costs, such as storage, handling, obsolescence and so on. Thus, inventory management deals with decisions related to supply and aims to realize the benefits of inventory with minimum costs. Inventory is perhaps one of the most significant controllable factors in operations and provides tremendous opportunities for performance improvements. The magnitude of this potential can be gauged by the amount of inventory held by firms. For example, as of March 1999, businesses in the USA held about US$1.1 trillion worth of inventories.[31] Firms such as Wal-Mart, Toyota and Dell have developed operational capabilities that, among other things, have helped to keep their inventories leaner in comparison to their competitors and thus compete effectively in the marketplace. For example, Dell turns its inventory over 80 times a year, compared with 10–20 times for its rivals.[32]

Basically, inventory management involves making trade-offs between inventory, capacity and knowledge/information. For example, better knowledge and information about customer demand leads to a reduction in demand uncertainty and the amount of inventory required. Similarly, a higher level of capacity increases the ability to meet demand from current production and reduces inventory needs. While the trade-offs involved are qualitatively well understood, the number of factors involved and their complexity makes the problem of determining optimal levels of inventory difficult. In practice, the problem is further complicated due to the large number of items handled by even small and medium-sized companies.

> *Inventory is perhaps one of the most significant controllable factors in operations and provides tremendous opportunities for performance improvements.*

As a result of continuing work in academia during the past 50 years, a wide range of models and systems have been developed to address a variety of issues in inventory. A significant part of the academic literature on the subject deals with the development of decision rules suitable for use in everyday operations. As a result, a good part of this work has been adapted and most inventory systems used in industry are based on this work. In this context, developments in PCs and IT have enabled the easy adoption of sophisticated tools by industry. For example, most enterprise resource planning packages provide a choice of models as part of the materials and planning systems.

While much of the work in inventory theory has been developed in the context of physical (manufactured) goods, many of the results are relevant for and applicable to service industries. For example, inventory models and results are at the core of the revenue management systems extensively employed in the airline and hotel industries.

conclusion

Our aim in this chapter was twofold. First, to present an overview of operations, bringing out the multifaceted nature of the function – a range of diverse activities, decision making at various levels, managing internal resources, in particular human resources, managing the interface with other functions, suppliers, immediate customers and so on. Second, to provide a flavour of the multiple key ideas that you will be exposed to in a core course in operations.

Today, the field of operations management continues to evolve and, in a number of cases, it has evolved into the new field of supply chain management by broadening the process perspective beyond the firm and establishing linkages with upstream and/or downstream activities. Supply chain management has come to be defined as the management of all aspects of providing goods to a consumer, from extraction of raw materials to end-of-life disposal and recycling, including manufacturing, physical logistics, and after-sales service and warranty issues.[33] Phenomenal developments in IT, enabling quick and accurate collection of data and the sharing of data and information, and strategic alliances with other players in the chain have strongly facilitated this process and have emerged as the drivers of initiatives for performance improvements in the entire supply chain. With several well-documented successes and increasing competitive pressures, we expect these trends to continue, perhaps even at a more rapid pace, offering exciting and challenging prospects to aspiring managers.

references/notes

1. Hounshell, D.A. (1991) *From the American System to Mass Production 1800–1932: The Development of Manufacturing Technology in the United States* (Baltimore, MD: Johns Hopkins University Press).
2. Drucker, P.F. (1954) *The Practice of Management* (New York: Harper & Row).
3. Sorenson, C.F. (1956) *My Forty Years with Ford* (New York: Norton).
4. Cray, E. (1979) *Chrome Colossus: General Motors and its Times* (New York: McGraw-Hill).
5. Abernathy, W.J. (1978) *The Productivity Dilemma* (Baltimore, MD: Johns Hopkins University Press).
6. Porter, M. (1996) 'What is strategy?', *Harvard Business Review*, Nov–Dec.
7. Skinner, W. (1969) 'Manufacturing – missing link in corporate strategy', *Harvard Business Review*, May–June.
8. Skinner, W. (1974) 'The focused factory', *Harvard Business Review*, May–June.
9. Hayes, R.H. and Wheelwright, S.C. (1979) 'Link manufacturing process and product life cycles', *Harvard Business Review*, Jan–Feb.
10. Anupindi, R., Chopra S., Deshmukh, S.D., Van Mieghem, J.A. and Zemel, E. (1999) *Managing Business Process Flows* (Englewood Cliffs, NJ: Prentice Hall) p. 26.
11. Maister, D. and Lovelock, C.H. (1982) 'Managing facilitator services', *Sloan Management Review*, **23**(4): 19–31.
12. Schmenner, R.W. (1986) 'How can service businesses survive and prosper?', *Sloan Management Review*, **27**(3): 25; Schmenner, R.W. (1990) *Production/Operations Management* (4th edn) (New York: Macmillan).
13. 'Bottleneck' is defined as anything that limits the system from achieving higher performance related to its purpose.
14. Krafcik, J.F. (1988) 'Triumph of the lean production system', *Sloan Management Review*, fall.
15. Shingo, S. (1989) *A Study of the Toyota Production System from an Industrial Engineering View Point* (rev. edn trans P. Dillon) (Shelton, CT: Productivity Press). See also Monden, Y. (1998) *Toyota Production System, An Integrated Approach to Just-in-time* (3rd edn) (Norcross, GA: Engineering & Management Press).
16. Cusumano, M.A. (1989) *The Japanese Automobile Industry: Technology and Management at Nissan and Toyota* (Cambridge, MA: Harvard University Press).
17. Suri, R. (1998) *Quick Response Manufacturing* (Shelton, CT: Productivity Press).
18. Womack, J.P., Jones, D.T. and Roos, D. (1990) *The Machine that Changed the World* (New York: Macmillan).
19. Womack, J.P. and Jones, D.T. (1996) *Lean Thinking: Banish Waste and Create Wealth in your Corporation* (New York: Simon & Schuster).
20. The 'five whys' in the TPS refer to the practice of asking 'why' repeatedly when problems occur to go beyond the symptoms and discover the root cause.
21. Kanban is usually a taglike card, which helps to control the production quantities in every process.

22. Goldratt, E.M. and Cox, J. (1992) *The Goal: A Process of Ongoing Improvement* (2nd edn) (Great Barrington, MA: North River Press).
23. Statistical process control is a methodology using graphical tools known as 'control charts' and it helps operators, supervisors and managers to monitor the quality of conformance and eliminate the special causes of variability in a process. This methodology grew out of Shewart's (Shewart, W.A. (1931) *Economic control of quality of manufactured product* (New York: D. Van Nostrand Company)) concept of statistical control: 'A phenomenon will be said to be controlled when, through the use of past experience, we can predict, at least within limits, how the phenomenon may be expected to vary in the future. Here it is understood that prediction means that we can state, at least approximately, the probability that the observed phenomenon will fall within the given limits.'
24. It is interesting to note that even though SPC principles have been known since the early 1930s, its wide adoption first occurred in Japan in the early 1950s under the influence of Deming ('What happened in Japan', *Industrial Quality Control*, August (1967) pp. 91–2. The adoption of SPC in the USA and Europe lagged behind for several years and picked up in the mid- 1980s, following clear evidence of Japanese leadership in the area of quality.
25. Feigenbaum, A.V. (1956) 'Total quality control', *Harvard Business Review*, **34**(6).
26. Garvin, D.A. (1988) *Managing Quality* (New York: Free Press).
27. Deming, W.E. (1982) *Quality, Productivity and Competitive Position* (Cambridge, MA: MIT, Center for Advanced Engineering Study).
28. Juran, J.M. and Gryna Jr, F.M. (1980) *Quality Planning and Analysis* (New York: McGraw-Hill).
29. Crosby, P. (1979) *Quality is Free* (New York: McGraw-Hill).
30. From Garvin, David, A. (1988) *Managing Quality: The Strategic and Competitive Edge* (The Free Press) p. 38.
31. Zipkin, P.H. (2000) *Foundations of Inventory Management* (New York: McGraw-Hill).
32. Bossidy, L. and Charan, R. (2002) *Execution: The Discipline of Getting Things Done* (New York: Crown Publishing).
33. Chopra, S., Lovejoy, W. and Yano, C. (2004) 'Five decades of operations management and the prospects ahead', *Management Science*, **50**(1): 8–14.

11 quantitative methods in business: making numbers work for you

professor clare morris

The term 'quantitative methods' (QM) refers to the broad range of mathematical and statistical techniques that can be applied to the solution of management problems.

The position of quantitative methods within an MBA programme differs somewhat from that of other disciplines such as human resource management or finance, in that the topic will not necessarily appear as a separate unit or module. Almost all MBA programmes will include some consideration of those aspects of quantitative methods that are useful in a business context. However, the way in which this element of the course is packaged varies considerably from one MBA to another. While some do include at least one separate unit or module in this area, titles may range from 'business statistics' through straightforward 'QM' to semi-disguised versions such as 'handling business data'. In other courses, the quantitative content is disaggregated and covered alongside other topics – operations management is one popular location. So, if you wish to assess the amount of quantitative material that is contained in a particular programme, you need to look in some detail at the content of the whole range of modules.

> The term 'quantitative methods' (QM) refers to the broad range of mathematical and statistical techniques that can be applied to the solution of management problems.

There are two reasons why this is the case. The first is that quantitative methods is not in itself a recognized functional area within most businesses, but rather a bunch of techniques and approaches that are of use across the whole range of business operations. So whereas it would be a very odd organization that did not have a department dealing with the accounting function, only a small proportion of companies will have an identifiable 'quantitative methods group'. Those which do tend to be in specialized sectors – such as credit scoring or market research – where the day-to-day business of the organization depends heavily on mathematical and statistical work. But the contact most managers will have with the subject will tend to be in the context of their own particular functional specialism – using statistical techniques to investigate production data, for example – and so the designers of many MBA programmes feel that the subject is best learned in those functional contexts, rather than in isolation. This is fine, as long as it is realized that most of the techniques are 'portable', and that a method learned within an operations management module may have equally valid applications within finance or marketing.

The second reason for the unusual position of QM within MBA programmes is that the subject is in the nature of a tool with which every educated manager needs to be familiar, and which can be used to tackle a wide variety of organizational problems. In this respect, the role of QM is not dissimilar to that of information and communications technology: you need to be comfortable in using the tools, and you will be a less effective manager if you have a morbid fear of spreadsheets or an anxiety about handling information of a numerical kind, but you will not be expected necessarily to have a high level of competence in the underlying theory.

There is conceivably a third reason why some business schools have moved away from packaging QM as a separate unit: it would be fair to say that it is the aspect of the MBA programme about which many students feel the greatest anxiety. For those who have not studied mathematics for 10 or more years, and who may have had unhappy experiences with the subject when they did study it, the prospect of having to study QM as a core component of the degree may be alarming. However, this anxiety is largely based on a misconception about the requirements of the subject. QM is most definitely not 'maths', and the level of technical mathematical facility that it requires is quite low; the parts of school-level mathematics on which you will need to draw probably do not go beyond what is studied in the second year of secondary schooling in most countries. Much of the detailed arithmetical work required will be carried out using appropriate IT – either the spreadsheets familiar to most managers, or more specialized software. The emphasis will not be on 'doing the sums', but rather on knowing what is a suitable method to use in tackling a given problem, and being able to interpret and apply the output of the mathematical technique in the practical context of that problem.

In fact, it is important to get away from some of the conceptions of mathematical work you may have developed in your previous study of the subject. The 'nuts and bolts' of calculations are rarely of importance, and in most assessments, you will not receive much credit for that aspect. Moreover, there are often no 'right answers' – there may, indeed, be a variety of methods that are equally applicable to a business problem, and they may offer the manager an equally wide range of 'answers'. The real art of the subject – and it is an art as much as a science – is in making effective use of those 'answers' in reaching a decision and taking effective action. From this point of view, 'quantitative thinking' might actually be a more suitable term than 'quantitative methods'.

So, if the subject isn't mathematics and it isn't about doing arithmetical calculations, then what is it and how is it important to good management? To answer these questions, we will look at a few examples of successful organizations that have made conspicuous use of quantitative thinking.

what qm offers organizations and managers

Quantitative methods can be used wherever there is information that can be presented in a quantified manner. This doesn't necessarily mean 'measured' in the conventional sense – the subject has a lot to offer in areas such as consumer preference testing of flavours in the food industry, which appear at first sight to be highly qualitative and subjective.

> One of the most successful quantitative initiatives of recent years has been the 'six sigma' approach to quality improvement.

It is probably true to say that the subject first found wide acceptance in the manufacturing sector, where the 'scientific' nature of production processes tends to lend itself more naturally to quantified methods. One of the most successful quantitative initiatives of recent years has been the 'six sigma' approach to quality improvement, which uses a range of relatively simple statistical tools – such as plotting of charts and investigation of relationships between different factors in a process – to effect substantial reductions in the levels of faults and failures among manufactured products.

A recent survey paper quotes the following outcomes of the introduction of the six sigma approach in two global corporations:[1]

Motorola

> in-process defect levels reduced by a factor of 200
> manufacturing costs reduced by US$1.4 billion
> fourfold increase in stockholders' share value.

Allied Signal

> new product introduction time reduced by 16%
> manufacturing costs reduced by more than US$1 billion.

It is interesting to note, however, that the same paper identifies 'management involvement and commitment' and 'cultural change' as two of the critical success factors in introducing the six sigma programme, thus reinforcing the point made above that it is the intelligent use of the methods in context, rather than the methods themselves, which is important.

There is nothing intrinsic to the methods used by these organizations that makes them suitable for use only in a manufacturing environment; indeed, there have been some notable successes for the methods in the service sector, although their application in service organizations probably requires more imagination and vision, and successful applications are often driven by one or two committed individuals. One such individual was the mayor of the US city of Fort Wayne, Indiana, where application of essentially the same methods as those used by Motorola and Allied Signal saved the city's taxpayers more than $3.5 million, while improving services such as road repair and refuse collection.[2]

> *Quantitative methods can also help organizations to obtain the optimum value from the vast resources of information with which today's electronic data capture methods can provide them.*

Quantitative methods can also help organizations to obtain the optimum value from the vast resources of information with which today's electronic data capture methods can provide them. For example, the British-based Financial Times Group used an approach known as 'data mining', which integrates statistical analysis with database technology, to obtain a better understanding of its global market. The measurable results of this exercise included:[3]

> a 75% increase in the email response rate for the Financial Times Group
> an increase of 182% in the leads generated by FT Your Money, the FT's personal finance section
> a 93% increase in registrations for the FT's Market Watch service.

Some businesses are, of course, founded on the use of quantitative methods. Market research companies are a case in point; without the underpinning provided by the theory of sampling, it would be impossible to select reliable samples, or draw valid conclusions from survey findings. If you have any doubts about the value the market, at least indirectly, places on these skills, you need only look at the recent sale to the French organization Ipsos of the opinion polling organization MORI, founded in 1969 by its present chairman (and highly respected statistician) Bob Worcester. According to the British *Independent* newspaper of 11 October 2005, Ipsos paid some £88 million for the purchase.[4]

However, while these success stories are impressive, it is probably true to say that the biggest impact of quantitative thinking in management comes through its everyday use by informed managers to improve their decision making – an unspectacular process that won't be reported in the media or attract journal articles, but nevertheless will have an enormous effect on management effectiveness and business performance.

major themes within quantitative methods

While individual quantitative methods units will differ widely in their detailed content, you can expect to find some common key concepts emerging. This section outlines the most important of these.

modelling

An idea that underpins many quantitative methods, particularly those generally embraced by the terms 'operational research' or 'management science', is the use of mathematics or statistics to *model* a practical business problem. In constructing a model, we understand that certain important features of the problem are reflected in the solution, while other less important aspects are not; the art, of course, lies in ensuring that you retain enough detail to capture the essence of the problem, but not so much that you render it so complicated as to be insoluble.

To make things more concrete, let's consider a simple example of the use of a model for a practical situation – the relationship between the number of units of a commodity sold each week by a retailer, and the weekly revenue received from the sales. Of course, this could be expressed verbally – you might say something like 'if we know the price for which each unit is sold, then multiplying that by the number of units sold gives the total revenue'. However, this is quite a lengthy explanation even for such a simple calculation (24 words, to be precise). A quantitative model enables us to put things more concisely. Here, if each item sells for £P, and the number of items sold per week is represented by 'n', then the revenue £R will be given by the equation $R = P \times n$, or just $R = Pn$.

You can see immediately some of the advantages of this way of modelling the situation. We can use the equation to find the revenue resulting from any level of weekly sales and any selling price. By using algebra to manipulate the equation, we can find out how many units must be sold at a given price to achieve a given revenue level – for example, if each unit sells for £3 and a weekly revenue of £1,500 is required, then 500 units must be sold. We can even use an alternative graphical format to represent the model, as shown in Figure 11.1.

Although this model is simple, it exhibits a number of the features you can expect to find in more complex quantitative models:

> The model represents a simplified version of reality. Thus, for example, we have assumed that each unit sells for the same price, and have ignored any matters such as bulk discounts; nor have we attempted to model aspects such as seasonal fluctuations in sales levels – we've assumed that the number of units sold per week is fixed.

> Several different types of model – here an equation or a graph – may be used to represent the same practical problem.

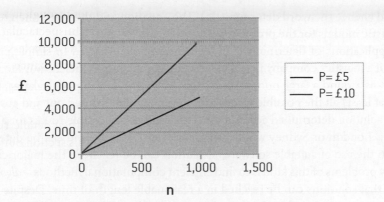

Figure 11.1 *A simple graphical model*

> Building and using the model requires us to have some prior information about the situation. Here we would need to know what price per unit was to be charged, and the number of units sold per week, in order to work out the weekly revenue.

> Aspects of the model may not fully reflect reality. In our graphical model, by drawing a continuous straight line, we have suggested that sales of fractional units are possible. However, this will not be the case for many commodities, for example cars, and so strictly speaking only the points on the line corresponding to whole number (or *integer*) values of 'n' will be meaningful in such cases.

> The model enables us to answer 'what if' questions, and explore the impact of varying the *parameters* of the problem – here, the price per unit and the level of sales.

> The same type of model can be used to represent many different practical situations. Here, what we have is called a *linear* model – when plotted graphically, it produces a straight line. Models of this kind are among the most widely used in a range of application areas. You might like to consider the problem of modelling the distance travelled in a given time by a car moving at a constant speed – you should obtain an equation and/or a graph mathematically identical to those in the revenue example, even though the context is completely different.

> Perhaps most importantly, the general features of the model reflect our intuitive feelings about the problem. The two lines in Figure 11.1, for example, show that the higher the price charged per unit, the more steeply the revenue line rises – not a very startling fact, but one which confirms that our model is realistic. It is important always to apply this kind of 'reality check' to the models you build – many students new to this area make the mistake of regarding equations, graphs and so on as 'just maths', and forget that they are supposed to be representing practical situations. Don't leave your experience and common sense at the door of your quants lectures!

deterministic vs stochastic problems

Under the label 'deterministic', we encompass those problems and situations where, once we have all the necessary information, we can arrive at a single definite result, which is not subject to the vagaries of chance. In the simple example above, once the weekly sales and the price per unit are known, the revenue for the week is completely *determined* (hence the word deterministic). The equation and the graph then represent deterministic models for the problem.

The applications of deterministic modelling are not restricted to simple problems, however; if a logistics company is seeking to discover the most efficient ways to route its delivery vans around a large number of customers in a wide geographical area, then (in principle at least) all the possible routes for the vans can be worked out and costed, and the 'best' solution determined accordingly. The number of possible routes for a city the size of, say, London or Sydney will be very large, but it is finite and can be determined. Thus, with the use of suitable software, a solution can be reached. The major challenge with many problems of this kind is to find efficient computational methods – *algorithms* – to ensure that solutions can be reached in a reasonable length of time. Despite the vast increases in computing power that have been achieved in recent years, this is still a very real issue for large-scale, real-life problems and an active area of research.

Stochastic problems are completely different in nature. They cover situations where an element of randomness is intrinsic to the nature of the question we wish to answer, and where ignoring that random element would be to render the problem trivial, and any solution useless.

One example with which everyone is familiar is that of planes arriving at a busy airport such as London Heathrow. Because of the volume of traffic, it is quite common for an arriving flight to have to circle above the airport for some time before being able to land. In an ideal world, all planes would depart and arrive exactly on time, take precisely the same predetermined time to disembark and load passengers and so on, so that the optimal schedule for flights could be worked out.

However, in practice, this is certainly not the case. Passengers check in late and delay flights; security checks may be carried out at short notice; weather conditions can cause flights to arrive either early or late; you can continue this list from your own experience. It is the unpredictability – the random or *stochastic* element – in the problem that needs to be tackled.

At first sight this might seem to be a hopeless task. If something is random, isn't it by definition impossible to predict? Well, yes and no. While it is not possible to predict an *individual* event in this kind of situation with a useful level of accuracy, it *is* possible to model *overall* patterns of behaviour. So, for example, by monitoring flight arrivals, a picture can be built up of how these vary relative to scheduled times – what proportion are more than 15 minutes early, between 10 and 15 minutes early and so on. This information can then be used to help determine what kinds of margins to allow between landings, and even to *simulate* patterns of arrivals over periods of days, weeks or months.

We are really talking here about another aspect of modelling, but in this case using stochastic models (also sometimes called *probabilistic*). Nor do we always have to rely on collecting empirical data, as in the example just mentioned; many situations conform, or with a little 'tweaking' can be made to conform, to one of a number of theoretical models known as *probability distributions*. One probability distribution with which many people are familiar is the well-known 'bell curve' or 'normal distribution', which provides a good model for many variables in different fields of application. Figure 11.2 shows how the normal distribution could possibly be used to model the variations in aircraft arrival times; the variable plotted on the horizontal axis is the number of minutes before or after the scheduled time of landing. One immediate point to note is that the centre of the distribution – representing the average of all the times – is not, as we might hope, at zero, but around +5 minutes, showing that there is a tendency for planes to arrive a little late – not serious on an individual level, but something which could well produce a big effect when cumulated over a day of operations. (I hasten to add that this is simulated, not real, data.)

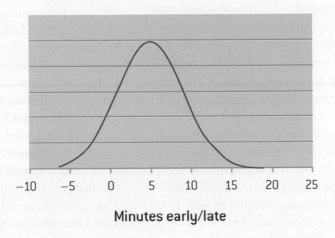

Figure 11.2 A normal distribution curve

It is probably fair to say that the great majority of business and management problems fall into the stochastic rather than the deterministic category, and this explains why the study of probability and probability distributions forms a cornerstone of many MBA courses in quantitative methods. Unfortunately, it is not easy, when approaching this topic for the first time, to jump straight into dealing with large-scale and realistic problems, which explains why some introductory courses on the subject appear to make use of rather simplistic examples. But don't be too ready to dismiss the whole area on that account; even if you have no ambition to reach the point where you will be able to construct your own complex stochastic models, having a good 'feel' for the basic ideas of probability will be an enormous help to you in structuring your thinking about business problems.

statistical significance

It could be argued that the concept of statistical significance simply forms part of the study of probability, but I choose to deal with it as a separate topic because it is probably the application of quantitative methods that you are most likely to bump into in your study of other disciplines. For example, you may be reading a research paper on an aspect of human resource management and come across a statement such as: 'The association between perceived degree of control over work patterns and level of job satisfaction was highly significant (p < 0.01).' Even the regular news media now often broadcast statements such as: 'Scientists have found a statistically significant difference in the reading ages of children who eat oily fish three times a week, compared with those who do not.'

How exactly is such a statement to be understood? In ordinary language, something that is 'significant' is important, meaningful, or potentially makes a large impact.

Unfortunately, statisticians are inclined to take words from everyday speech and make them mean something rather different. 'Significant' is not the only example you will encounter – 'confident' is another example.

So the term 'statistically significant' means roughly 'is unlikely to have arisen by chance'. Of course, 'unlikely' is another weasel word – the next obvious question is, exactly how unlikely? It is the quantification of this kind of statement that forms the basis for the study of statistical significance.

sampling theory

A closely related topic is that of *sampling*. If we always had complete information about a situation, then the question of chance, uncertainty or whatever you wish to call it would not arise. So, for example, if you know exactly how much every customer of a supermarket chain spends in a single visit during a given year – and this is the kind of information that can now be captured thanks to bar code scanning – then you can work out the average expenditure per customer for the year in question. However, in many cases, we do not have the luxury of complete information. You will be able to think of plenty of examples for yourself: market research and political opinion surveys are typically done using samples of 500–1,000 individuals; telephone interactions to call centres are routinely sampled for quality purposes; and much formal research (such as testing of new pharmaceuticals) is done on quite small samples.

Instinct tells us, quite correctly, that there is bound to be some uncertainty associated with any information based on sample – and therefore incomplete – information. The samples used in research situations, and in political opinion polling, are carefully constructed to make them as reliable as possible; nevertheless, if you read in your newspaper that 'a survey of 1,200 adults shows that 51% are in favour of on-the-spot fines for dropping chewing gum in the street', you would not immediately conclude that this means a majority of the whole population favours the fines. Another sample, carried out at a different location, might give a figure of 49%. Thus, while you might agree that 'the figure for the population as a whole won't be too far from 51%', it would be rash to put any money on that figure being *exactly* 51%. Then, of course, the further question naturally arises: just how far from 51% might the true figure be?

Sampling theory addresses these questions and provides a basis for drawing sound conclusions from sample-based data.

forecasting

At first sight, a business's need to predict the number of customers it may have in three or five years' time might seem more appropriately addressed by astrology than mathematics. Nevertheless, business planning depends critically on the ability to forecast many different parameters – from economic variables such as exchange rates to more industry-specific quantities such as the supply of a particular raw material, or the demand for a certain type of savings account.

> A business's need to predict the number of customers it may have in three or five years' time might seem more appropriately addressed by astrology than mathematics.

Although there is always going to be uncertainty associated with any kind of forecasting – and generally the uncertainty becomes greater the further ahead we are looking – many variables follow, more or less precisely, reasonably predictable patterns that we may expect to persist into at least the short-term future. Often the reasons for these patterns are easy to understand; for example there is a well-known curve called the 'bathtub curve' used to examine the rates at which items such as tyres fail in use. This curve is sketched in Figure 11.3, and you can see that it reflects a situation in which failure rates are high in the early stages of use (so-called 'infant mortality'); there is then a longer period when failure rates are low; and finally rates increase rapidly as items wear out at the end of their lifespan. A curve of this kind can be used to model and predict failure rates for a whole range of items.

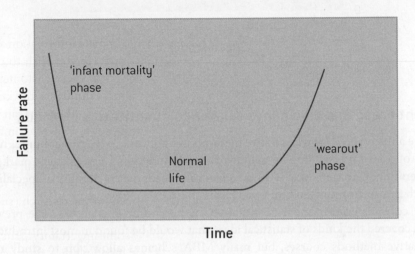

Figure 11.3 The 'bathtub curve'

Another well-known example is the case of 'exponential growth'. This term is often used colloquially to describe any quantity that grows rapidly, but its precise meaning refers to a quantity that grows in proportion to its own size. An obvious example would be the amount of money in an investment account earning compound interest.

These are just two examples from a wide range of models that can be used in forecasting – the Excel spreadsheet, for example, provides a range of curves for forecasting under its 'trendlines' option, which you may like to explore.

relationships

Many management problems involve examining the relationships between factors in complex situations, for example the impact that the base rate of interest has on the housing market, or the extent to which the speed at which a drill is operated influences the frequency with which the drill bit needs to be replaced. Sometimes the effect of a whole set of factors needs to be assessed simultaneously: thus companies providing credit-scoring services are interested in whether knowledge of someone's income, address, gender and so on enables an accurate prediction of their creditworthiness to be made.

Regression methods provide a means of tackling this kind of question in a quantified fashion. Starting from simple plots that can give us an idea of the relationship between two quantities (Figure 11. 4 shows such a plot for the drill bit example of the previous paragraph – what can you conclude?), these methods allow us to develop equations that best fit a particular set of data, to assess just how good the fit is, and to measure the strength of the relationship. They also allow us to predict the value of one quantity given the values of the factors to which it is related.

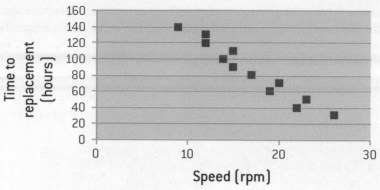

Figure 11.4 *Investigating a relationship*

management areas and disciplines related to quantitative methods

We have already seen that quantitative methods can appear in MBA programmes under a range of titles, and can crop up in quite disparate functional areas such as marketing and operations management. The basic subject also leads on to a number of specialisms, of which this section aims to give you a taste.

The core material in most quantitative methods units is *statistics*. The previous section covered the kinds of statistical ideas that would be found in most introductory quantitative methods courses, but many MBA schemes allow you to study more advanced statistical methods in an elective. The content of an advanced statistics elective might include *multivariate techniques* aimed at exploring the structure of large sets of data involving many variables. Popular multivariate techniques include:

> *Factor analysis,* aimed at reducing a large number of measured variables to a smaller set of meaningful factors, for example when examining consumer questionnaire data to identify the real factors underlying expressed consumer preferences.

> *Cluster analysis,* aimed at identifying distinct groupings of cases within a population, for example for market segmentation purposes.

> *Discriminant analysis,* aimed at identifying the factors that distinguish one subgroup in a population from another, for example when investigating why some credit customers default on their payments while others do not.

Another quantitative elective might be called 'operational research' or possibly 'management science'. Operational research (OR) is a term that covers a wide range of approaches to solving management problems – the Operational Research Society's website defines the subject as one which 'looks at an organization's operations and uses mathematical or computer models, or other analytical approaches, to find better ways of doing them'. Specific OR methods covered might include simulation, which uses computer-based models to imitate the operation of complex business systems; mathematical programming techniques, which deal with the optimization of a target variable (such as profit) in situations subject to a series of constraints; and so-called 'soft OR' approaches, which deal with effective ways of thinking about and structuring 'messy' real-life problems.

You will also find a strong quantitative element in some electives whose primary focus is one of the functional business areas: marketing, operations management and finance all make considerable use of specialized mathematical and statistical methods.

some hints on studying quantitative methods

If it is some time since you last studied any subject with numbers in it, you may be feeling some anxiety as to how you will cope with a quantitative methods course. Here are a few suggestions to help you develop a good learning strategy:

> Don't expect to be able to read a quantitative methods textbook in the same way as you would a novel, or even a textbook on, say, HRM. You will only get to grips fully with the material if you work with a pencil and paper to hand, following through any mathematical arguments or calculations and making sure that you know exactly how each step works.

> Quantitative subjects tend to be cumulative in nature – in other words, next week's lecture will probably build on this week's, rather than dealing with freestanding topics. So if there's something you don't understand this week, try to sort it out before the next lecture.

> Don't be afraid to use colleagues as a resource – one of the great things about the average MBA class is that it will contain people with all kinds of backgrounds and experience. So you will probably be able to find someone who is a whiz at anything involving numbers, with whom you can talk through the concepts you are learning.

> Beware of just going to the university library and grabbing a book with 'statistics' in the title from the shelf. Many topics in statistics – regression is one good example – can be studied at a wide range of levels, from very basic to the frontiers of research – and if the book you choose is at too advanced a level, you may become unnecessarily demoralized. So stick to what's on your reading list, or ask advice from your lecturer.

> Don't get fixated on 'the answer' – very often that's the least important part of the problem-solving process. Think about what the answer means in practice, whether it's realistic, whether there could be other equally valid answers.

> Be prepared to bring your experience and knowledge of other areas to bear in interpreting the solutions to quantitative problems. For example, if you are given some data about house prices and asked to calculate summary measures such as the mean, standard deviation and so on, your general knowledge will tell you that there tend to be more middling-priced houses, and fewer very expensive ones, on the market, so the summary measures will reflect, and be affected by, this fact.

> Don't be tempted to try to reduce everything to 'rules' – be prepared to think about *why* you are performing certain operations, not just *what* you should be doing. A simple example of what I mean here is the 'change side, change sign' rule, which you may have come across when learning how to manipulate equations – for example, if you are solving $x + 2 = 7$, the 'rule' suggests that the 2 'becomes' a -2 when you move it to the other side of the equation: $x = 7 - 2$. As it stands, this sounds pretty mysterious – *why* does a number acquire a minus as it flies over the equal sign? If you realize that in fact what you are doing is subtracting 2 from both sides of the equation – so as to maintain the 'balance' – then the step becomes logical rather than merely mechanical: $x + 2 - 2 = 7 - 2$, so $x = 7 - 2 = 5$.

> Don't worry about writing down lots of steps in an argument – no one will mind, and it's better to write down too much than to risk leaving a gap and thus taking a wrong turning. But do make sure that what you write down makes sense – not only to anyone reading it (such as the person marking the work), but also to yourself when you look back at it later. Generally, this means putting in plenty of words as well as numbers and symbols – you should be able to read a quantitative argument aloud exactly as you would a paragraph of English. And be sure that what you write is actually true – the 'you know what I meant' argument doesn't wash at this level.

a word about software

You will almost certainly be making use of a PC in your study of quantitative methods. Many MBA courses now use Excel as the major tool for this purpose, since most students will have had some experience of spreadsheets before starting the course. If you don't have much familiarity with Excel, or would like to put your understanding of spreadsheets on a more solid basis, there are many good texts to help you get started (see Chapter 19 'learning resources'). You would be well advised to engage in this familiarization before actually starting on the course.

Some courses, particularly for advanced study of statistics or operational research, may make use of more specialist software. SPSS is one of the most popular packages for serious statistical work, particularly in areas such as the analysis of survey data, while operational research techniques such as linear programming and simulation rely heavily on the availability of dedicated software. Commercial packages, which implement these methods, are often powerful and expensive, so you can expect to be able to access them via university systems, rather than purchasing a copy for use on your own PC.

current challenges for quantitative methods

It is possible, after studying an MBA quantitative methods course, to end up with the feeling that the subject consists of a neat bunch of techniques, and that the only remaining problem is the selection of the right technique to deal with a particular management problem. It is true that great progress has been made in developing effective quantitative tools, especially since the advent of powerful PCs has given managers access at their desks to software that can cope with large and complex problems. However, it would be quite wrong to think that no further research remains to be done.

On the technical side of the subject, work is going on to develop improved algorithms for all kinds of optimization problems, a large class of problems, which covers many apparently disparate practical applications ranging from routing of delivery vehicles to manpower planning. Primary research in this area tends to be done by mathematicians, and can be quite inaccessible to the non-mathematical specialist in its original form; however, the outcomes of such research find their way with increasing speed into commercial software.

The integration of 'softer' management methods with 'hard' statistical and management science techniques is also attracting interest. The strategy for quality improvement mentioned near the beginning of this chapter, 'six sigma', is a case in point: the approach involves the embedding of the use of statistical tools within a structured methodology for systematic business improvement.

Another development attracting increasing interest is so-called 'evidence-based management'. This derives its name from the 'evidence-based' approach to medicine, which now has widespread acceptance among practitioners, and which attempts to bridge the gap between research and practice by encouraging practitioners to base their decisions upon well-founded recent research, rather than depending solely on their own experience. In the management field, evidence-based practice is often contrasted with so-called 'opinion-based' practice ('I've been managing this area for 10 years, and I can tell you that what we need to do is ... '). The link with quantitative methods arises because the proper appraisal of research evidence requires an understanding of concepts such as statistical significance and sampling variability; the fact that many managers lack that understanding may help to explain why the outcomes of management research are often slow to find their way into standard practice, no matter how much potential they may offer for business improvement.

The ease with which data can now be captured electronically, and stored in large volumes, has given rise to another new area of work known as *data mining*. As is often the case when a discipline is subject to rapid development, it is difficult to find a universally agreed definition of data mining, but the version offered by the marketing agency AccuraCast (see http://www.accuracast.com/) is a good starting point:

Data mining uses a combination of machine learning, statistical analysis, modelling techniques and database technology to find patterns and subtle relationships in data. Data mining then infers rules that allow the prediction of future results based on these findings.

A typical client for a data-mining approach might be a supermarket chain, which has enormous data resources generated by point-of-sale data capture and wishes to exploit this so as to learn more about its customer base. Data mining might reveal, for example, that customers who purchase high-quality ready meals also tend to buy ready-washed salads; this information could then be used to inform a marketing strategy, such as offering a 'money off' deal on salads with the purchase of a ready meal. The advantage of the data-mining approach over many conventional quantitative methods for analysing the data is that it requires no initial hypotheses or assumptions about the data, and so can help to tease out previously unsuspected information. The downside (there always is one) is that it may be difficult to assess whether an apparent relationship discovered in the data is 'real' or simply an artefact of the battery of methods of analysis being applied.

The advantage of the data-mining approach over many conventional quantitative methods for analysing the data is that it requires no initial hypotheses or assumptions about the data, and so can help to tease out previously unsuspected information.

Finally, the concepts of *risk* and *risk assessment* are attracting much attention, not least from the popular media – for example, we read about the risk of a global 'bird flu' pandemic, or an asteroid striking the earth within the next century. Often the term is being used in a fairly loose way, but the business of quantifying risks and building those quantified estimates into decision making is very much a live topic of interest. The increasingly litigious and (so we are told) risk-averse nature of Western society means that organizations need to have ways of measuring the risks to which they are exposed. There are, not surprisingly, close links between the concept of risk and the ideas of probability and stochastic modelling mentioned earlier. Specific areas for development include ways of combining experts' subjective judgements of risk with a quantified approach – a particularly important process for new technologies where there may be little or no historical data to permit precise estimates of associated risks.

These are just a few of the areas where work is underway that has direct relevance to management applications. Perhaps one of the most fascinating things about mathematics and statistics, however, is that, over and over again, apparently 'pure' research, carried out solely out of interest in the subject, turns out (sometimes many years later) to have important applications in apparently unrelated fields. For example, there is a branch of mathematics called 'knot theory', which in many ways is about as abstract as the subject can get. But recently I spotted an advertisement for a mathematician specializing in this area to work on the development of new textiles. So who knows what branches of the subject may come to be of interest to future MBA students?

I hope that this chapter has given you some idea of the range, scope and importance of quantitative methods, not just within the MBA syllabus but also in the world of management at large. Should you wish to read more about what might be involved, refer to the learning resources chapter for some helpful titles.

references

1. Antony, J. and Banuelas, R. (2002) 'Key ingredients for the effective implementation of six sigma program', *Measuring Business Excellence*, **6**(4): 20–7.
2. http://www.minitab.com/resources/stories/FortWayneCaseStudy.aspx.
3. British Computer Society, *BCS Review Online 2003* at http://www.bcs.org.
4. 'Mori staff to share in £60m payout from Ipsos', *Independent*, 11 October 2005.

12 the accounting perspective

associate professor david trende

Whether we like it or not, accounting plays a part in all our daily lives. If you have ever invested in shares, bought a car or even rented a house or flat, you have probably used accounting information in some form or other to help you make a decision. In its simplest form, accounting involves keeping a historical record of the financial transactions that we undertake. In business, when managers want to use such data for decision making, they have to organize, classify and transform it into a range of different financial reports. There is a range of users of this information, both inside and outside the firm, who have to decide, for example, how to raise capital, what assets to acquire or dispose of and how to control and allocate costs.

The study of accounting is a core subject in the MBA curriculum. This reflects the need for managers to understand the way in which accounting numbers are produced and used. However, while knowledge of the procedural aspects of accounting is useful, it is *more* important that MBA students learn to question and understand the assumptions underlying the numbers and the judgements that others have made in arriving at those numbers. Armed with this understanding, students are then in a better position to make sure the accounting information they come across subsequently is relevant, reliable and useful – and, hopefully, reflects economic reality.

> Whether we like it or not, accounting plays a part in all our daily lives. If you have ever invested in shares, bought a car or even rented a house or flat, you have probably used accounting information in some form or other to help you make a decision.

This chapter is designed to give students an insight into the nature of accounting and who uses accounting information and why. Along the way, we examine some of the fundamental building blocks of accounting and introduce the most commonly used outputs of the financial accounting system: *the balance sheet, income statement* and *cash flow statement*. The chapter ends with a summary of the key challenges faced by many organizations when reporting on their performance to the broader investment community.

the nature of accounting

When I was a student, my accounting professor explained the role of the accountant using an analogy of the scorer at a cricket match. The scorer merely records what happens during the match, using a stylized uniform score sheet. The score is kept in a particular way so that each action in the game can be easily recorded as it happens and the result of the match can be determined at the end of play. The scoring method also allows description of the state of the match at any point in time during play.

The scorer is not a participant in the game, merely a recorder of what happens during the match. He does not bat, bowl, field or keep wicket. The scorer does not make up the rules of the game nor enforce those rules. The former is the province of the governing body of the game and the latter is the role of the umpires. During play the scorer is able to inform others of the state of play and at the conclusion of the game provides a summary of what occurred and the outcome of the game. Records of the game need to be kept because the participants want to know what has happened. In cricket, these participants comprise the players, the umpires, the spectators, cricket fans who didn't attend the game, commentators and the regulators.

This analogy depicts the accountant as merely a recorder of the action. Indeed, this 'stewardship' role in accounting has dominated the discipline for centuries. The primary expectation of accounting numbers was that they should reflect the facts of past occurrences. Hence, reliability of accounting numbers was regarded as paramount. Reliability is still highly prized today. However, it must coexist with the need for accounting numbers to assist a range of stakeholders in their decision making. These competing demands are what create most of the problems in modern accounting.

In the modern economy, there are many stakeholders in economic activity ranging from investors and employees (who provide the capital and labour essential to the creation of economic wealth) to the people managing organizations on behalf of others, both in the public and private sectors. In the former, through government on behalf of the community and, in the latter, through companies and other business structures on behalf of private investors. Other players in the economic chain include customers and suppliers, and a further raft of interested parties such as taxation authorities, industry and government regulators, lobbyists and activist groups such as environmentalists. All these stakeholders have a need for information about the elements and results of economic activity. Accounting provides much of the data and information they want.

There are two main branches of accounting. *Financial accounting* is aimed at providing information to external stakeholders, primarily owners. This reflects the origins of accounting associated with property rights. The purpose of this form of accounting is to give an overview of the results and position achieved by the entity being accounted for. It does not generally contain masses of detailed information but rather an encapsulated view of the results of past transactions. Readers may be familiar with the concepts of a balance sheet, income statement and cash flow statement. These financial statements illustrate the degree of summation and condensation implicit in accounting – each statement often reflects thousands of financial transactions that took place in a previous accounting period.

The other main branch is *management accounting*. It produces information needed by the managers of the enterprise. They need much more detailed and extensive financial information than the 'big picture' provided by the financial statements. The function of management accounting is to provide that greater level of detail about financial transactions and outcomes.

the characteristics of accounting information

In order to be able to use accounting information for decision-making purposes, users expect the information to exhibit four essential characteristics. First, the information must be *relevant* to the decisions that the users make. As we shall see, transactions are initially recorded at the number of dollars involved. Over time, due to inflation, the value of these dollars is eroded. Hence, assets valued at historical costs provide less and less relevant information to users as time passes. Economic decisions about such assets need information about current value (see Box 12.1).

BOX 12.1 Estimating the current value of an asset

For example, say you owned your own business and you bought a block of industrial land ten years ago for $1 million. Today someone estimates its market value is $3 million. Given that today's accounting standards permit your company to use either the original cost or the estimated market value, at what amount do you think your company should show the land in today's balance sheet?

Second, the information must be *reliable*. It must be free from bias and not somebody's guesswork. If we use current value as a more relevant number, someone must make an estimate of that value. Do you use the actual amount you originally spent or do you take the expert, but subjective, opinion of the valuer? These trade-offs between relevance and reliability are common in modern accounting.

Third, the information must be *understandable*. This requirement raises a particular problem for accountants. For a user to understand any particular accounting number, he or she needs to understand the derivation of that number. The set of concepts, principles and rules upon which accounting is built exists in order to be able to provide numbers to users without long-winded explanations about the source of the number and what it represents. This is perhaps partly why accounting is often criticized as being prepared by experts for experts.

Lastly, users want *comparability*, preferably both over time within the entity and over time between entities. It is now generally accepted that the accounting treatment of particular items should be consistently applied over time within a particular accounting entity. Comparability between firms is more difficult to achieve, as managers have the ability to adopt the accounting policies that they believe best meet the circumstances of their entity. There is therefore no guarantee that different entities will adopt the same accounting treatment for any particular item.

choices, estimates and judgements

The uninformed typically see accounting as a precise science rather than an art. Recording of financial transactions requires precision to ensure that errors are avoided. But when these data are transformed into information, choices, estimates and judgements are required.

The *double-entry bookkeeping* system (explained below) means that its outcomes are measured down to the last cent. This gives the impression that the figures must be right. However, the way in which choices, estimates and judgements are made means that the reported numbers are best estimates of reality rather than 'the truth'. This apparent precision of accounting numbers must always be recognized when accounting numbers are used as a basis for decision making.

The nature of business activities is very diverse. No two entities operate in exactly the same way. To facilitate good decision making, accounting information should reflect economic reality. This means that the particular circumstances of the individual accounting entity should be taken into account in deciding upon appropriate accounting treatments. Consequently, the accounting profession has allowed some choice of accounting treatment. This recognizes diversity rather than attempting to impose uniformity of accounting treatment across all entities.

The need for estimates, choices and judgements in accounting is nowhere more important than in depreciation. 'Depreciation' is the process by which tangible assets become expenses. For example, suppose that our firm bought a piece of machinery at the beginning of the year. This machine will last for a number of years and will ultimately be sold for scrap. Over its life, the machine will have directly cost the entity its purchase price less its scrap value. The machine contributes to the earning of revenue over its lifetime and therefore its net cost must be treated as expenses over that period. In order to get a realistic profit figure year by year, the net cost must be spread over the years of life of the machine. Thus, measuring depreciation requires the accountant to decide upon the life of the asset, the scrap or residual value at the end of its life, and how the amount to be expensed (depreciated) should be allocated to each year of its life. All these elements are uncertain and the accountant's decisions should be made conservatively.

It is the existence of choices, estimates and judgements in accounting that makes ethics an important issue. The modern emphasis on usable information rather than historical facts has brought ethics to the fore in accounting theory and practice. Once choices, estimates and judgements are necessary and allowed, the possibility of misuse of this freedom becomes a reality. Managers may use this freedom to make accounting choices, estimates and judgements in ways that produce accounting numbers that reflect what the managers consider desirable. However, accounting numbers are supposed to be about reflecting economic reality. These possibilities of creative accounting can only be addressed through professional and business ethics.

> *It is the existence of choices, estimates and judgements in accounting that makes ethics an important issue. The modern emphasis on usable information rather than historical facts has brought ethics to the fore in accounting theory and practice.*

Ethics is not about preventing fraudulent activity. In accounting, it is about the way in which choices, estimates and judgements are made. The problem with ethics is that you cannot legislate to ensure ethical behaviour. Ethics comes from within the person; acting in accordance with your moral code. It involves ideas of fairness, equity and freedom from bias. Ethical behaviour in an accounting context means making decisions about accounting numbers in the interests of providing economically realistic information to the users whose objectives accounting serves.

how accounting works

The first known text on bookkeeping was written in the late fifteenth century and described the recording and processing techniques still in use today. A robust recording system will have formal rules and procedures to ensure consistency of treatment and, in the case of accounting, processing procedures to ensure outcomes are consistent with the inputs to the system. A set of building blocks, discussed later, determine what will be allowed into the system, how it will be processed and, largely, the form of the financial statement outputs.

The bookkeeping system is built upon the truism that all the funds that an entity has (assets) must be equal to the sources of those funds (liabilities plus owners' equity). This describes the fundamental accounting equation used as the basis of all recording.

All transactions, items and events allowed into the accounting system must be recorded so that the accounting equation remains intact. For example, when your business bought the block of land for $1 million equal and offsetting entries were required in the records to increase one asset (land) and decrease another asset (cash). By so doing, the integrity of the accounting equation is maintained.

As other elements are processed in the system, the entity needs to decide what labels to use for all the different types of assets, liabilities and equity. The list of elements is called the 'chart of accounts'. Any input to the system will have equal and offsetting effects on the accounting equation. The first step is to record these inputs in a journal, a chronological record of events. Each element of the effects on the accounting equation arising from the transaction, item or event will comprise a single journal entry. At the end of the accounting period, the system will contain the effects of all inputs on assets, liabilities and owners' equity for the whole of the period. So a journal is simply an accounting diary. However, the data in the diary are not in a form that allows financial statements to be prepared. They are still in a raw state, unprocessed.

To produce summarized statements of performance, financial position and cash flows the raw data must be transformed, summarized and classified into a more usable form. The obvious thing to do is to summarize by putting like things together. A feature of business is that, while there are large numbers of transactions, there are relatively fewer different types of transactions. There are lots of sales, purchases, cash receipts, cash payments and so on. The second step is to create a record where like items are recorded together. A way of doing this is to have a separate record for each asset, liability and equity label. The information from the journal can then be transferred to this record. At the completion of this posting process, each separate record will have in it all the transactions, items and events that affected it during the period. Each of these separate records is an account and together the accounts comprise the ledger. Both the journal and the ledger contain the same information, but recorded in different ways. If we now want to know about cash flows for the year, all cash movements are recorded in the cash account. If we want to know about the cash flows of a particular transaction, we can find all the elements of that transaction in a journal entry.

> To produce summarized statements of performance, financial position and cash flows the raw data must be transformed, summarized and classified into a more usable form.

Periodically we should check the system to make sure that A = L + OE (Assets = Liabilities plus Owners' Equity). To do this we make a list of the balances of all the accounts in the ledger, add up the total of the assets and check this against the total of liabilities and proprietorship. This list is called a 'trial balance'.

At the end of the period when financial statements are to be prepared, we should ask whether the journal and ledger (together the books of account) properly reflect all the elements of profit or loss for the period and the right amounts of all the assets, liabilities and equity at the end of the period. It is likely that they will not and it is therefore necessary on the last day of the accounting period (balance day) to make adjusting entries to achieve this outcome (balance day adjustments).

Recording and processing data in the accounting system involves increases and decreases in the asset, liability and equity accounts of the entity. Centuries ago, a special labelling method was devised to record these increases and decreases – debits and credits. Debits and credits are nothing more than labels: they are simply directional indicators associated with changes in assets, liabilities and equity. Of themselves, they do not have any qualitative meaning. The method is built on two basic 'acts of faith'. An increase in an asset is called a 'debit', and the opposite of a debit is a 'credit'. It follows that if A = L + OE, then the sum of the debits must equal the sum of the credits. It also follows that asset accounts will have a debit balance, while liability and equity accounts will have a credit balance.

Suppose your business decided to revalue the previous example's block of industrial land to show market value in the balance sheet. On balance day, an adjusting entry will be needed increasing the carrying amount of the asset by $2 million (the increase in value) and increasing owners' equity by the same amount. Since the increase in value represents a holding gain rather than a 'real' profit, accountants record the increase as a separate part of owners' equity called an 'asset revaluation reserve' rather than including it in retained profits. Thus, a journal entry will be made as in Box 12.2.

BOX 12.2 **The asset revaluation reserve**

Debit	Land		$2,000,000
Credit		Asset revaluation reserve	$2,000,000

All these entries are made in the journal and then posted to the ledger accounts. The ledger account balances are then recalculated for the adjustments, and the resulting balances of each of the asset, liability and equity accounts will contain all the information needed to produce an income statement and balance sheet.

As managers, it is highly unlikely you will ever be required to perform bookkeeping tasks, but a knowledge of how accountants derive the numbers they provide to you will greatly assist you in your management tasks. It will also allow you to converse intelligently with accounting personnel.

accounting and the information age

The job of the bookkeeper through the ages has often been seen as a tedious and boring one. All transactions undertaken by the accounting entity were recorded by hand in the journal and manually posted to the ledger. The balance of each ledger account had to be determined at balance day to permit the preparation of financial statements. When hundreds, thousands or millions of individual transactions occurred during an accounting period, errors were inevitable. Errors are likely when tasks that must be performed precisely are undertaken for large volumes of essentially similar data over long periods of time. If data are recorded to the wrong accounts or in the wrong amounts, it will ultimately be reflected in errors in the financial statements, unless previously detected. Considerable effort was expended in trying to ensure that such errors were found and fixed. For example, the trial balance was a means of checking whether all transactions had been recorded in accordance with the accounting equation.

The invention of the computer revolutionized bookkeeping. The only manual task now required is the input of the market transactions, items and events of the entity and the specification of the adjustments needed at the end of each accounting period. Modern computer software ensures that the computer now performs all the intra-system procedures. Balances of ledger accounts, trial balances and even financial statements are available at the press of a button. Information technology has also enabled external data sources to be linked into the accounting system, providing a considerable expansion of the information available to management from the system.

key concepts in accounting

Over time, accountants have developed a number of key concepts and principles that underlie the practice of accounting. The concepts determine what is permitted as inputs to the financial accounting system, the way in which those inputs are processed, and the resulting outputs in financial accounting statements. The ideas discussed below are not an exhaustive set of all the ideas on which accounting relies for its form and content. They are, however, the key ideas that, together, explain most accounting outcomes.

the entity concept

Before any recording of financial transactions can be made, we must be able to identify the entity or unit for which accounts and reports are to be prepared. This concept, while self-evident, is the starting point for the design of any accounting system. Without it, we would not know what should be recorded and what should not. It ensures those financial transactions, items and events between the entity and others outside it (market transactions) are the only ones recorded.

The accounting entity can be anything we choose. It may be a person, a collection of people, an activity undertaken by the person or those people, a government, a business, a social organization or any other form that makes economic sense. All of us are involved, in one way or another, with activities that involve accounting entities. An accounting entity does not have to be a legal person. For example, you may be employed and also run a business in your spare time. You may choose to define your business activities as an accounting entity because you will need to know how successful they are.

> Before any recording of financial transactions can be made, we must be able to identify the entity or unit for which accounts and reports are to be prepared.

For business and accounting purposes, we can have a wide variety of entities but in any particular case we must define it in accounting terms before we can commence recording economic activity. You may be familiar with the most common forms of business entity. The sole trader is a person in business individually. A partnership is the common activities of a group of people for the same purpose. The company, a separate legal entity, is a widely used vehicle for business around the world.

monetary measurement

At one time or another, you may have had occasion to read the output of the accounting system, the financial statements comprising a balance sheet, income statement and cash flow statement. You would then know that at the end of every line of every statement is a monetary amount. This tells us that everything in the accounting system must be measured in money terms; and not just any sort of money, but a common monetary measuring unit. This is usually the currency of the country of residence of the accounting entity.

A little thought about this notion will lead you to realize that if something is not capable of being measured in money, then accountants will not allow it into the system. This is one of the primary reasons why people are not shown as assets on balance sheets.

The concept is simply saying that we must have a standard measuring unit. Thus, anything that cannot be measured in money terms cannot form an input to the financial accounting system.

the historical cost concept

The traditional historical cost accounting system is built on the idea that all transactions, items and events are to be recorded at the number of dollars involved in the transaction at the time it took place, that is, at historical cost. Thus, assets are recorded at the number of dollars required to acquire them at the point at which they are purchased. Only those transactions arising from dealing with a party external to the accounting entity give rise to an item to be recorded at historical cost.

It should be noted that over the years, accountants have approved of various departures from this historical cost concept. Nowadays, accounting standards generally permit a choice of accounting treatment.

'going concern' concept

This concept is usually expressed in terms of the accounting entity having an indefinite life. It really means that the entity will continue to operate until at least its planning horizon, rather than lasting forever. The concept reflects the fact that most businesses do continue; if not, we would value for liquidation purposes (going out of business) on balance day.

If we valued on the assumption of liquidation, both measurements of income and financial position would be quite different. For example, inventory may have to be sold as a job lot for much less than its cost when acquired in the ordinary course of business. Using the liquidation number to value inventory would result in a much lower value on the balance sheet and the potential loss would be shown on the income statement. If the business were expected to continue, this would be a misleading accounting treatment.

the dual aspect concept

The whole of the recording process in accounting is based upon this concept. In essence, it is saying that every transaction entered into by an accounting entity will have two equal and offsetting effects as defined by the fundamental accounting equation. Assets represent the things controlled by the accounting entity. The sum of all the assets represents amounts owed to someone. Liabilities and equities represent claims by people outside the accounting entity (liabilities) and by the owners (owners' equity).

Hence, the uses of all the resources of the entity (assets) must be equal to the sources of those resources (liabilities and equity). This dual aspect concept is the basis for debits and credits.

the time period concept

In order for the users of accounting information to get timely information enabling them to make economic decisions, it is necessary to report on the results of the activity of the accounting entity at discrete intervals of time. The time period concept simply means the period for which profit or loss is to be computed. In effect, the life of the business will be split into a series of discrete time periods.

This concept gives rise to many of the problems in accounting measurement. Most estimates are a result of a need to report at regular intervals. For example, on balance day, we must decide whether an incomplete transaction is to be ignored or whether part of it should be recognized.

recognizing revenues and expenses

Revenues are the resources that an entity earns from undertaking day-to-day operations (for example sales, fees). Revenues increase owners' equity; their equal and offsetting effects are an increase in assets or a decrease in liabilities. Generally, accountants recognize revenue at the earliest point in the accounting entity's operating cycle at which that revenue can be said to be earned, quantifiable and collectable.

Expenses are the costs incurred in generating revenue. Hence, once revenue is measured, we can determine which costs are to be matched against that revenue as expenses of the accounting period.

conservatism

Business is fraught with risk and uncertainty and accountants reflect this by being cautious in their evaluations. Accountants call this 'conservatism' or, if you prefer, 'reasonable pessimism'. It is based upon the assumption that statement users are risk averse.

Conservatism does not mean deliberate understatement of assets and income. Rather, it suggests that accountants should err on the downside where doubt exists. Hence, profits are never anticipated, while losses almost always are (see Box 12.3).

BOX 12.3 **An example of conservatism in accounting**

For example, a used car salesperson enters the accountant's office, saying: 'I have got this sale in the bag, we just haven't got a signed order yet.' The accountant replies: 'Well, before we treat this as a transaction, let's wait till we have the signed paperwork and have delivered the car.'

The concept implies a counterbalancing, cautious attitude to uncertainty to offset the optimism of executives. This concept is closely linked to the further accounting concept of objectivity. 'Objectivity' means freedom from bias, or able to be independently verified, or not subject to opinion. Accountants seek verifiable evidence (hence the use of the historical cost concept) rather than relying on opinions as to the number of dollars to be recorded in the accounts. The concept of objectivity is therefore aimed at producing information that users can regard as reliable and dependable, that is, can be relied upon as 'accurate' and realistic.

consistency

It is now generally accepted that the accounting treatment of particular items should be consistently applied over time. For example, where a particular method of depreciation is utilized in respect of a class of asset, the accounting entity should continue to do so in future years unless there are very good reasons for change. The object of this concept is to give consistency to the entity's reports over time, thereby promoting comparability.

It is important to recognize that consistency does not mean that everyone has to use the same methods or procedures in a given situation, or that there will necessarily be comparability between entities.

materiality

Accountants should report in the financial statements those things that are important to the users of financial information. Effort should not be wasted on those inconsequential things about which the users do not require information. Hence, materiality is a concept about relative importance.

In order to apply the concept of materiality to any particular item, it must be recognized that it has two dimensions. First, does the nature of the item make it material? Accountants regard bad debts as a material item irrespective of the amount of those bad debts. Second, is the item material because of its size? For example, expenditure of $100 on tea and coffee may be material for your social club but $100,000 spent by a major public company may not be material to them.

> *Accountants should report in the financial statements those things that are important to the users of financial information.*

It is important to recognize that materiality is not a concept seeking to exclude particular things from the accounts. It is a concept applied to financial reports to decide which items should be shown separately in those reports. For example, in the tea and coffee situation, the $100,000 for the major public company would be lumped together with all other non-material items as general expenses.

users of accounting information

As we have mentioned, a wide range of groups, both external and internal to the firm, have an interest in the output of accounting. While all have an interest in the performance and financial position of the accounting entity, each of them are interested in different aspects of those things.

Not least among the users are the owners and prospective investors in entities that pursue economic activity in the private sector. The managers of private sector entities (that is, those charged with the responsibility of managing resources to maximize the value of the owner's wealth) are largely motivated by a desire for profit. In the public sector, the government and its agencies are responsible for the efficient and effective use of the resources provided by the public.

Apart from those users with a direct connection to the accounting entity, there are many others in the wider environment with an interest in the entity. Not least among these are the government and its many agencies. A primary user of accounting information is the tax authority.

There are also users who interact with the accounting entity on a daily basis – customers, banks, suppliers and employees. Each of these users has an interest in the performance and financial position of the business enterprise. Customers want to deal with firms that are able to provide continuous reliable supply at acceptable prices. Suppliers want assurance that their bills will be paid on time. Employees are concerned about the security of their employment and the capacity of their employer to pay fair wages and provide proper working conditions.

external users: owners and investors

Business activity requires capital. This capital is used to acquire the resources that the entity needs in order to pursue its chosen activities successfully. Part of this capital may be described as *structural*; items such as land and buildings, plant and equipment. Most of these types of asset are tangible assets, although they may include intangibles such as brand names, copyrights, patents and goodwill purchased by the enterprise. In addition to structural capital, the entity will almost certainly need *working capital*, that is, the short-term funds required to sustain day-to-day operations (for example cash, inventory, amounts owed by customers). Obtaining short-term funds from others can effectively reduce the amount of the firm's funds that need to be invested in these short-term assets; for example obtaining credit from suppliers, effectively borrowing from employees by paying them at the end of the month. The net investment in these short-term items is what accountants define as 'working capital'.

A business entity has to make several key decisions. It must decide what business it is in (what sort of goods or services it will provide), what market(s) it wants to operate in and how these will be approached. These and many other decisions are part of business strategy. When the overall direction is clear, issues of financial strategy need to be addressed. How will the necessary resources be acquired and financed? Initially, capital will almost certainly come from investors. The subsequent raising of funds may come from those initial owners and additional investors (that is, *equity capital*) and/or be borrowed from financial institutions (that is, *debt capital*).

Owners and investors make decisions about their willingness to provide equity capital to a business. Providing such capital is more risky since an owner's right to a return of capital ranks behind all other creditors of the business. The capital may be lost through business operations and the owners have no recourse to anyone for compensation. Nor do owners have a right to a specified periodic return on that capital. Since owners take the ultimate risks, they expect higher returns on their capital than those who take lower risks, such as lending institutions. Lending institutions require a stated periodic rate of return (interest rate) and generally have recourse to assets to recoup their capital in case of default by the borrower.

> *Once investors have made their investment in a business, they become owners and must in future decide whether to maintain, increase or reduce that investment.*

The return required by owners (and potential investors) will take into account the risks associated with the investment, the probability of receiving returns on the capital and the timing of those returns as well as the risk of losing the capital. This required rate of return is known in accounting and finance circles as the *cost of equity capital*. It will be higher than the cost of debt capital since the risks to the lender are lower than those of owners or investors.

Once investors have made their investment in a business, they become owners and must in future decide whether to maintain, increase or reduce that investment. If the firm wishes to expand and requires additional capital, it may seek to obtain all or part of that capital from existing owners. Should the owners invest the further capital required? If the firm is not doing well, will the owners want to divest their ownership if a buyer can be found? These buy, sell or hold decisions are critical issues for owners.

One major source of information for owners and investors in making this equity investment decision is the *financial statements*. The *income statement* describes the surplus or deficit generated during the accounting period, the *cash flow statement* describes the sources and uses of cash and the *balance sheet* describes the financial position of the entity at the end of the accounting period. However, we must remember that these statements are a representation of history. They are not forward looking. In addition to knowing what has happened, owners and investors must make judgements about what they think will happen in the future. Owners and investors would certainly like managers to provide them with forecasts of income, cash flows and expected future financial position but such forecasts are rarely provided.

Another major purpose of accounting is to provide a means by which stakeholders, particularly owners, can monitor the stewardship of their resources by management. This monitoring function has become increasingly important over time as the dichotomy between ownership and control of resources has accelerated. For example, in companies listed on a stock exchange, the management who control the decision making about the use of economic resources are not usually the same people as the owners. Owners need to be convinced that the resources are managed in their best interests. This may not always be the case, as management can act in ways that transfer wealth from one set of stakeholders to another. For example, the issue of options to executives potentially creates such a transfer of wealth from owners to managers. Issues of this kind give rise to potential conflicts between stakeholders. The production and dissemination of financial statements is one way of monitoring, and possibly controlling, these conflicts.

> Another major purpose of accounting is to provide a means by which stakeholders, particularly owners, can monitor the stewardship of their resources by management.

A further way in which accounting information assists owners is by providing information that facilitates measurement of the performance of the entity and assessment of its financial health. Measures such as 'earnings per share' and 'return on equity' are widely used indicators of performance from an owner's perspective. The 'debt to equity ratio', the 'working capital ratio' and the 'net cash cycle' are examples of common measures used in assessing financial stability. These types of measure can be tracked over time, both within the firm and between firms. Trend analysis of this sort is a useful starting point for owners' and other stakeholders' estimates of future performance and position. Analysis of past performance and position using accounting information, and owners' estimates of future performance and position based on that analysis, are major elements of owners' 'buy, sell or hold' decisions about their equity.

internal users: senior executives, business managers

Managers are responsible for planning and controlling the activities of the business. To do this they need a great deal of information. Not only do they need big picture information about performance and financial position but also detailed information about each element of business operations. Information about elements of the business operations is the stuff of management accounting.

Plans made by management are generally translated into annual budgets. Budgets are the financial action plans for the business. These budgets form the basis for ongoing monitoring of performance of all aspects of the business during the coming year. Budgets are intended to be active management tools. Unless actual outcomes are compared to budgets, and variances adequately explained and acted upon, there is little point in setting a budget in the first place. Setting budgets is a time-consuming and difficult task. For established businesses, the most common form of budgeting is 'incremental budgeting'. For start-up businesses or those undergoing major restructuring, budgets are built from scratch: a process known as 'zero-based budgeting'. In incremental budgeting, results for the previous year provide the starting point from which estimates for the coming year are made. Most firms will prepare three budgets; a *profit budget*, a *cash flow budget*, and a *capital expenditure budget*. These budgets form an integral part of the management information system and most firms, particularly large ones, incorporate automatic monitoring mechanisms into their internal reporting systems. Actual results are usually compiled both monthly and year-to-date and compared to budget.

Budgets are both a big picture tool and a means of breaking down elements of the business. In controlling day-to-day operations, much of management's effort goes into the control of costs. While prices charged for goods and services are a product of demand, the firm's ability to control its costs has a considerable impact on the firm's profitability. Managers must therefore understand the behaviour of costs and the relationships between costs, volume and profits.

One of the simplest and most important cost dichotomies is between 'fixed' and 'variable' costs. Fixed costs remain the same over a given range of output. Variable costs rise or fall proportionally with output: a one-to-one relationship. 'Break-even analysis' is one of the most common applications of cost–volume–profit (CVP) relationships (see Box 12.4).

BOX 12.4 The relationship between costs, volume and profit

Suppose your firm is thinking of introducing a new product. The sales department estimates it will sell for $50 per unit. The production department says that fixed costs will rise by $100,000 if the new product is introduced and that the variable, or direct, costs of producing it will be $30 per unit. How many units will the firm need to sell in order to break even?

In our example, profit from the product will be equal to the number of units times selling price per unit less fixed costs plus the number of units times the variable cost per unit.

Algebraically, this can be written as:

$$P = SP \times X - (FC + [VC \times X])$$

Where   P = profit
           SP = selling price per unit
           X = number of units
           FC = fixed costs
           VC = variable cost per unit

Using this expression and setting profit to zero, we find that the firm will need to sell 5,000 units to break even.

A large part of management accounting is about costing. Depending on how the firm operates, managers need to know how much products, processes or jobs cost. Management accounting has developed costing systems for each of these applications. Firms that are more sophisticated use standard costing, whereby a standard cost for each cost component is set and regularly reviewed. Actual costs are then tracked against these standards.

Attaching costs to cost objects, such as products, sounds simple. In practice, it can be extremely difficult, requiring judgements and estimates. A simple example illustrates the nature of the problem. A firm manufactures a number of products from a rented factory located in an industrial suburb. The annual rental of the factory is fixed. In determining the cost of each of the products produced in the factory, how should the factory rent be dealt with? One option is to say that only those costs that vary directly with the output of products should be included in their cost. This is known as 'variable' or 'direct costing'. It would result in the factory rent being expensed for the period. The major alternative is to say that, in addition to variable costs, all the fixed cost traceable to production should be included in product cost. This is known as 'absorption costing'. Under this alternative, the factory rent must be allocated between products. How should this be done? There are many possibilities but no right answer.

The most recent approach to attaching costs to cost objects is called 'activity-based costing' or ABC. This method starts from the simple proposition that it is activities that cause costs to be incurred. In order to cost anything, therefore, the activities involved in that 'thing' should be identified. Once the activities are known, costs automatically follow (see Box 12.5).

BOX 12. 5 **Calculating the true cost of doing business**

For example, a Swedish company used ABC some years ago to find out whether they were making profits from all their customers. The study concluded that about half the customers were losing the firm money. This had not previously been obvious because no one considered all the activities, and therefore costs, associated with dealing with customers. By including all such costs, such as the cost of time spent dealing with customers' complaints, the true customer costs were revealed.

Problems can arise, however. With some products, tracing all the activities and the associated costs involved in producing them is simply not cost-effective. The solution is to choose a set of appropriate cost drivers that is usable as a substitute for individual activities. For example, in manufacturing a product, many activities may be traced to the amount of time spent on them. Time could then be selected as one of the cost drivers for that product.

Comment was made earlier about identifying variances between budgets and actual results. 'Variance analysis' is an important part of management's control of a business. If the budgets are unmet, the reasons for the variances should be identified and, where possible, remedial action instituted. This continuous monitoring and evaluation is an essential element of successful management.

The foregoing selection of management accounting's informational input to managers' day-to-day decision making gives you some insight into management accounting's role in the modern business enterprise.

globalization and accounting challenges

The accounting profession has encountered hard times in the past few years. The spate of corporate collapses around the globe at the end of the last century and the beginning of the new have highlighted the perceived deficiencies of accounting. There are those who interpret this as the 'end of the world', suggesting accounting must be the subject of major reform or consigned to the dustbin.

> The spate of corporate collapses around the globe at the end of the last century and the beginning of the new have highlighted the perceived deficiencies of accounting.

The reality is less dramatic but nonetheless concerning. A twenty-first century scandal to hit the airwaves, Parmalat Finanziaria in Italy, is but one in what is now quite a long string of major corporate failures. Enron and WorldCom come readily to mind on the international stage. These collapses raised concerns about the state of accounting because, in all these cases, there were no easily discernible signs in the published accounting information to suggest that failure was imminent. However, these failures must be seen in context. They represent a small fraction of the economic resources used by private enterprise. Using them to predict a general malaise in accounting falls into the trap of generalizing from the particular. In many cases, these failures were the result of fraud by members of the management, some of whom are now languishing in jail as a result, rather than deep-seated problems in accounting. Accounting cannot cause business failure. At worst, it can conceal economic reality and thereby contribute to such failures.

Notwithstanding this defence of accounting's role in corporate failure, many countries have reacted to the spate of corporate collapses in the past decade with new legislation. Most of this legislation deals with improved corporate governance rather than directly with accounting. For example, in the USA, the Sarbanes-Oxley Act of 2002 now requires senior management to sign off on the financial accounts, rather than just the directors.

Despite the many high-profile corporate failures, the accounting profession has not been sitting on its hands. Decades ago, it recognized that the globalization of business was an inevitable trend and that the profession needed to internationalize its standards. This process began in the middle of the twentieth century and has moved steadily forward. Initially, international accounting standards were very general, allowing a great deal of choice in accounting treatments. This approach was taken in order to get countries to sign up to the process of development of international standards without requiring them to abandon their current

> A set of standards issued by the International Accounting Standards Board, based in London, has now been adopted by many countries around the world, including the UK, most of the British Commonwealth countries, the member nations of the EU and many others.

treatments. This was necessary as accounting treatments varied dramatically around the world. Subsequent work on international standards was progressively aimed at narrowing these gaps. The dawn of the twenty-first century saw these efforts start to come to fruition. A set of standards issued by the International Accounting Standards

Board, based in London, has now been adopted by many countries around the world, including the UK, most of the British Commonwealth countries, the member nations of the EU and many others. This is a major beginning to the worldwide adoption of a common set of accounting standards.

Finally, if this chapter has piqued your interest in accounting, there are a plethora of books on the market to satisfy your interest, some of which are referenced in Chapter 19 'learning resources'.

13 finance

professor rob brown[1]

People have been thinking and writing about financial questions for thousands of years but it is only in the past 50 years or so that finance has been recognized as a discipline in its own right. Fifty years may sound like a long time but compared to other disciplines like economics (several hundred years) or mathematics (several thousand years), it is brief indeed. Despite its relative youth, finance has rapidly established itself as one of the indispensable foundations of management education and practice.

Finance has many parents but its main forebear is economics. Indeed, some regard finance as just a branch of applied economics. Although I think it is more than that, there is certainly some truth in this statement. Many of the founders of the discipline would have described themselves as economists and some of the seminal papers in finance appeared in economics journals. Yet many students find that finance requires a somewhat different set of skills to economics. In general, basic courses in finance tend to place greater emphasis on applications and are often taught and assessed with frequent use of fairly realistic numerical examples. They also demand a greater understanding of related disciplines.

overview of the structure of the finance discipline

The needs of MBA students were a major impetus in the development of finance. Naturally, the academics called on to teach it were not comfortable teaching unrelated 'facts' and they set about developing a coherent theory and body of knowledge in finance. Usually they kept a close eye on ensuring that the discipline they were developing would be of use to practitioners and students after graduation.

Conventionally, much of the discipline of finance falls into the subdisciplines of investments and corporate finance. *Investments* adopts the viewpoint of the individual investor, while *corporate finance* adopts the viewpoint of the corporation. To get a feel for what is involved, here are some typical questions that each subdiscipline considers:

investments

> What exactly is 'risk' and how can it be measured?
> How risky are ordinary shares (common stock) compared to bonds (interest-earning assets)?
> How much should I invest in shares and how much in bonds?
> How do stock prices behave over time, and why?
> What is the trade-off between the return an investor can expect and the risk he or she bears?

> Can financial prices such as interest rates, exchange rates and stock prices be predicted?
> Should I invest internationally as well as domestically?
> If I buy options as well as stocks, what happens to my risk and return?

corporate finance
> How much should a company borrow?
> How much of a company's earnings (profit) should be paid out as dividends?
> When is a good time to raise new capital for the company by issuing new shares?
> My company's equipment is wearing out – what is the best way to evaluate alternative replacements?
> What risks and returns may be expected if the company I manage expands overseas?
> Should the company sell options to the investing public and/or grant options to its senior employees?

You may have noticed that some of the topics listed under 'investments' appear to be similar to topics listed under 'corporate finance'. This is as it should be: the primary difference is the viewpoint, not the content. A facetious definition is that in an investments subject, we are hoping to buy a security for less than it is really worth, but in a corporate finance subject we are hoping to sell a security for more than it is really worth. Eventually, of course, these two viewpoints will be reconciled by market forces, since the price paid by the buyer is the price received by the seller.

In many MBA schools, once you have completed the basic finance course, you can then enrol in further finance courses. Usually, there will be an advanced investments course –perhaps called something like 'portfolio management' – and an advanced corporate finance course – perhaps called something like 'corporate financial policy'. There may also be specialist courses on offer, such as financial markets and instruments, international finance, real estate finance, derivative securities[2] and financial institutions management.

skills and knowledge needed to study finance

Many MBA schools set prerequisites for the basic finance course. Typical prerequisites are economics and/or accounting and/or quantitative methods. A basic appreciation of corporate law and tax can also help. Each of these is discussed briefly below.

economics

Finance and economics share a similar approach to modelling and reasoning. The principal assumptions in both basic finance and basic economics are that people act in a rational and self-interested way and transact in competitive markets. Both disciplines share similar methods of empirical testing. Usually, these tests take the form of statistical modelling using historical data.[3] Microeconomics, which deals principally with the consumer and the firm, is the most relevant part of economics for the study of finance.[4] But compared to basic economics, basic finance requires the student to have more specialized background knowledge. All students can relate to the economist's theory of the consumer because all students have practical experience as consumers. They know what it is like to make consumption choices when constrained by a budget.

But not all students have experience of what it is like to be an investor or what it is like to make financial decisions on behalf of a company. Those who do usually find that studying finance gives their experience greater meaning.

accounting

Because of the somewhat specialized character of finance, many students benefit from being exposed to some background knowledge and terminology of business before they study finance. The study of accounting can help to provide such a background. In addition, students and practitioners of finance benefit from having at least some knowledge of accounting because accountants provide data relevant to financial decisions.

quantitative methods

Some of the fundamental concepts in finance – risk for example – are statistical in nature. It is very hard to think of risk in any way that does not involve the statistical concept of probability. So the ability to think statistically is invaluable to the finance student. Similarly, some of the basic tools of finance – compound interest for example – are mathematical in nature. While students of basic finance do not need advanced knowledge of either statistics or mathematics, a serious deficiency in either area will make even a basic finance course quite hard going.

corporate law

Finance students do not need much knowledge of corporate law (or company law as it is known in some jurisdictions) but they do need to be clear on the fundamental concept of the separate legal personality of the company. In law, a company is a 'person' separate from the shareholders who own it. Being a legal 'person', a company can have objectives, make decisions and enter into contracts. It can sue and be sued. Of course, in practice, all these actions are actually taken by real (or 'natural') people on behalf of the company. These decision makers are meant to act in the best interests of the company. But suppose they only *pretend* to pursue the best interests of the company, when in reality they are pursuing their own interests? In that case, corporate decisions and policies can be fully understood only if we know something about the *personal* objectives of the people who run companies.

tax

Governments often take in tax between 20% and 50% of a taxpayer's income – in some cases, even more. Taxes must be collected in accordance with the law, but laws are subject to challenge and interpretation. When a business is small and uncomplicated, there is often little room for legal challenges, but as a business becomes larger and more complex, the scope for interpretation grows – and so does the opportunity to find legal ways to reduce tax. Unfortunately, tax considerations drive many financial decisions. Therefore, unless we know something about tax, many financial decisions will be difficult to understand.

the main ideas in finance

Corporate Finance by Richard Brealey and Stewart Myers is a well-known finance textbook, now into its eighth edition. It is prescribed in many MBA courses.[5] In their final chapter, Brealey and Myers provide their list of 'the seven most important ideas in finance'. Their chapter is well worth reading but, of course, it is designed for someone who has already read their book. The remainder of this chapter will give you the flavour of these seven ideas.

net present value

Net present value – known ubiquitously as 'NPV' – is a technique that can be used by companies to decide how much a proposed investment is worth. Suppose you are running a manufacturing company and you are considering whether to the replace your main piece of machinery. How should you reach this decision? Should you ask your accountant to calculate the effect on the company's profit next year? Or should you ask for the effect on profit in all future years? Or would it be better to estimate how long it will take to get your money back – the quicker, the better? The answer is that you may choose to do any or all of these things – but the most important thing you should do is calculate the NPV of buying and using the new equipment. But before we calculate NPV, we need to understand the principles involved, and to do that, we need to review compound interest, which is one of the foundations of NPV.

Suppose you have $1,000 to invest and your bank offers you an interest rate of 8% p.a., repayable in a lump sum after two years. In the first year, you will earn $80 in interest. This interest is added to your deposit, so it grows to $1,080. In the second year, you will earn interest of 8% × $1,080 = $86.40, taking your deposit to $1,080 + $86.40 = $1,166.40 at the end of the second year. The quick way to do this calculation is to use the compound interest formula:

(1) $\quad S = P(1+i)^n$

where S is the 'future sum', that is, the value at the end of the investment term

P is the principal

i is the interest rate per period and

n is the number of periods.

Using equation (1), we find $S = \$1,000 \times (1.08)^2 = \$1,000 \times 1.1664 = \$1,166.40$.

NPV turns this relationship upside down:

(2) $\quad P = \dfrac{S}{(1+i)^n}$

Equation (2) says that *if* we know an investment will produce a cash inflow (S) of $1,166.40 in two years' time, and *if* the rate of return (i) that we require on this investment is 8% p.a. (compound), *then* the value of this investment to us today (P) is:

$$P = \frac{\$1{,}166.40}{(1.08)^2} = \frac{\$1{,}166.40}{1.1664} = \$1{,}000$$

P is known as the investment's 'present value' – literally, its value to us now. If someone offered to sell us this investment today for, say, $990, then the *net* present value of the investment is $1,000 − $990 = $10. In this case, we would need to pay only $990 for something that is worth $1,000 to us. Clearly, this is a good investment. The NPV rule is simple: if the NPV is positive, it's a good investment; if the NPV is negative, it's a bad investment.

It's fortunate that in English, the letter P can stand for the three equivalent interpretations of equation (2): present value, principal and price. As we've just seen, P is the *present value* of a future sum, S. But it can also be thought of as the *principal* of a loan. If you are a lender, it is the amount you need to lend now if you want to be paid back a particular sum (S) in the future. If you are a borrower, it is the amount you can borrow today if you agree to pay back the amount S in the future. Less obviously, but just as importantly, P can also mean the price of a security. If a security promises to pay a lump sum of $1,166.40 in two years' time, then under the conditions assumed in the example, if the security were sold in a competitive market, the *price* it should fetch is $1,000. Competing buyers should bid up the price until the NPV of the security is zero.

Let's return to the company considering the installation of new equipment. To calculate the NPV, it will first need to forecast the cash flows that will result if it buys and uses the new equipment. Among other things, this requires forecasts of the cash outflows on labour, materials and repairs expected from operating the new equipment. Second, it will need to decide on the required rate of return (i), taking into account the risk of the investment. Third, it will need to calculate the NPV of the investment.[6] Of these, the third is much the easiest. There are many pitfalls and practical difficulties in the first two and they provide the raw materials of many MBA assignments.

the capital asset pricing model

The capital asset pricing model – usually just called the CAPM – was a major reason for William Sharpe, its inventor, being awarded the Nobel Memorial Prize for Economic Science in 1990.[7] But before we can look at the CAPM, we first have to look at portfolio theory, which is one of its foundations.

Portfolio theory was developed by Harry Markowitz in the 1950s.[8] A 'portfolio' is a collection of assets in which someone has invested. Centuries before Markowitz, it had been recognized that it was a good idea to invest in a range of assets.[9] But it was Markowitz who gave this advice a scientific foundation and showed how investors could get a better trade-off between risk and return.[10]

The capital asset pricing model – usually just called the CAPM – was a major reason for William Sharpe, its inventor, being awarded the Nobel Memorial Prize for Economic Science in 1990.

Markowitz assumed that each asset has its own probability distribution of returns. This means that we know the various outcomes that are possible from an investment, and we also know the probability of each of these outcomes occurring. The return it actually produces is like drawing a number from that distribution. The mean of the distribution is the asset's 'expected return' – roughly speaking, this implies that over a long period of time, an investor in the asset will earn a return equal to the expected return, or something very close to it. The risk of the asset is the spread or dispersion of its return distribution, as measured by the standard deviation. By making these assumptions, Markowitz was able to apply a range of standard statistical tools to the portfolio decision. Markowitz showed that as assets are added to a portfolio, the standard deviation of the return on the portfolio – that is, the risk of the portfolio – will tend to fall, at first rapidly and then more slowly. Moreover, the risk of a portfolio will *always* be less than the average of the risks (standard deviations) of the assets that make up the portfolio.[11] But, unlike risk, the expected return on a portfolio *is* simply the average of the expected return on each individual asset. As an investor diversifies his portfolio, risk falls but expected return doesn't – so no wonder investors diversify.

The driver behind this result is a measure known as the 'covariance' between returns on assets. If I choose at random two shares listed on the same stock exchange, their returns are likely to have a positive 'covariance'. Loosely speaking, this means that when the price of one share rises, the price of the other share is more likely to rise than to fall. So, typically, they rise and fall together – *but not always*. When they don't, one is up and the other is down. And when this happens, my total return isn't greatly affected. In other words, I've benefited from diversification. Markowitz showed that once a portfolio consists of a large number of different assets, the crucial factor when I add the next asset is not the standard deviation of that asset's return but the covariance between the return on that asset and the returns on the assets already in the portfolio.

This important result is often a stumbling block for students, so it's worth spelling out. If I invest in just one asset, my risk is completely determined by the standard deviation of the return on that asset. If I then add a second asset, the risk of my portfolio will be affected by *both* the new asset's standard deviation of return and the covariance between the return on the new asset and the return on my existing portfolio. But as I add more and more assets to my portfolio, the standard deviation of each extra asset matters less and less. Eventually, it hardly matters at all. Instead, the risk of my portfolio is affected more by the covariance between the new asset's return and the returns on the assets already in the portfolio. Hence, when making investment decisions, investors who are already well diversified should focus on how the returns on a proposed new investment will covary with returns on the investments already held.

Markowitz didn't stop there. Once we know how the risk and expected return on a portfolio is related to the risk and expected return of the assets in the portfolio, we should be able to improve our portfolio-building skills. Suppose you hold an equally weighted portfolio of shares in five different companies. This means you have put 20% of your money into each company. If I knew these assets' expected returns, standard deviations and covariances, I could easily calculate your portfolio's risk (standard deviation) and expected return. Further, it is almost certain that for the same five assets, I could use portfolio theory to find a different set of portfolio weights that would give you a higher expected return but the same risk. In other words, I could use portfolio theory to improve your risk–return trade-off. Better yet, I could suggest that you invest in a wider range of assets – why stop at five? – and you should do better still. Where does this process end? Should an investor go on diversifying – buying a wider and wider range of assets? In principle, the answer to this question is yes. But in practice, once you've invested in about 30 different assets, you've probably got nearly all the benefits that diversification offers.

The Markowitz message to the individual investor is clear – diversify, diversify, diversify. Suppose all investors did that. In such a market, what would determine asset prices? An answer is provided by the capital asset pricing model (CAPM). Typically, the CAPM is used to analyse stock prices, although in principle it applies to all assets. In the stock market, the dominant players tend to be the big, diversified investors such as pension funds, mutual funds and insurance companies. Accordingly, the market prices of stocks will tend to reflect their ability to bear risk. Hence, based on portfolio theory, a critical factor in determining the stock price should be how the return on the share covaries with returns on other shares in the investor's portfolio – in other words, on the covariance with the stock market in general. And this is indeed the result stated by the CAPM.[12]

In the CAPM, the price of an asset depends in part on its so-called 'beta risk', which is actually the ratio of two risk measures. The first risk measure is the covariance between the returns on the asset and returns on the market as a whole. In essence, this measures the risk of the asset when it is held as part of a fully diversified portfolio. The second risk measure is the variance of the return on the market as a whole. In essence, this is the risk of the market as a whole. Notice that beta risk does *not* depend on the standard deviation of the return on the asset. Why? Remember that if an investor has diversified his portfolio, then the standard deviation of any single asset is of virtually no significance to him. Hence, it does not affect the price.

According to the CAPM, beta risk is 'priced', that is, the investor is rewarded with a higher expected return for bearing it. No matter how thoroughly an investor diversifies, she or he cannot escape market-wide swings – by definition, they affect everybody. Because beta risk is unavoidable, it should be rewarded. But other risks can be avoided just by diversifying. These diversifiable risks are real and are borne by any investor who chooses not to diversify. But they are not rewarded. Investors cannot expect to be rewarded for bearing risks that do not have to be borne.

> No matter how thoroughly an investor diversifies, she or he cannot escape market-wide swings – by definition, they affect everybody.

Portfolio diversification is an excellent idea. You get reduced risk without sacrificing expected return. Is this a free lunch? Sorry, no. If the CAPM is right, then assets are priced *as if* all investors have diversified. So, diversifying your portfolio doesn't get you a free lunch; you simply get the reward that is commensurate with taking on the non-diversifiable (beta) risk that remains. But here's the sting in the tail: if you *don't* diversify, you will be underrewarded for the risks you bear. So, diversification isn't a free lunch, it's a properly priced lunch. Failing to diversify is like paying full price for lunch but getting only the children's meal.

In the years since Sharpe published the CAPM, researchers have considered other risk factors that may affect stock prices. Two factors have received particular attention. The first is the ratio of the book value of a company to its market value. The 'book value' is essentially the value of the company as measured in the accountant's financial statements. The 'market value' is its share price multiplied by the number of its shares on issue. The second is the size of the company. Many of the researchers who believe that these two factors are important also believe that the CAPM's beta is important too.

efficient capital markets

One of the more controversial claims made by many finance researchers is that, in general, capital markets are efficient. In this context, the term 'capital market' simply means a market in which financial assets are traded. Probably the best example is the stock market but the term encompasses markets for bonds, options and foreign exchange, to name just three. The term 'efficient' does not refer to production efficiency. We are not talking about how quickly your broker answers the phone or how much brokerage costs. Instead, we mean 'information efficiency'; how rapidly and how accurately a capital market reacts when it receives new information. The reaction is, of course, seen in the market price of the asset. For example, suppose that a stock market has high information efficiency. When information about a particular stock reaches that market, the next time the stock is traded, its price will jump to a new level – higher if the news is good and lower if the news is bad. The price reaction will be completed in a single movement. The price will not adjust gradually towards a new equilibrium, nor will it predictably overreact and thus become subject to later correction.

On this view, the stock market is not subject to irrational swings induced by passion and fashion. It may sometimes *look* like that, and maybe a lot of individuals who trade in the market may even *be* like that. But the market price will be a rational, calculated assessment of value, based on all available information. How could this possibly be? The answer lies in competition. Stock markets are highly competitive. There are numerous potential buyers and sellers and every buyer is trying to secure the lowest possible price, while every seller is trying to secure the highest possible price. Many try very hard to be better informed than their competitors, since better information means a better chance to spot an underpriced or overpriced stock. Suppose, contrary to market efficiency, that stock prices could be relied on to move gradually to a new equilibrium after new information is received. For example, if a share is trading at $10.00 and good news arrives, warranting a 7% increase in the price, the price adjusts first to $10.10, then $10.20, then $10.30 and so on until it reaches $10.70. Clearly, in such a market, there is a very simple trading rule that will make me very rich very fast: when good news arrives, be the first to buy and then sell when the adjustment process is complete. Of course, in a competitive market, I will not be the only person to latch onto this idea. Others will do it too. And we will all keep doing it until this reliable pattern is eliminated.

> One of the more controversial claims made by many finance researchers is that, in general, capital markets are efficient.

Efficient markets should not produce reliable price 'patterns' that can be exploited for profit. For example, there should be no reliable cycles in stock prices. Similarly, there should not be reliable trends following events such as the announcement of a company's annual profit. In the latter case, the market should form an unbiased expectation of what a forthcoming profit announcement will be, and then, when the announcement is made, react in a once-off manner – positively if the profit is higher than expected, or negatively if the profit is lower than expected.

Efficiency considerations should also eliminate arbitrage opportunities. An 'arbitrage' is the simultaneous trading in two or more securities to produce an immediate cash inflow at no risk. Put simply, an arbitrage is a money tree. A simple example of arbitrage is buying a share in one place for $20 and simultaneously selling it in another place for $21. Market prices should be set such that arbitrage is not possible.

This may not sound like a very potent statement but it is. Although it does not always enable us to state exactly what a price should be, it frequently allows us to rule out many thousands of possible price combinations on the grounds that they would create arbitrage opportunities.

Finance has many arbitrage-based pricing theorems. Some of the issues they deal with are:

> The rate of return on a firm's shares compared to the rate of return on its debt
> The price of an option relative to the price of the asset underlying the option
> The price of an option relative to the price of a different option on the same underlying asset
> The price of a swap contract relative to the price of related forward contracts
> The forward exchange rate relative to the spot exchange rate
> The change in the stock price when a dividend is paid.

Earlier I described efficient capital markets as a controversial area of finance. In my view, much of this controversy is unwarranted and rather misses the point. Let's put it into perspective. Are all stock markets *always* efficient? Of course not. Have they *sometimes* made pricing errors that should have been recognized as such at the time? Of course they have. Is arbitrage *always* impossible? Of course not. But these questions are rather silly because they are based on a purist's interpretation of efficiency. Efficiency is a *model* of capital market behaviour, and, like all models, it is imperfect. So let's ask some pertinent questions about capital market efficiency. How difficult is it to find genuinely profitable trading rules? Answer: very difficult, and for a great many people, impossible. How difficult is it to find and exploit a genuine arbitrage opportunity? Answer: very difficult, and for a great many people, impossible. Are any investors smart enough, or skilled enough, to 'beat the market' consistently? Answer: maybe some can, especially if they have access to superior information, or if they confine themselves to researching opportunities that most people ignore. But most ordinary stock market investors have little chance of beating the market consistently. Here, then, is my overall take on capital market efficiency: it isn't a perfect description of reality but it is close enough that most people, most of the time, should behave *as if* it were true.

value additivity

Sometimes known as the 'law of the conservation of value', value additivity simply states that present values add up. If a company invests in just two projects, A and B, then the total value is just the present value of A plus the present value of B.

Perhaps this law sounds obvious, but it isn't. I will first put the case *against* the law and then explain why the law is right after all. Portfolio theory tells us that diversification is an excellent idea for investors. Shouldn't the same hold true for companies? We could think of a company as a portfolio of projects. For example, Mega Industries might have three projects – a copper mine, an ice cream factory and a television station. By diversifying its interests in this way, Mega Industries is able to deliver to its shareholders the benefits of diversification. By the same logic, if Mega Industries is considering investing in a new project – say, buying a bank – it needs to consider how the returns on this new project covary with the returns on its existing investments in copper, ice cream and television. This process mirrors that of the investor considering a new asset to add to her or his portfolio. Hence, Mega Industries should not simply estimate each project's present value and sum them. It's more complicated than that.

Although this logic sounds clever and sophisticated, it's flawed. And this is good news, because project evaluation is hard enough without having to consider portfolio effects between projects. Diversification is indeed an excellent idea but even excellent ideas should be implemented in the most efficient way. The crucial question is this. Who is best placed to diversify an investor's portfolio: the investor himself, or a company in which the investor holds shares? The answer is obvious: it is the investor himself, not the company. If I am a shareholder in Mega Industries, and I wish to diversify by also investing in banking, I can do so very easily. I simply buy shares in an existing bank. The only extra cost will be a small percentage to cover brokerage, which will be a lot less than the extra costs involved in Mega Industries buying a whole bank. Moreover, if subsequently I wish to reverse my decision, I can do so very easily – a lot more easily than Mega Industries could sell its bank subsidiary. Finally, I am likely to be a better judge than the management of Mega Industries of the diversification I need. If I want to invest in banking, I will do it myself; I do not need or want Mega Industries to do it for me.

Does this mean that takeovers are always a bad idea? No. Takeovers undertaken by listed companies *purely* for the purposes of diversification are a bad idea but there are also good reasons for takeovers. For example, there are times when a company can improve its efficiency by taking over a competitor or a supplier. The buzz word here is 'synergy': the value of the total is greater than the sum of its parts. Synergy is thus the exact opposite of value additivity. It would be foolish to deny that synergies exist.

> Diversification is indeed an excellent idea but even excellent ideas should be implemented in the most efficient way.

But, like sightings of Elvis Presley and Tasmanian tigers, they are claimed more often than they are substantiated. The stock market itself tends to be dubious about the virtues of takeovers. Evidence from across the world is reasonably consistent on this point. When a takeover bid is announced, on average, shareholders in the target company gain, while shareholders in the bidder either gain nothing or lose. The consistent winners from takeovers are the individuals heavily involved in the process – the investment bankers, the lawyers and (since pay is often related to the size of the company) the managers of the bidding company.

capital structure theory

'Capital structure' refers to how a company chooses to finance itself. All companies require at least some funds to be contributed by the shareholders who own the company. Collectively, these funds are known as 'equity'. The most common way that shareholders contribute funds to establish a business is through the purchase of ordinary shares (common stock). Once the company is operating, shareholders automatically increase their contribution if they do not take out all profit in the form of dividends. Many companies also choose to raise capital by borrowing money. Debt comes in myriad forms: bank loans, bonds and commercial paper are three examples, each of which has numerous subcategories. The big question is a deceptively simple one: how much should a company borrow? In other words, what is the best mix of debt and equity?

Shareholders are the 'residual claimants'. They get whatever is left after everyone else has been paid. Hence, their return may be a little or a lot depending on how well the company has performed. Lenders get paid before shareholders and, unlike shareholders, they are usually entitled to a *predetermined* amount (the interest). The result of borrowing is known as 'leverage', which refers to the fact that, by borrowing, shareholders increase the variability of their return.

Leverage can be illustrated by a simple example. Suppose a company's assets are worth $200m, financed by $120m of equity and $80m of debt. The interest rate on the debt is 10% p.a., so the annual interest charge is $8m. Now suppose that in a typical year the company's profit before interest is $20m, in a good year it is $26m, and in a poor year $14m. What percentage rate of return do the shareholders earn in typical, good and poor years? Table 13.1 provides the answers.

Table 13.1 *Return on equity in poor, typical and good years*

	Poor year	Typical year	Good year
Assets	$200m	$200m	$200m
Earnings before interest	$14m	$20m	$26m
Interest (10% p.a.)	$8m	$8m	$8m
Earnings after interest	$6m	$12m	$18m
Return on equity (RoE)	$6m/$120m = 5% p.a.	$12m/$120m = 10% p.a.	$18m/$120m = 15% p.a.
Return on assets (RoA)	$14m/$200m = 7% p.a.	$20m/$200m = 10% p.a.	$26m/$200m = 13% p.a.

Compare the last two rows in the table. In a typical year for this company, the return on assets (10%) is equal to the interest rate. In this event, the return on equity (RoE) – that is, the return earned by the shareholders – is also 10%. In a good year, the return on assets (RoA) is 13%, which exceeds the interest rate, and the shareholders do better still and earn 15%. But in a poor year, the shareholders' return is only 5%, which is less than the return on assets (7%). From the shareholders' viewpoint, borrowing makes a poor year (RoA = 7%) even worse (RoE = 5%), but it makes a good year (RoA = 13%) even better (RoE = 15%). Remember from the CAPM that the definition of risk is a greater spread in outcomes. Clearly, borrowing increases the risk faced by shareholders.

The fact that something is risky does not mean it is a bad idea. Taking a risk is acceptable if sufficiently large rewards are on offer. So, the critical question is: are shareholders sufficiently compensated for the extra risk caused by borrowing? In a well-known paper, Franco Modigliani and Merton Miller gave their answer: yes, but no more and no less.[13] The shareholders' reward is exactly commensurate with the risk. Since there is nothing abnormal to gain (or lose) from borrowing, it shouldn't matter to shareholders whether or not the company borrows. One capital structure is as good as any other. The total market value of a company – that is, the market value of its debt plus the market value of its equity – is not affected by the *ratio* of debt to equity. Or, as finance teachers are wont to say, the value of a pie does not depend on how it is sliced.

> The fact that something is risky does not mean it is a bad idea. Taking a risk is acceptable if sufficiently large rewards are on offer.

Modigliani and Miller based their conclusion on idealized market conditions. Hence, we shouldn't jump to the conclusion that in practice capital structure is irrelevant. That would misinterpret the point of their work. Their genius lay in showing that, *of itself*, there is nothing special, magical, mysterious, desirable or detrimental about borrowing.

If borrowing has any of those characteristics, it must stem from the factors *omitted* from the Modigliani–Miller analysis. These factors include 'frictions' like company taxes, personal taxes, liquidation expenses and imperfect communication between market participants. Or there may be product gaps in the securities market: investors might pay a premium for some new variety of security that meets their previously unfilled needs. These are the kinds of factors that need to be considered when a company is considering how much to borrow.

option theory

In finance, the word 'option' means much the same as it does in everyday life. Someone is said to hold an option if they have a choice that they can exercise, or not exercise, as they wish. Quite often, these choices will expire after a given time. The classic option in finance is an option to buy shares. For example, the board of Jasper Printing may give its CEO, Freda Jones, an option to buy 100,000 shares in the company at $10 per share, exercisable any time in the next three years. Suppose that when Freda is given these options, the market price of a Jasper Printing share is $9. If, at any time in the next three years, the market share price exceeds $10, then Freda has a winner. Say the share price hits $12. Freda can exercise her options, which requires her to pay $10 for each share. That is, she pays 100,000 × $10 = $1m for shares that are worth 100,000 × $12 = $1.2m. So, if she wanted to, she could pocket $200,000. Of course, if the Jasper Printing share price never gets above $10 in the next three years, then Freda won't want to exercise the options. They will simply lapse. But when Freda was given the options, no one knew whether the share price would, or would not, exceed $10 in the coming three years, so the options were worth something when they were given to her. The question is: how much?

Fischer Black, Myron Scholes and Robert Merton answered this question in the early 1970s.[14] They showed that the value of many options depends on just five factors: an interest rate, two characteristics of the option and two characteristics of the 'underlying asset' (Jasper Printing shares in Freda's case). The interest rate is the default-free rate for the term of the option. In Freda's case, this could be measured by the yield on a three-year government bond. The two characteristics of the option are its exercise price ($10 in Freda's case) and its term to maturity (three years for Freda). The two characteristics of the underlying asset are its current market price ($9 in Freda's case) and its volatility. The last one requires some explanation. The prices of many financial assets like shares tend to move around over time. 'Volatility' is a measure of this tendency. In practice, volatility can often be measured reasonably well by looking at the return on the asset in the past and calculating the standard deviation. Unlike many financial models, the Black–Scholes–Merton option pricing model specifies a particular equation. For example, it doesn't just state that higher volatility means a higher option price. Rather, the option pricing model tells us exactly how much the option price should increase if the volatility increases by a certain amount. Such results are rare in the social sciences. In 1997, Robert Merton and Myron Scholes were awarded the Nobel Memorial Prize for Economic Science for their work on options.[15]

Options abound in the financial markets. There are options to buy (known as 'call

> Someone is said to hold an option if they have a choice that they can exercise, or not exercise, as they wish. Quite often, these choices will expire after a given time.

options') and options to sell (known as 'put options'). In addition to options on shares, there are options on bonds, foreign exchange, futures contracts, swap contracts, financial indexes, land and commodities. There are even options on options. In the Chicago Board Options Exchange (CBOE), more than 24 million option contracts were traded in 2005, valued at more than US$200 *trillion*. And, while the CBOE is the biggest option exchange, there are many other busy option exchanges around the world.

In part, option markets have developed in response to people's desire to gamble. If you want to, you can use options to increase your risk, so that you are likely to get very rich (or very poor) very fast. But that isn't the main reason for their growth. Options are a remarkably flexible and effective way for firms and investors to *manage* risk. In effect, an option buyer gets protection against the price of the underlying asset moving beyond the exercise price. The option seller is paid to accept this risk. In fact, in many cases, far from being a way to gamble, buying an option is very like buying insurance.

The principles of option pricing are also important, because lots of financial contracts either contain options or can be thought of as options. Examples include rights issues, warrants, convertible notes, convertible bonds, convertible preference shares, overdrafts, standby agreements, performance fees of various kinds and asset value guarantees. This list is by no means complete. Even corporate debt is like an option because the company has an option to default. If a company can afford to repay debt, it will choose to do so and then the stockholders keep whatever remains. If it cannot repay the debt, the stockholders walk away and the company's assets belong to the creditors.

> Remember that the NPV rule is to go ahead with an investment project if the NPV is positive.

There are also 'real options'. Remember that the NPV rule is to go ahead with an investment project if the NPV is positive. What happens next? In the NPV world, that's the end of it. Management's role is simply to accept or reject proposed investments, not to manage them once they are underway. If the project's cash flows turn out to differ from those that were forecast, then that's just the risk you took. Of course, the real world of management isn't like that. Managers are expected to respond as a project unfolds, scaling back investments that prove disappointing, expanding those that succeed, abandoning the disasters. All these actions are *real options* – management has options to scale down, expand, abandon and so on. There are also real options even before a decision is made on whether to accept or reject a project, for example there is an option to delay starting a project to allow a pilot study to be undertaken. Like financial options, real options have value. In investment decisions, they should be considered along with NPV.

agency theory

For many years, there was a fundamental inconsistency at the heart of corporate finance theory. While it was assumed that shareholders were motivated purely by self-interest, it was also assumed that company managers such as CEOs and board members would act purely in the interests of shareholders – even if this was contrary to their own personal interests – simply because that was their job. Some thinkers had noted this inconsistency long ago. In the late eighteenth century, Adam Smith, the 'father of economics', had criticized the corporate form in his book *The Wealth of Nations*, 'because companies were owned by one group (the shareholders) but managed by someone else'. But mostly, the inconsistency was ignored. In the late 1970s, it shot back into prominence with the publication of an important paper by Jensen and Meckling.[16] It has remained prominent ever since.

The basic idea is that when someone, such as a CEO, makes decisions on behalf of someone else, such as a group of shareholders, there is a principal–agent relationship. In this case, the CEO is the agent and the group of shareholders is the principal. Even though agents are legally bound to pursue the principal's interests, rather than their own, in reality, agents are self-interested just like anyone else. A wise principal acknowledges this fact and tries to *monitor* the agent's behaviour. But, in practice, monitoring is usually neither costless nor perfect. For example, shareholders often have little or no idea what the CEO does from day to day. As well as monitoring, principals may try to give the agent extra incentives to act in the principal's interests. These activities are referred to as 'bonding'. For example, the CEO may be given shares in the company to encourage the CEO to think and act like a shareholder.

The owner vs manager agency relation is only one of many encountered in finance. Another concerns lenders and borrowers. When a company borrows money, the funds come under the control of the company. If the company performs poorly, lenders may lose some or all of their money. In this case, the lender is the principal and the company is the agent. To protect themselves, lenders can take various actions such as inserting clauses in the loan agreement that give the lender the power to demand immediate repayment if the company does (or does not) take specified actions.

Many common financial decisions of CEOs, lenders and investors make little sense unless we first recognize that some kind of agency relation is in place. An understanding of agency relations also helps in the design of corporate policy. For example, agency theorists have been able to suggest the kinds of agent behaviours that principals should watch out for. They have also been able to suggest various monitoring and bonding mechanisms that can help to alleviate the problems inherent in agency relations.

the empirical evidence

Do these ideas actually work in practice? Yes, but some work better than others. By the standards of most social sciences, finance has an impressive list of achievements. NPV is used by nearly all major companies. Portfolio theory is widely understood and its main message implemented. The CAPM's insistence that the 'market as a whole' is an important factor continues to have widespread support, although many would add two or three other factors to the list. Nevertheless, 'beta' risk has become embedded in the vocabulary and practice of finance.[17] Market efficiency is controversial but it is still a brave (or foolhardy) person who claims that it is easy to beat the market. And mutual funds that don't try to beat the market have become very popular with investors. The stock market itself seems to agree that diversifying takeovers are questionable – and in recent years many companies have 'spun off' (sold) previous acquisitions that don't fit with their main business. Option pricing theory works so well that the websites of some exchanges provide links to option price 'calculators'.[18] Some option market authorities use option pricing models to estimate prices for administrative purposes. Some companies are starting to supplement their NPV calculations with real option valuations. While it is often hard to put a precise dollar value on agency

> By the standards of most social sciences, finance has an impressive list of achievements.

costs, there's little doubt that they exist. Agency costs help to explain many features of financial contracts that we see in practice.

One reason finance works so well is that financial markets are often close to the economic theorist's ideal of the competitive market. There are lots of well-informed, highly motivated buyers and sellers trading in markets that are usually easy to access and to exit. So, not surprisingly, the competitive model works well. Moreover, there are lots of accurate data to test the theories. Whereas a macroeconomist may get, say, four observations a year on GNP, or maybe 12 observations a year on national money supply, all of which are measured with error, finance researchers get thousands of accurately recorded prices every day.

Where to now for finance? There are many challenges still to be tackled but in my mind two stand out. These are capital structure and tax. Despite many years of concentrated work, by some of the best minds in finance, there is still a lot to learn about capital structure. As a result, we can advise on a capital structure decision with less confidence than we can advise on pricing an option. Tax plays an increasingly important role in finance research. The impact of tax on borrowing decisions and dividend decisions is the most obvious but there are others too. Yet, it seems to me, tax still plays a greater role in the practical world of financial decisions than it does in finance textbooks and finance research.

In conclusion, finance will test your problem-solving skills and your ability to put theory into practice. It will test your verbal, numerical and mathematical skills. It is demanding and some people find it pretty difficult. But it is essential knowledge for the MBA student and the practising manager. Best of all, it is fascinating and rewarding.

references/notes

1. This chapter was written during a sabbatical leave at the University of Manchester, UK. I am grateful for support given by the University of Manchester. I am also grateful to Moreen Anderson, Rayna Brown, Bonnie Buchanan and Stephen Easton for helpful comments. All remaining errors and infelicities are mine.
2. Derivative securities include forward contracts, futures contracts, options and swaps.
3. The technical term is 'archival data'. An example from economics is a database of national income statistics. An example from finance is a database of stock prices.
4. The other major subdiscipline of economics is macroeconomics, which deals with the economy as a whole, rather than with individual decision makers within the economy.
5. Despite its title, the book considers the viewpoints of both investors and companies. That is, in the terminology I have used in this chapter, it covers both investments and corporate finance.
6. It also requires the decision maker to consider continuing with the old equipment but I will ignore this complication.
7. The prize was awarded for contributions to the theory of financial economics and was shared equally with Merton Miller and Harry Markowitz, both of whom are mentioned below. John Lintner (died 1983) and Jan Mossin (died 1987) are often credited with having invented the CAPM at about the same time as Sharpe.
8. Markowitz, H.M. (1959) *Portfolio Selection: Efficient Diversification of Investments* (New York: Wiley).
9. A writer in the Babylonian Talmud recommended spreading one's wealth across real estate, business and cash – a very early recognition of the wisdom of portfolio diversification. See Tract Baba Metzia (Middle Gate) Part I, Chapter III.
10. Markowitz, H.M. (1952) 'Portfolio selection', *Journal of Finance*, 7(1): 77–91.
11. There is an exception. If returns are perfectly positively correlated, then the risk will be averaged.

But if the returns on two assets are perfectly positively correlated, they're essentially the same asset anyway.

12. Sharpe, W.F. (1964) 'Capital asset prices: a theory of market equilibrium under conditions of risk', *Journal of Finance*, **9**(3): 425–42.
13. Modigliani, F. and Miller, M.H. (1958) 'The cost of capital, corporation finance and the theory of investment', *American Economic Review*, **48**(3): 261–97.
14. Black, F. and Scholes, M. (1973) 'The pricing of options and corporate liabilities', *Journal of Political Economy*, **81**(3): 637–54; Merton, R.C. (1973) 'Theory of rational option pricing', *Bell Journal of Economics*, **4**(1): 141–83.
15. Fischer Black would undoubtedly have shared in the award had he not died in 1995.
16. Jensen, M.C. and Meckling, W.H. (1976) 'Theory of the firm: managerial behavior, agency costs, and capital structure', *Journal of Financial Economics*, **3**(4): 306–60.
17. For example, the New York Stock Exchange website provides beta estimates for US companies. See www.nyse.com.
18. For examples, visit the Chicago Board Options Exchange website (www.cboe.com) or the Australian Stock Exchange website (www.asx.com.au).

14 organizational behaviour

professor paul dainty

Managing people effectively is an essential aspect of operating a successful organization. Many companies have shown how considerable success can result from effective people management. Herb Kelleher, the CEO of Southwest Airlines, for example, has improved the performance of his airline through understanding why his employees behave the way they do. He involves his people in running the business, links superior performance to rewards and tries to create a work setting where employees enjoy coming to work and work hard to further their organization's goals and interests. As Kelleher's actions suggest, a solid understanding and appreciation of how people behave in organizations can have a major impact on the success of a firm.[1]

> Managing people effectively is an essential aspect of operating a successful organization. Many companies have shown how considerable success can result from effective people management.

Another example is GE, one of the world's most consistently successful companies. Jack Welch, the CEO who led GE for 20 years, also emphasized the importance of people to the business: 'We spend all our time on people. The day we screw up the people thing, the company is over'.[2] Sam Walton, the founder of Wal-Mart, believes that to be successful 'people are the key'.[3]

Research also suggests that people are 'the key' or at least one of the most critical components. Jeffrey Pfeffer and John Veiga, drawing on research studies of companies in the USA and Germany, highlight the financial benefit that comes from making employees a core focus of an organization's strategy, including increased sales, improved profits and increases in shareholder wealth. These benefits are a result of the implementation of high performance people practices. Indeed, they argue that extensive empirical research demonstrates that an 'irrefutable business case can be made that the culture and capabilities of an organization – derived from the way it manages its people – are the real and enduring sources of competitive advantage'.[4]

However, relatively few organizations seem to have taken this message on board. Based on their review of the research, Pfeffer and Veiga estimate that only a small proportion of contemporary organizations provide the right systems and environment to achieve a competitive advantage through people. They found that companies who produced outstanding results engaged in seven critical practices such as ensuring employment security, providing extensive training and high compensation systems. Moreover, all seven practices had to be implemented, comprehensively and consistently, for a company to benefit.

None of these hurdles seem insurmountable in themselves, but clearly there are many companies that are either not motivated or are unable to overcome these challenges. Why is this? Reasons highlighted by Pfeffer and Veiga include undue enslavement to short-term pressures that squeeze out longer term development and the view that people are a cost rather than an asset, which erodes trust, commitment and loyalty.

However, lack of will is not the only reason why companies fail to gain a competitive advantage through people. Understanding and managing behaviour within organizations is extremely challenging. People are complex. Each person comes to work with a unique view of the world based on their psychological make-up and experience. Consequently, the successful management of people requires an ability to understand and predict their behaviour. Moreover, this has to be done within a fluid work context characterized by rapid organizational change, increased diversity, swift and sophisticated technological advances and differing views of employee–employer relationships.

> *Understanding and managing behaviour within organizations is extremely challenging. People are complex.*

Indeed, even the experts acknowledge the challenges involved. Gregory Northcraft and Margaret Neale deliberately subtitled their text on organizational behaviour *A Management Challenge*, because they believe the uncertainty, conflict and complexity makes managing behaviour in organizations a difficult and particularly fraught activity.[5]

the essence of organizational behaviour

Challenges such as these are examined in detail through the discipline of organizational behaviour (OB). This subject also acts as the building block for other people-related subjects on an MBA programme. Stephen Robbins defines OB as the systematic study of the actions and attitudes that people exhibit within organizations.[6]

While most people embarking on an MBA may not be familiar with the academic discipline of OB, everyone is familiar with the subject matter. Our lives are characterized by involvement in a wide range of organizations, starting with school and including clubs, churches and corporations. Consequently, as Stephen Robbins argues, each of us is a student of behaviour. Since our earliest years, we have watched the actions of others and have attempted to interpret what we see. We have been 'reading' people most of our life. We watch what others do and we try to explain to ourselves why they have engaged in that behaviour. In addition, we often predict what they might do under different sets of conditions.

How effective these predictions are, of course, varies tremendously. Sometimes our assumptions are wrong and it doesn't matter too much. But there are many circumstances where the consequences of getting it wrong can be considerable. An example was the attempt by a unit of KPMG's Real Estate Services Group to entrench a number of staff in June 2002. What, on the surface, should have been a fairly straightforward activity took a turn for the worse through a lack of foresight. It started when details of a proposed redundancy package leaked out before it was discussed with affected staff. When discussions did take place, the redundancy packages offered to employees were a lot less than had been rumoured beforehand. On realizing there was a problem, KPMG's human relations group (who feared legal action from the disgruntled employees) decided to destroy all copies of the earlier, more generous packages. But with the catastrophes at Arthur Anderson and Enron in mind, managers reversed this decision when they considered the potential problems that might arise if documents

> *Our lives are characterized by involvement in a wide range of organizations, starting with school and including clubs, churches and corporations.*

had been destroyed which were relevant to future litigation. They decided to collect and keep all the relevant documents in a safe place.[7]

The insights gained from studying organizational behaviour can help in such situations. Studying OB would have highlighted the potential impact that inconsistent communication would have had on the retrenched employees and the possibility that they might still take legal action. It would also have helped in understanding the impact that these actions would have on the remaining employees and the potential for mistrust and lowered morale within the wider organization. As OB replaces intuitive guesses with systematically designed research studies, it highlights the consequences of making poor decisions. The field of OB demonstrates that most behaviour is not random and is usually purposefully driven. Behaviour is generally predictable if we know how an individual perceived a situation and what they see as important.

In addition to providing insights into an individual's view of the world and what motivates them, the field of OB also helps with understanding how bringing together the range of capabilities possessed by individuals in an organized form produces outstanding outcomes for some organizations and disaster for others. A review of almost any business newspaper or website will highlight both the latest developments and complete catastrophes. Indeed, on some days, you can get both. On the day Mercedes-Benz announced it was trying to stem its financial woes, BMW announced a surge in fourth quarter profits of 30%.[8] Understanding why some organizations are successful while others fail is also a major benefit of studying OB.

how organizational behaviour helps from a manager's perspective

Jennifer George and Gareth Jones point out that a working knowledge of organizational behaviour is important to individuals at all levels of the organization because it helps them appreciate the work situation and how they should behave to achieve their own goals.[9] Knowledge of OB is particularly important to managers. People are a central part of many definitions of what a 'manager' does. Probably the most common definition is 'someone who gets things done through others'. Managing people is not the only aspect of management, however. There are several technical dimensions to the role and the other chapters in this part of the book highlight these. Nevertheless, the people dimension is critical, as many of the theories and frameworks that have been developed to explain the managerial role highlight.

One of the most widely quoted contemporary frameworks describing what managerial work involves is that of Henry Mintzberg. In contrast to the classical view of management, which saw managers planning, organizing and controlling in a fairly stable environment, Mintzberg portrayed things differently. His research in the 1970s suggested that far from an orderly world, managerial work is much more fluid, chaotic and reactionary than had previously been portrayed. His framework (Figure 14.1) emphasizes the decision-making roles of managers (right-hand box).[10] But the ability to make good decisions depends on how well managers execute their 'informational' roles. The quality and amount of information that managers have depends on their interpersonal ability and how well they relate to people. Consequently, how well managers fulfil their 'interpersonal' roles has a major impact on their effectiveness.

> *The quality and amount of information that managers have depends on their interpersonal ability and how well they relate to people.*

Mintzberg's research, and the many subsequent studies done by others, highlights how critical the management of people is to managerial success. Organizational behaviour helps managers to perform these roles more effectively by improving their understanding, explanation and prediction of human behaviour in the work context. While OB does not provide definite answers, it can improve a manager's general prediction of what is likely to have a positive or negative impact. Good decisions can then be made if the manager has identified the critical information in a situation and understood the impact on important variables.

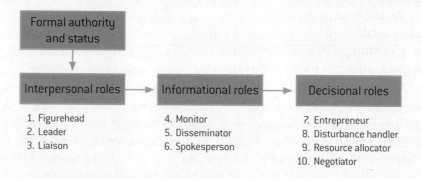

Figure 14.1 Mintzberg's managerial roles

The KPMG example outlined earlier illustrates this. Understanding the feelings of uncertainty in the Real Estate Services Group, and the possible tension in the broader organization arising from the ensuing redundancies, should have been of paramount concern to management. It would also have been important to account for the possible heightened emotional response from people losing their jobs with the self-image and financial loss involved. Having this information should then have influenced what and how management communicated the redundancy packages both formally and informally. Awareness of the critical characteristics of the environment, the key characteristics of the people involved and the essence of the problem would have helped in making better decisions about the redundancy process.

However, how decisions are made by managers is not merely an interesting academic exercise but has an important overall purpose. This purpose, noted by many writers, is to improve organizational efficiency and effectiveness. Effectiveness is the ability of an organization to accomplish an important goal, purpose or mission. Efficiency is the ability to maximize productivity per unit of resources (labour and capital).[11]

Robert Kreitner and Angelo Kinicki have four criteria for determining whether an organization is effective:[12]

1 Goal accomplishment: how well the organization meets or exceeds its goal

2 Resource acquisition: how well it acquires the necessary factors of production

3 Internal processes: how committed, satisfied and trusting the employees are

4 Satisfaction of strategic constituencies: how happy the stakeholders are.

Thus, the study of OB can help managers in executing the core aspects of their role. It does this by increasing awareness of how people are likely to behave in many different circumstances in organizations and as a result helps them to make good decisions about how to manage people and other resources to achieve organizational effectiveness.

organizational behaviour and associated people disciplines

The contribution to better management practice through the field of organizational behaviour and the study of people at work has its roots in the human relations movement and the Hawthorne studies of the 1930s (see Chapter 9). However, it was not until the late 1940s that the behavioural sciences developed as a formal area of study and not until the 1970s that organizational behaviour became formally established.[13]

As the term suggests, OB focuses on behaviour in organizations and draws on more established disciplines that study behaviour in all contexts. OB, consequently, is a mixture of several behavioural science disciplines that view organizations in slightly different ways. The main contributors are generally seen as psychology, sociology, social psychology and anthropology, along with other fields such as political science. Psychology is concerned with understanding individual behaviour, such as learning, perception and personality. Sociology concentrates on wider social systems and contributes to understanding broader communication processes, power and institutional conflict. Social psychologists are concerned with how the individual reacts to their environment, particularly at a group level, and looks at issues such as communication patterns and group dynamics. Anthropologists in their study of society and community behaviour have contributed to OB through their work on cultures and environments, showing how people from different countries and organizations may have different approaches and views of the world.[14]

However, while this is largely an enriching experience, the diversity of contributions has also brought with it a degree of confusion and overlap. In an attempt to clarify how these disciplines come together in studying work behaviour, Fred Luthans contrasts the level of the subject (macro or micro) with its approach (theoretical or applied), as shown in Figure 14.2.[15] As Figure 14.2 indicates, OB emphasizes the theoretical basis of the ideas and frameworks that explain work behaviour. The study of human resources emphasizes the application of many of the OB theories in both a functional and operational sense. Organizational development (OD) and organizational theory (OT) concentrate on the broader organizational context, including different organizational forms and organizational improvement.

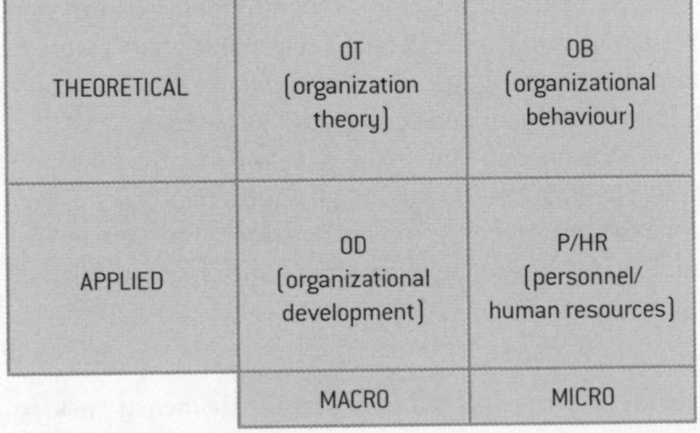

THEORETICAL	OT (organization theory)	OB (organizational behaviour)
APPLIED	OD (organizational development)	P/HR (personnel/ human resources)
	MACRO	MICRO

Figure 14.2 Disciplines explaining work behaviour

While this is still a generally accepted classification of the field, the fluidity and range of behavioural problems faced in organizations means that there will be overlap between these areas (and particularly between OB and HR) and some blurring between what is taught on MBA programmes. Indeed, in many business schools, the core behavioural subject on the MBA course may not be called organizational behaviour, but a variety of titles varying around the words 'human', 'people', 'management' and 'performance'. However, whatever the name, the field of OB tends to be the platform on which the other behavioural subjects are built, particularly subject electives on an MBA programme. Whether or not one pursues additional studies in the behavioural area, OB is essential for understanding the fundamental issues and proposing general solutions for managing people.

the major topics explored in organizational behaviour

There is a range of behavioural issues that influence an organization's effectiveness. Those that are explored through OB include differences in perception, learning, motivation, interpersonal communication, stress and conflict, group structure and processes, leadership style, power, work design and change processes. Stephen Robbins notes that because OB is specifically concerned with employment-related situations, it also emphasizes behaviour related to jobs, work absenteeism, employment turnover, productivity, human performance and management.[16]

These topics are usually considered at three levels of analysis, as there are often different nuances that affect behaviour at each level. Each level, individual, group and organizational, is considered below.

individual level

Individual performance is the single unit on which overall organizational performance depends. Understanding individual behaviour is therefore critical for effective management. Some of the issues involved are illustrated by the case study of Tony Lacy in Box 14.1.

BOX 14.1 Tony Lacy (1)

Tony Lacy had been a manager for several years in a major financial consultancy firm. He had 10 junior consultants reporting to him. Michael Pearson, one of his consultants, had worked for Tony for the past two years. Recently Tony received work back from Michael that had several errors in it and overall he felt that Michael's work had been quite poor. He had to spend time correcting the errors, which had been time-consuming and frustrating, particularly from an experienced consultant like Michael.

This had been the second time in the past two months that Tony had received work from Michael that had been substandard. Tony turned a blind eye to it the last time, but now feels that this cannot go on. Moreover, Tony had noticed that Michael had been coming into work late recently. Tony felt he had no alternative but to speak to Michael about his poor work and timekeeping.

On the surface, Tony has a fairly straightforward task in front of him. It is clear that Michael needs the feedback, both in order to help himself and to ensure that overall performance of the department is maintained. However, to accomplish his task successfully, Tony needs to be careful about making assumptions about the reasons for Michael's slide in performance. How would you approach the situation? As you will see from Box 14.2, the situation looks quite different from Michael's point of view.

In order to manage the situation successfully, Tony needs to have thought about a number of individual behavioural issues. He needs to understand the context and conditions that have given rise to Michael's reporting errors and timekeeping issues. Tony needs to understand how differences in perception can give rise to different views about a situation. He needs to explore how clear Michael is about what is expected of him and his role. Tony needs to understand what motivates Michael and what rewards are available to him and how well these have been communicated.

BOX 14.2 Tony Lacy (2)

Having worked for Tony Lacy for two years, Michael Pearson felt he had made a strong contribution to the department. Michael felt he produced high-quality work, often under pressure. He frequently worked long hours in the office trying to meet tight deadlines.

Over the past few months, the demands seemed to have increased. He recently produced a piece of work for Tony in a time period that he felt no one else could have completed. Although the long hours involved in completing the work had personal family implications, he had been prepared to put up with this inconvenience in order to progress his career. Because he had been working such long hours, he had not been able to complete some normal family chores and had been arriving a little later for work than usual.

Michael had been frustrated recently not so much by the long hours but by the lack of recognition of his contribution and any positive feedback. He was looking forward to raising the issue in the meeting that Tony had recently requested. Michael felt he should ask about possible bonus payments, or other rewards, and whether he might be eligible for these.

Additionally, Tony needs to understand how stress can have a positive and negative impact on performance. He also needs to think about work/life balance and what consequences there might be for getting these wrong. He might also consider Michael's personality and how emotional he might be if he felt he was misunderstood by his manager. Tony may need to reflect on how well he listens and is prepared to probe to understand the issues involved. Finally, Tony needs to think about the potential decisions he might make and the implications of these both for Michael and the impact it might have on the rest of his department.

It is unlikely that many people will go through this checklist before every meeting with their staff. But having some understanding of organizational behaviour attunes the manager to the potential problems that might arise by making superficial assumptions and jumping into a situation with an 'obvious' solution in mind.

group level

The way people behave in work groups is often different to the way they act when they are alone. The communication patterns and relationships between group members can be different to those developed on a one-on-one basis. Groups can develop their own patterns and expectations, or norms, about what is acceptable within a group. Norms on how conflict is managed, what can and cannot be spoken about, how much participation is encouraged and how other groups are viewed are often distinct and different characteristics of work groups. Moreover, the ways in which groups are led is particularly important to their success. These points are illustrated by the case of the CSS company in Box 14.3.

BOX 14.3 **The CSS company**

Jane Watson was the MD of a UK computer software solutions firm, CSS. The firm was part of a European group with headquarters in Germany. Jane, along with the other members of the senior management team, met in Frankfurt every month to discuss company issues. The company had only recently begun to recover from the heady days of the dot.com boom era and had gone through a lot of restructuring. However, there was still much to do and the German CEO had made it clear what needed to be done, particularly in the UK arm of the business.

Jane often felt uncomfortable in the senior team meetings. Conversations were often very polite and she felt that not all the members of the senior team were pulling their weight. She felt particularly under pressure from the CEO because of the UK's poor performance, but couldn't believe that other MDs were not facing the same problems. However, because the team only met once a month and then only for a few hours, it was difficult to really know the true extent of the problems faced in other European countries. The CEO ran the company with an iron hand and while it was possible to raise some thorny issues, most were kept off the agenda. Jane had been trying to raise issues of cross-subsidization for months, which she believed put the UK arm at a disadvantage in comparison to the other subsidiaries.

Jane often thought about the contrast between the European team and her own management team in the UK. The group met frequently and the meetings would often go way past their allotted time. Everything and everybody was discussed and she often had to dampen down the group's antagonism to some of the other European teams. Several of her managers worked on cross-European projects and they would often relay stories about the mistakes made by their European counterparts. They were particularly upset by the company's cross-subsidization rules and the lack of sympathy in Frankfurt for change. The group often socialized together and Jane couldn't help feel that, despite the problems with the UK business, she had a first-class team.

The case of CSS illustrates a number of issues in managing work groups. Both the teams in Germany and the UK have strengths and weaknesses. The European CEO is clear about the path the company needs to take and keeps tight control over his senior management team. However, the 'team' seems to operate more as a group of individuals, with a lack of open discussion and trust between the senior managers, than an effective work team. The CEO seems to be using the group more for information swapping than for frank discussion, collaboration and decision making.

Jane operates with her work team in a more open and honest way, but it may not be any more effective than the more controlled senior management team. Jane's group seems to be focused on the unfairness of their situation rather than solving the UK's problems. It is possible that their norms of cooperation and openness lull them into believing they are effective.

Clearly more data about the two work teams and the issues they face would be needed to draw any concrete conclusions about how their performance might be improved. Nevertheless, the case illustrates that when dealing with work groups, the role of the leader is particularly critical. It is important that he or she is both clear about the purpose of the group and the way it should be managed. What is discussed and the way it is discussed are particularly important in group effectiveness. The norms created by groups can be both positive and negative, which affect how the group deals with its own problems and reacts to the outside world. Leadership style, group dynamics and norms, power, politics, trust and conflict are all issues that affect groups and these are explored through the organizational behaviour subject.

organization level

The third level of analysis is at the 'organization' level. This includes an understanding of organization structure (the formal reporting relationships and groupings), organization culture (the generally accepted way people think and behave in the organization) and the process and systems that guide behaviour overall. Some of the issues at this level are illustrated by the case study of Optus and Telstra in Box 14.4.[17]

BOX 14.4 Optus and Telstra

The telecommunication industry in Australia was originally dominated by a government-owned monopoly, now known as Telstra. In the 1990s, the government deregulated the market in order to increase competition, improve services and cut prices. Several reforms were introduced, including the awarding of a telecommunications licence to Optus in 1991. Other countries, including the UK, had similar experiences in the telecommunications industry at that time.

Telstra was a large, bureaucratic organization operating like a government department. Unions had a strong presence in Telstra and played an important role in the industry. In contrast, Optus was more like a start-up company with a much smaller workforce and without a history of unionization. It was decided to break from the traditional employee–management arrangements found in Telstra. Unions had only a minimal role at Optus.

Optus aimed at taking market share from Telstra by competing in terms of price and customer service. To do this, Optus wished to create a company that was efficient, customer focused and dynamic. Optus executives believed they could do this by creating a flat organization structure, union-free environment and performance-based pay system for all levels of employees, not found at Telstra. They also implemented several strategies to develop what Optus executives argued was a unique culture, emphasizing values of leadership, achievement, teamwork, empowerment and customer satisfaction. Close attention was paid to recruitment and selection. Optus attempted to recruit employees first on attitude and, second, on technical competencies. As a result, approximately 90% of Optus's new employees were between 20 and 25 years old, with a high percentage of recent university graduates. Senior management believed that younger candidates would be less likely to carry cultural baggage from another enterprise.

By the mid-1990s, Optus had won approximately 14% of the long-distance market and a third of the mobile phone market. Some of the major reasons for the company's success were the development of a cohesive and positive corporate culture and a set of work practices that influenced all employees.

Whether one agrees with the approach Optus took or not, the case illustrates how a company managed several organizational components with a specific objective in mind. Optus deliberately set out to create a culture that defined the appropriate behaviour desired from its employees, the internal relations and values. It also set out to create what it saw as a 'positive' culture in contrast to the more bureaucratic culture found in Telstra at that time. In general, the research on organizational culture indicates that a positive culture can improve organizational effectiveness, while a negative culture can considerably inhibit the contributions of individual and group members.

> *Organizational change is the planned attempt to improve the performance of the organization through changing individuals, groups and/or major organizational components such as culture and structure.*

The case also highlights the additional elements that affect behaviour at an organizational level. In addition to an organization's culture, an organization's structure, job design, technology and systems, including reward and financial reporting systems, impact on organizational performance. Exploring ways of aligning these aspects and the implications of adopting one approach over another (as this case illustrates) are also considered in the field of OB.

Managing these broad processes in organizations, however, is not straightforward and there are no guarantees of success. Nevertheless, the study of organizational behaviour highlights the major organizational components that need to be addressed in improving organizational performance. Additionally, and equally important, the discipline is not only concerned with identifying the major organizational elements but how to change them. Organizational change is the planned attempt to improve the performance of the organization through changing individuals, groups and/or major organizational components such as culture and structure. Implementing change in a way that is most likely to lead to improved performance is also a major area of study in OB.

It is also important to remember that these three levels of analysis are linked. Individual performance is related to group performance, which is related to overall organizational performance. Consequently, in looking at behavioural problems, it is important to be aware of the potential implications and knock-on effects in other parts of the organization. Performance at one level may affect what happens at other levels, and it is often necessary to review the team context and the organizational reward systems in order to solve, for example, an individual's lack of motivation. Being able to see the broader implications of managerial decisions and the time frame over which they might occur are critical OB skills.

current challenges for ob

The areas touched on in this chapter are broad ranging and the OB courses on the MBA will explore many of them in more depth. However, there are some contemporary behavioural challenges faced by managers that are worth highlighting here. This illustrates that the field is an applied subject and offers insights and guidelines to some of the most critical issues faced today.

instability and change

One issue is in managing the sheer volume and constant nature of change. Twenty-five years ago, a high degree of order and stability would be expected in the work environment of most people. A major reorganization might be experienced once or twice in an individual's working life. In contrast, the twenty-first century has been notable for, and will continue to be characterized by, change as a continuous activity.

In addition to experiencing large change interventions, such as downsizing or reengineering, most managers will also have to manage constant, incremental and ongoing readjustments within the workplace. Generation X and Y employees are coming to corporations with different philosophies towards work than the baby boomers. There are more women and minority groups in the workplace and the legacy of corporate restructuring, outsourcing and the use of temporary staff is changing the traditional concepts of loyalty and organizational commitment. Moreover, global competition constantly licks at the heels of the inflexible or slow to change.

Additionally, as Robert Kreitner and Angelo Kinicki point out, teams are pushing aside the individual as the primary building block of organizations.[18] Command and control management is giving away to participative management and empowerment. Egocentric leaders are giving away to customer-centric leaders. Employees are increasingly being viewed as internal customers. The new employment contract expects individuals to be a creative self-starters and team players capable of doing a variety of jobs with a diverse array of people. Pay is increasingly tied to results, not to years on the job. Individuals will be expected to take charge of their own career and act more like partners than employees, as discussed in Chapter 8. The new and the old approaches are contrasted in Table 14.1.[19]

Table 14.1 Evolution of the twenty-first century manager

	Past managers	Future managers
Primary role	Order giver, privileged, elite, manipulator, controller	Facilitator, team member, teacher, advocate, sponsor, coach
Learning and knowledge	Periodic learning, narrow specialist	Continuous lifelong learning generalist with many specialties
Compensation criteria	Time, effort, rank	Skills, results
Cultural orientation	Monoculture, monolingual	Multicultural, multilingual
Primary source of influence	Formal authority	Knowledge (technical and interpersonal)
View of people	Potential problem	Primary resource
Primary communication pattern	Vertical	Multidirectional
Decision-making style	Limited input for individual decisions	Broad-based input for joint decisions
Ethical considerations	Afterthought	Forethought
Nature of interpersonal relationships	Competitive (win–lose)	Cooperative (win–win)
Handling of power and key information	Hoard and restrict access	Share and broaden access
Approach to change	Resist	Facilitate

Change affects organizations at all three levels of analysis outlined earlier. At an individual level, work will be characterized by the need for continuous learning, more creative and innovative thinking and greater flexibility. At the group level, the continuous forming and reforming of work teams in order to meet specific client requests, found in consultancy firms like McKinsey, will become more widespread. At the organizational level, most organizations will be in a constant state of flux. British Airways posted a £200 million pre-tax loss in the 2002 financial year, which resulted in cutting 13,000 jobs, slashing short-haul routes and cutting head office costs by one-third. A few years ago this would have been seen as a tragedy, but increasingly this, and the ensuing restructuring that the company faced, is seen as commonplace.

However, while change has become a contemporary phenomenon, the ability to manage change does not seem to have moved at the same pace. A study of 300 medium to large European companies by the consultants AT Kearney found that less than 20% of their change management programmes achieved success.[20] While not being the complete panacea to organizational problems, a study of OB can certainly provide important insights into how change should be implemented, how to overcome resistance to change and how best to create a culture that is more likely to lead to overall success.

managing for competitive advantage

Equally demanding is not just the ability to manage rapid change, but to do so in a way that improves on the status quo and enhances the organization's competitive advantage. Competitive advantage can be created in several ways. It can come through increasing efficiency, improving quality, creativity and innovation or better customer responsiveness. In a survey of over 1,700 managers from 36 countries by the American Management Association, 'customer service' and 'quality' ranked as the corporate world's top two concerns.[21] OB can assist in improvements in all these areas, but two will be mentioned in particular here.

The first is in improving quality. Often discussed in subjects on operations management, quality has also long been seen as an issue that is dependent on how people are managed. Indeed, the total quality management (TQM) movement, which developed during the 1980s and 90s and has had a dramatic impact on the quality of goods and services worldwide, is often defined as an employee-driven improvement process. While the goals of TQM are to create highly loyal customers and minimize the time taken to respond to problems, they also have a strong people component. These include developing a culture that supports teamwork, the design of work systems that increases work motivation and job satisfaction and a focus on continual improvement.[22]

The ongoing development of quality initiatives has also continued to emphasize the management of people. One of the most notable of these initiatives since TQM has been the six sigma quality programme developed by Motorola and most publicized by GE. Six sigma is the ability to operate at a quality level of 3.4 defects per million operations. To make this seemingly impossible target achievable, people need to be constantly thinking about new ways of working, which is an issue that runs throughout OB.

The challenge for managers is to create work environments where creativity and change are the norm rather the exception.

To be ahead of the game, managers need to create cultures where quality initiatives like this can thrive. Indeed, this highlights the second area of competitive advantage, that of creativity and innovation. Companies like Dell, 3M, IBM, Apple, Amazon.com and many others stay at the top of their industries because of their ability to innovate in the way they develop products, bring them to market, or service their customers. Sometimes their amazing creativity goes unnoticed, but what often does become noticeable very quickly is when companies fail to innovate. The demise of companies like British Leyland and others was partly due to tired products delivered in tired ways.

This shows that in some organizations employees can be innovative, flexible and change oriented, while in others change is seen as threatening and negative. The challenge for managers is to create work environments where creativity and change are the norm rather the exception. The field of OB provides many ideas and insights to help achieve this aim.

workforce diversity

Within this overall change milieu, several issues stand out as particular challenges for managers in the coming years. The first of these is managing a diverse workforce. Diversity is concerned with the difference that arises from factors such as personality, age, gender, disability, race, ethnicity, religion, diversity of thought, sexual orientation and socioeconomic background.

> *The challenge is to understand how diversity within an organization affects the way groups and individuals relate to each other and then for the organization as a whole to respond to different needs and perceptions.*

Many companies are experiencing dramatic changes in the make-up of their workforce. For instance, 21% of the 35,800 employees of Australia Post are culturally and linguistically diverse and have emigrated from over 100 countries.[23] However, by itself, knowledge of the demographic composition of a company is of little use. The challenge is to understand how diversity within an organization affects the way groups and individuals relate to each other and then for the organization as a whole to respond to different needs and perceptions.

Numerous organizations have responded positively to these issues, by implementing diversity policies and creating a culture that values difference. More companies have gone beyond ensuring that no employee is disadvantaged because of difference and have looked at ways of benefiting from workforce diversity. The American law firm Dewey and Levine, for example, has expanded its range of work to reflect the broader interests of its own workforce, taking on cases particular to some minority groups that it would not normally have considered.[24]

However, despite the efforts made by many companies, diversity will provide many challenges in the future. Indeed, in many ways, we have only scratched the surface in understanding and effectively managing these issues. For example, a company which prides itself on its approach to diversity is GE. However, an article in the *New York Times* reported: 'Of the 20 businesses that provided 90 percent of G.E.'s earnings in 1999, only one is headed by someone who is not white.' Jack Welch accepted that GE wasn't 'where we want to be yet'.[25] Neither, quite possibly, are a lot of the other model companies.

> *If managed effectively, diversity can enrich an organization by allowing a range of ideas and approaches to be applied to many different problems. However, where diversity is not managed appropriately, there is a much greater chance of conflict, miscommunication and dissatisfaction among some employees.*

If managed effectively, diversity can enrich an organization by allowing a range of ideas and approaches to be applied to many different problems. However, where diversity is not managed appropriately, there is a much greater chance of conflict, miscommunication and dissatisfaction among some employees. While the field of OB may not provide easy answers to the challenges of managing a diverse workforce, it does help in sensitizing managers to the issues and provide potential roads forward.

globalization

Related to this is the challenge of managing globalization. This has particular implications for the management of people. Managers have to become capable of working with people from different cultures for two reasons. The first is related to the diversity challenge discussed above. More and more domestic work environments are characterized by people from all over the world. This also implies that customers and consumers will be more international in their outlook and companies will have to respond to these differing needs.

The second issue likely to be particularly significant for ambitious and mobile MBA graduates is in working overseas and managing in a global environment. Many multinational and international companies not only have to manage activities in several countries, but also coordinate activities across national boundaries. This requires that managers, possibly with one cultural view of the world, have to understand how to motivate and lead employees within a different cultural context. However, many companies have not yet fully come to terms with the challenge. Daniel Meiland, the executive chairman of Egon Zhender International has commented:

We have always talked about the global executive, but the need to find managers who can be effective in many different settings is growing even more urgent. In addition to looking for intelligence, specific skills and technical insights, companies are also looking for executives who are comfortable on the world stage … And yet we have a lot to learn … Many companies haven't been all that successful at developing global executives from within … The intentions are good, but the fact is, practice hasn't caught up with intent.[26]

The development of global managers is a challenge that will accelerate as the world economy expands and more companies grow to meet this challenge. The field of OB can give insights into finding solutions for many of the individual, team and cultural imperatives that confront global organizations.

leadership and empowerment

There are literally thousands of published research papers on the nature of leadership and the term has taken on a multitude of meanings, encouraging managers to be everything from coaches and facilitators to visionaries and role models.

Possibly one of the most challenging ongoing requirements of managers is to become effective leaders. Except for the political and military arenas, leadership was largely only of academic interest until the mid-1980s. Since then, however, it has become (and will continue to be) a subject of critical practical importance.

It is important because the turbulent economic environment in which most companies operate requires those in positions of responsibility to provide direction and motivation in a chaotic world. However, what form that direction and motivation takes is of considerable debate, as noted in Chapter 7. There are literally thousands of published research papers on the nature of leadership and the term has taken on a multitude of meanings, encouraging managers to be everything from coaches and facilitators to visionaries and role models.

As a result, the boundaries between the responsibilities and roles of the manager/leader and the employee/associate have become blurred. The dominant trend has been towards empowering employees; giving them much more accountability and control over their work environment, with the subsequent loss of decision-making power by those leading them. Consequently, both employees and managers have had to learn how to work with different relationships and responsibilities.

> Despite the ambiguity and changing nature of the leadership/management role, it is vitally important that the new age managers explore their own leadership strengths and limitations.

The thrust towards pushing decision making down the organization and empowering employees is unlikely to take a step backwards. But it is also unlikely that the 'right' style of leadership will be found for all circumstances. As the reasons for Carly Fiorina's demise at Hewlett-Packard continue to be debated and Doug Daft's lack of presence at Coca-Cola discussed, what does seem to be clear is that there are many different roads to leadership success or lack of it. Whether it be celebrity leaders, like Jack Welch and Michael Eisner, or leaders with more humility like Robert Iger at Disney, leadership in the twenty-first century can take many and varied forms.

Despite the ambiguity and changing nature of the leadership/management role, it is vitally important that the new age managers explore their own leadership strengths and limitations. While it is unclear whether leadership can be taught, collectively we have a much better understanding of the nature of leadership than we did 20 years ago. The field of OB can provide MBA students with many insights into what leadership involves and potential ways of developing the appropriate skills.

the new employee contract: loyalty and motivation

One of the reasons why leadership in work organizations has become particularly challenging is because of the restructuring that many firms have undergone. The move to leaner organizations, with the perception that people are expendable, has resulted in many employees becoming less committed to their organizations. Indeed, IBISWorld predicts that in another 20 years or so many of us will be contractors working for virtual companies, with loyalty towards our peers and colleagues rather than an employer.[27]

> One of the reasons why leadership in work organizations has become particularly challenging is because of the restructuring that many firms have undergone. The move to leaner organizations, with the perception that people are expendable, has resulted in many employees becoming less committed to their organizations.

Even today many writers perceive a shift in the employment contract – the psychological calculation of the contribution the individual makes for an assumed reward or return. Kreitner and Kinicki suggest that there has been a shift from a 'relational contract' to a 'transactional contract'.[28] They argue that for employees committed to lifelong learning, working smarter rather than harder and making their own opportunities, the new employment contract situation is positive. Promotions will be fewer and slower than before because of a flatter organization with fewer layers. But lateral moves from one project or function to another will provide lots of challenges for those who get results. However, this will only be positive, even for those employees who have come to terms with the new psychological contract, if companies uphold their end of the deal.

Chris Lee and Jean Bethke Elshtain highlight a survey of 3,300 Towers Perrin staff, which found that most respondents were willing to take responsibility for their careers and for producing value for the company, as long as the company delivered meaningful rewards for goals achieved, support for skill development, honest communication about mutual objectives and reasonable flexibility in the work environment. But employers weren't delivering consistently: 41% of respondents disagreed when asked if policies were administered fairly and consistently, 45% did not think their company hired the most qualified people for jobs and 52% saw a gap between pay and the level of performance the company demanded. Organizations tend to get what they give. Companies that fail to deliver on the main factors perceived to be central to the new psychological contract will reap the results in terms of a downturn in loyalty, motivation and trust.[29]

> the challenge for managers is to maintain employee commitment to the organization while implementing the changes needed to stay globally competitive

Unfortunately, the Towers Perrin experience may not be unusual. A Watson Wyatt survey in 2002 of 13,000 workers in the USA found that fewer than two out of five employees trust senior leaders.[30] Thus, the challenge for managers is to maintain employee commitment to the organization while implementing the changes needed to stay globally competitive, an issue at the core of OB.

ethical behaviour

There have been many recent events throughout the world that have raised the issue of ethical business behaviour. These have ranged from the collapse of major corporations to the jailing of CEOs because of their illegal and inappropriate actions. Bernard Ebbers of WorldCom, Dennis Kozlowski at Tyco International and Jeffrey Skilling of Enron will all go down in history for their fraudulent behaviour rather than their business acumen. Even Martha Stewart, the homemaking guru, received a jail term for lying to Federal investigators.

> It is difficult to establish whether behaviour has become more unethical or more people are being caught, although the latter seems more likely. Certainly, what seems to have been acceptable 20 years ago is not acceptable today, whether this be the harassment of individuals in the workplace, covering up defective products or destroying documents that implicate wrongdoers.

It is difficult to establish whether behaviour has become more unethical or more people are being caught, although the latter seems more likely. Certainly, what seems to have been acceptable 20 years ago is not acceptable today, whether this be the harassment of individuals in the workplace, covering up defective products or destroying documents that implicate wrongdoers. Indeed, it is not just illegal behaviour that can ruin careers, as the sacking of Harry Stonecipher as CEO of Boeing in March 2005, shows. His relationship with a member of staff, which transgressed his own code of conduct, indicates, at least in some quarters, the raising of the ethical bar to new heights.

As Jennifer George and Gareth Jones point out, ethics establishes the goals that organizations should pursue and the way in which people inside organizations should behave to achieve them.[31] Ethics also defines an organization's social and moral responsibility towards individuals or groups outside the organization that are directly affected by its actions. However, there are no universal guidelines on what is good ethical behaviour and the line between right and wrong will often be blurred.

This means that managers cannot define away ethical dilemmas. However, what they can do, through studying OB, is minimize their occurrence and create a climate where employees can work productively, safely and with as little ambiguity as possible around the boundaries of what is and is not tolerated by the organization.

conclusion

This chapter has provided an outline of some of the main benefits of studying organizational behaviour and how it can help MBA students as current and future managers in overcoming the many challenges faced in working with people. The subject is wide ranging, but one that will reap considerable benefits from thoughtful and regular reflection of the issues. While the subject does not provide certainty, it does provide insight and possibilities. While studying the field cannot guarantee you will become a role model manager, it will certainly enable you to become better than you are today.

> While studying the field cannot guarantee you will become a role model manager, it will certainly enable you to become better than you are today.

references

1. George, J.M. and Jones, G.J. (1996) *Understanding and Managing Organizational Behaviour* (New York: Addison-Wesley) pp. 1–2.
2. Stewart, T.A. (1999) 'Who will run GE?', *Fortune*, 11 January, p. 27.
3. Luthans, F. (1995) *Organizational Behaviour* (New York: McGraw-Hill) p. 3.
4. Pfeffer, J. and Veiga, J.F. (1999) 'Putting people first for organizational success', *Academy of Management Executive*, **13**(2): 37–49.
5. Northcraft, G.B. and Neale, M.A. (1994) *Organizational Behaviour: A Management Challenge* (Orlando, FL: Harcourt Brace) p. 5.
6. Robbins, S.P. (2000) *Essentials of Organizational Behaviour* (Englewood Cliffs, NJ: Prentice Hall) p. 2.
7. *Australian Financial Review*, 4 June 2002.
8. *Australian Financial Review*, 1 April 2005.
9. Op. cit. George and Jones (1996).
10. Adapted from Mintzberg, H. (1973) *The Nature of Managerial Work* (New York: Harper & Row) pp. 54–99.
11. Op. cit. Northcraft and Neale (1994) p. 5.
12. Kreitner, R. and Kinicki, A. (2001) *Organizational Behaviour* (New York: McGraw-Hill) pp. 77–380.
13. According to Luthans, F. (1995) *Organizational Behaviour* (New York: McGraw-Hill) p. 12.
14. Robbins, S.P. (2000) *Essentials of Organizational Behaviour* (Englewood Cliffs, NJ: Prentice Hall) p. 3.
15. Luthans, F. (1995) *Organizational Behaviour* (New York: McGraw-Hill) p. 15.
16. Op. cit. Robbins (2000).
17. From Simmons, D.E., Shadur, M.A. and Bamber, G.J. (1996) 'Optus: new recruitment and selection in an enterprise culture', in J. Storey (ed.) *Blackwell Cases in Human Resource and Change Management* (Oxford: Blackwell) pp. 147–59.
18. Op. cit. Kreitner and Kinicki (2001) p. 8.
19. From Kreitner and Kinicki (2001) op. cit., p. 8.
20. *The Age*, 25 November 2002.
21. 'AMA global survey on key business issues', *Management Review*, December 1998, p. 30.
22. Tosi, H.L., Mero, N.P. and Rizzo, J.R. (2000) *Managing Organizational Behaviour* (Oxford: Blackwell) p. 180.
23. *Australia Post's Workforce Becomes More Diverse*, www.auspost.com.au, February 2003.
24. From Thomas, D.A. and Ely, R.J. (1996) 'Making differences matter: a new paradigm for managing diversity,' *Harvard Business Review*, September/October, p. 85.
25. Bond, N., *Next Step*, www.diversityatwork.com/articles/Diversity100.htm.
26. 'In search of global leaders', *Harvard Business Review*, August 2003, pp. 38–45.

27. *Australian Financial Review*, 16 July 2002.
28. Op. cit. Kreitner and Kinicki (2001).
29. Lee, C. and Bethke Elshtain, J. (1997) 'Trust me: employees' trust in their employers', *Training: The Human Side of Business*, 34(1). 20.
30. From the Watson Wyatt website – www.watsonwyatt.com – 17 August 2003.
31. George, J.M. and Jones, G.J. (1996) *Understanding and Managing Organizational Behaviour* (New York: Addison-Wesley) p. 19.

15 marketing

professor michael baker

Marketing is an enigma:

> It is the foundation of the modern global economy, but is often seen as some kind of 'selling with knobs on'.
> It is the oldest of the business practices, but among the newest, if not the newest, of the business disciplines.
> It is a philosophy of business, and a practical business function.
> It is seen as past its sell-by date, and the driving force behind commercial success.

And so we could go on. In this chapter, our aim is to explore these apparent contradictions with a view to explaining why it is that Peter Drucker, one of the founding fathers of modern management, should assert: 'There are only two functions of a business – innovation and marketing.'

To begin with, we will offer a brief history of the origins and evolution of the modern marketing concept, as we believe knowledge of these is vital to understanding, and possibly explaining, our enigma. It will also help to account for the plethora of definitions of marketing. Next, we will address the question of the role of marketing in the modern economy and the modern organization. This is a particularly pertinent issue at the present time, as the emerging economies of Brazil, Russia, India and China (the BRIC countries) challenge the dominance of the affluent postindustrial economies of the USA, Western Europe, Japan, Australasia and so on. Third, we will explore the contribution of marketing to the strategic direction of all organizations – public and private, for profit and not-for-profit, large and small. And then we will look at the application of marketing to day-to-day operations through the management of the so-called 'marketing mix'. Finally, we will speculate on marketing's role in the future.

a brief history of marketing

It is beyond doubt that modern civilization owes its existence to the practice of marketing. Even in the subsistence economies of prehistory, when life was 'nasty, brutish and short', marketing offered a better standard of living than could be achieved through attempts at self-sufficiency. Long before the discovery of agriculture or the domestication of animals, gender encouraged role specialization, with males responsible for hunting and security, and females for gathering and child rearing. But the real breakthrough in human development occurred when specialization extended to the performance of the many tasks necessary for survival. The benefit of task specialization is that it increases output or productivity so there is more of everything to go around. But, for this

> It is beyond doubt that modern civilization owes its existence to the practice of marketing.

to happen, specialists must be able to exchange their surpluses for goods and services provided by others. Now, the gains from task specialization will soon be dissipated if we have to spend a lot of time trying to make contact with persons with a coincidence of wants – we each have something the other needs so we can negotiate an exchange. Obviously, we need a central place where anyone with something to exchange can meet up with other like-minded individuals, and this place is the *market*.

Over time, increased specialization encouraged permanent settlement in locations with natural advantages and trade between them. To manage this trade, a medium of exchange (money) had to be created, as had writing and accounting to keep a record of stocks and transactions (Phoenicians, *c*.4000 BC). In time, the search for greater variety and choice prompted trade between nations, exploration and wars. However, the great breakthrough in economic growth came in the eighteenth century with the Industrial Revolution in Great Britain.

The Industrial Revolution, which gave birth to modern society, was the consequence of three major developments:

❶ The application of science and technology to production and distribution.

❷ The division of labour.

❸ Entrepreneurial management.

The division of labour was described eloquently by Adam Smith in his *Wealth of Nations* (1776). Smith's description of this primitive production line identified at least ten different tasks:

One man draws out the wire, another straightens it, a third cuts it, a fourth points it, a fifth grinds it at the top for receiving the head; the head requires two or three distinct operations; to put it on is a peculiar business, to whiten the pins is another; it is even a trade by itself to put them into the paper.

Two points are of particular significance in this step forward. First, organization is required to bring together the men, provide a workplace and source raw materials. Second, the enormous increase in output reduces the price of the product, necessitates the development of channels of distribution to make it available to those with a demand for it, and leads to the exploitation of a much larger market. It also means that the 'factory' tends to produce standardized products and no longer makes to the order of individual customers.

The 'rediscovery' of marketing and the emergence of the modern marketing concept is generally attributed to the USA in the 1950s. As we shall see, several prominent names are associated with this event; a key contributor being Robert Keith, who followed a historical approach in identifying what has become known as the 'three eras' conceptualization – production, sales and marketing.[1]

Keith identified these three different eras based on the evolution of the Pillsbury Company in the USA. Pillsbury was, and still is, a manufacturer of bakery products, a category of what are generically termed *fast moving consumer goods* or 'fmcg'. In the mid-nineteenth century, its emphasis was on increasing supply and reducing costs – the primary characteristics of a 'production orientation'. As new companies entered the market and competition intensified, more emphasis was given to selling differentiated products, but this differentiation was based on what the firm could make using its existing technology and assets. So the distinguishing feature of a 'sales orientation' is '*selling what we can make*'.

But, with the potential for excess supply as a result of rapid economic growth, it became clear that selling harder needed to be replaced by selling *smarter*. Selling smarter means that, before committing yourself to the sale of a new product in the hope of maintaining competitiveness, you need first to establish what it is the customer wants. In the days of craft industry, this was relatively simple – the potential customer discussed their wants with you, and you produced what they had specified. But, with industrialization and the concentration of production in factories, a physical separation developed between producer and customer, which, in time, became a psychological separation too. As long as demand exceeds supply, then customers can't afford to be too choosy, and have to buy what is available. But, as variety and choice increase, customers will prefer those sellers whose offering most closely matches their needs – usually those who are closest to the customer – and others will go out of business for lack of custom. So, in order to restore and maintain competitiveness, a new strategy is called for, based on determining what the customer wants and then *making what we can sell*. It is this that we call a 'marketing orientation'.

Keith's description of the evolution of Pillsbury and the identification of three eras is not universally accepted. Gilbert and Bailey dismiss this so-called 'traditional view' and comment:

Such a view infers that a sales orientation did not exist during (or before) the production era but came into being as a result of supply exceeding demand. Similarly, it suggests that marketing practices were not developed until it became apparent that pushing goods on to the market was not as effective as focusing on the provision of satisfaction.[2]

In order for the two suppositions above to be true, the 'marketing era' school of thought makes the following inferences:

> Neither sales nor marketing practices were fully applied in business until towards the end of the production era, which lasted until the 1930s.
> Sophisticated marketing practices were not incorporated into business operations until the 1950s.
> There was little or no competition in the marketplace during the production era when demand exceeded supply.
> Firms gave little thought to marketing before and during the production era.

Clearly, these suppositions are unrealistic – you only have to vist the souk in Cairo or a bazaar in India to realize immediately that merchants have always worked hard to sell their wares. Whether or not this amounts to what we call marketing today is a matter of debate.

Nowadays most people regard marketing as synonomous with selling. In fact, the verb 'to market' has both a transitive and an intransitive form, one meaning 'to buy' and the other 'to sell'.

Nowadays most people regard marketing as synonomous with selling. In fact, the verb 'to market' has both a transitive and an intransitive form, one meaning 'to buy' and the other 'to sell'. So marketing is really about both buying and selling. It is claimed that the popularity of the term marketing came about because Procter & Gamble needed a name to describe the integration of its operating divisions responsible for advertising, promotion, trade and so on into a single overarching function. P&G asked: 'What do housewives say?' The answer: 'I am going to do my marketing today' – hence marketing.

defining marketing

While it is clear that marketing has been practised for millennia, interest in it as a subject of formal study only developed in the second half of the nineteenth century in the USA, in association with the rapid development of agriculture and industry. In turn this led to the establishment of 'land grant' universities in states with farm-based economies, and business schools in universities in industrial cities like Pittsburgh and Chicago. The first professorial chair in the subject was created at the Wharton School of the University of Pennsylvania in the 1880s and was soon followed by many more. To begin with the focus was on production and distribution as these were the principal challenges – how to increase output and make that output available to those with a demand for it.

As we have seen, this emphasis changed in the 1930s and again in the 1950s as the focus switched to selling and then marketing as we know it today. Below we offer a selection of definitions of marketing from 1920 to the present day in chronological order:

1 The function of marketing is the establishment of contact.[3]

2 Marketing is the process of determining consumer demand for a product or service, motivating its sale and distributing it into ultimate consumption at a profit.[4]

3 Marketing is not only much broader than selling, it is not a specialized activity at all. It encompasses the entire business. It is the whole business seen from the point of view of its final result, that is, from the customer's point of view. Concern and responsibility for marketing must therefore permeate all areas of the enterprise.[5]

4 Marketing is distinguishing the unique function of the business.[6]

5 Marketing is the performance of business activities that direct the flow of goods and services from producer to consumer or user:[7]
> Marketing is the creation of time, place and possession utilities
> Marketing moves goods from place to place, stores them, and effects changes in ownership by buying and selling them
> Marketing consists of the activities of buying, selling, transporting and storing goods
> Marketing includes those business activities involved in the flow of goods and services between producers and consumers.

6 Marketing is the process whereby society, to supply its consumption needs, evolves distributive systems composed of participants, who, interacting under constraints – technical (economic) and ethical (social) – create the transactions or flows that resolve market separations and result in exchange and consumption.[8]

7 Marketing is the set of human activities directed at facilitating and consummating exchanges.[9]

8 Marketing is concerned with the creation and maintenance of mutually satisfying exchange relationships.[10]

9 The purpose of a business is to create and keep a customer.[11]

10 Marketing is the business function that identifies current unfilled needs and wants, defines and measures their magnitude, determines which target markets the organization can best serve, and decides on appropriate products, services, and programmes to serve these markets. Thus, marketing serves as the link between a society's needs and its pattern of industrial response.[12]

11 Marketing is both a set of activities performed by organizations and a social process. In other words, marketing exists at both the micro- and macro-levels. Micro-marketing is the performance of activities that seek to accomplish an organization's objectives by anticipating customer or client needs and directing a flow of need-satisfying goods and services from producer to customer or client. Macro-marketing is a social process that directs an economy's flow of goods and services from producers to consumers in a way that effectively matches supply and demand and accomplishes the objectives of society.[13]

12 Marketing is the management process responsible for identifying, anticipating and satisfying consumer's requirements profitably.[14]

13 Activities that facilitate and expedite satisfying exchange relationships through the creation, distribution, promotion and pricing of products (goods, services, ideas).[15]

14 Today we see the marketing concept as a statement of organizational culture, an agreed-on set of shared values among the employees of a company representing a commitment to put the customer first in all management and operations decision making. It calls for everyone in the organization to think about their job in terms of how it delivers value to customers.[16]

15 Marketing is selling goods that don't come back to people who do. (Anon)

16 The delivery of a standard of living. (Anon.)

17 Marketing is an organizational function and a set of processes for creating, communicating and delivering value to customers and for managing customer relationships in ways that benefit the organization and its stakeholders.[17]

As we progress through this chapter, many of the ideas encapsulated in these definitions will arise. The problem is that most of the definitions are not particularly memorable – especially those that try to include everything, like 10, 11 and 12 – while those that don't are usually too vague to be of much practical use. However, as Keith Crosier observed, after reviewing more than 50 definitions in the 1970s, we can see that they fall into three distinct categories. First, there are definitions that conceive of marketing as a *process*. Second, there are those that see marketing as a *concept* or *philosophy of business*. And, third, there are those that emphasize marketing as an *orientation*.

The 'marketing as a process' school dominated thinking in the late nineteenth century through to about 1930. It was strongly associated with the land grant universities in the USA, with a concern for the selling and distribution of primary agricultural products, and the new business schools, mainly endowed by wealthy industrialists who had strong interests in industrial products and what we now call business-to-business marketing (B2B). Individual consumers were of limited interest and the economic concepts of competition and market forces commanded most attention.

The 'marketing as a concept' school began to emerge in the 1930s, when the experiences of the Great Depression made it clear that producers could not continue to expect an ever-growing demand to absorb all their output when competing mainly on price and the sale of largely undifferentiated products. Clearly, adopting the assumption that consumers are homogeneous did not reflect the reality. The theory of perfect or monopolistic competition began to give way to the theory of imperfect competition, and an acceptance that consumers are heterogeneous. This being so, it is necessary to develop an understanding of consumer needs, and then create products and services to satisfy them – the essence of the marketing concept. In turn, this directed attention towards the behavioural sciences, and particularly psychology and sociology. However, the main emphasis was on demand stimulation through advertising and personal selling.

the marketing concept and marketing management

The best known description of the modern marketing concept appeared in a seminal article by Ted Levitt called 'Marketing myopia'. Levitt opens by stating: 'Every major industry was once a growth industry', but he goes on to point out that many such industries are now in a state of stagnation or decline. The reason – 'a failure of management'.[18]

Simply put, Levitt's thesis is that new industries come into existence because innovators and entrepreneurs discover new and better ways of meeting people's needs. As this becomes known, customers gradually switch their allegiance from the old to the new, and the old industry declines while the other grows to take its place. Thus, like biological organisms, every product and every industry has a life cycle, hence the 'product life cycle' concept (PLC). In my view, this is both an original and powerful idea, appreciation of which is vital to the avoidance of 'failures of management' due to myopia. But this view is not held universally, as many critics see the PLC as misleading and incapable of implementation.

In essence, the product life cycle concept proposes that every product and service, if it runs to its full term, comprises four major phases, as illustrated in Figure 15.1.

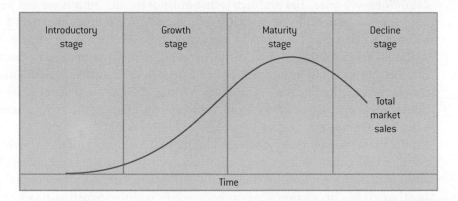

Figure 15.1 The 'normalized' product life cycle

Now, the qualification 'if it runs to full term' is rarely, if ever, found – certainly not among those who are critical of the idea. As with biological organisms, it is clear that many are stillborn or die in infancy – hence the high failure rate for new products. However, if they do survive infancy, it is likely that they will enjoy a normal life expectancy and experience growth, maturity and decline. It is also clear that, depending on the species (type of product), the actual length of each phase may vary enormously.

Second, our 'normalized' PLC has a shape similar to that of a normal distribution, but when one plots sales against time (the parameters of the PLC), such a smooth curve rarely results for any given product or service. This should not be surprising because, as the law of large numbers makes clear, if we repeat an action many times, such as tossing a coin or throwing a dice, the laws of probability lead us to expect that a plot of the results, in terms of combinations and permutations, would assume that of a normal distribution, confirming the deterministic nature of the process.

Third, critics assume that the PLC is an immutable process and not amenable to (managerial) intervention. Clearly, this assumed flaw must be invalid, because if it were true, then all PLCs would assume the same shape, which we have agreed they don't. So, as with human lives, an accident or an unforseen event may terminate a life prematurely, while medical care may extend it significantly.

So the critics dismiss the PLC because they cannot use it as a predictive device for any given product or service, failing to appreciate that no actuary would ever presume to predict the life expectancy of a named individual, while being perfectly happy to write a policy averaging the life expectancy of all persons of a given age. And even then, pestilence, famine or war could distort the projection.

The reality is that the PLC is a guide to strategic thinking that emphasizes the inevitability of change and the importance of continuous innovation to survive. In illustrating the concept, Levitt used some examples that have not stood the test of time – the revival of the railways and electric street cars being cases in point. But his underlying message remains true: 'When a man goes into a hardware store to buy a ¼" drill, he needs a ¼" hole'. Only as long as the ¼" drill remains the most satisfactory means to the desired end will it remain in demand. The day that Black & Decker launch their new hand-held laser drill that can make holes of any chosen diameter (and depth) in any material you care to think of, the twist drill industry is as dead as the dodo.

Management's failure is to think of means rather than ends, of products rather than customers:

The view that an industry is a customer-satisfying process, not a goods-producing process, is vital for all businessmen to understand. An industry begins with the customer and his needs, not with a patent, a raw material, or a selling skill. Given the customers' needs, the industry develops backwards, first concerning itself with the physical delivery of customer satisfactions. Then it moves further backwards to creating the things by which these satisfactions are in part achieved. How these materials are created is a matter of indifference to the customer, hence the particular form of manufacturing, processing, or what have you cannot be considered as a vital aspect of the industry.[19]

marketing: philosophy and function

Levitt's 'Marketing myopia' is intrinsically concerned with marketing as a philosophy of business – a guiding principle that argues that supply is subservient to demand. The adoption of this principle is often referred to as being 'marketing oriented', but, in recent years, a distinction has begun to develop between a *marketing* orientation and a *market* orientation. While this may appear to be a semantic quibble, it is an important one, for reasons we will try to make clear.

As we have seen, the marketing era is regarded as the logical successor of the preceding production and sales eras, which emphasized the creation of an increased supply to keep up with a rapidly growing demand. But, as a result of technological innovation and a slowing down of population growth, a potential for excess supply developed that called for more careful attention to customers' needs. In the days of craft industry, potential customers interacted directly with suppliers and specified their wants precisely. But, as Adam Smith's example of the pin-making industry shows, the division of labour and the establishment of factories led to mass production of standardized, undifferentiated products. To dispose of this vast increase in supply, manufacturers had to access much larger geographical markets, new channels of distribution, and employ the services of salesmen and intermediaries – wholesalers and retailers to reach their potential customers. This increase in physical distance between the producer and consumer also led to a psychological distance and it was this that prompted the need to rediscover the marketing concept.

So long as demand exceeds supply, most customers will be willing to accept what the seller has to offer. But, when the position is reversed, the only way in which sellers can encourage customers to prefer their offerings over their competitors is to differentiate them in some meaningful way. Of course, what is 'meaningful' depends entirely on what the intending buyer perceives it to be; the only sure way to establish this is to eliminate the psychological gap by making direct contact with potential buyers. The emphasis now is on making what we can sell rather than selling what we make.

In mass markets for undifferentiated goods, demand is determined by availability and price. So, when such goods are freely available, price becomes the sole determinant, and the firm with the lowest costs will dominate the market. This is a strategy of cost leadership and it was the one pursued by Henry Ford in creating and then dominating the mass market for automobiles between 1910 and 1925. When Ford first conceived of mass assembly as a means of making low-cost cars widely available, his ambition was to sell a car for $500 – greatly below the going market price. Ford had no idea how many cars he could sell at this price, but you don't need a doctorate in economics to know that the lower the price, the greater the quantity demanded and vice versa – a relationship illustrated by the 'normal' demand curve in Figure 15.2.

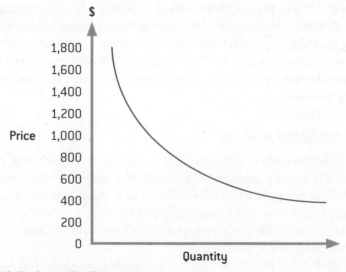

Figure 15.2 The 'normalized' demand curve

By 1916, Ford had two-thirds of a greatly expanded US auto market and was selling his Model T for $258 – a price no other manufacturer could match. From Alfred Sloan's *My Years at General Motors*, we know that this was precisely the problem facing the Product Policy Committee when it met in April 1924 – in fact, GM could not make a car at Ford's selling price.

Now whether GM's decision was based on formal consideration of the normal demand curve or not, the logic of it was. Consider Ford's selling price estimated at $250 and GM's manufacturing cost at $350, as shown in Figure 15.3; every unit of demand to the left of these points is prepared to pay more for a differentiated product. So, if you would like a coloured car rather than Ford's universal black, the question is 'How much would you be prepared to pay?' Probably not $100. However, GM conceived of producing a range of models with different specifications and price points, and introducing new models every year so everyone could tell how old/new your car was. Further, to encourage new sales, GM offered to buy back your old car in part exchange, which it could then resell, often for less than the cost of a new, but undifferentiated Model T.

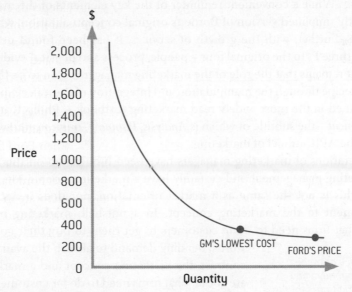

Figure 15.3 Ford vs GM's demand curve

GM had adopted a strategy of market segmentation and developed a range or portfolio of products catering for the needs of customers with varying needs and buying power. Sloan wrote:

Having thus separated out a set of related price classes, we set forth an intricate strategy which can be summarized as follows: We proposed in general that General Motors should place its cars at the top of each price range and make them of such a quality that they would attract sales from below that price, selling to those customers who might be willing to pay a little more for the additional quality, and attract sales from above that price, selling to those customers who would see the price advantage in a car of close to quality of higher-priced competition. This amounted to quality competition against cars below a given price tag, and price competition against cars above that price tag.[20]

Now, all firms are not large enough to have a range of products for every segment, and they will choose a 'focus strategy' and target specific niche markets. Irrespective of which strategy you follow, the seller needs to differentiate their output from their competitors – product differentiation – and to do so have adopted the practice of branding.

All these strategies and practices existed prior to the formal articulation of the marketing concept in the 1950s, raising the question 'What changed then?' Essentially, the pent-up demand for consumer goods created by the Second World War was satiated in the USA, and competition had become acute in domestic markets. To survive under these conditions, and avoid the consequences of a deflationary spiral, one must understand the needs of the market precisely and what it is that motivates customers to behave the way they do. Based on this understanding, one can then tailor the *product* to the needs of one's target market, make it available in a convenient *place* at an attractive *price* and communicate these facts through appropriate *promotion* – hence the '4Ps' of the marketing mix.

The notion of the 4Ps was popularized by Eugene McCarthy in his standard textbook *Basic Marketing*, which has been the foundation of the marketing curriculum for almost 50 years.[21] While a convenient reminder of the key elements of the marketing mix, it is a greatly simplified version of Borden's original conceptualization, which has twelve elements. Further, with the growth of services, it has been found necessary to add another three Ps to the original four – people, process and physical evidence. However, the point remains that the role of the marketing manager is seen to be the creation of a unique recipe through the manipulation and integration of the mix elements. This view is enshrined in the most widely read marketing textbook – Philip Kotler's *Marketing Management* – the subtitle of which is *Analysis, Planning, Implementation and Control*.[22] Hence the APIC model of marketing.

Generations of marketing managers have been brought up on the Kotlerian view of marketing management and certainly have a marketing orientation. But, as hinted earlier, this is not the same as a market orientation, nor does it necessarily reflect commitment to the marketing concept. In a nutshell, marketing management is about what firms need to do *to* customers to get them to buy their goods – in other words, bending demand to absorb the available supply. By contrast, the marketing concept and a market orientation are about what firms need to do *for* customers to earn their patronage, goodwill, trust, commitment and, ultimately, their loyalty. In recent years, this apparently fine distinction between doing things *to* people and *for* people has become encapsulated in what is known as 'relationship marketing'.

The key difference between marketing management and relationship marketing is that the former is a functional approach to physically managing the marketing mix elements, while the latter promotes the view that, to be successful, an organization needs to bend all its efforts to the satisfaction of its customers – a cultural or philosophical view derived from the marketing concept.

the origins of relationship marketing

During the 1980s, marketing suffered what McKinsey described as a 'mid-life crisis'.

From being the driving force behind competitive strategy, marketing was seen to have lost its edge, with one firm's marketing activitities cancelling out another's. This was not a new phenomenon. In 1970, Charles Ames published a paper in the *Harvard Business Review* entitled 'Trappings vs substance in industrial marketing', in which he addressed criticisms from senior management in industrial, or business-to-business (B2B) firms, that while marketing appeared to underpin the success of fast moving consumer goods firms, it didn't seem to work for them.[23] Ames' explanation was that they had mistaken the 'trappings' of marketing – especially advertising and promotion – for the 'substance' – the identification of customer needs and the creation of goods and services to satisfy them. In the absence of an equivalent or better product, no amount of promotional effort would persuade a buyer even to consider buying from such a firm. To be successful in a competitive market, one must be seen to offer additional values to those that define the basic product or service, and it is the creation of these that is the main challenge for the prospective seller. Traditionally, product life cycles were longer but, as a result of firms seeking to gain a sustainable competitive advantage (SCA) through the creation of observable attributes and features, increased emphasis was given to technological innovation and new product development (NPD). The problem with observable attributes and features is just that – your competitors can see them too, benchmark them, improve on them and launch a new, improved version of their own. So, continuous NPD has become essential for survival – success calls for something more.

> To be successful in a competitive market, one must be seen to offer additional values to those that define the basic product or service, and it is the creation of these that is the main challenge for the prospective seller.

The important point to remember is that what qualifies as 'something more' is based on the perception of the buyer. In 1924, Melvin Copeland of the Harvard Business School published a classification of goods based on the buyer's perception of them – convenience, shopping and specialty goods.[24] Convenience goods are usually low-cost items that we buy frequently, often with little conscious thought or effort – hence they are known as low involvement goods. By contrast, shopping goods cost more, are purchased less frequently and often differ from one another in important ways that change over time. The purchase of such goods incurs medium to high involvement on the part of the buyer. Finally, specialty goods are those that have a particular significance for the buyer and always have high involvement. The point about specialty goods is that to others they may be seen as convenience or shopping goods – if you will only drink Coca-Cola and accept no other cola-flavoured drink, then it is a specialty good for you. Most of us literally couldn't care less and will accept the brand available. To understand what creates what has been called the 'unique selling point' (USP), or 'just noticeable difference' (JND), we need to have a clear understanding of what motivates buyer behaviour. It is for this reason that the study of buyer behaviour – both individual and organizational – is at the heart of the marketing process. Further, in order to determine why buyers behave the way they do, and to identify the specific factors that differentiate their behaviour, it is necessary to undertake qualitative research in addition to the more familiar quantitative studies based on geodemographics and objective measures.

As a result of such research, it has become clear that buyers use many kinds of subjective information in coming to a decision. Such information consists of activities, interests and opinions – hence AIO research. Based on AIO, it has become clear that in order to manage the huge amounts of information to which we are exposed, we develop patterns of habitual behaviour by 'chunking' this information. Perhaps the most obvious example of this is the importance of brand names and corporate reputation for decision making. Recognition of this has resulted in what is generally referred to as 'relationship marketing.'

Thirty years ago, as one of the founding professors of marketing in the UK, I was asked for a single-sentence definition of my subject. Based on six years' experience of selling in the steel industry, and ten years studying and teaching marketing, I suggested: 'Marketing is concerned with the creation and maintenance of mutually satisfying exchange relationships.'[25] In other words, a win–win approach to business as opposed to the zero-sum view of marketing management, which conceives of competition involving 'winners' and 'losers'.

Now it is quite clear that there are many kinds of relationships, from close to distant; but, in a marketing context, they are usually seen as the former kind where there is a close interaction between the parties to an exchange. Accordingly, we may think of a hierarchy of relationships starting with transactions, based on self-interest, moving on to those where the buyer trusts the seller to deliver the desired satisfactions and so develop a preference for that seller and become committed to them. Ultimately, this will lead to loyalty, in which case the seller's product may be regarded as a specialty good. Thus, when you experience a need for a given product category, the seller's name will automatically be the first to come to mind.

To encourage and sustain loyalty, many sellers have developed systems to reward repeat buyers, for example frequent flyer schemes and store loyalty cards. Collectively, such activities are designated customer relationship management or CRM. Given that the majority of purchases we make are low involvement and nearer to the transaction end of the relationship spectrum, it might be more correct to call such programmes customer *satisfaction* management. There is also the problem that, in many cases, CRM is a direct descendant of marketing management, as the idea of *managing* a relationship implies a desire to exercise control over it, which is not consistent with the marketing concept's notion of mutual satisfaction.

For relationship marketing to work, it must be seen as the basis for all business practice – as an orientation or philosophy to which all members of an organization subscribe. To develop such a marketing culture, it is necessary to practise internal marketing, the purpose of which is to have 'motivated and customer-conscious employees'. Employees, who are seen as internal customers and their jobs as internal products, should work in an organization that 'creates an internal environment which supports customer consciousness and sales-mindedness among their personnel'.[26] Employees need to become 'ambassadors for the organization',[27] as the 'quality of the service and the quality of the service providers are inseparable'.[28] The more competent the customer contact personnel, the better the service–business–client relationship will be, which will culminate in the service organization receiving a positive reference.

The aim of internal marketing is to:

increase job satisfaction, increase productivity and decrease absenteeism ... and to train personnel to enhance their skills and to encourage a customer orientation; and to supervise and evaluate their performance.[29]

Views such as these would seem to suggest that marketing is everybody's business, and raises the question as to the transferability of the marketing concept to other contexts.

transferring the marketing concept

By now, the distinction between marketing as a philosophy and marketing as a function should be clear. A final question that needs to be addressed is the extent to which both philosophy and function may be transferred to other non-business situations. The issue was broached first by Philip Kotler and Sidney Levy and they concluded that marketing ideas and practices are transferable to other contexts.[30] Since then, this view has been confirmed by the ubiquity with which 'marketing' is applied to almost every field of human endeavour – even religion and universities seem to find it important.

The problem is that the everyday interpretation of 'marketing' tends to emphasize persuasive communication, and usually fails to identify the research process necessary to establish how to design effective messages that will encourage the desired behaviour. On the other hand, practitioners in various subfields, like arts marketing, cause-related marketing, political marketing, sports marketing, social marketing, retailing and so on, are usually well versed in both the philosophy and practice of marketing.

Retailers build up databases that link individual purchases with their loyalty card details and use these for stocking and promotional decisions. Charities of all kinds profile the gift-giving behaviour of those who support their causes and target them with carefully designed and timed messages to trigger further donations. Using sophisticated geodemographic data, political parties concentrate nearly all their electioneering efforts on marginal constituencies that will determine the outcome of an election. In a nutshell, all these organizations seek to profile the needs and behaviour of their intended audience, so that they can segment it, target the segment(s) of interest and then position their own offering so that it will stand out and, hopefully, be preferred over all other similar competitive offerings.

A moment's reflection will confirm that our definition of marketing is equally applicable to all – by entering into an exchange, both parties seek to gain satisfaction of their needs. Perhaps, because of its commercial overtones, marketing should seek to adopt another name or, more to the point, make a better job of marketing itself.

positioning

In common with most of the other basic ideas introduced in this chapter, the concept of positioning is both a simple and intuitively appealing one. In essence, positioning means the achievement of a unique place in a competitive market for a particular product, such that some worthwhile subgroup of consumers perceive you to be different in some meaningful and important respect from all other competitors. In order to determine the position of a product – whether one's own or a competitor's – the first step must be to establish what are the key criteria or attributes that consumers use to judge performance and distinguish between the competitive offerings available to them. Once these key attributes have been defined, a survey may be undertaken to find out how consumers perceive each of the different brands in terms of the relevant criteria. This information may then be plotted using pairs of dimensions, such as price and performance, to determine the position of the ideal product (lowest price/highest performance) and the actual position of the products surveyed, as shown in Figure 15.4.

By plotting one's own and competitors' products in this way, one is able to identify what features and attributes may be used to differentiate them in the mind of the buyer. To do so, the marketer must develop a unique marketing mix based on the ingredients available. As with cooking, one can develop numerous recipes from the same ingredients but, in the final analysis, it is the way you do this – the implementation – that determines how successful you are. As the well-known British chef Rick Stein observed: 'A recipe should be a tune to which you can sing your own song.'

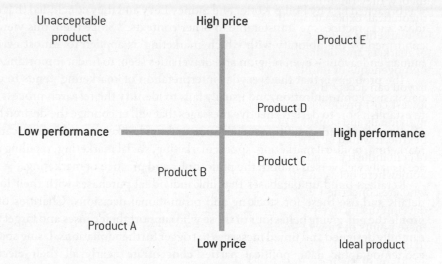

Figure 15.4 *Product positions in a competitive market*

quo vadis?

In a plenary address to the World Marketing Congress in 2001, Jagdish Sheth, one of marketing's most influential thinkers, observed that: 'The future of marketing has always been determined by outsiders.' This being so, it might be dangerous for a marketer to try and predict where his discipline might be going in future.

What Sheth had in mind is the fact that, in the absence of a universally accepted and overarching 'theory of marketing', the major advances in thought and practice have been introduced by 'outsiders'. For example, in the 1930s when marketing was struggling to cope with the effects of an economy in recession, it was the appointment of behavioural scientists as professors of marketing that led to a whole new perspective on the subject. The reason that this occurred is that then, as now, 'business studies' was a major academic growth area and there was a scarcity of qualified persons to fill the vacancies. During the 1930s, many highly qualified academics from other social sciences – economics, psychology, sociology and so on – were fleeing Europe to escape Naziism. On reaching the USA, however, they found there were no opportunities in their core discipline and so had to turn to related or 'cognate' subjects, of which marketing is one.

For many years now, I have argued that marketing is a synthetic discipline – not in the sense that it is an artificial substitute for something else, but in the real sense that other professional disciplines like architecture, engineering and medicine are synthetic disciplines.[31] Originally, 'synthetic' referrred to the act of synthesizing or integrating related ideas into a more powerful and holistic explanation of a phenomenon, and it is this that is the defining characteristic of professional practices – they are concerned with finding solutions to problems as they exist in the real world, not in the abstract. So marketing is an integrated and applied social science that has its foundations in subjects like anthropology, economics, psychology and sociology, each of which is fully recognized as an established discipline in its own right based on accepted theoretical principles.

But the problem with the 'single' disciplines is that, in order to develop acceptable theory, they often have to assume away or 'control' factors that might impact on the theoretical explanation. Buyer behaviour – of central importance to the practice of marketing – is a case in point. In economics, in order to analyse the functioning of markets and define the nature of competition, it is assumed that all products are homogeneous or undifferentiated – as are all potential customers. If, and it is a very big if, you can accept these assumptions, then it is clear that buyers will always choose the lowest cost producer. By contrast, psychologists are concerned with the behaviour of individuals and consider they are just that – different from one another. While this may be true, it would be very costly to make everything to order – as was the case in the days of craft industry – and supply would be severely restricted, as would population growth. Somewhere between these viewpoints we find the sociologists and anthropologists, who are concerned with how human beings socialize with one another in groups and develop distinctive patterns of behaviour. Somehow, the marketer has to reconcile all these points of view in deciding what strategy the organization should adopt and how to implement this through the management of its marketing mix.

Many of the most influential ideas in marketing strategy are based on the thinking of Michael Porter, whose 'five forces' model of competition is to be found in virtually every MBA course on offer.[32] Not many people know that Porter too was a 'refugee', in his case from Harvard College where he was studying industrial economics to Harvard Business School where he was able to develop this school of thought in original directions with immediate appeal to practising mangers. Economics, too, has languished as a discipline in recent years as students have preferred to study more applied business subjects, with the result that many economists and econometricians have migrated into business studies, including marketing. Perhaps it is unsurprising that one of the hottest topics in economics today is 'behavioural economics', a welcome development as someone unkindly said that 'an economist is someone who knows the price of everything, and the value of nothing'.

> Perhaps it is unsurprising that one of the hottest topics in economics today is 'behavioural economics', a welcome development as someone unkindly said that 'an economist is someone who knows the price of everything, and the value of nothing'.

Another problem with marketing as a discipline is that it identifies the need for new approaches to management and then allows others to take them over. Customer relationship management has been pre-empted by information technologists, TQM by production engineering and internal marketing by human resource management. And, if we are not careful, what is currently considered the most important research issue in marketing – marketing metrics – will be taken over by the bean counters.

In looking to the future, Sheth identified four contextual causes that need to be addressed by marketers. First, there is the need to evolve new methods and techniques to deal with the ever-increasing importance of services in the postindustrial economies. Second, there is a need for much clearer measurement and accountability to confirm the contribution of marketing to competitive performance – the marketing 'metrics' mentioned earlier. Third, there is the need to recognize the internet as a new channel of communication and distribution, and incorporate it into our strategic thinking.

And fourth, we have to recognize that for the first time ever there are five generations living in an economy and think through the implications of an ageing population and its impact on lifestyle and consumption. To these, we would add environmental or 'green' issues, concerns for social responsibility and ethical corporate behaviour, and the challenge of the emerging economies.

If marketers are to meet and resolve these challenges, then they need to be customer focused, build long-term relationships with customers, and think of their lifetime value as opposed to their short-term profitability. In other words, observe the golden rule – do unto others as you would be done by – and create and maintain mutually satisfactory exchange relationships.

references

1. Keith, R.J. (1960) 'The marketing revolution', *Journal of Marketing*, January.
2. Gilbert, D. and Bailey, N. (1990) 'The development of marketing: a compendium of historical approaches', *Quarterly Review of Marketing*, winter.
3. Cherington, P.T. (1920) *The Elements of Marketing* (London: Macmillan – now Palgrave Macmillan).
4. Brech, E.F.L. (1954) *Principles of Management* (2nd edn) (London: Longman).
5. Drucker, P. (1954) *Practice of Management* (New York: Harper & Row).
6. Ibid.
7. Converse, P.D.H., Huegy, H.W.M. and Mitchell, R.V. (1965) *Elements of Marketing* (Englewood Cliffs, NJ: Prentice Hall).
8. Bartels, R.B. (1968) 'The general theory of marketing', *Journal of Marketing*, **32**: 29–33.
9. Kotler, P. (1972) *Marketing Management* (2nd edn) (Englewood Cliffs, NJ: Prentice Hall).
10. Baker, M.J. (ed.) (1976) *Marketing: Theory and Practice* (London: Macmillan– now Palgrave Macmillan).
11. Levitt, T. (1983) *The Marketing Imagination* (New York: Free Press).
12. Op. cit. Kotler (1972).
13. McCarthy, E.J. and Perrault Jnr, W.D. (1994) *Basic Marketing* (8th edn) (Homewood, IL: Irwin).
14. Chartered Institute of Marketing.
15. Marketing Association of Australia and New Zealand.
16. Webster, F.E. (1992) 'The changing role of marketing in the corporation', *Journal of Marketing*, **56**: 1–17.
17. American Marketing Association, 2004.
18. Levitt, T. (1960) 'Marketing myopia', *Harvard Business Review*, July–August.
19. Ibid.
20. Sloan, A.P. (1965) *My Years with General Motors* (London: Sidgwick & Jackson) p. 69.
21. McCarthy, E.J. (1996) *Basic Marketing* (Homewood, IL: Irwin).
22. Kotler, P. (2003) *Marketing Management: Analysis, Planning, Implementation and Control* (11th edn) (Englewood Cliffs, NJ: Prentice Hall).
23. Ames, C. (1970) 'Trappings versus substance in industrial marketing', *Harvard Business Review*, July–August.
24. Copeland, M.T. (1923) 'Relation of consumers' buying habits to marketing methods', *Harvard Business Review*, April.
25. Op. cit. Baker (1976).
26. Gronroos, C. (1982) *Strategic Management and Marketing in the Service Sector* (Helsinki: Swedish School of Economics and Business Administration).
27. Lewis, B.R. (1989) 'Customer care in service organizations', *Marketing Intelligence and Planning*, **7**(5).
28. Chase, R.B. (1978) 'Where does the customer fit in a service operation?', *Harvard Business Review*, **56**.
29. Op. cit. Lewis (1989) pp. 18–22.
30. Kotler, P. and Levy, S. (1969) 'Broadening the concept of marketing', *Journal of Marketing*, **33**.
31. Baker, M.J. (2006) *Marketing: An Introductory Text* (7th edn) (Helensburgh: Westburn Publishers) p. 8.
32. Porter, M.E. (1985) *Competitive Advantage: Creating and Sustaining Superior Performance* (New York: Free Press).

16 macroeconomics and public policy

associate professor mark crosby[1]

As I sit down to write this chapter, I see an article in the business section of the *Financial Times* detailing how Cable & Wireless is considering a series of acquisitions abroad. On any given day, there are likely to be a number of such decisions being made by companies large and small. Obviously, in considering these acquisitions, the acquirer will carefully examine factors such as the calibre of the management and the quality of the business to be acquired, but one factor that will be critical to the success of the acquisition decision will be the quality of the macroeconomic environment in the host country. So how should management go about building an understanding of the macroeconomic environment? The discipline of macroeconomics tries to understand the forces shaping the 'big picture' in an economy – meaning that rather than focusing on individual businesses, macroeconomists focus on trends in a particular industry, or in the economy as a whole. Critical to an understanding of the macroeconomy is an understanding of the public policy framework. How does the US Federal Reserve make the decision as to whether or not to change interest rates, and how will such a change affect other global economies?[1] In an increasingly interconnected world, it is imperative to understand how these decisions are made and what impact they will have on local economies and businesses.

> The discipline of macroeconomics tries to understand the forces shaping the 'big picture' in an economy – meaning that rather than focusing on individual businesses, macroeconomists focus on trends in a particular industry, or in the economy as a whole.

One of the features of macroeconomics is that competing theories are used to try and understand the world around us. These competing views will mean that students need to work hard to develop their own intuition about which model best describes the issue they need to examine. To some extent, these competing views are rooted in different political or ideological positions, but there is the added complication that the data used by macroeconomists to analyse the macroeconomy does not always come with a unique interpretation. For example, macroeconomists would all agree that sometimes markets do not work very well.[2] The question is how many markets 'fail', and whether this matters for the models that we use to study the macroeconomy. These competing theories explain the common perception that economists have more answers to any particular question than there exist economists. Despite these competing views, there are also strong areas of agreement among macroeconomists, and economists more generally.

In this chapter, first we will describe some trends in the global economy in the past 30 years, and use this historical lens to illustrate the types of question addressed in the discipline of macroeconomics. The chapter will then outline the theoretical frameworks used by macroeconomists and, in particular, detail the fundamental principles that underpin macroeconomic analysis, before concluding with some current and future issues in macroeconomics. We will begin our journey through economic history in China in 1979.

history and background

Today, hardly a day goes by without a politician or a businessperson thinking about issues such as China's booming manufacturing growth and the impact of this growth for world trade and local manufacturers, or whether China's exchange rate is giving it an unfair advantage over local firms in international markets. But in 1979, China was on the mind of very few businesspeople. After China's Communist Party took power in the country in 1949, China was closed to the rest of the world as far as business and trade were concerned. Over the subsequent 30 years, China remained a very poor, isolated country, but in 1979 China's leader Deng Xiaoping initiated a series of reforms to China's economy. These reforms have been incremental, but since 1979, the reforms add up to a significant change from a highly centralized and bureaucratic socialist economy to an economy that is quite market oriented and open to trade.[3]

For a businessperson, the rise of China raises a number of questions. First, many managers see an economy with 1.3 billion people, with GDP growth of more than 9% per year since 1979, and draw the obvious conclusion that China

> Probably the first thing that any student of macroeconomics learns is how to measure and understand gross domestic product (GDP).

is an important market to consider (either to enter, to sell goods or perhaps to acquire businesses in). But will GDP continue to grow at 9% per year? Probably the first thing that any student of macroeconomics learns is how to measure and understand gross domestic product (GDP). GDP is a measure of production in an economy, and understanding how this basic measure is calculated is the first step towards understanding the drivers of economic growth.

Once a student has mastered the measurement issues surrounding GDP, the next step is to think about how to understand economic growth in an economy. Economists think of growth as being driven by an accumulation of economic inputs, such as the workforce and the number of machines and factories in an economy. In the case of China, the incredible economic growth that has been achieved since 1979 is understandable once one examines the economy from the economic growth accounting perspective. This framework also allows a businessperson to address the question of whether the China growth story can continue, and therefore whether China is a good place for a foreign businessperson to invest.

In the West, 1979 saw the election of Margaret Thatcher in the UK, and the following year saw the election of Ronald Reagan in the USA. Reagan and Thatcher were intellectual soulmates who fundamentally changed the structure of the economies of both countries, but after gaining office, one of the first tasks of both Thatcher and Reagan was to try and reduce *inflation*.[4] The Bank of England and the Federal Reserve are responsible for *monetary policy*[5] in the UK and the US respectively, and have the authority to take action to try to control inflation. In the UK, the Bank of England was charged to try to reduce the growth of the money supply, while in the US, then Federal Reserve Chairman Paul Volcker was given authority by President Reagan to do whatever it took to reduce inflation. The result of the actions of the central banks in both cases was high interest rates and a recession.

The high interest rates of themselves made life extremely difficult for many businesses, but when combined with a recession (negative growth in GDP), many businesses were forced into bankruptcy or at best found limited profitability through the early 1980s. In macroeconomics, the decisions made by central banks are studied under the topic of monetary policy – how central banks make decisions with regard to interest rates and what the role of a central bank is, and should, be.

Another feature of the Reagan and Thatcher governments was the commitment to smaller government. This commitment translated into significant cuts in individual income tax rates in both countries and also a commitment to deregulate the economy. Since the 1980s, many countries have adjusted the structure of their tax systems so that individual income tax rates are lower than 25 years ago. In many countries, these income tax cuts have been offset by the introduction of consumption taxes, so that goods have been taxed more heavily. These changes in the tax structure have affected incentives to work and incentives to consume certain types of good that are taxed more, or less, heavily in different countries. It is important for managers to be aware of these tax structures in different countries, as they not only affect accounting profit, but also can affect the optimal structure of salary packages and working conditions, as well as the relative desirability of different types of production technique.

Deregulation of the economy had a dramatic impact on almost every business in the US and the UK. Deregulation directly affected industries such as the airlines, banks and telecommunications, which were opened up to competition and had many rules and regulations regarding business conduct amended or abolished. But even for industries not directly affected by deregulation, the impact on businesses was profound. Many costs fell, as competition led to cheaper plane fares and phone bills. But cheaper fares also made it easier to access foreign markets, as well as making it easier for foreign competitors to access local markets. The impacts of deregulation on the business landscape were profound, and it is important to note that deregulation was not restricted to just the UK and the US. Left-wing governments in New Zealand and Australia instituted wide-ranging reforms to the economies of those two countries, with deregulation being at least as widespread as in the UK and the US. Even continental Europe deregulated industries such as the airlines and telecommunications, although regulations with respect to labour and some other markets remain more restrictive than in the English-speaking countries. More recently, deregulation has occurred even in traditionally heavily regulated economies, such as India. In India, reforms to sectors of the economy such as manufacturing and retailing have opened up these markets to foreign companies, as well as enabling better access to the global economy for some low-cost Indian manufacturers, and for Indian entrepreneurs in sectors such as information technology.

Economic reform in the 1980s also saw economies become more closely interconnected. Clear evidence of this came in October 1987, as a fall on US share markets quickly led to falls on most other OECD share markets.[6] In response to these share market collapses, the Federal Reserve in the US, along with other central banks, acted quickly to cut interest rates and enable easier access to bank loans, so as to try and minimize the impact on business from falls in share prices. This loose monetary policy was, in fact, very effective, as the impact of the stock market crash on the general business environment turned out to be small.

While the direct impact on the macroeconomy of the stock market crash was small, progress on reducing inflation was halted by the loosening of monetary policy in late 1987 and 1988. By the end of 1988, it had become clear to many central banks that the focus of monetary policy should return to inflation reduction, and thus monetary policy was tightened. High global interest rates, and a number of other mostly country-specific factors, led to a global economic slowdown beginning in late 1989, with many countries such as the US and the UK going into a deep recession. The combination of high interest rates and low or negative economic growth created a challenging business environment within all OECD economies. In the US, the manufacturing sector in particular was hard hit, while in the UK the City of London fared poorly from the late 1980s into the early 1990s, as property prices fell and financial markets were weak.

At the same time as tight monetary policy was exacerbating recessions in much of the English-speaking world, the economy of Japan began a dismal decade as far as economic performance was concerned. After peaking at just under 40,000 in December 1989, Japan's Nikkei Index began a decline that saw it fall to less than 8,000 in 2003. Falling prices then hit Japanese property markets, decimating the wealth of Japanese corporations and citizens. The impact on Japan's macroeconomy was devastating; consumers stopped buying and firms stopped investing. Having been considered the miracle economy throughout the 1970s and 80s, the Japanese economy in the 1990s became a case study in macroeconomic mismanagement. For businesses exporting to Japan, the business environment became extremely challenging. And for firms within Japan, most of the 1990s saw falling goods prices and declining sales. From a business perspective, being able to understand the failings of Japan, and predict whether economic reforms there would eventually lead to better economic performance, is a critical input to decisions such as whether to refocus attention on the Japanese market, or whether to abandon Japan and focus attention on other economies such as China's.

> Since the early 1990s, most OECD economies have been able to maintain low inflation, which is a key ingredient to the relatively stable economic growth and low interest rates enjoyed since then.

Outside Japan, recovery from the recession of the early 1990s was well underway by 1992, and the advantage of the high interest rates of the earlier few years was that inflation was now very much under control. In an attempt to lock in the benefits of low inflation, many countries restructured their central banks to make them more independent of government. This independence was designed so that central banks could focus on maintaining low inflation without having to suffer from political interference to cut interest rates for political purposes. Since the early 1990s, most OECD economies have been able to maintain low inflation, which is a key ingredient to the relatively stable economic growth and low interest rates enjoyed since then.

The 1990s were, however, a decade where the sometimes negative consequences of integrated *global capital markets* became clear.[7] As further liberalization and deregulation of markets continued, many developing countries were encouraged to open up their capital markets and enjoy the benefits of low global interest rates. Thailand was a typical example of this pattern, with many local corporations and banks enjoying access to cheap US dollar-denominated loans from international banks and other sources. The problem, however, was that a change in Thailand's exchange rate in July 1997 led to a dramatic worsening of the balance sheets of much of Thailand's corporate sector, as the cost of financing US loans increased overnight. With foreign lenders not knowing if these Thai corporations were bankrupt or insolvent, there was a stampede for the door by foreign lenders. This crisis then spread to Indonesia, Malaysia and Korea, with a similar devastating effect on businesses in those countries.[8]

Understanding the detail of the Asian crisis requires a solid understanding of how fixed and flexible exchange rate systems work. It is fair to say that not many economists foresaw the Asian crisis, but once one understands the basics of exchange rate economics, it is straightforward to see the risks implicit in a high level of foreign currency-denominated debt. A fixed exchange rate needs to be understood as a type of regulated fixed price, similar to, say, rent controls that might be studied in microeconomics. To maintain a fixed exchange rate, a country's central bank needs to be able to supply any extra demand for foreign exchange in the foreign exchange market. A problem in this type of system is that central banks sometimes run short of reserves. In this situation, exchange rates can often move dramatically, with potentially disastrous consequences for firms who do not take notice of the warning signs.

> Understanding how fixed exchange rates work is critical as part of the decision-making process around investing in countries such as China or Malaysia today.

Understanding how fixed exchange rates work is critical as part of the decision-making process around investing in countries such as China or Malaysia today. China's exchange rate is likely to appreciate significantly against the US dollar over the course of 2007. Unlike Thailand in 1997, where the central bank was running out of reserves and was eventually forced to devalue the currency, China's central bank is rapidly accumulating foreign currency. In this situation, China can afford to make its currency more valuable (appreciation), without running any risk of running out of reserves. Knowing how a fixed exchange rate system works, it is easy to see why further appreciation of the Chinese currency is likely to occur.

The recession of the early 1990s also saw a significant change in global inflation rates. With economies performing poorly, firms found it a difficult environment to raise prices, and so inflation rates in many countries, such as the US, the UK and Australia, fell to low, single-digit levels for the first time in two decades. With central banks now having greater independence in many countries, the gain in lower inflation has been locked in to this day. Today, inflation is still variable, but is not often above 4–5% in most OECD countries. The benefit to businesses is that lower inflation means lower interest rates and a more stable and predictable macroeconomic environment.

After recovering from recession in the early 1990s, most English-speaking economies enjoyed rapid economic growth and rising equity prices. In the US in particular, GDP growth in the second half of the 1990s was high, and equity prices grew at rapid rates. One of the explanations for this expansion, in the US and elsewhere, was the growth of the 'new economy'. Computerization was finally becoming a reality for most businesses, and the World Wide Web and other innovations in computer software and hardware were helping businesses become more productive. This 'IT revolution' is still having dramatic effects on almost every business, but the macroeconomic impacts are still a subject of some debate. From about 1997, many macroeconomists were arguing that prices for US equities were above fair value. Most prominent of the critics was Robert Shiller from Yale University, whose book *Irrational Exuberance* argued that prices for many assets were subject to reaching excesses on occasion as individuals bought into hype rather than fundamentals.[9] He was of the view that US stock prices fit the picture of irrationally high prices from about 1997.

Proponents of the new economy view tended to focus on the large productivity gains being had by firms right across the macroeconomy. If firms could grow faster, and the macroeconomy was going to grow faster, then surely equity prices should grow quickly? But one of the basic principles of finance is that the fundamental value of a share is the (discounted) value of future dividends, which will be related to the future earnings of a company. The problem for the new economy story is that prices and earnings for IT companies were not growing quickly in the late 1990s, even though the economy was growing quickly. In many cases, IT stocks did not yet have positive earnings at this time. In March 2000, the Nasdaq (an index of high-tech stocks) began a fall from initially over 5,000 to less than 2,000 within two years. Investment in the IT sector of the economy has fallen in most countries from 1999 levels. Of course, for companies in the IT sector of the economy, the years since 2000 have been difficult, but for most other businesses computer prices have continued to fall and IT support is becoming easier to access and cheaper. Indeed, the rise of outsourcing is supporting the trend to cheaper and high-quality IT services. In studying the IT revolution, a student will learn macroeconomic concepts such as productivity and will also build on frameworks studied in microeconomics and in finance.

key concepts in economics

The previous section outlined some trends in the world economy over the past 30 years. Despite the general nature of the discussion, it is clear that a solid understanding of both these historical trends and an understanding of the various forces at play are invaluable to business managers. Understanding interest rate and exchange rate movements, as well as the actions of central banks and regulators, is critical to making correct business decisions. With the global economy becoming increasingly interconnected, it is also important to understand macroeconomic developments and trends in markets quite distant from home.

> Understanding interest rate and exchange rate movements, as well as the actions of central banks and regulators, is critical to making correct business decisions.

The theoretical frameworks used in macroeconomics are similar to those used in microeconomics. There is a sense in which the macroeconomy is just the sum of all the individual participants in the economy, although it turns out that some of the principles studied in microeconomics need to be amended in order to understand the macroeconomy. In the introductory textbook *Principles of Economics* by Greg Mankiw, it is argued that there are 10 central ideas that unify economics.[10] These ideas cut across microeconomics and macroeconomics, but it is illustrative to briefly discuss all 10 ideas as a way of showing how economists analyse the economy. The 10 ideas are:

> *People face trade-offs*: This is a principle that economists use to study how people make choices. If we want to consume more goods, for example, we need to work harder and so forgo leisure.

> *The cost of something is what you give up to get it*: Here the idea is that everything has a cost, whether monetary or not. Going to business school has monetary costs (the fees), but also the cost of not being able to work. Therefore, in making the decision to study at business school, this opportunity cost of not working needs to be included along with the fees.

> *Rational people think at the margin*: In many applications in business, it is the marginal cost or benefit, rather than the total cost, that is relevant. Imagine that a

firm spends $2 million to develop a new product, only to find that the market is smaller than initially thought. Should another $1 million be spent to get the product to market? In making this decision, it is only the additional $1 million that should be considered in making the decision as to whether to continue. The $2 million has already been spent, so should be irrelevant to the continuation decision.

> *Trade can make everyone better off*: Economists are generally in favour of free trade, as this is seen as a way of maximizing the total output of all economies. Trade enables individuals and countries to specialize in what they are good at, thus maximizing the wealth of nations.[11]

> *Markets are usually a good way to organize economic activity*: Economists believe that the self-interested actions of private individuals most often lead to good outcomes, both as far as the individual, and society more generally, are concerned. Markets fail sometimes, but economists have strict criteria for assessing whether intervention in a market is warranted or not, and for choosing the right form of intervention. This leads to the next principle.

> *Governments can sometimes improve market outcomes*: Major reasons for markets not working well are a lack of competition, a problem in a market with pollution or other 'externalities' that affect third parties. Governments can improve these market failures by regulating, creating more competition or other means.

> *A country's standard of living depends on its ability to produce goods and services*: There are vast differences in income levels and living standards across countries, and understanding these differences is the domain of macroeconomics. Productivity is the amount of goods and services produced using an hour of a worker's time, and explaining differences in productivity is a major task of macroeconomics.

> *Prices rise when a government prints too much money*: The idea here is pretty simple; when you buy a good using money, you are exchanging paper notes (or claims to notes) for goods. If everyone has lots of these paper notes, then you will need to exchange a lot of notes for goods – prices will be high. Understanding the relationship between money, interest rates and prices is a fundamental topic in macroeconomics.

> *Society faces a short-term trade-off between inflation and unemployment*: This trade-off has become known as the Phillips curve. The basic idea here is that reducing inflation requires a sacrifice in higher unemployment. Understanding the size and nature of this trade-off is important to understanding monetary policy and the actions of central banks.

Different economists might come up with a slightly different list, but there is no question that these are fundamental principles of economics. It can also be seen that some of the principles are microeconomic (relating mostly to individuals), while others are macroeconomic (relating to the entire economy). However, some of the principles utilize both microeconomic and macroeconomic ideas (such as the principle regarding the benefits of free trade), and all the principles utilize similar theoretical frameworks. To illustrate the theoretical frameworks, we now discuss some specific examples.

The frameworks that macroeconomists use to analyse issues are usually simple mathematical models, and in the MBA classroom, these models are most often presented in graphical form. Models allow students to apply principles studied in one context to a different but related context. For example, in studying the deflation (negative inflation) that has recently created problems in Japan, the 'aggregate demand/ aggregate supply' model could be utilized (see Figure 16.1). This model enables students to see how changes in economy-wide demand and supply conditions translate into changes in economy-wide price changes and GDP growth. Such a model can then be used to study Japan's deflation, as well as the implications of the IT revolution in the US on inflation there, or inflation and GDP developments in other countries.

The aggregate demand curve is based on the idea that in the macroeconomy as a whole, the level of demand for goods and services will vary inversely with the overall price level in the economy (you will learn why this is the case in the course of your MBA programme). The overall level of supply of goods and services in the economy will, on the other hand, be positively related to the overall price level. These two assumptions lead us to the aggregate demand (AD) and aggregate supply (AS) curves below.

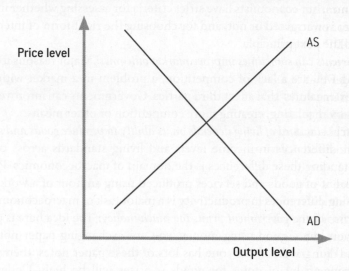

Figure 16.1 *The aggregate demand/aggregate supply model and Japanese deflation*

Deflation is a fall in the price level, and this can occur if the level of AD falls (shifts to the left), or if AS increases (shifts to the right). Japan's deflation has been caused by falling AD. You would then also study why this deflation tends to persist, and why deflation tends to be associated with a weak economy and rising unemployment. The low inflation in the US in the late 1990s was associated with rising AS, which was related to strong productivity growth during this period. This is a good situation for an economy to be in; the economy grew strongly and unemployment fell, but inflation remained low.

Another topic for study in macroeconomics is economic growth theory. In order to examine the prospects for economic growth in a country, a student would learn to use some models of growth, along with some growth accounting. Models of 'economic growth' build from simple models of the firm in microeconomics. In microeconomics, a firm is described as having a number of fundamental inputs in the production process. Workers (or labour) are combined with capital (machines, plant and equipment, and buildings) in order to produce final goods for sale by the firm. The firm needs to choose how much capital and labour to use, and how much output to produce on the basis of existing prices, wage levels and interest rates.[12]

In thinking about economic growth, economists utilize the same framework used in the theory of the firm; in a sense, the macroeconomy is treated like a very large firm, with output, or GDP, produced according to how much labour and capital is available in the economy. The growth of the economy will then be determined by the growth of capital and labour in the overall economy. Growth accounting then uses this framework to describe how economic growth occurs. For example, it might be estimated that 60% of GDP growth in the past decade was due to growth in capital in the economy and 40% was due to technological progress. With little population and workforce growth, growth in the labour force cannot be a significant contributor to economic growth. This analysis can then be used to think about growth prospects for a country like China. In China, the more widespread availability of machines and factories (capital) has been the major driver of economic growth since 1979, and most economists would believe that capital accumulation should continue to lead to high economic growth in China for at least the next decade. This will see China's level of GDP per person catching up to levels in middle-income countries such as South Korea.

A model that is used to tackle a range of analytical problems is the 'supply and demand' framework. In short, the value of a good depends on the available supply of the good and how much people want the good (demand). A good that is in plentiful supply, such as water, will tend to have a low price, while a good in short supply, such as diamonds, will sell for a high price. On the demand side, the more people there are demanding a particular good, the higher the price that a seller will be able to charge. This model is used in a range of applications in macroeconomics, a good example being the simplest model of foreign exchange rates. What caused the value of the US dollar to rise in the late 1990s? The short answer is the rising demand for US dollars by foreigners, who wanted to buy US shares. In the foreign exchange market, it is the supply and demand for local currency that determines the exchange rate. If there is too great a supply of local currency, the value of the local currency will fall (*depreciation*).[13] Such a rise in the supply of local currency might be caused by a desire by local citizens to rebalance their portfolios away from owning local bonds to owning more foreign bonds. As you can see, exchange rate theory builds from the supply and demand framework in microeconomics, but also turns out to be closely related to theories of portfolio choice studied in finance.

The supply and demand framework is also used to study *interest rate determination* (see Figure 16.2). The rate of interest that you are charged to borrow will depend on how many individuals and firms are looking to borrow money, and how many people are trying to lend money (savers). If more people try to borrow money, interest rates will tend to rise, while if more people save, interest rates will tend to fall (the market will improve for borrowers).

The supply and demand framework allows a student to think about interest rates in an economy. The supply of loanable funds will depend on how many individuals and firms are saving. It is probable that people save more as interest rates rise, so the supply of savings curve will be upwards sloping (S). The demand for these loanable funds will, on the other hand, depend negatively on the interest rate; at high interest rates, borrowers will find it too expensive to borrow money. The actual interest rate in the market will be where demand equals supply, at r* below.

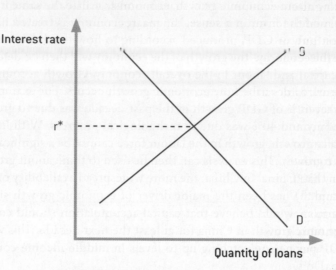

Figure 16.2 *Interest rate determination*

Imagine now that the number of savers in the economy rises – perhaps because more baby boomers are worried about financing their retirement. A rise in savings (shift to the right in the S curve) will lead to lower interest rates. This has in fact been one explanation for relatively low interest rates globally over the past few years.

The relevant issues for a business manager to study in the discipline of macroeconomics will depend to some extent on the home country of the business manager and the industry in which the business is being conducted. But the theoretical frameworks used to examine one country or industry will be easily transportable to other countries or industries. While these models will always be a simplification compared with the complexity of the real world, macroeconomic models provide extremely powerful frameworks for understanding economic issues. In a typical course of study, students might be exposed to three or four different models, capable of explaining all the major macroeconomic aggregates in any economy, such as the level of GDP and its growth, the rate of unemployment, the inflation rate, interest rates and exchange rate behaviour. Once a student has mastered these models, they will find an analysis of macroeconomies to be quite straightforward.

looking forward

The discipline of macroeconomics provides business managers with the conceptual frameworks necessary to understand the local and international economies. This understanding is helpful when predicting future trends in important macroeconomic variables, such as interest rates, that have a critical impact on most businesses. Students will also become aware that a sound understanding of macroeconomics leads to a healthy scepticism with regard to forecasting, which can, ironically, lead to better decision making. Such an understanding enables a business manager to think about likely scenarios for the macroeconomy and examine the implications of those scenarios for business. A couple of examples that illustrate both the difficulty of forecasting but also

> The discipline of macroeconomics provides business managers with the conceptual frameworks necessary to understand the local and international economies.

illustrate how macroeconomics puts structure on scenario analysis are as follows. One of the best models for forecasting exchange rates is the *random walk model*. It predicts that the best forecast of the exchange rate in 12 months' time for any currency pair among flexible exchange rate countries is simply today's exchange rate.[14] To a non-economist, this forecast often seems too simple – surely the pound has been falling against the euro for the last year, and therefore it is likely to continue to slide, or perhaps to revert to a more normal level? However, macroeconomists with a statistical bent (called econometricians) have found that nothing convincingly beats the simple random walk model when it comes to exchange rate forecasts. And this is a lesson that businesses routinely miss. Many large businesses have made significant losses from the assumption that the exchange rate would change in a predictable way. Businesses need to understand that exchange rates do change, but often in quite unpredictable ways – good scenario analysis is sometimes extremely useful in the context of the implications of exchange rate changes for a business.

An area where there might be more hope for the forecaster is in interest rate forecasting. Do we need to be worried about double-digit interest rates in the near future severely impacting firms' borrowing costs? The short answer is that this is unlikely in most OECD countries. With inflation now under control and central banks determined to maintain low inflation, interest rates are likely to remain in the 5–8% range that economists would consider to be normal (or neutral) when inflation is around the 1–4% range. Once again, a basic understanding of central bank behaviour and monetary policy will easily lead a student to this conclusion.

What about economic growth in the future? Can China continue to grow and what will be the implications of this growth for commodity and share prices worldwide? Here again, our economic models give us more guidance – economic growth theory would suggest that China is capable of growing at near double-digit rates for at least another decade or two, as it catches up to income levels in countries like South Korea and, perhaps eventually, even the US.

In short, macroeconomics provides useful frameworks that enable us as business managers to anticipate possible outcomes and take actions that are optimal in the face of these outcomes.

references/notes

1. The US Federal Reserve is the official body responsible for setting monetary policy in the US.
2. Economists are quite specific about the meaning of a market not working well – a good example being that prices are too high because there is a lack of competition.
3. For an interesting discussion of the economic progress of China since 1979, see Prasad, E. (2004) 'China's growth and integration into the world economy', IMF Occasional Paper 232.
4. Inflation is a measure of average rates of price increase in an economy.
5. Monetary policy involves the setting of a policy interest rate, or money supply in an economy. All interest rates in an economy will tend to follow interest rates controlled more directly by the central bank.
6. The Oganization for Economic Co-operation and Development was established in 1961 and now comprises 30 nations.
7. Since the early 1990s, firms have been increasingly able to fund their activities offshore. Global capital markets allow borrowers to find capital cheaply and easily without being restricted to only local banks and equity markets.
8. See Radelet, S. and Sachs, J. (1998) 'The East Asian financial crisis: diagnosis, remedies, prospects', *Brookings Papers on Economic Activity*.

9. Shiller, R. (2005) *Irrational Exuberance* (Princeton, NJ: Princeton University Press).
10. Mankiw, N.G. (2004) *Principles of Economics* (Belmont, CA: Thompson Southwestern).
11. This is one of the oldest principles of economics, going back to Adam Smith's *The Wealth of Nations*, first published in 1776.
12. See Barro, R. and Sala-i-Martin, X. (2003) *Economic Growth* (New York: McGraw-Hill) for a readable introduction to economic growth theory and the empirical literature regarding economic growth.
13. Depreciation is a fall in the value of a currency, for example when the British pound depreciates from US$1.60 to US$1.50 per pound.
14. See for example Frankel, J. and Rose, A. (1995) 'Empirical research on nominal exchange rates', in G. Grossman and K. Rogoff (eds) *Handbook of International Economics*, vol. 3 (Amsterdam: North Holland).

international finance

professor gonzalo chavez

International finance is a subject we intuitively link to international trade. Compared to the current notion of globalization that the term 'international' invokes, the early perception of an international transaction was more to do with the amount of time it took to move physical goods from one continent to another. However, today's international transactions are no longer limited to the exchange of finished goods with other locations.

Multinational corporations have gone beyond accepting their domestic resource limitations and now acquire physical locations abroad in order to make use of the natural and human resources in other countries. This type of investment where assets are acquired and management control exerted is termed *foreign direct investment* (FDI). Similarly, *outsourcing* now allows firms to hire providers that offer a better and more cost-efficient service instead of having to develop and train their own personnel. An example is India, which now supplies hardware design and software development services to international firms. This country now designs mobile phones and flat-screen TVs for European and US firms. Both sides benefit: international firms save on costs and suppliers benefit from the integration they ultimately experience with their clients. An example of this is the closer scrutiny faced by the foreign production facilities of many multinational firms with regard to child labour laws, something which would probably not have occurred without the presence of the multinationals.

> By buying securities issued by firms or governments around the world, countries with an excess supply of savings can help to finance the growth opportunities of countries that experience a deficit of funds.

International finance also includes *portfolio investments*, which relate to the buying and selling of securities such as stocks and bonds, and which do not imply management control. By buying securities issued by firms or governments around the world, countries with an excess supply of savings can help to finance the growth opportunities of countries that experience a deficit of funds. Firms with new project ideas can thus have access to global providers of funds instead of being constrained by the limited suppliers of funds at home. All in all, international links, while creating challenges, certainly move us towards mutual dependency.

This chapter builds on some of the basic concepts presented earlier in Chapter 13 on finance. You may recall that two subdisciplines in finance were presented – investments and corporate finance. When we examine *international* investments (although we use the same theoretical framework to consider the risk and return capabilities of assets), investing abroad now widens the benefits as well as the risks. If we do not find firms with sufficiently high-growth opportunities at home, we can certainly find developing economies that provide them. However, investing abroad also carries a potentially higher risk of political or social instability. International investments also imply that part of our profits will now be denominated in foreign currency, generating exposure to currency-driven losses when foreign currency falls in value relative to our home currency.

Similarly, the corporate finance questions analysed in Chapter 13 are also relevant from an *international* corporate finance perspective. International corporations still need to make financing decisions that will optimize their cost of capital. However, international markets now allow firms to obtain funds through many more sources than just those at home, thus allowing for a lower cost of capital. You may also remember that project investment decisions in a national or home setting required that we generate forecasts and apply discounted cash flow analysis tools such as net present value (NPV). In an international setting, this decision process will require additional analyses. Again, since investing in a foreign project implies investing in another country, our investment project's revenues will probably be denominated in a currency that is different from our home currency. Thus, understanding currency movements and trends now becomes important. In addition, investing in a foreign business environment implies a change in the level of risk we now bear, so we will need to adjust our required return so that it adequately reflects country risk. This required return would also be a function of regulatory and tax-related considerations that frequently change when firms do business abroad. Finally, the use of derivatives was previously offered as a way of managing risk. In an international finance context, options and other derivative securities such as futures, forwards and swaps are now used to hedge *currency* risk.

Thus, going to an international setting implies adjustments to both the numerator and the denominator of the equation presented in Figure 17.1. In finance, we are constantly trying to maximize *value*, which is estimated by dividing expected cash flows by the cost of capital. Therefore, my first key point is as follows: international finance is concerned with understanding and managing the manner in which these two components are altered in a multinational setting.

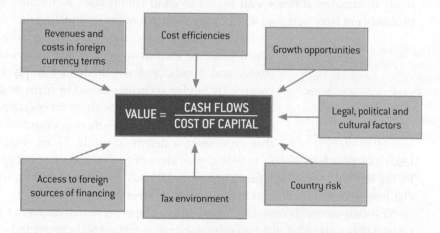

Figure 17.1 What changes when we consider an international setting?

how international finance relates to other business areas

Doing business abroad is a consequence of a close interaction between all functional areas. For example, there may be a strategic opportunity for a firm to increase market share through an expansion to another geographic market. Thus, the role of marketing is to make sure that increased sales are achieved through an enhanced interaction between the firm, its clients and its providers abroad. The sales forecasts that result will be critical in determining the expected cash flows that will be assigned to the project. Simultaneously, this increased sales opportunity also implies investment and production costs related to the setting up of the new production facilities, an analysis provided by operations. Human resources analyse the hiring, training, management and auditing of employees and the expenses these entail. The economic consequences of implementing this project are organized in a structured and coherent manner by the accounting department and so on.

To determine whether this project is ultimately feasible, the information provided by the other corporate functions is compiled and a financial analysis of the risks and benefits that the business idea offers implemented (Figure 17.2). Revenues and costs must be estimated and the role of currency volatility incorporated in the feasibility analysis. The level of risk in the new business environment will also be incorporated as a profitability hurdle rate that must be satisfied if the project is to be accepted. With this information, an NPV analysis is then carried out and the subsequent acceptability determined. This decision thus requires an understanding of international finance issues. With corporations making an increased use of international mergers and acquisitions as a way of achieving greater growth and competitiveness, international financial management is becoming more the rule, rather than the exception, in today's business environment.

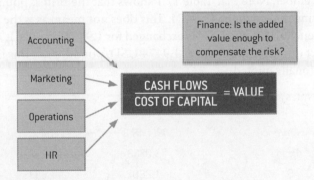

Figure 17.2 Finance and other functional areas

In this chapter, we will touch on some of the building blocks of international finance. First, we present the metrics and calculations related to the exchange rate. We then move on to present models that explain equilibrium relationships (known as 'parity conditions') that link inflation and interest rates with foreign currency movements. We examine how parity conditions are connected with the macroeconomic reality of countries. This implies understanding the information and relationships within the balance of payments accounts reported by nations so as to identify currency and economic trends. These previous parts affect the numerator (cash flows) of our value equation (Figure 17.1). We then turn our attention to how the denominator (cost of capital) needs to be estimated. Having concluded the basics of international asset valuation, we then introduce the benefits of geographical diversification by providing a natural multinational extension of portfolio theory. Lastly, we explore the use of derivative securities in order to hedge currency risk.

the exchange rate: what is it, how do we measure it?

The exchange rate is nothing but a price: the price at which we can exchange one currency with another currency. As of November 2006, 1 euro was being exchanged for 1.27 US dollars. We can then say that the exchange rate is 1.27 USD/1€ (1.27 US dollars per 1 euro). If we quote a currency rate in these terms, US dollars per 1 unit of currency A, then we are using an *American* quote. We can also invert this number so that we express it as 1/1.27 = 0.78 €/USD (0.78 euros per 1 US dollar). This latter quote is said to be expressed in *European* terms, although it is not exclusively applicable to European currencies. For example, 120 yen/USD is also a European quote.

Similarly, exchange rates may be expressed as *direct* or indirect quotes. A direct quote presents the rate of exchange in terms of home currency units per one foreign currency unit. Thus, a New York trader quoting the UK pound as 1.94 USD/pound is providing a direct quote, since his home currency is in the numerator. In contrast, a trader in Melbourne would provide an *indirect* quote for the Australian dollar if she was to quote it as 0.60 euros/AUD, since the euro (numerator) is not her home currency. In general, one observes currency quotes in indirect terms, with the exception of the UK pound and the euro.

Table 17.1[1] presents the *spot*[2] exchange rates of world currencies against the US dollar, the euro and the UK pound as observed in the *Financial Times* on 29 November 2006. Printed information shows market data as of the previous day, so the closing mid European quote for the Argentinean peso relative to the USD was 3.0788 pesos/USD on 28 November. Note that Table 17.1 shows that the British pound's quote under the dollar closing mid column is 1.9474. This does not mean, as is the case for most of the other currencies, that one USD is exchanged for 1.9474 pounds. It is actually providing the indirect quote for the dollar as 1.9474 USD/pound, since this is the way the pound is conventionally quoted.

Table 17.1 Exchange rates for world currencies

Country	Currency	DOLLAR	EURO	POUND
Argentina	Peso	3.0788	4.0487	5.9956
Australia	A$	1.2802	1.6835	2.4930
Bahrain	Dinar	0.3770	0.4958	0.7342
Bolivia	Boliviano	7.9950	10.5139	15.5695
Brazil	R$	2.1834	2.8713	4.2520
Canada	C$	1.1318	1.4883	2.2040
Chile	Peso	530.150	697.174	1032.41
China	Yuan	7.8400	10.3100	15.2676
Colombia	Peso	2318.00	3048.29	4514.07
Costa Rica	Colon	517.000	679.881	1006.81
Czech Rep.	Koruna	21.3034	28.0150	41.4862
Denmark	DKr	5.6685	7.4544	11.0389
Egypt	Egypt £	5.7188	7.5205	11.1367

Country	Currency	DOLLAR	EURO	POUND
Estonia	Kroon	11.8980	15.6465	23.1703
Hong Kong	HK$	7.7757	10.2255	15.1424
Hungary	Forint	195.677	257.325	381.061
India	Rs	44.6875	58.7663	87.0245
Indonesia	Rupiah	9185.50	12079.40	17887.80
Iran	Rial	9233.00	12141.90	17980.30
Israel	Shk	4.2866	5.6370	8.3477
Japan	¥	116.235	152.855	226.356
One month		115.776	152.471	225.503
Three month		114.841	151.663	223.746
One year		111.174	148.166	216.274
Kenya	Shilling	70.1800	92.2903	136.669
Kuwait	Dinar	0.2892	0.3804	0.5632
Malaysia	M$	3.6400	4.7868	7.0886
Mexico	New peso	11.0388	14.5166	21.4970
New Zealand	NZ$	1.4798	1.9461	2.8819
Nigeria	Naira	128.000	168.327	249.262
Norway	NKr	6.3104	8.2985	12.2889
Pakistan	Rupee	60.8000	79.9551	118.402
Peru	New sol	3.2245	4.2404	6.2794
Philippines	Peso	10.0050	66.6116	07.1666
Poland	Zloty	2.9124	3.8299	5.6715
Romania	New leu	2.6384	3.4696	5.1380
Russia	Rouble	26.34440	34.6437	51.3023
Saudi Arabia	SR	3.7504	4.9320	7.3036
Singapore	S$	1.5498	2.0380	3.0180
Slovakia	Koruna	27.0469	35.5680	52.6711
Slovenia	Tolar	182.259	239.680	354.932
South Africa	Rand	7.1718	9.4312	13.9663
South Korea	Won	930.800	1224.05	1812.64
Sweden	SKr	6.9049	9.0803	13.4466
Switzerland	SFr	1.2083	1.5890	2.3530
Taiwan	T$	32.6500	42.9364	63.5826
Thailand	Baht	36.3100	47.7495	70.7101
Tunisia	Dinar	1.3000	1.7096	2.5316
Turkey	Lira	1.4753	1.9400	2.8729
UAE	Dirham	3.6731	4.8303	7.1529
UK (0.5135)	Pound	1.9474	0.6753	–

Country	Currency	DOLLAR	EURO	POUND
One month		1.9478	0.6761	-
Three month		1.0183	0.6778	
One year		1.9454	0.6851	-
Uruguay	Peso	24.2950	31.9492	47.3121
USA	$	-	1.3151	1.9474
One month		-	1.3170	1.9478
Three month		-	1.3206	1.9483
One year		-	1.3327	1.9454
Venezuela	Bolivar	3539.53	4654.66	6892.88
Vietnam	Dong	16083.00	21149.90	31320.00
Euro (0.7604)		1.3151	-	1.4809
One month		1.3170	-	1.4790
Three month		1.3206	-	1.4753
One year		1.3327	-	1.4597

Table 17.1 also presents the exchange rate between world currencies and the euro and the pound.[3] An exchange rate of two currencies that does not include the USD is called a cross rate. Cross rates may be estimated by following this simple rule: if you wish to estimate a cross rate in terms of currency A per every unit of currency B, then simply divide the European quote of A by the European quote of B. The example below (taken from the *Financial Times*, 29 November 2006) shows how we would find the cross rate between the Argentinean peso and the British pound in terms of pesos per pound. As may be observed, our estimation yields the same cross rate as the one directly read from Table 17.1 under the euro column for the Argentinean peso:

European quote for the peso :   3.0788 pesos/USD
Eurpean quote for the British pound :   0.513505 pounds/USD

$$\text{Cross rate (pesos/pound)} = \frac{\text{European quote for peso}}{\text{European quote for pound}} = \frac{3.0788\ {pesos}/{USD}}{0.513505\ {pounds}/{USD}} = 5.9956\ {pesos}/{pound}$$

An observation of a live currency quote information panel will show that there is quite a lot of activity surrounding major currencies, with the most active exchange rates changing many times every minute. When a currency's value evolves so that it is subsequently worth *more* units of foreign currency, then we say it has experienced an *appreciation* of its value. If subsequent exchange rates show that a currency is worth *less* units of foreign currency, then it has experienced a *depreciation* of its value.

For example, let's take the euro's evolution against the US dollar. Table 17.1 shows the euro trading at 1.3151 USD/euro. Twelve months before, the euro was being exchanged at 1.1800 USD per euro. If we wish to estimate the euro's change with respect to the USD, we need to make sure all quotes are such that the euro is the currency being quoted (the denominator position). Once this is achieved, we calculate the change in price with respect to its initial value. Below we show how to calculate whether the euro appreciated or depreciated with respect to the USD:

Quote as of Nov 28, 2005 : $1.1800 \, \text{USD}\!\big/\!\text{euro}$

Quote as of Nov 28, 2006 : $1.3151 \, \text{USD}\!\big/\!\text{euro}$

Euro's change : $\dfrac{\text{USD at end} - \text{USD at beginning}}{\text{USD at beginning}} = \dfrac{1.3151 - 1.1800}{1.1800} = 0.1145 = 11.45\%$

Because of the positive sign observed in our result, we can conclude that the euro has appreciated by 11.45% against the US dollar. How, then, has the USD fared against the euro? Our intuition is probably telling us that it must have depreciated. To confirm this, let's repeat our estimation. Before doing so, remember that we are now estimating the *dollar's* evolution, so the quotes must be such that the USD is in the denominator. We find these quotes by inverting the ones we already have, as shown below:

Quote as of 28 Nov, 2005 : $\dfrac{1}{1.1800 \, \text{USD}\!\big/\!\text{euro}} = 0.8474 \, \text{euros}\!\big/\!\text{USD}$

Quote as of 28 Nov, 2006 : $\dfrac{1}{1.3151 \, \text{USD}\!\big/\!\text{euro}} = 0.7604 \, \text{euros}\!\big/\!\text{USD}$

Euro's change : $\dfrac{\text{€ at end} - \text{€ at beginning}}{\text{€ at beginning}} = \dfrac{0.7604 - 0.8474}{0.8474} = -0.1027 = -10.27\%$

As expected, the result is negative, implying that the USD has indeed depreciated against the euro. However, you may also notice that the magnitude is not the same. The euro has appreciated 11.45% against the USD but the USD has only depreciated 10.27% against the euro. These two effects should differ since, if this were not the case, a currency that appreciates by 150% with respect to another would imply that the second should equally depreciate by 150% with respect to the first. This is not possible, since a depreciation of 100% would already mean that the currency is worthless (value = 0). Currencies may fall in value, but they never reach a point where they do not have any value. In fact, if indeed currency A appreciates by 150% with respect to currency B, this implies that B has depreciated only by about 60% with respect to currency A.

Finally, let's again look at Table 17.1: it also provides one month, three month and one year exchange rates for the most actively traded currencies such as the yen, UK pound, US dollar and euro. These are called *forward* rates. Forward rates are the rates that we can lock in today in order to carry a currency transaction in the future. Thus, Table 17.1 indicates that a European investor could set up an agreement (*forward contract*) to buy British pounds, three months from now, at a fixed exchange rate of 1.4797 euros/pound. If the pound happens to appreciate against the euro during this three-month period, the European investor would be unaffected by this appreciation since he has a forward contract that provides the pounds at a fixed price of 1.4797 euros per pound. Of course, the story does not end as happily if the pound in fact depreciated against the euro and the investor is still required to fulfil his side of the agreement. Unfortunately, unlike other instruments such as currency options contracts, forward contracts generate an obligation. Having said this, the reader should remember that the assumed motivation for using the forward contract was to remove currency uncertainty and not for speculation.

parity conditions: how do we relate currency movements and macro-variables?

Having discussed how we measure changes in the exchange rate, the next issue is to identify the variables that affect exchange rate movements. The relative demand and supply that one currency has with respect to another is a consequence of the exchange of goods and services between nations. If the rest of the world heavily demands a country's goods and services, then its currency will appreciate relative to other currencies. This follows the rule that anything that is heavily demanded will increase in price.

> If the rest of the world heavily demands a country's goods and services, then its currency will appreciate relative to other currencies.

However, in addition to the commercial trade between nations, other factors such as political or social conditions may prompt investors to exit a country (and thus sell their currency holdings) in order to trade or invest their funds in a more stable environment. During the Mexican political and financial crisis of 1994, many international holders of financial instruments denominated in Mexican pesos sold their holdings in order to invest their funds in, say, US Treasury securities. The end effect was that these investors provided an excess supply of pesos (sold pesos) and created an excess demand for dollars. The excess supply of pesos made the Mexican currency fall in value (depreciate) against the US currency.

In spite of the myriad of factors that may potentially affect exchange rates, there are a series of relationships between macroeconomic variables and the exchange rate, termed *parity conditions*, which provide tools of analysis that help us determine how exchange rates should behave. As is the case with most concepts, it all begins with a simple idea: in this instance, 'the law of one price', which is expressed by the following equation:

$$S_{Baht/Yen} = \frac{PRICE_{Baht}}{PRICE_{Yen}}$$

The law of one price equation basically states that goods with equal characteristics should be worth the same, independent of location. If this were not true, then market participants could implement *arbitrage* by buying the good in the cheaper location and simultaneously selling the same good in the more expensive location. This process would continue until the excess demand of the good in the cheaper location ultimately increases its price (if everyone wants to buy the same good, its value increases). Simultaneously, the increase in the supply of the good in the more expensive transaction will eventually lead to an excess supply that ultimately lowers its price. Thanks to this process, the lower price increases while the higher price falls until they reach the equilibrium price level. At this equilibrium price, no one can implement arbitrage profits.

Of course, the reader will argue that there is a missing component in our example: different goods in different locations are expressed in their respective currencies. So where is the link that makes one price possible? The answer is found in the exchange rate. Imagine the following situation: one ounce of gold costs 624.30 dollars in the US and 490.64 euros in the EU. For the law of one price to hold, it must occur that the price of gold in the EU, when transformed to dollars, must exactly equal the price observed in the US. Below is a sample equation illustrating the law of one price:

$$490.64€ \times S_{USD/€} = 624.30 \ USD$$

Therefore,

$$S_{USD/€} = \frac{624.30 \ USD}{490.64 \ €} = 1.27 \ USD/€$$

What this implies is that the rate at which we should exchange euros and dollars must be such that one euro is worth 1.27 USD. When this happens, a good worth 490.64 euros is transformed into 624.30 USD. You may recall that the actual November 2006 quote for the euro was 1.27 USD. Thus, the prices in these two countries do seem to be consistent with the law of one price.

This result seems to provide a powerful tool with which to forecast exchange rate movements. All we have to do is find a common good between two countries, determine the exchange rate that would make the law of one price hold, and then simply compare it to the actual currency quotes in the markets. For example, our calculations indicate that one euro should be exchanged for 1.27 USD. Thus, if the euro is currently traded in the markets at 1.10 USD per euro, then we can forecast a euro *appreciation* since its equilibrium price should reach 1.27 USD. Under these conditions, one would readily buy as many euros as possible at 1.10 and simply wait until the euro reaches its fair value.

There is one caveat, however, with the law of one price. It assumes that there are no transaction costs or barriers that increase the cost of arbitrage transactions. Thus, market participants can easily exploit price differences between countries, no matter how small these differences are. After all, no taxes or transaction costs exist. The reality in world markets is quite different. There are transaction costs, tax differences and currency controls that increase the cost of arbitrage transactions. These market 'imperfections' may prevent the benefit obtained from exploiting the price difference being worth the effort. Thus, prices may not be corrected. In addition, not all goods can be arbitraged away. A Big Mac in downtown Sydney may be less expensive than one found in Madrid's main plaza. However, this does not necessarily imply that we can exploit the arbitrage by buying Big Macs in Sydney and selling them in Madrid. There is simply no secondary market for hamburgers (at least I wouldn't buy one).

In spite of the limitations of the law of one price, people come up with interesting tools with which to forecast exchange rate movements based on this rule. All you have to do is find an asset that has the same characteristics across market locations. One well-known attempt is the Big Mac Index. With the presence of McDonald's around the world, one can argue that local currency prices of a Big Mac coffee provide a comparison with which to apply the law of one price. In fact, *The Economist* periodically publishes these indexes.

The law of one price is just one of several relationships that are used to explain both the behaviour and determinants of exchange rate movements. Here are other parity conditions.

purchasing power parity

Purchasing power parity (PPP) is a modified version of the law of one price. However, instead of indicating that the exchange rate is such that it makes all prices equal, it indicates that exchange rates will *change* according to changes in the general price levels of countries (that is, π = inflation). The following equation illustrates PPP:

$$\frac{S_t}{S_0} = \left(\frac{1+\pi_{home}}{1+\pi_{abroad}}\right)$$

The PPP forecasts that countries with higher rates of inflation will also experience a depreciation of their currencies. In other words, countries whose prices grow more rapidly should observe their currency depreciating so that, when transformed to other currencies, the relative prices remain unchanged.

For example, say the expected annual inflation rates in Brazil and the US are 6% and 3% respectively, then PPP indicates that the Brazilian reais' spot rate should change in such a manner that reflects the inflation rate differences between the two countries. If the current rate at which reais and US dollars are traded for immediate delivery (the *spot* rate) is S_0 = 2.16 reais/USD, then the spot rate a year from now, S_1, will be as shown below:

$$S_1 = S_0\left(\frac{1+\pi_{home}}{1+\pi_{abroad}}\right) = 2.16\left(\frac{1+0.06}{1+0.03}\right) = 2.16(1.029) = 2.22\,Reais/USD$$

A frequent question is that, in using the PPP formula, how does one know what is considered home and what is abroad? In addition, which currency's change in price is it that we are estimating? The short answer is that we should look at the exchange rate we are using and identify the currency in the numerator and the denominator. To find *home*, simply look at the currency in the numerator. To find the currency we are quoting, look at the denominator. In our example, we started using a spot exchange rate of 2.16 reais/USD. Thus, home is Brazil (the numerator). The USD (denominator) is the currency whose change in value is being forecasted by PPP.

the fisher effect

The Fisher effect (FE) states that the nominal interest rates earned by investors should provide a real rate of return r (compensation for delayed consumption) and an inflation-related return π (compensation for the loss of purchasing power). Thus, if an investment offers a 9% return in a location that presents an inflation of 3%, then the real return the investment offers is of 6%. Thus, in addition to earning a 3% return to compensate for any loss of purchasing power due to inflation, the investor is earning 6% as compensation for putting his money to work. Below is the FE equation:

$$i = r + \pi$$

A consequence of FE is that nominal interest rate differences between countries should follow their respective inflation differentials. In short, countries with higher inflation levels should also present higher nominal interest rates. This is because higher inflation (if real rates are unchanged) requires that higher nominal rates must be offered in order to continue attracting investors. If this were not so, investors would actually lose wealth. As an example, earning a 10% nominal rate of return when inflation is 7% implies a real rate of 3% (10% = 3% + 7%). However, earning the same 10% when inflation rises to 14% would effectively mean that the investment offers a negative real return of –4%.

the international fisher effect

The international Fisher effect (IFE) is a natural consequence of the PPP and FE. PPP states that exchange rates are affected by inflation differentials, while FE indicates that nominal interest rates are also affected by inflationary differences. We close the circle by stating that the changes in spot rates must also be affected by nominal interest rate differences. Below is the IFE equation:

$$\frac{S_t}{S_0} = \frac{1 + i_{home}}{1 + i_{abroad}}$$

interest rate parity condition

The interest rate parity (IRP) condition takes the IFE a notch further by stating that forward rates are a function of nominal interest rate differences. There is, however, one major difference between IRP and the other parity conditions. IRP is a technical trading rule that must hold in the currency markets in order to avoid arbitrage opportunities, while the other parity conditions are equilibrium models that hold in equilibrium. Below is the IRP equation:

$$\frac{F_t}{S_0} = \frac{1 + i_{home}}{1 + i_{abroad}}$$

balance of payments

Remember that a company's financial statements are useful in that they show the economic consequences of doing business at a microeconomic level. In the case of nations, the equivalent of financial statements is the *balance of payments* (BoP) account. The BoP reflects the economic consequences of all transactions that occur between the residents of a country and their foreign counterparts. This information is presented following double-entry bookkeeping principles where all transactions have a matching offsetting entry. Additionally, because it covers all transactions during a specific period of time, the BoP is more a cash flow indicator rather than the snapshot typically provided by a firm's balance account. However, the BoP is useful for a more pragmatic reason: it provides information that helps managers and investors to determine trends in economic growth, generate expectations concerning currency evolution or catch signals of potential regulatory or tax-related changes.

The BoP is composed of the current and capital accounts,[4] as well as the official reserves and the net errors and omissions account. The *current account* tracks transactions whose flows occur within a one-year time frame, and which reflect the flow of goods (merchandise trade) and services (travel and financial services), income that is received or paid (dividends received from investments abroad or salaries paid to non-residents) and, finally, unrequited transfers (see Table 17.2). The latter indicate any transfer of funds that is not a consequence of providing a good or service. Remittances, the funds sent by immigrant residents to their countries of origin, may be considered as unrequited transfers.[5] Although the current account balance is frequently linked to the trade balance, it is not always the case that a country with a trade surplus/deficit automatically shows a current account surplus/deficit.[6]

Table 17.2 Sample current account transactions

Australian exporter sells wine to US client	Credit in Australian trade balance
US government bond pays interest to Japanese holder	Debit in US income account
Resident of Spain sends funds to family in Colombia	Debit in Spanish unrequited transfers account

The second account we will emphasize is the *capital account,* which tracks government debt and all capital market transactions such as FDI or portfolio investments (see Table 17.3). Any transaction involving the purchasing or sale of bonds and stocks would be entered under portfolio transactions within the capital account. The acquisition of property and plant by foreign firms would be part of FDI investment.

Table 17.3 Sample capital account transactions

Thailand selected as location for the new production facilities of a US firm	Credit in Thailand's FDI account
UK investor purchases bonds issued by the US government	Debit in UK's portfolio account

Because of double-entry bookkeeping, the capital account helps to explain a large part of the evolution observed in a nation's current account. For example, if a German firm exports 100,000 euros worth of wine to a US importer, this will generate a credit in Germany's current account (export of merchandise goods). On the opposite side of the transaction, the US importer makes the 100,000 euro payment to the German exporter's bank in New York. This increases Germany's foreign deposits, which is classified as capital leaving Germany, so it generates a debit in its capital account. In a similar manner, a surplus in the capital account generates a deficit in the current account, since the portfolio of assets sold to foreigners will ultimately generate an outflow of funds, through the current account, in the form of interest or dividend payments. In the same manner, a net FDI investment inflow will generate a current account outflow in the form of repatriated earnings.

Finally, the *international reserves account* is where all foreign currency transactions are included and the *net errors and omissions account* is a plug-in that shows the magnitude of funds that have not been tracked and would have made the BoP balance. Thus, as the name says, the balance in the BoP is really the result of all components balancing out. Below is the BoP equation:

Balance of payments = current account + capital account + international reserves + errors

There is an interesting relationship between exchange rate systems and the manner in which the BoP evolves. Assume a country like China adopts a *fixed exchange rate system* at 7.8 Chinese yuan per USD. If China experiences a net surplus of foreign currency (net balance of current and capital accounts is positive) because of a large trade surplus, then the higher ratio of foreign currency per yuan will make the yuan appreciate in value. To maintain the fixed rate, the Central Bank of China will need to use yuan to buy foreign currency (Chinese international reserves increase), thus creating an excess supply of yuan that will lower its value back to the 7.8 target exchange rate. If, on the other hand, China experiences a net deficit, then there is a deficit of foreign currency that would make the yuan depreciate. To correct this, the Bank of China will sell foreign currency (Chinese international reserves decrease) in order to buy yuan and bring its value back to 7.8 yuan/USD. Thus, a fixed rate system implies the use of reserves to maintain peg.

In contrast, *floating exchange rate systems* allow the exchange rate to fluctuate according to market forces and thus do not have the same effect on a country's international reserves. If a net surplus occurs in China, the oversupply of foreign currency would simply make the yuan appreciate in value. This would in turn reduce exports and increase imports so that the surplus is reverted back to 'equilibrium'. Under a deficit condition, the scarce foreign currency would imply yuan depreciation, something which would ultimately be corrected by more exports, thanks to cheaper yuan.

> Under a floating exchange rate system, a country with a net deficit condition will experience a currency depreciation, while a surplus will generate an appreciation.

To summarize, under a floating exchange rate system, a country with a net deficit condition will experience a currency depreciation, while a surplus will generate an appreciation. Under a fixed exchange rate system, a country with a net deficit condition will experience a reduction in its international reserves, while a surplus will generate an increase of international reserves.

Our example above does reflect a common trade issue in Chinese–US relations. Since China is a net exporter, its surplus condition would normally imply a yuan appreciation under a floating rate system. However, the US argues that China, in order to not lose exports (its main economic driver), intervenes in order to maintain an undervalued yuan. This keeps Chinese goods at a price advantage, to the detriment of the US, which bears a large trade deficit with respect to China.

The US has gone from a virtually zero current account deficit in the early 1990s to a deficit of more than 700 billion dollars by the end of 2005. This would imply a USD depreciation. In fact, the USD has depreciated by more than 10% against the euro in the 12 months prior to November 2006.

However, for a long time, the USD was apparently not affected by its large deficit condition. Why? To answer this, remember that a net current account deficit implies that the US pays more than it receives, so it needs to seek financing to pay its short-term obligations. This extra financing comes from an inflow in the capital account in the form of purchases of debt instruments issued by the US government. In fact, to finance its current account deficit, the US needs to have investors purchasing its securities to the tune of 2–3 billion dollars per day!

Fortunately for the US, foreign investors seem to have a large appetite for US securities. However, a weakening USD may prompt foreign investors to consider a reduction of their dollar holdings, since some of the large buyers of US debt are Asian central banks.[7] By purchasing these securities, the Chinese Central Bank is financing the US and, simultaneously, keeping its yuan low by selling yuan and demanding USD.

As can be seen, Chinese intervention in the markets does indeed maintain a devalued yuan, but it also helps the US fund its investment needs. Although there are those who argue that a higher yuan would solve the US current account deficit, it is estimated that a yuan appreciation would only solve about a third of the US current account deficit problem. Fiscal discipline is also a requirement for lower deficits.

As may be observed, BoP analysis can provide important information concerning currency movements. As an example, a country that adopts a fixed exchange rate, runs a current account deficit and has low levels of international reserves will generate a 'red light' in relation to concerns for currency depreciation. Its deficit condition will make the country use up its reserves in order maintain the fixed exchange rate. However, low reserves may imply that the country may be unable to continue the peg, and thus resort to a devaluation (the crises in Argentina, Mexico and Asia were consequences of this type of condition).

Similarly, the evolution of the capital account can provide an indication of FDI and portfolio investment trends that help managers to forecast more flexible regulation conditions. In contrast, the setting up of barriers to entry for investment funds can signal a business environment that is not yet receptive to international flows and even prone to nationalistic measures.

international investments

When we invest abroad, we are explicitly investing in financial instruments, commodities or assets. However, we are also implicitly investing in the foreign currency. To observe how this is so, let's go back to our earlier calculation of the euro's appreciation against the US dollar. You may recall that, by November 2006, the euro had experienced a 12-month appreciation of 11.45% (see Table 17.4).

Table 17.4 The evolution of the euro against the USD during a 12-month period

Estimated annual appreciation and depreciation for each currency	
	Spot rate (USD/euro)
Nov 2005	1.1800
Nov 2006	1.3151
Euro appreciation against the USD	11.45%
USD depreciation against the euro	10.27%

If a European investor had purchased a USD-denominated financial instrument that offered a 10% return back in November 2005, she would presumably observe her account balance grow by 10%. If she invested 1,000 euros, this would mean that, at the spot rate of 1.18 USD/euro, she would have invested a total number of dollars equal to 1,000 euros × 1.18 USD/euros = 1,180 USD. A 10% return on this initial investment implies that 1,180 USD × (1.10) = 1,298 USD would be in her account after the 12 months. However, because she is a European invested in US dollars, she now needs to transform these USD holdings to euros. Given that the dollar has depreciated by 10.27% with respect to the euro, what is her net euro return? The two equations below help us to find the answer:

$$r_{euros} = (1 + r_{USD})(1 + g) - 1$$

g = USD change relative to the euro = −10.27%

Thus,

$$r_{euros} = (1 + 0.10)(1 - 0.1027) - 1 = -0.013 = -1.3\%$$

This can be more easily appreciated in Table 17.5. As the table shows, our euro investor ends up with a net loss of 1.3%. She invested 1,000 euros but ended up with 987 euros a year later. This result is a consequence of the compounding effect of earning a negative currency return on top of the positive return received from the actual investment. In this case, the depreciation effect dominated the investment's 10% return.

Table 17.5 The impact of investing in a depreciating currency

	Investment in euros	Spot rate (USD/euros)	Investment in USD
This table presents the net euro return earned after investing 1,000 euros in the US, earning a 10% return in dollars, but also experiencing a USD depreciation of 10.27% against the euro.			
Nov 2005	1,000 euros →	1.1800 →	1,180 USD
Nov 2006	987 euros ←	1.3151 ←	1,298 USD
Return	−1.30%	−10.27%	10%

Things would have been quite different for a US participant investing in Europe at 10%. In this case, the US investor would have received his 10% plus the benefit of investing in a currency that appreciated by 11.45% relative to his home currency. The equation below shows how to calculate the impact of investing in an appreciating economy, giving a net USD return on this hypothetical European investment:

$$r_{USD} = (1 + r_{euros})(1 + g) - 1 = (1.10) x (1.1145) - 1 = 22.59\%$$

g = euro change relative to the USD = 11.45%

Again, in more detail, Table 17.6 shows how a US investor would ultimately receive 1,226 dollars for his 1,000 USD investment. This is due to the compounding effect of earning a currency appreciation return on top of the return received from the actual investment.

Table 17.6 The impact of investing in an appreciating currency

	Investment in USD	Spot rate (USD/euros)	Investment in euros
This table presents the net USD return earned after investing 1,000 USD in Europe, earning a 10% return in euros, but also experiencing a euro appreciation of 11.45% against the USD.			
Nov 2005	1,000 USD →	1.1800 →	847 euros
Nov 2006	1,226 USD ←	1.3151 ←	932 euros
Return	22.59%	11.45%	10%

In summary, therefore, when we invest abroad, this implicitly implies investing in a foreign currency. Any appreciation in the foreign currency will increase any return earned abroad, while any currency depreciation will reduce it.

The impact of currency movements is one aspect of investing abroad. There is another aspect that is related more specifically to diversification. As you may recall from Chapter 13, finance theory assumes that we are all diversified investors. Diversification implies the use of assets that are not perfectly correlated with each other in order to achieve higher levels of return for the same level of risk or, symmetrically, lower levels of risk for the same level of returns.

Remember that diversification can be visually observed by observing the best risk–return combinations of our portfolio holdings in a bidimensional plane, with return in the vertical axis and risk in the horizontal axis (see Figure 17.3). The result is a curve known as the 'efficient frontier'. As we include more stocks from different industries, we observe that the convexity of our efficient frontier approaches the vertical axis. In other words, we bear lower risk levels while maintaining the same portfolio return.

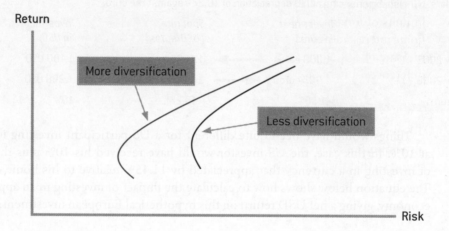

Figure 17.3 The efficient frontier

If diversification benefits can be attained by investing across domestic industries, imagine the potential of investing across industries and geographic locations. Just as the differences in the regulatory, economic, political and social environments between countries present a challenge, these same differences offer attractive rewards, since economies reacting in different ways to the same shocks provide the conditions that help us to diversify and reduce portfolio risk.

the cost of capital

An important component of any effort to create value is to correctly estimate the return (or hurdle rate) that should be required from investments. You may recall that the return we require should be a function of the amount of risk we bear. If it's not, we may destroy value in our decisions. For example, if we require too high a hurdle rate, then we will reject projects that would have otherwise added value. If our hurdle rate is too low, then we will accept projects whose return is not enough to compensate the cost of the funds used, so value is destroyed. Since our hurdle rate is also a function of how much we need to pay our providers of funds, a second important component of value creation is to choose the mix of debt and equity securities that minimizes our cost of capital. A lower cost of capital means that we will find a larger universe of acceptable, value-enhancing projects.[8] The cost of capital component of an international finance course will therefore deal with a correct estimation of the cost of capital, as well as a description of our financing choices.

What then changes in the cost of capital estimation in international projects? In general, investing in a business environment with different regulatory, political and cultural characteristics adds risk to our investments. If so, a *country risk premium* (CRP) to the return we would normally require is added as a way of requiring higher compensation for the higher risk of going abroad.

Although, in theory, the finance models used to estimate returns, such as the capital asset pricing model (CAPM), should reflect any additional risk, barriers to a free flow of international trade make it necessary to include a CRP.

A final adjustment to the way we estimate the cost of capital is in the manner we apply models such as the CAPM. For example, are the foreign project's cash flows expressed in units of foreign currency? If so, what input variables should be used, the investor's home interest rates or the interest rates observed in the target foreign country? Does our measure of risk require any adjustments? How do we account for the effect of inflation differences? International finance deals with these important considerations.

the right financing mix

To create value, management's concern is not just the maximization of cash flows. It is also important to minimize the cost of capital. When the right mix of debt and equity is found so that the cost of capital is minimized, we say we have found our firm's *optimal capital structure*. Clearly, the lower the cost a firm pays for the funds lent by stockholders and debt holders, the better. Additionally, it is important for firms to have access to liquid markets so that they are able to maintain or change this mix as needed.

> To create value, management's concern is not just the maximization of cash flows. It is also important to minimize the cost of capital.

Multinational firms that are able to seek financing abroad enjoy a potential advantage on both counts. Being able to borrow in different countries and currencies allows global firms to make use of the best interest rate conditions. Lower cost conditions may also arise because of tax or regulatory-related advantages. In addition, borrowing in foreign currency may actually provide a cost reduction effect from potential currency fluctuations or simply facilitate a better hedge of currency risk.[9] Such a hedge would occur if a firm invests and borrows in the same foreign currency, thus matching its foreign assets and liabilities.

In addition to accessing bank loans from international markets, borrowers can access bond and equity markets around the world. The international bond market is one place where high-quality issuers such as well-known corporations borrow by issuing debt securities. Firms can issue eurobonds[10] and thus borrow US dollars in Japan. They can also borrow in other countries' home currencies by issuing foreign bonds. Thus, a Japanese firm issuing a dollar-denominated bond in the US would be using a foreign bond called a 'Yankee bond'. If a US firm issues a foreign bond in Japan (yen-denominated), the bond is termed a 'Samurai bond'.

Firms can also choose to issue equity in larger and more developed markets. Although expensive, access to foreign equity markets provides other benefits in addition to a possible lower cost of financing. For firms that base their business activity in countries with small and illiquid stock markets, issuing equity abroad allows them to circumvent their home market's limited capability to provide funds. Additionally, firms may decide to issue stock in more developed and transparent markets to send a signal of higher quality. By satisfying more stringent corporate governance requirements than those of their home market, these international issuers effectively differentiate themselves from other firms in their home market. This would potentially allow a lower cost of equity, since investors generally recognize higher quality by demanding lower compensation.

To issue equity abroad, a firm can arrange for a bank to issue a global depository receipt (GDR) that represents, say, 10 of its ordinary shares. The GDRs would be issued in euros, pounds or dollars and in more than one country. If the GDR was issued in euros, the holder would receive the dividend payments provided by the 10 shares in that same currency, after the original foreign currency payments have been exchange rate adjusted. American depository receipts (ADRs) are similar to GDRs, except that they are dollar-denominated and only issued in the US.

derivative securities

Currency movements will affect a multinational firm's cash flow generation capability, since these alter the home currency value of revenues and costs experienced abroad. For example, a euro appreciation may increase a Korean firm's salary expense for its manufacturing facility in Spain. If the cost cannot be transferred to consumers, this will reduce profits. This kind of exposure to exchange rate volatility is termed *economic exposure*. Another way currency fluctuation affects firms is by generating *transaction exposure*, which occurs when existing financial commitments are negatively or positively affected by currency changes. Providing a fixed foreign currency-denominated price to foreign clients generates this type of exposure, since the time lag that exists between the price quote and the moment the foreign currency payments are received may expose the seller to potential losses if the exchange rate changes. Depending on the foreign location, losses and gains due to currency movements may also generate tax and accounting-related gains or losses that ultimately may produce changes in the cash-generating potential of an overseas operation. The latter case is an example of *accounting exposure*.

> Currency movements will affect a multinational firm's cash flow generation capability, since these alter the home currency value of revenues and costs experienced abroad.

Because managers and investors are continually exposed to exchange rate fluctuations, financial markets have created instruments to manage or *hedge* currency risk. These instruments, called *derivatives*, include options, futures, forwards and swaps. Their generic name comes from the fact that they derive their value from the price evolution of an asset termed the *underlying asset*. You may remember that Chapter 13 described a stock option contract that 'Freda' receives. In this example, the underlying asset was Jasper Printing's stock price. If the stock price went up, Freda's options were worth more, while a stock price fall could render Freda's options worthless. In the case of currency derivatives, the underlying asset is a currency. Thus, a euro options contract's underlying asset is the euro. Since options were discussed in Chapter 13, we will briefly turn our attention to forwards and futures contracts.

As stated previously, a forward contract is an agreement between two parties to exchange an asset at a specific time in the future and at a price agreed upon today. These instruments are custom-made contracts, since the maturity and asset type are the result of our personal requirements. An example of a forward contract is agreeing to buy one million Korean won, 20 days from now, at a price of 1,218 won per euro. In doing so, you eliminate currency risk since the exchange rate is fixed. An important characteristic of forwards is that, unlike options, these are contractual *obligations*, so we do not have the choice of letting the contract expire unused. Therefore, 20 days from now, you have the obligation to buy the won at the agreed price.

Although forward contracts are useful hedging instruments, they contain several unwanted characteristics. Forwards make you bear credit risk, since your counterparty may default. In addition, if you decide that you no longer have any need for the forward, it is difficult to find someone willing to purchase it under the same conditions you found useful. Is response to this, *futures contracts* were created by organized exchanges. Futures are forward contracts whose terms have been standardized so that each contract has specific maturity dates, underlying asset types and contract size. In addition, these instruments are marked to market on a daily basis so that the losses and gains are determined during the life of the contract, instead of waiting until the contract matures. For example, euro futures contracts mature in March, June, September or December and trade at multiples of 125,000 euros. Thanks to the standardization and the marking to market, a futures position may be closed at any point in time and the credit risk is no longer borne.

conclusion

In conclusion, international finance deals with the manner in which value is affected by doing business abroad. In this context, we mentioned that just as there are potential growth and diversification benefits when investing at an international level, the other side of the coin is that country risk and the value impact of currency volatility needs to be measured, forecasted and managed. We measured it by conceptually introducing how the exchange rate is determined and measured. We introduced exchange-related forecasting topics that covered the analysis of macroeconomic conditions (balance of payments) to more quantitative tools such as parity relationships. The managing of this risk was introduced through the use of derivative securities as hedging instruments. The good news was that most of the conceptual structure used in finance is applicable in an international context. However, the reader must remember that both the numerator and the denominator of our 'value' equation require adjustments when going abroad.

> *Just as there are potential growth and diversification benefits when investing at an international level, the other side of the coin is that country risk and the value impact of currency volatility needs to be measured, forecasted and managed.*

So what are the issues that challenge current research in international finance? Of course, work is being carried out in all areas. However, let me share a couple of research concerns that have become more relevant with globalization. The first topic deals with the manner in which corporate governance standards affect value. As access to multinational financing increasingly becomes a necessity, firms and countries need to signal to international investors that their interests will be exposed to credible institutions, transparent information and enhanced investor protection measures.

For example, listing a stock in a developed market may carry with it the intention of signalling greater commitment to enhanced governance standards, since listing implies satisfying more stringent governance requirements. If investors do perceive this as a signal of greater quality, they will in turn require less compensation, lower the firm's cost of capital and thus increase the firm's value. The interesting research questions thus deal with determining whether in fact such signals of commitment increase firm value and provide more liquid markets. If so, what are the governance measures and country conditions that drive this value increase? This is an important question for any firm or country competing for funds at an international level.

There is a second point of interest regarding the role of globalization in the development of countries. International remittances now allow innovative banks to develop relationships with micro-entrepreneurs and other receptors of remitted funds instead of passively assuming the role of a simple (albeit expensive) provider of electronic transfers. Financial institutions now facilitate business and mortgage loans using remittances as collateral. Thus, funds that were generally spent in pure consumption now become sources of small business opportunities that enhance people's lives and stem forced migration. The trend then is to explore how successful micro-credit policies can be adapted to larger lending structures so that they have a wider impact on employment and people's well-being.

references/notes

1. Material sourced from the *Financial Times*, 28 November 2006.
2. Exchange rates valid for transactions that call for immediate payment and delivery.
3. There are also many web-based sources of exchange rate information that are quite user-friendly, such as http://www.xe.com/ucc/
4. The International Monetary Fund actually uses the capital and financial accounts separately, but for explanation purposes, I use the former term as all-inclusive.
5. Although ignored in the past, remittances now exceed 100 billion dollars per year and are equivalent to the aggregate GDP of the 66 smallest world economies. For many countries, remittances are now their main source of hard currency, exceeding even their own exports.
6. Chile is a net exporter and so presents a trade surplus. However, because this nation is also an attractive investment location, its income account was at a deficit in some years due to the outflow of funds as payments to foreign investors. Since the income deficit dominated the trade surplus, its current account showed a net deficit.
7. A 24 November 2006 announcement that the Central Bank of China, holder of the world's largest international currency reserves (1 trillion dollars), was going to diversify its portfolio by reducing its USD holdings caused dollar depreciation in the markets.
8. It is not the same thing to require a 12% return from projects as it is to require 30%. We will find far fewer ones in which to invest in the latter case.
9. If a Japanese firm is able to borrow in a currency that depreciates against the yen, this would have the effect of reducing the yen-denominated cost of debt.
10. A eurobond is a security issued in a currency other than the currency of the country where the issue takes place.

18 business strategy

professor colin white

It is difficult to define strategy with any precision since it is a complex notion: there are almost as many definitions as there are individual commentators. Whole books have been devoted to its definition.[1] In its simplest conception, strategy is a unifying idea that links purpose and action, or, putting it more subtly:

a coordinated series of actions which involve the deployment of resources to which one has access for the achievement of a given purpose.[2]

Alfred Chandler, the first theorist of business strategy, defined strategy in the area of business as:

the determination of the basic, long-term goals and objectives of an enterprise, and the adoption of courses of action and the allocation of resources necessary for those goals.[3]

Sometimes the strategy is in the mind of a grand strategist; it is not written down, not spelt out in any detail, it is implicit, communicated by word of mouth, sometimes to a small team of senior managers. The strategy may unfold with events and be adjusted quickly and in unanticipated ways. This is often the case with the founder of a successful enterprise, such as Bill Gates (Microsoft), Geoff Bezos (Amazon.com), Richard Branson (Virgin) or Ingvar Kamprad (IKEA). It is not unusual for a CEO to adopt this approach in a crisis when all energy is concentrated on turning around an enterprise, as with Carlos Ghosn and Nissan. However, it is much better for the decision makers in mature enterprises not under threat to make the strategy explicit, thereby institutionalizing the strategy-making process. However flexible the strategy, its main features must be written down and widely and clearly communicated.

> *All successful organizations have a good strategy, and succeed largely because of it.*

All successful organizations have a good strategy, and succeed largely because of it. Having a good strategy does not guarantee success, unless, that is, it is defined in a meaningless way to be synonymous with success. A good strategy makes success more likely, whereas a bad strategy makes failure inevitable. Having a good strategy helps to clarify strategic intent – what an organization is trying to achieve – by indicating the resources that are required. In this sense, strategy is simply good operational management, placed in a dynamic setting.

a brief history of the concept

Strategy's significance extends beyond the world of corporate strategy, having relevance to all areas of human activity. It had its origins many centuries ago in the distinction made by military theorists between strategy and tactics, which almost exactly parallels the distinction between strategy and current business operations.[4] The military analogy encourages a narrow conception of strategy – that it is something handed down from above and highly competitive, just like the battlefield.

The application of strategy to the business area took time to take hold. An early emphasis in economic theory on competition limited the scope for independent choice of strategy by enterprises. In a fiercely competitive environment, it was felt, strategy is imposed on the survivors – there is little scope for independent choice. Only with the emergence of the modern business enterprise in the late nineteenth century, increasingly large and operating in a context of oligopoly, did it become obvious that there was room for strategy making in the business area. Indeed, survival came to depend on having a good strategy. Chandler was the first theorist to explore the development of strategy making, emphasizing the relationship between strategy and the structure of an organization.[5] The first explicit strategy maker, during the 1920s in response to the previous success of Henry Ford, was Alfred Sloan, the well-known CEO of General Motors.

The main development of strategy as an academic subject occurred after the Second World War, and the changing emphasis in strategy has reflected the changing business environment, in particular the move from an environment in which demand exceeded supply to one in which the reverse held. Business consultancies, such as the Boston Consulting Group or McKinsey's, and individual academics, such as Michael Porter, were important in providing the tools of good strategy making and guiding the direction of strategy making. The design theory of strategy making, probably the earliest systematic theorizing about strategy, referred to the need both to consider what an enterprise *should* do and what it *can* do. It considered as equally important questions, how to position the enterprise and what it can do, focusing on both the external and internal environments of the enterprise.[6] However, the pendulum moved strongly in favour of the positioning approach in the 1980s and on to the external environment with the publication of *Competitive Strategy* by Michael Porter in 1980 and again, in 1985, with *Competitive Advantage*.[7] The 1990s saw the focus of interest shift back again to the resources of the firm described by Gary Hamel and C.K. Prahalad in terms of core competencies and expanded upon a few years later in *Competing for the Future*.[8] Perhaps a fresh synthesis is needed.

> The changing emphasis in strategy has reflected the changing business environment, in particular the move from an environment in which demand exceeded supply to one in which the reverse held.

the essence of strategy

There are a number of steps critical to strategy making. Some of these are preparatory to the formulation of an actual strategy, best called 'strategic analysis'.[9] For example, reading (interpreting) the general and competitive environments is critical to the twin aims of identifying, creating and maintaining competitive advantage, and identifying and controlling risk. Such a reading involves scanning and monitoring developments in the general environment as well as forecasting and assessment. These steps help to position the enterprise appropriately, ensuring that it engages in the right activities, producing the right products for the right markets.

There are other, equally important steps – it is necessary to identify the resources accessible to the enterprise, the capabilities that these resources in different combinations make possible, and the core of distinctive competencies that an enterprise already possesses or could easily develop. Such steps involve the identification of what the enterprise can, rather than what it should, do.

Both are necessary sets of steps but the starting point is controversial. Do you start with the external or the internal environment, with what you *should* or what you *can* do?

It is common to separate other strategic activities, notably formulation, implementation and monitoring. In the 'classical conception', formulation of a strategy precedes its implementation, which in turn precedes its monitoring. However, not all strategy is handed down from above in the classical manner. With an 'emergent' strategy, one which comes as much from below as from above, there is an input from many, if not all, members of staff throughout an organization. In the emergent conception, the sequence of activities can be reversed: monitoring precedes implementation, which precedes formulation, or rather reformulation. In practice, the three activities occur simultaneously and are difficult to separate. Analysis is also inherent in all three activities.

who are the strategists?

In the classical conception, there is often just one strategist. In the emergent conception of strategy, all employees are makers of strategy or, in the jargon of management studies, 'strategizers'. An emergent strategy requires the empowerment of all staff in an organization since they are all ultimately responsible for the making of the relevant strategy. Each strategizer has a domain in which he or she can make decisions and therefore make strategy. In that domain, they have scope for initiating part of the strategy. For many, the domain is small, but together, many small decisions and innovations can turn an indifferent strategy into one that is dynamic and successful. The higher in an organization the decision maker is located, the larger this domain.

There is always a need for someone in the upper parts of the organization to coordinate the strategy process. It is critical to align the decision making in all domains. This requires good coordination and communication skills and subtle leadership in the strategy-making process.

different perspectives of strategy making

Strategy:

> Requires looking into the future and confronting relevant uncertainties. It may be impossible to forecast exactly what is likely to happen but it is necessary to limit the uncertainty to which an enterprise is exposed.

> Aims for a balance between stability and flexibility in how the enterprise responds to changes in its environment. Strategy guides rather than directs; bends and gives according to the pressures of a changing environment; and accommodates change of various kinds.

> Invites such change by continually asking new questions, rather than providing answers to old questions; it is for the creative, for the imaginative lateral thinkers who make their own future. In particular, it considers how an enterprise can innovate in a way that removes potential competition, if only temporarily.

> Is holistic and integrative, providing the big picture, the organizing framework in which operational decisions are made and their outcomes interpreted. It provides coherence in all business management and administration.

> Is path-dependent, focused on the uniqueness of every unfolding experience

and recognizing the degree to which small events can have an influence well beyond that envisaged. It takes full account of the individuality of the experience of any enterprise.

> Is interactive, both horizontally and vertically, between the inside and the outside of an organization and the different specialized divisions that characterize the modern business enterprise, and between different levels of an organizational hierarchy.

> Is about iteration, the repeated communication and reciprocal exchange of information, information that is continuously refined and turned into knowledge, information about external possibilities and internal capabilities.

> Is a learning process.

The emergent conception of strategy emphasizes the importance of learning in any effective strategy making. There is a twofold sense in which learning is a key element of any emergent strategy and strategy making in general. First, the process of strategy making is itself learned. To develop and realize a strategy is not an easy task. Some enterprises, such as General Electric, have a long history of strategy making, having pioneered many relevant techniques and having suffered many of the inherent difficulties of strategy making.[10] Some enterprises are much better at strategy making than others. Second, the changing content of any particular strategy is also the result of learning. It reflects a positive response to emerging opportunity and risk. In both senses, the enterprise is truly a learning organization.[11]

strategic thinking, strategic management and strategic planning

Strategic thinking is everywhere, strategic management is common, notably in finance or marketing, but strategic planning is rare.

One of the first schools of strategy making is described as the planning school; in this conception, strategy is seen as synonymous with planning. It is wise to define strategic planning more precisely, as the formulation and implementation of comprehensive, detailed and written plans with clear time horizons. Strategy is not planning, but for its realization it may involve what is often called 'planning'.

> Strategic thinking is everywhere, strategic management is common, notably in finance or marketing, but strategic planning is rare.

Strategy is much more about strategic thinking and strategy management than about strategic planning. It is about defining the vision (strategic thinking) and achieving it (strategic management). It is also about finding the degree to which operational management should be strategic. Only when strategic management becomes fully comprehensive, enveloping all enterprise operations, does it truly become strategic planning.

At the heart of all good strategy making is strategic thinking, which is akin to entrepreneurship or the more recently invented term 'intrapreneurship', both of which emphasize innovation. Strategic thinking is a creative activity, involving the use of imagination and intuition, requiring lateral as well as vertical thinking, and dealing with divergent and convergent problems – those with more than one solution as well as those with only one. It is about vision, as much about remaking the environment of an enterprise as accepting that environment as a given. It involves the application of new ideas (Microsoft or Amazon.com) or, perhaps more often, old ideas in a new combination (IKEA or Cirque du Soleil). At the core of any good business strategy is a new and effective business model, which may revolve around a completely new product (Hutchison 3G mobiles), an old product with a new combination of attributes (Southwest Airlines), or a new organizational principle (Dell). Good strategy involves identifying desired change and managing that change.

Strategic thinking is not about ideas with no practical application and no possibility of a significant return. It is about the application of reason to the realization of new strategic ideas and the achievement of operational effectiveness. Strategic thinking tests an idea against the real world, considering how a vision can be realized. Its success rests on the application of existing best-practice management techniques and therefore on strategic management. Strategy is about seizing relevant opportunities and controlling the associated risk. Strategic management is about controlling threats to the achievement of strategic targets and anticipating problems. Every opportunity is associated with risk, which must be controlled. Opportunity and risk are two sides of the same coin.

how strategy helps from a manager's perspective

Learning how to make good strategy improves the performance of all managers, whatever their function. Being involved in making strategy gives a sense of direction or purpose to operational decisions. Managers can better understand where they are going and the relevance of what they are doing. All operational activities require a strategic context, just as much as strategy, and its continuous renewal needs to be guided by emerging operational requirements and problems. Without a strategy, the ship would be rudderless, but it is not very helpful to steer the ship into dangerous waters.

Strategy helps managers in two principal ways, one cognitive and the other more practical. Strategy suggests to managers how to think about the development of the enterprise, and to conceptualize various challenges. The initial challenge concerns defining the direction in which an enterprise is moving. Strategy deals with the biggest of all managerial problems – how to define a vision for an organization and how to achieve that vision. If a mission statement is to have any meaning, then it must reflect the strategy of the organization. It assists in the careful articulation of strategic targets and in defining what is relevant to the monitoring of a strategy. It provides the organizing framework for the allocation of the resources available to the organization and for defining those vital resources that are lacking and can only be accessed in a limited number of ways – through the market, acquisition of another relevant enterprise or strategic alliances. With the help of strategy, the manager can see the big picture, and even contribute to the drawing of that big picture. It provides a systematic perspective for setting relevant targets and underpins the need for planning the use of resources.

As an academic discipline, management assists managers to conceptualize all sorts of problems, notably the recurrent problems that they confront. The application of an academic approach is possible only where there is enough in common between situations to make them amenable to a similar analysis; they can be conceptualized in a way that is easily understood. Many business dilemmas are repeated, recurrent problems, which never go away, such as when to grow and when to contract, when to cooperate and when to compete, or how to participate in international business.

All theorizing in the social sciences, of which management studies is an increasingly important part, is concerned with finding a way of reconciling the unique with the general. The use of case studies or, more accurately, case histories is designed to apply general concepts to unique situations. Theorizing helps to define and redefine those problems. It is also prescriptive, in that it seeks to show managers what to do, or rather how to work out for themselves what to do. The all-embracing nature of strategy reinforces this view of the role of academic studies. Auditing strategy is a critical learning activity for those wishing to understand how to develop a successful enterprise and the role that strategy has to play in running such a successful organization.

Since the enterprise is a coalition of stakeholders of various kinds, including suppliers, managers, workers, strategic allies (or, in the jargon of the economist, 'complementors'), government and the local community, any strategy must take account of the different interests and influences of a wide variety of relevant strategic players. It allows the decision makers to move away from oversimplified assumptions such as short-term profit maximization, which privileges only one of the stakeholders, the owners. It helps to determine the time horizon for which decisions are made and for which the profit level is relevant. Since strategy integrates all functional skills, it helps the manager to put everything, and everyone, in an appropriate place. It shows how the different divisions and activities combine in the achievement of business success. It places the annual business or corporate plan in its proper setting. It assists in the process of integrating all the stakeholders and all the specialist units within an enterprise in the realization of enterprise objectives, helping an organization to integrate various attempts at planning.

The involvement of the various stakeholders in strategy making helps to empower them. Such involvement is a precondition for using their familiarity with different aspects of the operation of an enterprise to improve a strategy and thereby enterprise performance. The empowerment of all stakeholders, including employees, both managers and workers, who are involved in the making of a good emergent strategy, gives every manager and worker a strong sense of worth, a sense of where in the organization he or she is placed and what contribution can be made. It also empowers all the stakeholders, allowing them to participate in the strategy-making process. All those involved in an enterprise, employees and stakeholders, become part of the process of strategy making. Good strategy making requires less command and direct control, but more communication and coordination. It requires the channelling of conflict, even the creation of consensus, in the making of strategy.

> Good strategy making requires less command and direct control, but more communication and coordination.

strategy and associated disciplines

It is possible to view strategy from a number of different, but not incompatible, perspectives, some involving different academic disciplines. Strategy, like management studies in general, is interdisciplinary in approach. A young discipline inevitably borrows theory from others. The nature of the problems under consideration determines the discipline that is relevant and almost inevitably suggests different disciplines. It is not difficult to see the enterprise as a social or organizational unit or the venue for political activity, that is, bargaining or negotiation, or to see that marketing and the resulting product differentiation require psychological analysis. However, most commentators on strategy tend to see an enterprise primarily as an economic organization, concerned with allocating resources in a way that generates income.

Economics is the discipline that has given most to strategy. The most commonly cited authorities are those who have an economics background and have contributed to understanding strategy making by applying economic ideas to management problems. Most outstanding is the work of Michael Porter who was the pioneer in systematically applying economic theory to strategy from the 1980s onwards. This is most apparent in his emphasis on positioning the enterprise, which introduces the relevance of the forces of competition in determining which markets offer the highest returns. Another area Porter pioneered was the selection of generic strategies. The main choice lay between product differentiation and cost minimization, seen as mutually exclusive. However, much of Porter's analysis suffers from a weakness of economic theory: it is static rather than dynamic in its approach. Strategy is concerned with the dynamic world of change.

Economists have contributed a number of other useful concepts, including the concept of 'valued added'. The aim of strategy is both to create significant value for the consumer, and to distribute that value among stakeholders in a way that increases their commitment to contributing to the future creation of value. The concepts of economic value added (EVA) and market value added (MVA) are often explored in more detail on the strategy curriculum of an MBA programme.[12]

It is useful to conceptualize and systematize the different perspectives that exist within the area of strategy. One illuminating approach is described below. It incorporates the economic perspective, but recognizes the existence and importance of other perspectives. It selects two distinguishing criteria, motivation and whether a strategy is handed down from above or emerges from below. The distinction between strategy being handed down by the grand strategizer and strategy emerging from all levels of the enterprise has already been made – it is an important distinction. For an economist, the obvious motivation for strategy is profit, but this privileges one stakeholder group, the owners. Other stakeholder groups, including managers, may have other motivations, such as growth, status, power, employment opportunities, even tax revenue: hence the use of the term 'pluralist'. There are four possible combinations, shown in Figure 18.1.[13]

	Source Single – Profit maximization	Motivation Pluralist
From above	Classical	Systemic
From below	Evolutionary	Processual

Figure 18.1 Different approaches to strategy

The 'classical' approach is the conventional description of strategy making. An emphasis on profit maximization places strategy squarely in the camp of the economists, since this is the main assumption of neoclassical economic theory. Such profit maximization may be the deliberate intention of the grand strategizer (classical strategy) or the result of competition forcing all decision makers to act as if they were maximizers (evolutionary strategy).

The 'evolutionary' view sees competition as moulding strategy, just as natural selection moulds the evolution of species, leaving little room for discretionary strategy making. Any failure to maximize profits would lead an enterprise to be taken over through a raid in the capital market.

The 'systemic' approach allows for the different motivations and attitudinal and institutional contexts that characterize the various cultures in the world, but still assumes that the strategy is handed down from above. There is obvious scope for those who study different cultures to make a positive contribution. Historians have a particular role to play here, especially economic historians, in interpreting the nature of strategy in different countries.

The 'processual' approach, a perspective that puts the emphasis on the process of strategy making rather than its content, allows for both pluralist motivation and emergent strategy. This is a more realistic approach. It gives space for a variety of disciplines, since it focuses on important constraints that influence the process of strategy making, which might be cognitive or psychological, political or social, as well as economic. In this approach, the skills and knowledge of the political theorist, the sociologist or psychologist are obviously relevant.

Sometimes different perspectives are given the designation of separate schools, but this is to overformalize the differences.[14] It is possible to identify as many as 14 different schools: they usually focus on different, and rather narrow, aspects of the complex activity of making a strategy.[15] They often focus on the insights in understanding strategy derived from applying concepts from different disciplines, including economics, sociology, psychology, political theory and even ecology. Such approaches are often consistent with each other since they relate to issues that are separate but not mutually exclusive. They add to our understanding of what strategy is and how to achieve a good strategy. Sometimes the schools focus on the content of strategy, sometimes on the procedures of strategy making. Sometimes they are descriptive or analytical, sometimes prescriptive.

the major areas explored in strategy

Since strategy is by aspiration comprehensive in its coverage, it is possible to include all major managerial issues in strategic analysis, but this is to adopt a quasi-imperialist orientation. Strategy is not synonymous with management. There are various ways in which the main areas of strategy can be classified. The following are the generic strategies and strategic dilemmas and are key issues that must be dealt with in any theory of strategy.[16]

how to create and maintain competitive advantage

At the core of any strategy is an attempt to create competitive advantage and then to maintain that advantage. This is best achieved by the achievement of uncontested market space and an emphasis on continuous value innovation.[17] For all successful enterprises, there is a combination of cost minimization and product differentiation, which allows them to outcompete others. Innovation allows a simultaneous achievement of what appear to be contradictory strategies, when viewed in a static context.

Whether the focus is on Southwest Airlines, Cirque du Soleil, Dell, IKEA or Amazon. com, the initial aim is to differentiate an enterprise from its competitors in such a way as to remove them as competitors. The key focus is on the attributes of a product or service, which successfully differentiate the product or service of an enterprise from those of competitors by satisfying the desired utilities of consumers, but also gives the supplier cost advantages. Often this involves disruptive innovation rather than sustaining innovation.[18] This allows the gaining of a significant number of customers and a profit margin, which allows the making of a significantly above-normal profit over a long period of time.

how to control risk

Creating and maintaining competitive advantage is the positive side of strategy making and controlling risk is the negative side. Yet they are both critical aspects of strategy. Controlling risk involves a number of activities, including the assessment of risk and the selection of an appropriate response to that risk.

> *Creating and maintaining competitive advantage is the positive side of strategy making and controlling risk is the negative side. Yet they are both critical aspects of strategy.*

The assessment of risk includes identification, measurement and monitoring. An essential part of risk control is to have a strategy that generates information about opportunities and threats. The alternative responses to such risk include avoidance, management and mitigation, or simply leaving a risk uncovered because it is the kind of risk that is characteristic of the relevant industry. Strategy involves choices about the resources required for assessment, the nature of any response, and the way in which risk control is linked to strategy making in general. Clearly, a good risk control strategy is an integral part of overall strategy. For example, any airline must have a planned response to events such as those of 11 September 2001 or to large increases in the price of aviation fuel.

One approach of increasing interest to strategy is the 'real options' approach, which allows the incorporation of uncertainty into the valuation of investment projects and encourages an interpretation of strategy as the identification and working out of a range of linked options to initiate relevant investment projects.[19] Any strategy can be seen as managing a portfolio of investment projects at various stages of development, most obvious in the pharmaceutical industry. Some of the different options involve flexibility in staging or phasing, such as when to exploit a mineral deposit or real estate, others are insurance options, such as the possibility of exit, both temporary or permanent, the use of alternative inputs, for example energy sources, or the production of different outputs, such as cars with different design features, or, even more importantly, growth options, including any research and development project.

what is the optimum size and growth rate of an enterprise?

There appears to be an inexorable increase in the size of organizations, even an iron law of oligopoly, which says that every market is eventually dominated by a small number of enterprises. In the early stages of development of a new product or industry, there may be many suppliers, but this is temporary. Competitive markets almost invariably lead to consolidation, which changes the nature of that competition, and occurs most rapidly in an economic downturn. During recessions, small enterprises are more likely to fail than large enterprises. The interaction of the strategies of the enterprises within an industry drives the history of an industry, determining the number of players, the level of capacity and price, and the amount spent on marketing or research and development.

There are clear advantages and disadvantages to size. The main disadvantages arise from a loss of manoeuvrability and failures of coordination and communication. Even economies of scale and scope often justify much smaller enterprises. The advantages of size are not so much a matter of such economies as of increased financial clout, greater competitiveness, and improved negotiating ability, notably in lobbying government for desired policy changes.

If an enterprise is too small, it needs to grow. It can grow organically, by investing in projects that expand the enterprise, or it can grow by merger or acquisition. The latter strategy is, in practice, often a failure, at least for the acquiring enterprise, making it essential to consider carefully the strategic implications of such a strategy.

If the enterprise is too large, then it is necessary to divest. Strategic divestment is as important as strategic acquisition to the successful operation of any enterprise. GE, one of the most successful companies in the world and one that has pioneered using strategy in innovative ways, has a ruthless policy of divestment in which a business unit must be number one or two in the world or have great potential in a new technical area to avoid such divestment.[20] BHP, the largest Australian company, has divested its steel division and both divestor and divestee have separately thrived.[21] However, divestment is too obvious an admission of failure, or at least too often interpreted as such, to be as attractive as acquisition. There is a clear asymmetry between the desirability of expansionary and contractionary acts, which partly explains the tendency for enterprises to get bigger and bigger and also the difficulties of some large enterprises.

how to integrate the enterprise to achieve strategic targets

A universal problem in the realization of any strategy is the principal/agent problem, which exists at all levels of an enterprise. A principal hires an agent to carry out a particular task. There must be suitable institutional and motivational frameworks relevant to motivating both principals and agents to work within the framework of a strategy.

A problem arises when the principal and agent have very different interests and different motivations, or when there are serious asymmetries of information. Typically, the agent knows much more than the principal about the circumstances under which he or she is completing the relevant task. It is possible for the agent to pursue his or her own interests and not those of the principal. There may also be asymmetries in investment in the relationship, which further complicate the nature of the fulfilment of the task. In order to persuade individuals to implement a strategy in an effective way, it is necessary to solve the principal/agent problem. For example, a major industry superannuation fund that used estate agencies to handle the leasing or maintenance of the buildings in which it has invested might find real conflicts of interest. Or a university endowment fund, such as Harvard's, which uses professional money managers, might be faced with a similar dilemma.

when to cooperate and when to compete

There has been a proliferation of strategic alliances in the international business environment, alliances often between enterprises of different countries. The alliances cover all kinds of activities from financing major investments or technical projects to problem solving in a highly specific way. They reflect a variety of motivations from controlling risk to gaining access to complementary resources, which the relevant enterprise lacks. They are sometimes for short periods of time and sometimes the prelude to a merger. Even the fiercest of competitors find it necessary on occasion to cooperate with their competitors, such as those operating in the area of e-commerce on solving security problems. It is possible to cooperate in some areas, such as research and development or marketing, and to continue competing in other areas.

For example, there are numerous ways in which the Australian wine industry, probably the single most successful sector of the Australian economy, has worked together to improve both the image and production of Australian wine. This cooperation has been conducted under the umbrella of at least 11 different industry-wide organizations. There are generic advertising campaigns yet individual wineries continue to compete with each other. The Australian wine industry is an example of the clusters that Michael Porter has argued are so important, which, when well organized, derive the advantages of both large and small size. Such clusters are important in sectors as diverse as the high-tech enterprises of Silicon Valley to the ceramic industry of Italy.

what mode of entry to choose in entering international business transactions

Many a small enterprise is born global – it engages in international transactions from its very inception. For example, the creation and continuing success of Airbus required international sales from the beginning. Almost without exception, larger enterprises are engaged in international transactions. Even if they are not, they must consider the repercussions of competition from abroad and the activity of foreign enterprises in their own economy. Engagement with the international economy makes it doubly important to have a strategy in which particular projects have a carefully defined place. It is common to draw a decision tree (Figure 18. 2) that shows what might be either a choice made at a given moment of time or the learning experience and strategic pathway of an enterprise that is steadily increasing its commitment to international business transactions.[22]

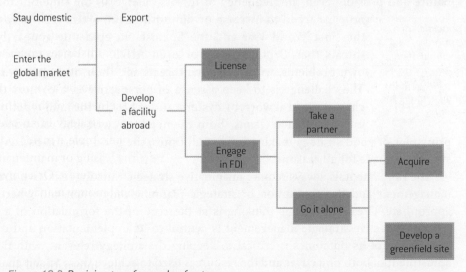

Figure 18.2 *Decision tree for mode of entry*

The choice of mode may reflect the nature of the overall strategy adopted by an enterprise. There are many factors that determine the choice, but the obvious ones are return and risk, between which there is often a trade-off. For example, the possibility of strict black empowerment laws may incline mining companies to invest in countries other than South Africa, unless the return is extremely high. Other relevant factors include the commitment of resources, the degree of control over product quality, or even the direct and indirect barriers to particular modes of entry. For example, the attitude and actions of the Chinese government, at various levels, make it unlikely that automobile producers would export to China from outside facilities: joint ventures within China are the preferred method of entry.

current challenges in strategy

Today, the main challenge to the making of good strategy is to keep in mind its fundamentals at a time when there is enormous pressure to forget them. These fundamentals never change, despite assertions to the contrary. Today, the times are said to be more turbulent, more volatile and more competitive than during any previous period. It is claimed that terrorist attacks and natural disasters, such as the tsunami of Boxing Day 2004, have completely changed the environment of threat. It has even been argued that the technical changes in communications, which have given birth to e-commerce, are revolutionizing business in an unprecedented way, even changing the underlying economic laws that govern business success and pricing. It has been claimed that globalization has changed the world dramatically, leading to hypercompetition. All in all, it has been argued that the risk environment is much more threatening for all enterprises and has changed the rules of good strategy making.

It is difficult to accept that the need to manage change is any greater today than it has been in the past or that globalization and the communications revolution have really changed the fundamentals. The exaggerations associated with the dot. com revolution have been made more realistic by the crash. After all, in a historical perspective, the telegraph was more revolutionary in its effects than the internet. The nature and possibly even the frequency of threats change all the time but there is no clear trend to increase or diminish in importance. In retrospect, the First World War and the Spanish flu epidemic appear bigger threats than September 11 or even AIDS. All periods have their own problems, with their own threats and their own opportunities. The challenge is to keep a sense of perspective in a context that is characterized at worst by hysteria and at best by the loud repetition of unsubstantiated claims about the need to rewrite the rule book. The principles of good strategy making hold at all times, the good and the bad. A good strategy is made for all seasons.

> The principles of good strategy making hold at all times, the good and the bad. A good strategy is made for all seasons.

The fundamentals always require imaginative strategic thinking, effective strategic management and the application of strategic planning only when and where it is appropriate. Creative strategic thinking is at the core of the formulation of a good strategy, effective strategic management is central to its implementation and careful monitoring of its outcomes is critical to keeping the strategy relevant, with flexible adjustment of both objectives and the resources used to achieve them to suit changing circumstances. The managers of enterprises must explore the ways in which these fundamentals can be satisfied, given the unique circumstances of the enterprise. Each strategy is specific to time and place, and to a particular enterprise.

The key challenge is to encourage creativity in a way that promotes innovation and helps the enterprise to maintain competitive advantage. There is a temptation to continue to use a successful business model and therefore successful strategy, although the environment in which the enterprise is operating is changing and making that business model inappropriate. Success breeds failure because of the tendency to stick to a status quo that has served the enterprise well. Strategic drift is a major source of difficulty for an established enterprise. Such drift, as a result of which a strategy moves seriously out of line with the changing environment, is likely to lead eventually to a serious turnaround situation, with sales and profits falling. It is important to maintain an emphasis on innovation, particularly in the good times when it is easier to provide the relevant resources. It is also important to divest when times are good, not when it is difficult to do so.

> The great importance of intrapreneurship creates a need for appropriate space for innovators and for the championing of the innovators by those who can incorporate the resulting innovations into a strategy.

Strategy forces decision makers to accept the unpalatable truth that luck is opportunity recognized. Strategy helps them to recognize, or even make, that opportunity. In order to gain uncontested market space, the enterprise needs to continue to focus on those key attributes of a product that differentiate it from others and make it appealing to consumers, to encourage all to pursue this goal, and to build ongoing innovation into the system. The great importance of intrapreneurship creates a need for appropriate space for innovators and for the championing of the innovators by those who can incorporate the resulting innovations into a strategy.

One approach, which offers a genuinely strategic approach to making individual investment decisions, is that which likens investment decision to financial options and uses similar budget appraisal techniques. Such an approach places a value on the flexibility that characterizes investment decision making and therefore strategy making. After all, any strategy consists of a portfolio of investment projects of differing maturities. One challenge is to incorporate this approach not just in the appraisal of investment projects but also in strategy making in general. These investment projects must be considered together, not individually. It is important to incorporate uncertainty or risk into the joint appraisal of such investment projects.

A challenge that is evident from the number of dramatic failures to confront the problem, notably the collapse of Enron, is the need to move beyond the emphasis on a simple short-term performance indicator, such as the growth of earnings before interest, tax, amortization and depreciation, as the sole strategic target. The slavish pursuit of the bottom line has led to all sorts of bad behaviour, but worse, it has led to a tendency to place finance before strategy rather than the reverse. A good strategy, imaginatively formulated and well implemented, will produce good financial results, but the strategy should come first. The financial framework then reflects the strategy that has been made. The bottom line is not to be ignored, but its state will reflect the quality of the relevant strategy. It is more realistic to accept for monitoring purposes the balanced scorecard approach, which considers the performance of the enterprise in a range of different areas including finance but also customer satisfaction, and includes as important indicators well ordered internal processes and the capacity to learn and to innovate. Under this approach, it is possible to use as many as 20 different key performance indicators to monitor the realization of a strategy, as it recognizes the complexity of the targets that any realistic strategy must set.

There are more obvious immediate challenges. Strategy making can easily fall into one of a number of dangerous traps, which must be avoided.[23] These dangers reflect the weaknesses that can beset any enterprise. At all times there is a challenge to avoid falling into one of them. Even the most successful strategy makers sometimes fall victim. For example, GE has worried throughout its strategic history about the dangers of an excessive institutionalization of strategy: the strategic processes can easily become overbureaucratized.[24]

Sometimes strategy making is pursued without any real commitment, with the key people going through the motions and doing only what is expected. There is no real effort put into producing a feasible strategy and the end product later gathers dust on the shelf. Such tokenism is all too common. It sometimes reflects a fear on the part of senior managers of giving away too much discretion in decision making; it sometimes reflects a mental laziness on the part of managers who do not wish to confront the problem of making choices. They postpone the making of any such choice until the last minute.

The opposite danger is to attach too much importance to strategy by a process of overbureaucratization, in which there are too many meetings, too many reports and too many statistics. Strategy making becomes an end in itself, absorbing too many resources and the time and energy of key decision makers. Part of such a danger is the adoption of fads, just as common in the making of strategy as in any management area. Almost all management ideas are at some time a fad, including strategy, if viewed as a solution to all problems.

> Almost all management ideas are at some time a fad, including strategy, if viewed as a solution to all problems.

Sometimes the strategy is highjacked by one individual and becomes a vehicle for uncontrolled ambition. The example of Jean-Marie Messier and Vivendi illustrates this.[25] At other times, strategy is a simple reproduction of the past, which reinforces the innate conservatism of once successful organizations. Past trends are extrapolated. Strategy is built around previously successful business models. Strategy thereby institutionalizes strategic drift. Alternatively, a strategy sometimes focuses solely on the negative side, ignoring the positive side of new opportunities. It becomes an obsession with the threats and risk and with counteracting those negative influences. In other cases, strategy simply validates the business plan, which is concerned with the bottom line and reflects an obsession with short-term profit maximization.

Sliding into any of these traps can lead to the discrediting of strategy for key stakeholders. In reality, such a slide discredits a particular kind of strategy making, rather than strategy making in general.

conclusion

In recent years, it is no accident that in the area of management studies, strategy has been the focus of great attention. There is consequently a larger literature on strategy than on any other single management idea. In any MBA programme, strategy has a central role – it is always a core subject. In some programmes, there may also be a number of electives relating to various specialized aspects of strategy making. Strategy provides a, if not the, unifying framework in which other management functions must place themselves.

Theoretically, strategy is one of the area's most significant big ideas, since its very definition raises all sorts of issues about what an enterprise is trying to do and its interaction with the various environments in which it operates; practically, it is an idea with implications for performance that are critical to the survival and success of the enterprise. Good performance reflects a good strategy more than any other single factor. The realization of a good strategy has continued to be a necessary, but not always a sufficient, condition for significant business success. There are other necessary conditions such as the hiring of competent staff or the continuing existence of an external environment favourable to the relevant strategy. The quality of the enterprise personnel, who have as one of their tasks the implementation of such a strategy, is important. An exciting new strategy may simply be badly executed. Any strategy has to be formulated creatively, implemented well and monitored carefully. Bad implementation can ruin the best of plans. The relevant environmental circumstances may also change in an unanticipated way. Bad timing is a problem for some strategies. The strategy may be a winner but it is introduced at the wrong time, perhaps before successful execution is possible, possibly true of Hutchison and 3G mobiles. There are not always first mover advantages; sometimes there are significant first mover disadvantages. Plain bad luck can undo the best of strategies.

> Theory relating to strategy is becoming more sophisticated and more rigorous. There are many directions in which the study of strategy making might go in the future.

Theory relating to strategy is becoming more sophisticated and more rigorous. There are many directions in which the study of strategy making might go in the future. The real options and the balanced scorecard approaches are just two new developments that suggest future directions.[26] They represent pathways that have been opened up in recent years. There is still enormous scope for the further development of the study of strategy.

references

1. Mintzberg, H. (1994) *The Rise and Fall of Strategic Planning* (Hemel Hempstead: Prentice Hall); Mintzberg, H., Ahlstrand, B. and Lampel, J. (1998) *Strategy Safari: A Guided Tour Through the Wilds of Strategic Management* (New York: The Free Press).
2. White, C. (2004) *Strategic Management* (Basingstoke: Palgrave Macmillan) p. 5.
3. Chandler, A.D. (1962) *Strategy and Structure: Chapters in the History of Industrial Enterprise* (Cambridge: MIT Press) p. 13.
4. Sun Tzu (1971) *The Art of War* (New York: Oxford University Press); von Clausewitz, C. (1984) *On War* (trans. J. Howard and P. Paret) (Princeton, NJ: Princeton University Press).
5. Op. cit. Chandler (1962).
6. Learned, E.P., Christensen, C.R., Andrews, K.R. and Guth, W.D. (1997) *Business Policy: Text and Cases* (Homewood, IL: Irwin).
7. Porter, M.E. (1980) *Competitive Strategy: Techniques for Analyzing Industries and Competitors* (New York: The Free Press); Porter, M.E. (1985) *Competitive Advantage: Creating and Sustaining Superior Performance* (New York: The Free Press).
8. Prahalad, C.K. and Hamel, G. (1990) 'The core competencies of the corporation', *Harvard Business Review*, **70**(3): 79–83; Hamel, G. and Prahalad, C.K.(1996) *Competing for the Future* (Boston, MA: Harvard Business School Press).
9. Mellahi, K., Frynas, K.G. and Finlay, P. (2005) *Global Strategic Management* (Oxford: Oxford University Press) p. 7.
10. Vaghefi, M.R. and Huellmantel, A.B. (1999) *Strategic Management for the XXIst Century* (London: St Lucie Press) see Chapter 2, Strategic leadership and General Electric.

11. Quinn, J.B. (1992) *Intelligent Enterprise: A Knowledge and Service-based Paradigm for Industry* (New York: The Free Press).
12. Ghemawat, P. (1999) *Strategy and the Business Landscape: Text and Cases* (Reading, MA: Addison-Wesley)
13. Adapted from Whittington, R. (2001) *What is Strategy and Does it Matter?* (2nd edn) (London: Routledge).
14. Op. cit. Mintzberg et al. (1998).
15. Op. cit. White (2004) pp. 17–20.
16. Op. cit. White (2004) particularly Parts 2 and 3.
17. Kim, W.C. and Mauborgne, R. (2005) *Blue Ocean Strategy: How to Create Uncontested Market Space and Make the Competition Irrelevant* (Boston, MA: Harvard Business School Press).
18. Christensen, C.M. (1997) *The Innovator's Dilemma* (Boston, MA: Harvard Business School Press).
19. Amram, M. and Kulatilaka, N. (1999) *Real Options: Managing Strategic Investment in an Uncertain World* (Boston, MA: Harvard Business School Press).
20. Welch, J. (2001) *What I've Learned Leading a Great Company and Great People* (London: Headline).
21. Op. cit. White (2004) pp. 408–13.
22. Op. cit. White (2004) p. 532.
23. For a more detailed analysis, see White (2004) op. cit., pp. 616–18.
24. Op. cit. Welch (2001).
25. Johnson, J. and Orange, M. (2003) *The Man Who Tried to Buy the World: Jean-Marie Messier and Vivendi Universal* (London: Viking). Three extracts published in the *Guardian*: 'A fairytale beginning of Vivendi', 24 June 2003; 'The night the music died', 25 June 2003; 'The day the undertaker called', 26 June 2003.
26. Kaplan, R.S. and Norton, D.P. (1996) *The Balanced Scorecard: Translating Strategy into Action* (Boston, MA: Harvard Business School Press).

learning resources

3

19 learning resources

introduction

The book chapters give insights into the personal and functional capabilities that can be developed on a postgraduate management degree programme. However, some of you may feel you need a greater understanding of what the subjects cover before starting your course. Also, the more enthusiastic among you may wish to explore some of the areas in greater depth. The suggestions in this section are meant to help you do both. As with the chapters, none of the references are meant to replace the material you will be presented with on your degree programme. However, the more familiar you are with the subjects before you enter the lecture theatre, the easier your learning will be. For those of you already familiar with some of the topics, the resources suggested below may help give you a more detailed picture of the various subjects on your MBA.

part 1: studying the subject

chapter 1 why take an MBA?

There are numerous journals, books and websites containing information about MBAs and the ins and out of postgraduate management education. Some of the publications are almost out of date before they are printed as the area is developing quickly. For the publications suggested below, the most recent editions are indicated.

If you have not yet decided which business school to attend, publications that can help include:

> *Official MBA Handbook 2005/2006* by Michael Pilgrim and Claire Sharp (Financial Times/Prentice Hall, 2006).
> *Guide to MBA Programmes 2006* (11th edn) (Peterson's Guides).
> *Which MBA?: A Critical Guide to the World's Best MBAs* by George Bickerstaffe (18th edn) (Prentice Hall, 2006) which includes schools outside the US.
> *The Wall Street Journal Guide to the Top Business Schools 2006* by Ronald Alsop and *Wall Street Journal* staff (Random House) which tends to emphasize American schools and the views of corporate recruiters.

In addition, many major financial and business papers and journals devote space to business education in general and MBA students and their issues in particular. Indeed, two publications, *BusinessWeek* and the *Financial Times* have had a considerable impact on academic business education in the past 10 years by producing ranking tables of business schools.

The *BusinessWeek* Business School website is at www.businessweek.com/bschools, and the *Financial Times* website is at www.ft.com/businesseducation/mba. The main websites of both publications produce a wealth of business information and commentary on current issues.

Other sites worth looking at are:

> The Economist Intelligence Units site 'Which MBA Online' at http://mba.eiu.com which provides background information on the world's top 100 MBA programmes.
> The QS TOPMBA site www.topmba.com which has good information for MBA applicants and MBA students. You will also find details here of the World MBA Tour, which has participation from over 400 business schools each year.

In addition, the site at www.transworldeducation.com gives information on studying around the world including business courses, as does www.infozee.com/channels/mba/ and www.mba-courses.com.

chapter 2   maximizing the MBA experience

If you are interested in developing your management skills, there are many useful books on the subject, including:

> *The 7 Habits of Highly Effective People* by Stephen Covey (Fireside, 1990) which although published some time ago, has many useful ideas for managing oneself.
> *A Manager's Guide to Self-Development* by Mike Pedlar, John Burgoyne and Tom Boydell (McGraw-Hill, 2001).
> *Developing Management Skills* by Kim Cameron and David Whetten (Pearson Custom Publishing, 2005).

The manager's world is constantly changing. You may also wish to consider your longer term development and the kind of environment your MBA should equip you for in the future. Books that attempt to give a picture of the trends in management, leadership and a range of different business scenarios include:

> *Leadership and Management in the 21st Century:* Business Challenges of the Future edited by Cary Cooper (Oxford University Press, 2005).
> *Management 21C: Someday We'll All Manage This Way* edited by Subir Chowdhury (Financial Times/Prentice Hall, 2000).

In contrast, a business event that had a considerable impact and provides a picture of what management in the future should not be like is the Enron scandal. *The Smartest Guys in the Room: The Amazing Rise and Scandalous Fall of Enron* by Bethany McLean and Peter Elkind (Penguin, 2003) provides an insight into the saga. The TV documentary of the same name produced by Alex Gibney in 2005 displays the main characters and events and also the people who successfully challenged the misconduct.

chapter 3   developing a learning capability

Chris Argyris's article 'Teaching smart people how to learn' (*Harvard Business Review*, **69**(3) 1991) is well worth reading. It describes the defensive barriers that professional people can put up to learning.

Joe Landsberger's website 'Study guides and strategies' at http://www.studygs.net provides study guides on a range of topics including distance learning.

Books elaborating on the mechanics of learning journals and logs include:

> *Learning Journals: A Handbook for Academics, Students and Professional Development* by Jennifer Moon (Routledge, 2006) which gives advice on journal writing on academic courses and for professional development.

> *Learning Log* by Tony Nutley (Lulu.com, 2006) which takes a workbook approach to reflecting from experience.

Two books that will help with working with case studies are:

> *The Case Study Handbook* by William Ellet (Harvard Business School Press, 2007).

> *Learning with Cases* by James Erskine, Louise Mauffette-Leenders and Michale Leenders (Richard Ivey School of Business, 2001).

In completing research-based projects, the books you consult will depend on the kind of research you are undertaking. There are a plethora of books addressing management research issues to varying depths and different degrees of accessibility. Some of the more user-friendly works include:

> *Business Research Methods* by Alan Bryman and Emma Bell (Oxford University Press, 2004).

> *Postgraduate Research in Business: A Critical Guide* by Sarah Quinton and Teresa Smallbone (Sage, 2006).

> *Doing your Dissertation in Business and Management: The Reality of Researching and Writing* by Reva Berman Brown (Sage, 2006).

> *Guide to Management Research Methods* by Mandy van der Velde, Paul Jansen and Neil Anderson (Blackwell, 2004).

> *Research Skills for Management Studies* by Alan Berkeley Thomas (Routledge, 2004).

chapter 4   developing a problem-solving capability

There is a great deal of material both in paper and electronic form that helps with problem solving and creative thinking. Writers such as Edward de Bono, who developed the areas of lateral and parallel thinking, and Tony Buzan, who developed mind maps, have had considerable influence on improving thinking processes and their books are well worth reading. Their websites are at www.edwdebono.com and www.buzan.com.au.

Other books worth considering include:

> *Creative Management and Development* edited by Jane Henry (Sage, 2006).

> *Creative Problem Solving for Managers: Developing Skills for Decision Making and Innovation* by Tony Proctor (Routledge, 2005).

> *The Mind Gym: Wake up Your Mind* by Mind Gym (TimeWarner, 2005) which takes an innovative approach to developing different ways of thinking.

> *Bad Thoughts: A Guide to Clear Thinking* by Jamie Whyte (Corvo Books, 2003).

> *A Field Guide to Good Decisions: Values in Action* by Mark Bennett and Joan McIver (Praeger, 2006).

Websites that contain material on problem solving and puzzles include Jim Loy's Puzzle Page at www.jimloy.com, which contains a range of classic and more recent puzzles. Another good puzzle site that also includes Einstein's riddles is http://

hlavolamy.szm.sk/brainteasers/ and a website that outlines a range of different thinking techniques is at www.mindtools.com.

chapter 5 developing an emotional capability

Daniel Goleman is probably the person who is most notable for heightening awareness of emotions in relation to job performance and how they can be used to positive effect. The book that has had the most impact is:

> *Emotional Intelligence: Why It Can Matter More Than IQ* by Daniel Goleman (Bantam, 2006) which was recently published as a 10th anniversary edition.

Possibly one of the most successful writers on stress is Cary Cooper. His most recent book takes a practical approach to coping with stress and contains many valuable tips on time management, exercise, nutrition and relaxation:

> *How to Deal with Stress* by Cary Cooper and Stephen Palmer (Kogan Page, 2007).

There are many books on exercise and diet and most of them have varying degrees of credibility. One which has some scientific basis is:

> *Eat, Drink, and Be Healthy: The Harvard Medical School Guide to Healthy Eating* by Walter Willett and P.J. Skerrett (The Free Press, 2005).

There are also many books on mental self-help and positive thinking. Some of the older books still work well for some people, such as:

> *The Power of Positive Thinking* by Norman Vincent Peale (Running Press, 2002).
> *The Mind Gym*, noted in Chapter 4, which also has sections on positive thinking.
> *Resilience at Work: How to Succeed No Matter What Life Throws at You* by Salvatore Maddi and Deborah Khoshaba (AMACOM/American Management Association, 2005) which is from the developers of mental hardiness.

Dealing with conflict also has a wealth of material, but a recent book which puts conflict into a leadership context is:

> *Leading Through Conflict: How Successful Leaders Transform Differences into Opportunities* by Mark Gerzon (Harvard Business School, 2006).

chapter 6 developing an interpersonal capability

There are some classic texts in this area. For example:

> *How to Win Friends and Influence People* by Dale Carnegie (Vermilion, 2007) was first published in 1936.
> *People Skills* by Robert Bolton (Touchstone, 1986) which also has many useful ideas and can be found in some libraries and through internet booksellers.

More recent general communication skills books with a business emphasis include:

> *Face-to-Face Communications for Clarity and Impact* (Harvard Business School Press, 2004).
> *Managing Business and Professional Communication* by Carley Dodd (Pearson/Allyn and Bacon, 2004).

> *Communication Skills for International Students in Business* by Tracey Bretag, Joanna Crossman and Sarbari Bordia (McGraw-Hill, 2007).

For those of you who need help with business presentations, two useful books are:

> *Creative Business Presentations: Inventive Ideas for Making an Instant Impact* by Eleri Sampson (Kogan Page, 2003) which encourages the need to look beyond PowerPoint as the main solution to improving presentations.
> *The Results-Driven Manager: Presentations that Persuade and Motivate* (Harvard Business School Press, 2004).

chapter 7 developing a leadership capability

Charles Manz is possibly the person most associated with the idea of self-leadership, outlined in two co-authored books:

> *Mastering Self-Leadership: Empowering Yourself for Personal Excellence* by Chris Neck and Charles Manz (Prentice Hall, 2006).
> *Company of Heroes: Unleashing the Power of Self-leadership* by Charles Manz and Henry Sims (Diane Books, 1999).

Other books focusing on developing personal leadership skills are:

> *Dilemmas of Leadership* by Tudor Rickards and Murray Clark (Routledge, 2005).
> *The Leadership Odyssey: A Self-development Guide to New Skills for New Times* by Caroline Napolitano and Linda Henderson (Jossey-Bass, 1997).
> *Self-directed Behaviour* by David Watson and Roland Tharp (Wadsworth Publishing, 2006) which has been around at least since the 1970s, but is one of the few books in the area of personal development, which, while aimed at self-help, is based on empirical research studies.

Books on a similar theme emphasizing the personal change process are numerous. One of the most well-known writers who has written about transition and change in a business context is William Bridges. Two of his most popular books are:

> *Transitions: Making Sense of Life's Changes* (Da Capo Press, 2004).
> *Managing Transitions: Making the Most of Change* (Perseus Books, 2003).

In the area of public leadership, recommendations are harder to make as the number of books on this subject are vast. However, a good starting point is:

> *A Force for Change: How Leadership Differs from Management* by John Kotter (Free Press, 1990). This draws a distinction between leaders and managers, which has possibly been one of the most significant and enduring.

Others choose to reflect on the qualities of great leaders. For example:

> *Inspiring Leadership: Learning from Great Leaders* by John Adair (Thorogood, 2003).
> *Leading Coherently: Reflections from Leaders Around the World* by Nancy Stanford-Blair and Michael H. Dickmann (Sage, 2005).

Two recent books on the subject, both applicable to MBA students but which take different approaches to leadership, are:

> *Why Should Anyone be Led by You?: What it Takes to be an Authentic Leader* by Rob Goffee and Gareth Jones (Harvard Business School Press, 2006).
> *Inspiring Leaders* edited by Ronald Burke and Cary Cooper (Routledge, 2006).

chapter 8   developing a career management capability

The journal and newspaper websites that specialize in MBA issues, such as *BusinessWeek* and the *Financial Times*, will also have information on career development and job search. There are also a range of industry indexes giving information on companies and their products, which can help in selecting an area to work in. Increasingly, websites are sprouting up, providing a range of career information, such as www.vault.com, an international career information site.

As with some of the other areas covered in this book, career management also attracts a wide range of publications and authors. Indeed, some publishers such as WetFeet have a suite of books covering a range of topics. As they are published in the USA, some of the books may not be completely relevant if you are outside America, but the books can get you started in many different career areas:

> *Killer Cover Letters and Résumés: The WetFeet Insider Guide* (WetFeet, 2003).
> *Negotiating Your Salary and Perks* (WetFeet, 2004).
> *Industries and Careers for MBAs* (WetFeet, 2004).

One of the classic texts in career management and one that is still valuable is:

> *What Color is Your Parachute?: A Practical Manual for Job-hunters and Career-changers* by Richard Bolles (Ten Speed Press, 2003).
> *The What Color is Your Parachute Workbook: How to Create a Picture of Your Ideal Job or Next Career* by Richard Bolles (Ten Speed Press, 1998) is a workbook that goes with the above text.

Other books relevant to MBA students, but with different approaches, include:

> *Finding Your Way with an MBA* by Susan Cohen and Don Hudson (John Wiley, 2001) which, as well as offering practical advice, also outlines the experiences of MBA graduates from a range of different industries.
> *Managing Yourself for the Career you Want* (Harvard Business School Press, 2004) which has advice on a range of topics from different authors.
> *Knock 'Em Dead 2007: The Ultimate Job Search Guide by Martin Yate* (Adams Media Corporation, 2006) which includes job search and interviewing tactics, networking and online research.
> *Discovering Your Career in Business* by Timothy Butler and James Waldroop (Perseus, 1997) includes a business career interest inventory.
> *The Vault MBA Career Bible: 2007 Edition* (Vault, 2006) which is an annual review of MBA career paths and hiring trends in major industries for MBAs.

part 2: core topics in business

chapter 9   periods and perspectives in management

Exploring the historical background and context of management is done well by a number of authors. One of these is Stuart Crainer, who has written several books on management education. Two of his books that consider management ideas in a historical context are:

> *Key Management Ideas: Thinkers that Changed the Management World* (Pitman/Financial Times, 1998).
> *The Ultimate Business Library: 75 Books that Made Management* (Capstone, 2000).

Along a similar vein is:

> *The Evolution of Management Thought* by Daniel Wren (John Wiley, 1994) which traces the evolution of management thought from its earliest days to the present.

Books that combine the views of different thinkers and management theory include:

> *Business: The Ultimate Resource* by Daniel Goleman (Perseus, 2002) which provides extracts from 70 of the most influential business books written throughout history.
> *Great Minds in Management: The Process of Theory Development* edited by Ken Smith and Michael Hitt (Oxford University Press, 2005). This is a panorama of the key ideas in management theory and also offers reflections on the process of theory development.
> *The Concise Blackwell Encyclopedia of Management* by Cary Cooper and Chris Argyris (Blackwell, 1998) which is a reference guide to the management sciences itemizing over 900 concepts.
> *Management Speak: Why We Listen to What Management Gurus Tell Us* by David Greatbatch and Timothy Clark (Routledge, 2005) which examines how management gurus disseminate their ideas.

If you are not yet sure how theory helps practising managers, it is worth reading 'Why hard-nosed executives should care about management theory' by Clayton Christenson and Michael Raynor (*Harvard Business Review*, September 2003).

chapter 10 operations management

Some of the production and operations management textbooks may be too detailed to explore at this stage, although, as with the other functional subject areas, there is nothing wrong with thumbing through a textbook to get a feel for the subject. A couple of books which provide an overview are:

> *Operations, Strategy, and Technology: Pursuing the Competitive Edge* by Robert Hayes, Gary Pisano, David Upton and Steven Wheelwright (Wiley, 2004).
> *Operations Management: Strategic Context and Managerial Analysis* by Terry Hill (Palgrave – now Palgrave Macmillan, 2000).

If you are at the early stage of an MBA, several books that will introduce you to the subject in a general, rather than technical way, are:

> *The Goal: A Process of Ongoing Improvement* by Eliyahu Goldratt and Jeff Cox (North River Press, 1992) which is a readable business novel about how a manager turns around a failing manufacturing plant.
> *Lean Thinking: Banish Waste and Create Wealth in Your Corporation* by James Womack and Daniel Jones (Free Press, 2003) which describes their business system model derived from streamlined production processes. It contrasts manufacturing strengths and weaknesses in several industries.

> *The Machine That Changed the World: The Story of Lean Production* by James Womack, Daniel Jones and Daniel Roos (Free Press, 2007) which is written in a similar vein.
> *The Toyota Way: Fourteen Management Principles from the World's Greatest Manufacturer* by Jeffrey Liker (McGraw-Hill, 2003) which is written for a general audience, but explains the management principles and business philosophy behind Toyota's worldwide reputation for quality and reliability.
> *Reengineering the Corporation: A Manifesto for Business Revolution* by Michael Hammer and James Champy (Collins, 2004) which is a seminal work, in which the authors outline the concept of process re-engineering.

chapter 11 quantitative methods

For some students, dealing with quantitative methods and statistics can be a daunting prospect. If you are concerned about recalling basic mathematical ideas, and would like to brush up a little before starting your MBA course, try:

> *Essential Mathematics for Business and Management* by Clare Morris with Emmanuel Thanassoulis (Palgrave Macmillan, 2007) which is a straightforward text that assumes no prior mathematical knowledge and covers the essential mathematical skills needed by business students at MBA level.

These books may also help to get you started:

> *Quantitative Approaches in Business Studies* by Clare Morris (Pearson Education, 2003) which is an accessible introduction to the effective use of mathematical and statistical techniques in business, requiring only minimal prior mathematical knowledge.
> *Statistical Thinking: Improving Business Performance* by Roger Hoerl and Ronald Snee (Wadsworth/ITP, 2001) which is illustrated with case studies and applies statistical thinking to business processes.
> *Statistical Thinking for Managers* by J.A. John, David Whitaker and David Johnson (CRC Press, 2001) which is an introductory text in business statistics, which takes a practical approach, outlining statistics concepts with a minimum of mathematics.
> *Quantitative Methods for Business, Management and Finance* by Louise Swift and Sally Piff (Palgrave Macmillan, 2005) which is designed for business students taking an introductory course on quantitative methods and starts with no assumptions about students' knowledge.
> *Seeing Through Statistics* by Jessica Utts (Duxbury Press, 2004) which aims to develop statistical literacy through real-world applications and emphasizes ideas rather than calculations.

The more recent books above have companion websites. But you may want to explore statistics using a CD package. Books that do this include:

> *Modern Business Statistics with Microsoft Excel* by David Anderson, Dennis Sweeney and Thomas Williams (Thomson/South-Western, 2006) which is a business statistics text that balances a conceptual understanding of statistics with a real-world application of statistical methodology.
> *Complete Business Statistics with Student CD* by Amir Aczel (McGraw-Hill/Irwin, 2005) which offers sections on regression analysis and updated cases on companies around the world, using Excel.

> *Statistics for Managers Using Excel and Student CD Package* by David Levine (Prentice Hall, 2007) which has applications from accounting, finance, marketing, management and economics and emphasizes managerial decision making.

In addition, an MBA maths tutorial and workbook can be found at www.mbamath.com. Also worth considering is the *MBA Survival Kit* by GMAC (McGraw-Hill/Irwin, 2001). This is a series of CD programmes providing an introduction to finance, accounting, quantitative skills and statistics and is designed specifically for those entering an MBA programme. It is a self-directed learning package that explores the core quantitative skills used across functional business areas within different companies.

chapter 12 accounting

The majority of introductory accounting textbooks are one of two types: books dealing only with financial accounting; and texts covering both introductory financial and management accounting. The former are generally prescribed in tertiary courses containing a major in accounting and the latter in many MBA programmes where there is only one core course in accounting.

Books that provide an introduction to the subject include:

> *Accounting: What the Numbers Mean* by David Marshall, Wayne McManus and Daniel Viele (McGraw-Hill/Irwin, 2005) which is written for non-accounting students, emphasizing the basics in a step-by-step approach, starting from what accounting information is to how managers use it.
> *The Accounting Game: Basic Accounting Fresh from the Lemonade Stand* by Darrell Mullis and Judith Orloff (Sourcebooks, 1998) which is an entertaining book that gives a basic understanding of accounting for those with no prior knowledge of the subject.
> *Essentials of Accounting* by Robert Anthony and Leslie Breitner (Prentice Hall, 2006) which is a self-teaching introduction to financial accounting that introduces balance sheets, income statements and statements of cash flows along with explaining important accounting concepts and terms.

Although not aimed solely at MBA students, the following books provide an accessible introduction to the subject:

> *Finance and Accounting for Non-financial Managers: All the Basics You Need to Know* (5th edn) by William G. Droms (Perseus Books, 2003).
> *Finance for Non-financial Managers* by Gene Siciliano (McGraw-Hill, 2003).
> *The Essentials of Finance and Accounting for Non-financial Managers* by Edward Fields (Amacom Books, 2002).

chapter 13 finance

The academic subject of finance addresses a different but related range of issues and topics. The following books provide guidance on the subject:

> *Principles of Corporate Finance* by Richard Brealey, Stewart Myers and Franklin Allen (McGraw-Hill/Irwin, 2005) which is one of the leading texts on the theory and practice of corporate finance.
> *Business Finance* (9th edn) by Graham Peirson, Rob Brown, Steve Easton, Peter

Howard and Sean Pinder (McGraw-Hill, 2006) which is a widely used textbook that clearly explains and demystifies the finance area and is comprehensive in approach.

› *A Random Walk Down Wall Street* by Burton Malkiel (W.W. Norton, 2007) which was first published in 1973 and is still considered to be one of the better books in introducing the principles of risk and return, investment and portfolio strategies.

› *Financial Intelligence: A Manager's Guide to Knowing what the Numbers Really Mean* by Karen Berman and Joe Knight (Harvard Business School Press, 2006) which covers essential concepts such as income statements, balance sheets, cash flow statements, the mechanics of analysis: calculating ratios, return on investment and working capital, but in a way that is straightforward to understand.

› *Corporate Finance: Core Principles and Applications* by Stephen Ross, Randolph Westerfield, Jeffrey Jaffe and Bradford Jordan (McGraw-Hill/Irwin, 2006) which aims to cover the essentials of corporate finance, but at a level that is understandable by the widest possible audience.

› *Corporate Finance: Principles and Practice* by Denzil Watson and Antony Head (Financial Times Management, 2003) which provides an introduction to the core concepts and key topic areas of corporate finance in an approachable, 'user-friendly' style. Covers the finance function and three decision areas in finance: investment, financing and dividends.

chapter 14 organizational behaviour

One of the most popular organizational behavioural texts that will give you an overview of the subject is written by Stephen Robbins. The latest version is:

› *Essentials of Organizational Behaviour* by Stephen Robbins and Tim Judge (Prentice Hall, 2007).

Other texts that also explore some of the major topics in the area include:

› *Organizational Behavior: Key Concepts, Skills and Best Practices* by Angelo Kinicki and Robert Kreitner (McGraw-Hill/Irwin, 2005).

› *Managing and Organizations: An Introduction to Theory and Practice* by Stewart Clegg, Martin Kornberger and Tyrone Pitsis (Sage, 2004).

In addition, you may wish to explore subject areas within the overall discipline such as the area of human resources. Dave Ulrich has been a leader in this field for many years and has produced a range of readable and influential books such as:

› *The HR Value Proposition* by Dave Ulrich and Wayne Brockbank (Harvard Business School Press, 2005).

› *Human Resource Champions: The Next Agenda for Adding Value and Delivery Results* by Dave Ulrich (Harvard Business School Press, 1997).

Also worth exploring are books that, while not normally considered to be organizational behaviour books, have a lot to say about the way people are managed within a business context. Examples of this approach are:

› *Good to Great* by Jim Collins (Random House, 2001).

› *Built to Last: Successful Habits of Visionary Companies* by Jim Collins and Jerry Porras (Collins, 2004) .

The text that has possibly most dominated the marketing subject and which will give you a flavour for the different topics in the area is Philip Kotler's *Marketing Management*. The latest edition is written with Kevin Keller (Prentice Hall, 2005). Kotler is one of the few authors (along with Warren Bennis in the leadership area) whose name is on a par with the academic subject area itself and carries enough weight to be able to get away with titles like *Kotler on Marketing* (Free Press, 2001).

In addition, there are also many good books describing the marketing subject. Others you might consider are:

> *Marketing Strategy and Management* (Palgrave Macmillan, 2007) and *The Marketing Book* (Butterworth-Heinemann, 2002) both by Michael Baker, who has written extensively in the area.

> *Marketing Mistakes and Successes* by Robert Hartley (John Wiley, 2007) which is a case book looking at some of the marketing problems and achievements of companies like Dell, McDonald's and Harley-Davidson.

> *Marketing: A Complete Guide* by Malcolm MacDonald and Martin Christopher (Palgrave Macmillan, 2003) focusing on MBA courses in particular.

chapter 16 macroeconomics and public policy

In addition to thumbing through the books suggested below, a good way to get a general feel for macroeconomics is to read the quality business press on a regular basis. Several journals such as *The Economist* focus specifically on the subject. Much of what is written, for example on fiscal policy and exchange rates, does not go into the theoretical background, but by regularly reading the quality press, your understanding of the major terms and issues will improve. Also, from time to time, some journals carry 'briefing articles', which explain some of the theoretical concepts in accessible language.

Books that will introduce you to the subject include:

> *Macroeconomics: Understanding the Wealth of Nations* by David Miles and Andrew Scott (John Wiley, 2005) which deals with sophisticated economic issues, but in a manner that can be understood by anyone taking a course in macroeconomics.

> *Commanding Heights: The Battle for the World Economy* by Daniel Yergin and Joseph Stanislaw (Simon and Schuster, 2002) which is a clearly written analysis of the new world economy, describing the world's modern political and economic development.

> *The Undercover Economist: Exposing Why the Rich Are Rich, the Poor Are Poor and Why You Can Never Buy a Decent Used Car!* by Tim Harford (Oxford University Press, 2005) which is, as you will detect from the title, a playful book that treats complex economic theories in an interesting way.

> *The Economics of Public Issues* by Roger Miller, Daniel Benjamin and Douglass North (Addison Wesley, 2005) which complements courses in economics, political economy, public policy and social issues.

> *The Making of Economic Policy: History, Theory and Politics* by Steven Sheffrin (Basil Blackwell, 1991) which is also worth looking at if you can get hold of it.

This is a technical subject that has been included in the book to give students a flavour for some of the more advanced issues they will be able to pursue on an MBA. Books that will give you more insight into the area include:

> *International Financial Management* by Jeff Madura and Roland Fox (Thomson Business Press, 2007) which provides clear explanations with real-world applications, although it presumes an understanding of basic corporate finance.
> *Global Corporate Finance* by Suk Kim, Seung Kim and John Cotner (Blackwell, 2006) which provides students with the practical skills needed to understand global financial problems and techniques.
> *Multinational Finance* by Kirt Butler (South-Western, 2003) which is easy to read and follow and covers the major international finance topics in an integrated fashion.
> *Multinational Finance* by Adrian Buckley (Financial Times Management, 2003) which is aimed at MBA and other postgraduate courses in international financial management. This book has a strong European orientation.

chapter 18   business strategy

There are many texts in the area that will give you a flavour of the subject. Some of these include:

> *Exploring Corporate Strategy: Text and Cases* by Gerry Johnson, Kevan Scholes and Richard Whittington (Prentice Hall, 2005) which is comprehensive and one of the leading texts in the area.
> *Strategy and the Business Landscape* by Pankaj Ghemawat (Prentice Hall, 2005) which offers a contemporary, although historically grounded, perspective on the field of strategy and is aimed particularly at MBA students.
> *Strategic Management* by Colin White (Palgrave Macmillan, 2004) which is a comprehensive text that focuses on applying strategy in practice using a wide range of international case examples.
> *Essentials of Strategic Management* by J. David Hunger and Tom Wheelen (Prentice Hall, 2006) which is a shorter book, but one that concisely explains the most important concepts and techniques in strategic management.
> *Strategic Management: Creating Value in Turbulent Times* by Peter FitzRoy and James Hulbert (John Wiley, 2004) which is aimed at MBAs and takes a managerial perspective on strategic management.

Additionally, you may wish to take a look at some of the books that have helped to define the area. Two of these are:

> *Competitive Strategy* by Michael Porter (The Free Press, 2004) which has been translated into 19 languages. When it appeared in 1980, it had a major impact on the theory, practice and teaching of business strategy throughout the world.
> *Competing for the Future* by Gary Hamel and C.K. Prahalad (Harvard Business School Press, 1996) which encourages managers to be more than 'maintenance engineers' worrying only about process such as budget cutting and re-engineering, but to focus on tomorrow's competition and opportunities.

name index

A

Adair, J., 329
Allen, F., 333
Alsop, R., 325
Ames, C., 269
Anderson, N., 327
Ansoff, I.H., 170
Argyris, C., 28, 99, 326, 331

B

Bailey, N., 261
Baker, M., 335
Bandura, A., 126
Bell, E., 327
Bennett, M., 327
Bennis, W., 129
Berman Brown, R., 327
Bernanke, B., 97–8
Bethke Elshtain, J., 255–6
Black, F., 236
Bolles, R., 330
Bolton, R., 328
Boydell, T., 326
Braddick, B., 128
Branson, R., 95
Brealey, R., 228, 333
Bridges, W., 329
Brindle, M.C., 168, 177
Brockbank, W., 334
Brown, R., 333
Bryman, A., 327
Buckley, A., 336
Burgoyne, J., 326
Burke, R., 330
Buzan, T., 327

C

Cameron, K., 326
Cameron, S., 37–8
Carnegie, D., 328
Casey, D., 61
Champy, J., 169, 332
Chandler, A., 170, 307, 308
Chowdhury, S., 326

Christopher, M., 335
Churchill, W., 132, 165
Clark, M., 329
Clark, T., 331
Clement, S., 117
Cohn, S., 149
Collins, J., 334
Cooper, C.L., 78, 326, 328, 330, 331
Copeland, M., 269
Covey, S.R., 326
Cox, C., 78
Cox, J., 331
Crainer, S., 7, 11, 13, 170, 330–1
Crosby, P., 174, 190, 191
Crosier, K., 263

D

Daft, D., 255
Dearlove, D., 7, 11, 13
de Bono, E., 59, 65–6, 327
De Meyer, A., 20
Deming, W.E., 174, 190
Dodd, C., 328
Drucker, P.F., 170, 177, 181, 259

E

Easton, S., 333
Ebbers, B., 256
Edison, T., 67
Eichinger, R., 127
Einstein, A., 60, 67, 68, 327–8
Eisner, M., 255
Elkind, P., 326
Ellet, W., 327
Erskine, J., 327

F

Fayol, H., 168, 172, 178
Feigenbaum, A.V., 190
Fiorina, C., 255
Fong, C., 11, 14
Ford, C., 82
Ford, H., 181–2, 266
Friedman, M., 78–9

subject index

Page numbers in **bold** denote pages with figures or boxes